D1544173

Belief and Worship
in Native North America

Belief and Worship in Native North America

ÅKE HULTKRANTZ

Edited, with an Introduction, by
CHRISTOPHER VECSEY

SYRACUSE UNIVERSITY PRESS
1981

CHAPTERS 1 and 4 are reprinted, with permission from *Native Religious Traditions*, ed. Earle H. Waugh and K. Dad Prithipaul, *Studies in Religion 8* (1979) (Waterloo, Ontario: Wilfred Laurier University for the Canadian Corporation for Studies in Religion). CHAPTER 2 is from a lecture held at the XIIth Congress of the International Association for the History of Religions, Stockholm, August 1970, and is reprinted from *Temenos* 7 (1971) (Turku, Finland: Finnish Society for the Study of Comparative Religion). CHAPTER 3 is reprinted from *Ethnos* 21, nos. 3–4 (1956) (Stockholm, Sweden: Etnografiska Museet). CHAPTER 5 is reprinted from *Studies in Shamanism*, ed. Carl-Martin Edsman, 1 (1967) (Åbo, Finland: Donner Institute, Scripta Instituti Donneriani Aboensis). CHAPTER 6 is reprinted from *Temenos* 14 (1978) (Turku, Finland: Finnish Society for the Study of Comparative Religion). CHAPTER 8 is reprinted from *The Supernatural Owners of Nature*, ed. Åke Hultkrantz, *Stockholm Studies in Comparative Religion* 1 (1961) (Stockholm, Sweden: Acta Universitatis Stockholmiensis). CHAPTER 9 is reprinted from *Studies in Comparative Religion* (Spring 1970) (Pates Manor, U.K.: Perennial Books Ltd.). CHAPTER 10 is reprinted from *Ethnos* 19, no. 1–4 (1954) (Stockholm, Sweden: Etnografiska Museet). CHAPTER 11 is reprinted with permission, from *Studies in Religion/Sciences Religieuses* 9, no. 2 (1980) (Waterloo, Ontario: Wilfred Laurier University for the Canadian Corporation for Studies in Religion). CHAPTER 12 is reprinted from *Syncretism*, ed. Sven S. Hartman, 3 (1969) (Åbo, Finland: Donner Institute, Scripta Instituti Donneriani Aboensis). CHAPTER 13 is reprinted from *Religious Symbols and Their Functions*, ed. Haralds Biezais, 10 (1979) (Åbo, Finland: Donner Institute, Scripta Instituti Donneriani Aboensis). CHAPTER 15 is reprinted from *New Religions* 7 (1975) (Åbo, Finland: Donner Institute, Scripta Instituti Donneriani Aboensis).

Library of Congress Cataloging in Publication Data
Hultkrantz, Åke.
Belief and worship in native North America.
—
Bibliography: p.
1. Indians of North America—Religion and Mythology. I. Vecsey, Christopher T. II. Title.
E98.R3H79   299'.78   81-18356
ISBN 0-8156-2248-1   AACR2

Manufactured in the United States of America

Åke Hultkrantz is Professor of Comparative Religion and head of the Institute of Comparative Religion, University of Stockholm, and author of more than a half-dozen books and 200 articles on American Indian religion.

Christopher Vecsey is Assistant Professor of History at Hobart and William Smith Colleges and co-editor of *American Indian Environments: Ecological Issues in Native American History.*

CONTENTS

Persistence and Change

Bibliography

INTRODUCTION

Christopher Vecsey

IN THE BOOK THAT FOLLOWS one of the world's foremost scholars of American Indian religions has gathered fifteen articles on native North American religions for an American audience. Students of the history of religion, anthropology, American Indian studies, and folklore will find useful information in this book, both in the data it presents and in the way it presents them.

The author of these articles is a Swedish professor, the chairman and director of the Institute of Comparative Religion at the University of Stockholm. He has published some three hundred papers—including thirteen books—on the history of religion and ethnology. His publications have appeared in all the major languages of Europe, centering on methodology of religions, Indian religions and cultures, and circumpolar religions in general, including that of the Scandinavian Lapps. He performed field work among the Lapps in 1944 and 1946, and among the Shoshoni and Arapaho Indians of Wyoming between 1948 and 1958. In addition, he conducted some field work among Northern Plains Indians in 1977. He has taught widely outside his native land, serving as visiting professor in the United States, Hungary, Austria, Scotland, and Canada, as well as lecturing throughout Europe.

Åke (pronounced AW-kee) Gunnar Birger Hultkrantz was born in Kalmar, Sweden, in 1920. He studied in Sweden, earning degrees in ethnology (1946) and the history of religions (1948). He completed his dissertation at the University of Stockholm in 1953 and has served there as docent and then professor ever since. He, his English wife Gerry, and their two daughters live on a wooded suburban island, Lidingö, six miles from downtown Stockholm.

Although Professor Hultkrantz brings to the following collection his long and erudite research regarding Indian traditions, he also brings an enthusiasm for Indians that predates his adult scholarship. Like many Swedes (and Germans, French, and Britons), Hultkrantz grew up fascinated with Indian lore. The romantic image of the noble Indians has held sway for more than a century in Europe and persists today.

As a youth Hultkrantz read avidly about Indians. By his teens he was reading Swedish translations of adventures of Indian life by European and American writers such as James Fenimore Cooper, Karl May, Francis Parkman, George Catlin, and Edward S. Ellis. The books had, he says, a "childish ethic" but were a "revelation" to him. He marvelled at Indians who could—at least in romance—place an ear to the ground to hear at great distance, who could read animal signs in disturbed twigs, who could sense a change in the weather by gauging the breezes and scrutinizing the clouds. Even more, he was fascinated by the medicinal and religious aspects of Indian life depicted in these books. He remembers reading of a medicine-man, leaping and swaying in order to effect a cure on a patient. Even as a youth Hultkrantz wished to understand such phenomena; he recalls, "I wanted to analyze this."

In school he maintained his interest in the mysteries of American Indian life. He did not care much for the political and military sides of history but kept his curiosity for the mysterious and the unusual. For a while he concentrated on the Lapps (an area of interest which he maintains to this day), but at the University of Stockholm his professor, Ernst Arbman, thought this field too narrow. He encouraged Hultkrantz to pursue his major love, the Indians. Hultkrantz followed Arbman's advice: "A dam had broken. I threw myself over the literature on Indian religion. I was in the blessed isles. I loved it." He has devoted himself to Indian religions ever since, and he assesses, "I have had the happiest of lives with my studies, learning in a scholarly way what had attracted me from childhood."

From his first to his most recent publications, Hultkrantz has translated his devotion to his subject matter into erudition. Moreover, the romantic image of Indians as lovers of nature, as people at harmony with their world, has persisted through his works. His first publication (Hultkrantz 1947) surveyed Indians and other "nature-folk"; his latest article (in a book entitled—in Swedish—*They Took Our Land*), published by a Swedish "Indian Club" to which he belongs, is on the topic of "Indians as Nature-protectors" (Hultkrantz 1981).

As Hultkrantz's romanticism has persisted, so has that of his fellow Swedes. "We Swedes are crazy for Indians," he remarks, "we always have been." Swedish youths and even grown-ups continue to set up teepees in the woods around Stockholm, playing at being Indians. Advertisements in Swedish newspapers picture Indians in headdresses and face paint, gazing at canoes on the waters.

In Hultkrantz's own office we find a Shoshoni headdress, a buffalo skull complete with sagebrush and sweetgrass offerings, a bust of a Dakota Indian, drawings by Indians Hultkrantz has known, a Seneca turkey feather, and Black Elk's meditation eagle feather (a gift from Professor Joseph Epes Brown, who studied under Hultkrantz at the University of Stockholm). These coexist with his mountain of volumes, from first editions of Henry Rowe Schoolcraft to publications of the Bureau of American Ethnology. Not only is the mix of artifacts and bibliophilia symbolic of Hultkrantz's dual—romantic and scholarly—involvement with Indians, but set amidst his formal parlor with Victorian furniture, chandeliers, and parquetry, the overall substance contains the feral within the formal, as does Hultkrantz's scholarly life. From his home he takes regular jaunts through the spruce, pine, and birch woods. In northern Sweden he goes mountain climbing. Like his fellow Swedes he is a doting, de-voted nature-lover, and this quality shows through in his writings amidst the edifice of footnotes. He comments, "My life is much more than books. I have a good time. I have a delightful family life. I have the natural world around me. I have my joys beyond my studies."

He describes himself as an "antiquarian." He loves Indian traditions and is not so interested in the secular pow-wows of recent vintage. He does, however, try to keep up with current Indian affairs. He is inquisitive about Indian politics, treaty rights, and land claims. He is knowledgeable about recent Indian legislation in America, and he subscribes to Indian publications like *Wassaja* and *The Indian Historian* that keep him abreast of contemporary Indian events. He considers himself a "friend" of the Indians in a sincere and yet self-deprecating way, realizing that he can do little as an outsider to help them in their struggles to maintain their sovereignty and cultures.

As much as he is a romantic, he does not want to "convert" to Indian ways. He finds such a scenario "ludicrous." "Their values and their ways," he says, "developed from their conditions. We can learn from them, surely, but we cannot expect to become them. I am moved by the Indian concern for harmony and balance with nature in its more general sense, but we Europeans cannot adopt all Indian nature-ways in detail." He remarks that "part of the confusion of modern western life is our inability to lead authentic lives. We feel the need to find ourselves. Surely we will not succeed by copying other people, even those as admirable as American Indians whose ways we respect."

In order to encounter Indian traditions face to face, Åke Hultkrantz conducted field work, beginning in 1948. With money from the Vega Fund of the Anthropological and Geographical Society of Sweden and from the Swedish-American Foundation, he journeyed to the Wind River Shoshoni reservation in Wyoming. He chose the Shoshoni partially because of the romantic attraction of Plains culture but primarily because scholars knew almost nothing about them. He wanted to find out something new. In addition, he knew that their social structure was simpler and more easily studied than that of other Plains groups. What he did not know was that the Shoshonis had maintained more of their traditions than most other Plains tribes because of their relative isolation. He was lucky to find much of their old religion intact (Hultkrantz 1966b: 66). He would have chosen the Ojibwas, whose territory is most like his own in Sweden—the birch and conifers and bogs and lakes—but Ruth Landes and A. Irving Hallowell had already "claimed" that field.

Before reaching the Shoshonis, Hultkrantz stopped in Chicago, where one anthropologist told him that he should "go home to Sweden" and leave Indians to the American researchers. A kind of scholarly Monroe Doctrine prevailed, an attempt by some ethnologists to "keep the natives as an American domain," but Hultkrantz invaded and captured the field, with the cheering encouragement of the masters of anthropology of the time, Robert Lowie, Paul Radin, Alfred Louis Kroeber, and Leslie Spier. They all applauded this Swede on his intellectual quest. On the other hand, he met with resistance from competing (as they saw it) fieldworkers who looked with distrust on an ethnologist who was interested primarily in religion.

His two main interests in fieldwork were: (1) to reconstruct the pattern of the old Shoshoni religion within its cultural background, and (2) to examine the process of acculturation within religion. In short, his aim was "to gain knowledge about the structure and function of religion in a primitive community" (Hultkrantz 1966b: 66, see 67). As a fieldworker Hultkrantz busied himself with ecology, economics, social and political organization, but religion was (and has remained) his central subject.

When he began his field work, he "didn't know anyone any-where, but I made acquaintances." An Episcopal clergyman at Wind River put him up. He tried using a horse to travel to the various Shoshoni camps, but he admits that he "never was very good"; so, he bought a bicycle and pedalled across the sandy sagebrush from group to group. In 1955 he returned for another six months, a little wealthier, and purchased an automobile, learned how to drive, and obtained his first driving license.

He came equipped with lists of questions from ethnographic guidebooks, which he began to fire methodically at the Shoshonis. The Indians found this process distasteful and balked at answering. He also came equipped with gifts of cigarettes and tobacco for informants, and he was rebuffed by Indians who wanted hard cash, having been "spoiled" by other ethnologists who rewarded their in-formants lavishly. Hultkrantz remembers depleting his money so thoroughly that on his way home he was forced to sleep in dollar-a-night motels, until he learned to ration his funds more wisely. He learned also to avoid the direct questioning recommended in the field work guides and instead to gather his data through relaxed conversa-tion. He learned that to mention, for example, a Swedish folk belief in the "lady of the woods" would prompt the Shoshonis to recount their comparable beliefs (Hultkrantz 1966b: 70–73). Being a foreigner was probably an advantage for him, since the Indians were just as curious about the exotic habits of his countrymen (whose traditions he romanticized for the Indians) as he was about theirs. Through such conversations, and through laborious study, he learned the basic outlines of the Shoshoni language, for which to this day no published dictionary or grammar exists. He reckons that half of his time among them was taken in language lessons (Hultkrantz 1966b: 76). He was a good listener; he sat and heard stories, letting his informants disagree with or amplify each other's testimony. In the process he made friends and gathered enough source material to serve him for the next thirty years and more.

And yet not all his experiences were pleasant. He found him-self embroiled in the factional disputes of his informants. Some Shoshonis would not speak to him, urging their fellows to ignore his requests for information. One young man on the reservation threw a hatchet at him, attempting to scare him off from attending a religious ceremony (Hultkrantz 1966b: 76). Still, his quiet persistence pre-vailed, and he returned in 1955, again for the summer in 1957, and for some weeks in 1958, expanding his field to include the Wyoming Arapahos.

Between 1958 and 1968, however, he was unable to return to

the States. After that time it was more difficult for him to enter the Shoshoni reservation for field work or social visits. The political climate on the reservation had changed. Younger, more politically sharpened Shoshonis did not welcome ethnologists. As a result, he has been "completely disconnected" from the Shoshonis since 1958. He tries to conduct some small field work wherever he goes in the States, especially on the northern Plains, but except through mutual contacts his association with his Shoshoni informants has been severed.

His field work may have been curtailed in the late 1950s, but his scholarship flourished and continues to produce fruit. When he published his dissertation (Hultkrantz 1953), he paid for it completely with his own and his family's money, taking out a loan of 20,000 Swedish krona, "a remarkably enormous sum at the time" he observes. Few resources existed for the publication of scholarship in Sweden at that time. Today in Sweden it is much easier for scholars to have their works printed, many of them in English.

Through the last three decades Professor Hultkrantz has proven himself to be a consummate scholar. After hundreds of articles and more than a dozen books, he is still vigorously productive. At present he has three books on the way: a monograph on the American Indian peyote religion, a long-awaited volume on shamanism in North America, and in 1981–82 he will serve for twenty weeks at the Department of Religious Studies at the University of Aberdeen in Scotland as a visiting professor, delivering the Gifford Lectures, the most prestigious invitational post worldwide in religious studies. He has entitled these lectures—which will be published as a book—"The Veils of Religion," referring to the human use of symbols to comprehend the supernatural.

Besides these three books, on the side desk in his home study lies a stack of perhaps fifty of his manuscript articles which are forthcoming in various international journals. He believes that scholarship (not his own scholarship in particular; he is a modest man) serves humanity. As a result, he engages in his work with fervor and without cease. He is a restless creator who is incredulous that someone would not know what to study: "My trouble is that life is too short. I have too much I want to do and know." He confesses that he is afflicted with a "lust to write."

Hultkrantz has made his own way in the scholarly world. He admits that from his student days, "I haven't had any heroes." He wanted to conduct his investigations regarding tribal and folk religions according to his own method. As a result he has established in his own writings a cross-referencing to his other publications, a mighty fortress of interconnected observation, a veritable intellectual world-view with coherence and continuity over his productive lifetime, a unified corpus of data and theory.

As a professor at the University of Stockholm, he has trained his graduate students not to follow his methods but to succeed at their own. His students say that he is a fair and kind colleague who adjusts his pedagogy to suit each student's strengths and needs. He allows his students to speak their own minds and to go their own ways, with his blessing: "I don't expect anyone to go about his work in the way I have." Likewise, he has avoided the bitter debate with other scholars over method and results. He is chary with overbounding praise, but he recognizes generously the contributions of others. He has enjoyed the various approaches others have brought to the study of tribal religions, while not embracing their ways himself.

He characterizes his own work as "academically rigourous," aiming toward objectivity. He perceives that American students of Indian religions are often involved in personal searches for meaning and wholeness. They—typically American in their belief that ideas should be put to work—want to know to what practical and spiritual uses these Indians' ideas can be put. Hultkrantz is not searching for spiritual enrichment through his study. Rather, the religious phenomena he studies excite his academic curiosity for their own sake, as examples of human religiosity.

In many ways he is a typical Swede—in his romanticism regarding Indians, and in his scholarly bent toward historical and phenomenological rigor, eschewing the speculation of the Germans and the psychologizing of the Americans. He is as heavy-gaited as other Swedes are in their scholarship. And yet he enjoys the license of American publications. For examples he refers to the uses of Freud and Jung in American academic writings as "madness" but also "great fun" which Swedish scholars never feel free enough to consider, much less write for publication.

He is also typically Swedish in that he has looked beyond his national and linguistic borders to the works of scholars from other cultural traditions. He is conversant with German, French, Hungarian, English, and Russian schools of erudition, putting to shame the parochialism of American academics who are all too often ignorant of the languages and traditions of study beyond America and England.

It is ironic, then, that Professor Hultkrantz, who is far more cosmopolitan than any American student of American Indian culture or religion, feels isolated from the mainstream of American Indian studies. His books have been published primarily in Sweden (although frequently in English), and they have often been ignored by Americanists who might have benefitted from his knowledge. He believes that publishing in Sweden—with little or no advertising—has retarded acceptance by the rest of the world, particularly America.

Nevertheless, he is internationally known and respected. He has received offers, for instance, from universities in the United States to become research professor. He has preferred, however, to remain in his familiar, secure island home where he feels isolated, but from whence his works are reaching at last across the continents. The academic world has begun to mark a path to his door. Non-Indians—folklorists, anthropologists, students of comparative religion—and Indians visit his home. Film-makers ask his advice on their upcoming plans to parachute into the Amazon to interview medicine-men. A Canadian Indian hockey player, passing through Stockholm on a tournament, spends the evening at Hultkrantz's gracious home to discuss contemporary religious matters. Recognition for his work is growing, and it is hoped that this book will increase the American awareness.

The articles in this book date from three decades, from 1954 to 1981. Through this time Hultkrantz says that he has changed his views on many subjects, but his method—an empirical phenomenology that takes into consideration historical, cultural, and ecological influences to understand American Indian religions—has remained constant. He is neither like Paul Radin, his early friend in America, who took a third of every book he wrote to correct the opinions he had expressed in his previous book. Neither is Hultkrantz like Alfred Louis Kroeber, another friend from the field work days, who claimed that he had not changed a single idea in over fifty years of publishing.

Although his opinions on particular matters have changed over time, throughout his career Hultkrantz has sought one goal: "to elevate the research on native American religions to a scientific level equal with that of the studies of Old World religions." Two decades ago Hultkrantz wrote that "North American religions supply a treasure trove of data on primitive religion and should therefore be intensively used in phenomenological studies of religion." He went on: "It is impossible to reach reliable theories in comparative religion if the religious materials have not been mapped and related to historical, social and environmental factors in North America and elsewhere" (Hultkrantz 1965a: 107). This is precisely what the author has tried to do throughout his career, and it is the core of the following collection.

The book makes two major contributions to scholarship. First, it provides phenomenological, ecological, and historical perspectives, using methods which are not too common in the United States, and thus can serve as a methodological primer. And second, it includes North American Indian religions as worthy members of the religions of the world. To join North America to a full part of the history of religion; that, he says, has been his "great ambition." He has always contended and continues to assert that we cannot understand religion without including tribal religions like those of American Indians. At the same time, he maintains, we cannot understand Indians without understanding their religions. This book aims to accomplish an understanding both of religion and American Indians through the study of Indian religious phenomena.

He has brought to his task a thoroughgoing Swedish phenomenology. For him "the phenomenology of religion is . . . the systematic study of the forms of religion, that part of religious research which classifies and systematically investigates religious conceptions, rites and myth-traditions from comparative morphological-typological points of view." He states that "the great task of the phenomenologists of religion . . . is to make careful inventories of religious categories throughout the world, providing in this way a complete atlas of the morphology of conceptions, rites and myths" (Hultkrantz 1970b: 74–75, 78).

His phenomenological method precludes any judgment regarding the truth or untruth of religious beliefs; in effect, he attempts to bracket out his own assumptions about the nature of the physical or supernatural worlds in order to understand what his subjects believe. He is not interested in stating what religion should be in essence, but instead he wants to learn what religion consists of by observing objectively the religious phenomena as believed and practiced by American Indians and others. In so doing he tries to avoid value judgments and sets his mind to observation and comparison of data.

Only after understanding the religious phenomena and what they mean to the people whose phenomena they are, can the phenomenologist make more theoretical considerations about their religious import in the broader, comparative realm. Hultkrantz carries out this method exactly. Each article in this book is a painstaking examination of religious phenomena as found among certain people—for example, the Wind River Shoshoni of Wyoming. Only at the end of each article does the author allow himself the freedom to discuss the ramifications of the materials he has gathered. Based on his wide-ranging findings, he compares phenomena across national and ethnic borders where historians and anthropologists often fear to tread (Hultkrantz 1970b: 80–81). The result is to understand the phenomena themselves—concepts of deities, initiation ceremonies, and the like—as well as the function of the phenomena in Indian culture and history.

The impatient reader will perhaps be frustrated. Hultkrantz's comparative method requires thoroughness of research and documentation. A few scattered examples will not do for him; rarely does he generalize from one or two examples. Hence, the reader who wishes that Hultkrantz would get to his point is perhaps missing the author's point: the evidence must be placed before the reader in full before any conclusions can be drawn. Hultkrantz has done his homework and his field work; both show clearly in his voluminous writings, in his bibliography, and in his references to informants' testimonies.

Hultkrantz's phenomenology is grounded in an unyielding empiricism. Rejecting fancy theories and pretty language, he is a plain empiricist who avoids the easy generalization, who takes in all the diversity of detail he has recorded, who hopes not to violate anything that has passed before his observant eyes by leaving it out or twisting it into an unrepresentative theoretical framework. He rebuts philosophers and speculators of all stripes by demanding to see their data. He sticks to the position that he can say only what his informants and written sources have said; he can go no further than his data.

Hultkrantz is a phenomenologist, but he recognizes that he cannot separate historical and ecological influences on religion from religion itself. The phenomena, history, and the environment all intermingle. He has attempted to separate them out, and then put them together again, in order to understand the forces that influence American Indian religions as well as the religions themselves. In this sense he is an intellectual historian, one who takes into account the interconnections between ideas and events without reducing ideas to a function of events. He is interested in the role that religious ideas and practices have played in American Indian history, as well as in the phenomena of ideas and practices themselves. As an intellectual historian he is interested in the content of religious ideas: what do they say? He wants to know who holds these ideas within a group: is there consensus amongst the members of an Indian nation, or is there disparity in ideas and practices? He is also interested in how the ideas are used by the people who hold them. He is curious about the contexts—ecological and historical—which surround religious ideas, but he refuses to reduce religion to its context. In short, he takes religious ideas seriously for themselves but without separating them from the world out of which they spring.

Professor Hultkrantz has tried to encompass the fields of religious studies, history, folklore, and anthropology, bringing them back together into the unity they once had before this century (Hultkrantz 1956b). He belongs to anthropological, ethnohistorical, folkloric, and comparative religion associations both in this country and abroad, and it is significant that he has written two major books on methodology. One, *General Ethnological Concepts* (1960a), is a dictionary of anthropological terminology, an encyclopedic guide to the student of ethnography who wishes to know more about the field than what is taught in American anthropology programs. The other, *Metodväger inon den Jämförande Religionforskningen* (1973c), is a thorough survey of the comparative study of religions: its definitions, documentation, systemization, and methodological approaches. He has proven himself a master of two academic worlds that match his two advanced degrees: ethnology and the history of religion. Like other European historians of religion, he considers himself an anthropologist, at least in the broadest sense of the word (cf. Hultkrantz 1977a: 86). Moreover, he is both a field worker and a book scholar. Wherever he goes in the States he tracks down both native informants and unpublished manuscripts. He understands the models of the social sciences, even when he does not follow them, favoring instead a more "humanistic devotion" to his subjects rather than theoretical frames, employing an "intuitive process of controlled imagination" in addition to data collection. He regards himself an anthropologist and a historian, in sum a "humanistic student of comparative religion."

Nevertheless, in America he has received criticism and neglect both from the historians of religion, who either find American Indian phenomena unimportant, or who do not want to consider the cultural contexts for religious phenomena; and from the anthropologists, who deny the validity of religion as a subject matter in its own right. Standing between the religionists and the ethnologists, Hultkrantz will not divorce religion from culture, but equally he will not allow a cultural determinism to corrupt his phenomenology. He avoids reductionism, therefore, on both sides. He will not reduce religion to its contexts; neither will he reduce religion to its phenomena. In his view there is more to religion that the religious elements in it. At the same time he has chided anthropologists, especially "the younger American scientists for whom names such as

Lowie and Radin already belong to the unreadable past" (1966b: 68), for denying the importance of religion in tribal culture. The "new ethnology," Hultkrantz today believes, has taken up his interest in belief systems. He feels somewhat justified in the tradition he began with *Conceptions of the Soul among North American Indians* (1953), which received harsh words from some American anthropologists who could not understand why anyone would be interested in document-ing a phenomenology of belief. "They couldn't understand what I was up to," he recalls, "but now others are doing, thirty years later, what I was doing then."

In a situation in which historians of religion have entered the field of tribal religions and anthropologists have entered the field of the so-called "high cultures," the two groups have come into rivalry, and the social scientists have resented the religionists (Hultkrantz 1977a: 81). Many anthropologists have said that the problems of reli-gious studies are irrelevant; the concepts of scholars in religion are founded on subjective, Christian taxonomies and motifs (sin, soul, godhead, etc.); they have little or no knowledge of the workings of culture. Hultkrantz agrees that some of their deficiencies are real, and some students of religion have deserved the abuse they have received from the anthropologists. Some of his fellows in comparative religion show a frightening lack of interest in the cultural bases of religion, and others have shown an antiscientific bias that is "alarming" (Hultkrantz 1977a: 84, cf. 87–91). However, the crux of the matter is that for the anthropologists, in Hultkrantz's view, "Religion is . . . denied any value in itself; it is a vehicle of institutions, attitudes and relations explained by the socio-cultural matrix. Historians of reli-gion, by contrast, tend to consider religion as an entity *sui generis*" (Hultkrantz 1977a: 85). Religionists grant autonomy to religion, while "many anthropologists seem to take it for granted that religion is an illusion of the mind" (Hultkrantz 1977a: 93). This, for Hultkrantz, is a dangerous position, one which denies the important effect that reli-gious beliefs and practices have on tribal people like American In-dians. Although many Indian groups have traditionally no word for "religion," they often have a concept of the supernatural and of proper relations with the supernatural as they conceive it. By trying to ignore this universal fact, anthropologists have warped their findings to fit their own subjective, possibly atheistic prejudices.

Professor Hultkrantz says that he writes, to a degree, in the Swedish Lutheran tradition, with a Kantian bent. He has purposely used the language of religions rather than that of the anthropologists in order to describe and analyze American Indian religions in the following book. The title of the work, *Belief and Worship in Native North America*, indicates that the terminology of the churches prevails, even though his method has been that of the ethnologist scholar. He uses the common-day language of religions, implying that Indian religions are comparable (but, of course, not identical) to Christian and other religious traditions.

Hultkrantz ascribes primacy in his description of religion to the role of belief. He shows in the course of the book that beliefs are essential to a religion, and although some might say that such a view betrays a Christian heritage, he asks why we should think that Indians and other tribal peoples are mindless, going through ritual motions without an idea in their heads (cf. Hultkrantz 1966b: 74). The view expressed by some anthropologists seems foolish to Hultkrantz, that the rituals of tribal peoples precede their beliefs. He suggests that the opposite is true, even though abstractions of religion get lost and confused over time. Throughout this work he shows that an interpenetration exists between belief and worship in American Indian religions, past and present.

The first section of the book, "Belief and Myth," reasons that religion is based on beliefs and values, both conscious and unconscious. These are the most important parts of a religious system, since they provide basic motivation for the action of religion; they make the religion what it is, since action by itself can not be called religious without a content of belief in the supernatural to propel it. For Hultkrantz it is vital to recognize that religion "does not consist of mindless rituals; it is not simply people going through the motions, or an empty headed thrill."

In the first chapter, "Myths in Native North American Religions," he indicates that myth is primarily a religious concept and should be understood religiously above all else. It is a model for human behavior, a paradigm for human life, based on supernatural actions. At the same time, myths are not synonymous with religion. Myths contain some but certainly not all of the beliefs of a religious system. They can compartmentalize religion and turn abstractions into stories for the easier understanding of the people of the belief group; however, as stories—which reflect culture beyond religion— they can frequently reflect religious beliefs only obliquely. In brief, religious belief transcends the epics of its mythology, and its mythology extends beyond its religious core.

In "The Structure of Theistic Beliefs among North American Plains Indians," he takes up in a more systematic way the content of religious beliefs. In this Hultkrantz shows his phenomenological interest in classification of theistic beliefs. He also reveals a bulwark of his system, based on long empirical observation: tribal religions invariably concern a concept of the supernatural. He has argued elsewhere (Hultkrantz 1980a) that the definition of religion is inexorably tied to such a concept. American Indian groups without exception posit the existence of another order beyond the normal one, and their religions are an attempt at communication with such a supernatural order. Therefore, the supernatural is an essential category of Indian religions.

One of the difficulties of defining the supernatural for any Indian group, much less for the continent as a whole, is the fluidity of categories in various situations. Indians have not been Aristotelians; their concepts change in different situations. Religion to them is not a mechanical philosophy. Rather, it is active and changes to meet different situations. In "Configurations of Religious Belief among the Wind River Shoshoni," Hultkrantz demonstrates that individualism among some Indian tribes, especially the hunters, leads to a diversity in religious belief that defies generalization. In addition, the religious beliefs of a person can change over a period of time and from situation to situation. As a fieldworker, Hultkrantz has found this to be so among the Wind River Shoshoni. In this article he shows, for instance, that in Shoshoni belief the creater of mythology is different from the creator of Sun Dance conception. In general, then, a "configuration" of religious beliefs exists—a set of different and differing religious conceptions, one of which might dominate the others at any one time. Furthermore, there is not necessarily a coherence within the configuration. The theorist of holism in culture will be disappointed to learn that myths and other religious beliefs do not always form neat complementary units.

Although Hultkrantz has granted primacy to belief, many of his scholarly articles have been concerned with religious activity: worship, or more generally, ritual. He has stated that ritual actions by themselves are not religious; only with a content supplied by ideas do they attain the level of the religious. However, he has also seen that discontinuities can exist, not only within a configuration of beliefs but also between belief and action. Rituals have the function of making actual, putting into motion, the beliefs of a religious configuration; however, they do not necessarily correlate neatly with beliefs, although there is interaction between the two realms. In his second section, "Worship and Ritual," Hultkrantz concentrates on the ritual activity of Indian religions.

He notes that not all religious ritual action is worship—a

proper regarding of the worth of the supernatural—although much of
it is. Worship is a type of ritual but not the only one. The Spirit Lodge,
for example, is not always concerned with worship, although the cult
of the dead almost certainly always is. For Hultkrantz worship is not
necessarily subjugation before the supernatural. It can be silent meditation or petition by sympathetic harmony. The many types of worship fill the entire book.

In "Ritual in Native North American Religions," Hultkrantz
describes the symbolic action of religion, in which beliefs are acted
upon and transposed into motion. Not only does he show the connections between belief and ritual, but he also suggests that human verbal deficiency in the face of the supernatural, the inability to grasp the
supernatural through veils of symbols, has led religious people like
American Indians to dramatic, expressive acts. Not being able to say
all that they believe, the American Indians create ritual, presenting to
the supernatural a polysemous, wordless worship.

The focus of the following chapter, "Spirit Lodge, a North
American Shamanistic Séance," is a type of rite, the purpose of which
is to bring humans into contact with the supernatural for divination.
The Spirit Lodge has diffused from its central Algonkian center across
most of northern North America. Hultkrantz has traced its growth
and analyzed its most salient features and in so doing has provided a
definition of shamanism in North America: a social and religious
institution in which a person with the aid of helping spirits attains a
trance and communicates with the supernatural for the good of the
community, often (but not always) for the purpose of curing disease.

In "The Cult of the Dead among North American Indians,"
Hultkrantz corrects the mistaken notion that American Indians have
had little cult regarding their dead. He shows that especially in the
Southwest among the Pueblos, but commonly across the continent,
Indians have held the conviction that the dead have the power to help
or harm the life pursuits of the living, and as a result the living have
made it their business to worship their dead, even when they have
regarded them with dread. Hultkrantz has thus broadened his
phenomenology of the supernatural to include certain spirits of the
dead, whom the living need to placate, serve, and coerce, in order to
aid in the existence of living humans.

The issue of connections between the supernatural, religion,
and the pursuit of human continuance is central to the third section of
the book, "Ecology and Religion." One of Hultkrantz's greatest innovations and successes has been in the realm of the ecology of religion.
Between 1955 and 1958 he became aware of the ecological bases of

Shoshoni culture, including religion, and he became convinced of the "fundamental importance of natural ... conditions to religious development" (Hultkrantz 1966a: 133; cf. Hultkrantz 1966b: 69). He observed that the Eastern and Western Shoshonis had separate traditions that corresponded to two different ecosystems as well as divergent historical influences. As a result he tried to map the ecological dimensions of Indian religiosity, avoiding the materialistic reductionism of such an enterprise, concluding that "environment stimulates religious forms" (Hultkrantz 1966a: 142), but refusing to say that environment causes religion itself. He has regarded this interest in ecology and religion as an "intellectural drama" in which he joins materialist interpretation without becoming a slave to it.

Hultkrantz has placed emphasis on Indians' creativity, feeling, imagination, placed into religious action, through a threefold system of integrating ecology and religion. At the first level, he posits that some religious beliefs and activities are directly concerned with the gain of sustenance. At a secondary level, a group's subsistence activities help form a social structure, which is then reflected in the organization of the group's religion. Third, the morphology of the religion, the symbols, and other religious forms borrow from and reflect the natural environment and the activities associated with subsistence pursuits. All three levels of integration are possible between religion and ecology (see Hultkrantz 1976b), and all three levels are seen in the four articles of this third section.

In "Feelings for Nature among North American Indians," the author takes on the issue of whether Indians have been conservationists and asks what feelings they have had for their natural surroundings. He finds that Indian nature-attitudes have been directly concerned with their specific surroundings and subsistence activities and have not been based on all-encompassing regard for natural beauty. Indians have selected specific aspects of nature for their worship and care. But on a more metaphysical plane, nature has revealed the supernatural and thus has been deserving of Indian respect. Hultkrantz finds that Indians have not been conservationists in any systematic way. They have protected parts of nature which they love (as it fits their subsistence, culture, and religious configurations), but they have wasted other portions. The author also shows that white intrusions have fractured Indian feelings for nature in many cases.

Since Indian ecological religion has been integrated with sustenance, it comes as no surprise that for Indians, who were by and large hunters at first contact with whites, their religion has reflected their hunting concerns. As "The Owner of the Animals in the Religion of the North American Indians" demonstrates, Indians have perceived a type of supernatural which can be called an animal guardian or owner of nature, whose powers control the gaining of game, and the concept of which shows the life-promoting dimension of Indian religions. In this chapter Hultkrantz establishes a typology of animal guardians and indicates the three-levelled integration between Indian ecology and religion.

In "Attitudes to Animals in Shoshoni Indian Religion," Hultkrantz focuses on one tribe, showing both their feelings for nature and their tribal categories for supernaturals of nature. In so doing, he uses his field work to complement his book work, creating an emic Shoshoni typology for animals and a tribal view of prescribed relations between humans, deities, and animals.

"The Indians and the Wonders of Yellowstone" shows another side of human-nature relations, demonstrating that Indians do not always think fondly of nature; indeed, they can be quite frightened by it. Yellowstone, with its amazing hot springs and geysers both repelled the Indians of the area and attracted them for specific occasions, like vision-quests. In short, the wonders of Yellowstone were seen by the local Indians as sacred ground, veils of the supernatural, the proper sites for religious pursuits, whereas in mundane situations the area was to be avoided.

In the fourth section, "Persistence and Change," Professor Hultkrantz takes into consideration the historical influences on Indian religions, documenting the ways that Indian traditions have altered over time, and equally how they have continued to this day. Just as in his ecological theory he is careful not to imply that environmental contexts have been the sole and necessary cause of religious phenomena, in this section he separates the historical contexts for movements like the Sun Dance, Ghost Dance, and peyote religion, from their religious motivation and morphology. He is not content to label these movements "nativistic" or to say that they arise from "relative deprivation," but rather he shows how the movements presented certain concepts of the supernatural and recommended modes of worship, in short, how these movements were religious. Hultkrantz shows that Indian peoples have had religious as well as environmental, political, and social needs, religious needs that have changed and persisted over time, and which require periodic renewal through movements which may have other dimensions, but which must be considered preeminently religious, especially when their primary aim is to establish or maintain communication with the supernatural.

In "The Problem of Christian Influence on Northern Algon-

kian Eschatology," he examines how Christianity has made inroads to
Algonkian Indian beliefs regarding the afterlife, and how traditional
Indian eschatology has persisted. He indicates how Algonkians have
often combatted Christianity by using Christian eschatology against
itself, for example, by claiming that Indian converts will not get to the
Christian heaven (because they are Indian) and will be denied their
place in the Indian heaven (because they are Christian). Finally,
Hultkrantz shows that the concepts of retribution of sins after death
and the Supreme Being as the god for the dead seem surely to be
Christian influences on Algonkians.

Hultkrantz's article on Algonkian eschatology points out his
command of literary sources over a wide geographical area; his next
three articles narrow the focus to one group, the Shoshonis of Wyoming. In "Tribal and Christian Elements in the Religous Syncretism
among the Shoshoni Indians of Wyoming," he looks at the process
and content of religious syncretism and finds that the Shoshonis have
adopted limited aspects of Christianity (for example, eschatological
beliefs), that Christian theology is little understood, and that nominal
church membership is prevalent. At the same time, peyotism has
made strong inroads, and the Sun Dance has become a focal point
for summer rituals, replacing the old vision-quests and shamanistic
rites. The result is that numerous religious complexes exist at Wind
River: at least three Christian denominations, peyote religion, Sun
Dance, and various sorts of traditional belief and worship. Factionalism and ideological confusion have been results where Christianity has functioned to weaken the old without replacing it with
something viable.

"The Traditional Symbolism of the Sun Dance Lodge among
the Wind River Shoshoni" takes even a closer look at Wind River
religion. Hultkrantz demonstrates that the Sun Dance, although a
recent innovation among the Shoshoni, possesses for them many of
the traditional religious symbols of their tribal faith. At the same time
it has Christian symbolism, which was added to make the religious
complex more palatable to missionaries and other non-Indians in authority. For the Shoshonis today the Sun Dance is a renewal ceremony with cosmological significance, not a religion by itself, much
less a "nativistic" cult. Its purpose is to communicate with, to worship, the supernatural and thus is essentially religious.

Again concentrating on the Shoshonis in "The Changing
Meaning of the Ghost Dance as Evidenced by the Wind River
Shoshoni," Hultkrantz takes up a most complex issue: what is the
meaning of a ritual to its participants? He asks what is the religious

content, the belief, behind the movements of Ghost Dance worship? At the same time, he addresses the question of what happens to a religious movement when its prophecy fails. He follows the evolution of the Ghost Dance, from its ideology in the Orpheus myth and its dance patterns in the seasonal round dance, through the Prophet Dance and other antecedents, to its flourishing and demise. Today, he notes, among the Wind River Shoshonis the Ghost Dance has either continued as a ritual to bring about reunion with the dead and world renewal, or (for most) it has reverted to a traditional round dance entertainment.

After three articles based on his field work, Hultkrantz returns to a broader field, the "Conditions or the Spread of the Peyote Cult in North America." In this final chapter, a foretaste of his forthcoming book on the peyote religion and a demonstration of the evenhanded method that highlights his work, he reviews theories which attempt to explain the origin and essence of peyotism. Some have seen the movement as a response to white domination, as a weapon against Christianity, as a refuge for the culturally lost, as a function of changed Indian conditions and poverty, just about everything except as a religious movement. Without denying any one feature or explanation, Hultkrantz maps out the attracting and obstructing elements that influenced Indians across the western part of the continent to accept or reject the movement. He emphasizes that above all else it was a religion that offered people in religious disarray a means of communication with the supernatural, as variously conceived. For thousands of Indians it has provided a convincing belief and an inspiring mode of worship.

Thus in the course of fifteen chapters Professor Hultkrantz evinces the scope of North American Indian religions, from the systems of belief and worship to their ecological and historical contexts. This introduction only summarizes the contours of the book and cannot substitute for its rich documentary texture.

In preparing the book and particularly the introduction for publication, the editor received aid from Hobart & William Smith Colleges to facilitate interviews with Professor Hultkrantz in Stockholm. Unascribed quotations in the introductory text derive from those interviews. It is hoped that this volume will serve the needs of its author, its publisher, and its readers, and will promote the further study of American Indian religions.

BELIEF AND MYTH

1

Myths in Native North American Religions

ANY EFFORT TO DISSECT AND CLASSIFY THE MYTHS of the North American Indians in a short presentation must necessarily be selective and superficial. Not only is the concept of myth as such highly controversial and therefore difficult to handle, North American tales which may pass as myths are extremely numerous. Some of them have been dealt with in detailed, bulky monographs, but most of them have either been published in collections of tales or have not been published at all: they exist as manuscripts in the files of the Smithsonian Institution or other public or private archives. Many mythological tales are still part of the traditional store of narratives told on Indian reservations.

It is not my intention to try to embrace all this material here, to account for scholarly achievements and the range and dimensions of North American Indian myths. My object is more specific, as the title of the chapter reveals. In my consideration these myths have not received in all respects the scholarly treatment they deserve. My aim is therefore to outline the religious import of North American myths. In contradistinction to most colleagues in anthropology and folklore, I consider "myth" to be primarily a religious concept. Consequently, its place in religion and its meaning should be sought for first of all. To my understanding this analysis has been used very sparingly, whereas historical, formal, and psychological investigations have been performed quite frequently.[1] In proceeding from a religio-scientific point of view, we may arrive at important conclusions as to the types of myths, the role played by myths, their relations to the ritual and to belief systems. Moreover, it can be shown that each cultural area of North America has a myth system that corresponds to historical and ecological factors.

The reader should be aware of the fact, already made clear, that in the face of an enormously abundant material the following account can only be very selective. First of all, I have used material with which I am well acquainted and which has been discussed earlier in my literary production. If this means a slight predilection for myths from the Plains and Basin areas, it cannot be helped.

Mythological Research in North America

Myth is, as I said, primarily a religious concept. This statement will no doubt be questioned by opponents: why should a tale, a myth, be analyzed solely from the viewpoint of its religious contents when there are so many other aspects that could be applied? "Myth" is a *terminus technicus* in many disciplines (cf., e.g., Chase 1949). Literature, history, folklore, anthropology all contend that the subject of myth properly belongs within their own domain. Myth is oral "literature," or folktales, or speculation about natural occurrences, or untrue statements about the world around us. With the exception of the latter category, all the others are products of scholarly thinking over a long time.

It may be advantageous here to look back upon the approaches to North American myths and tales that have been in current use up until now (cf. Dundes 1967: 61 ff.; Hultkrantz 1966–67b: 21 ff.). Disregarding euhemerism and other early western ways of understanding the myth, it was the symbolism of O. T. Müller and the *Naturmythologie* of Max Müller and others that constituted the prevailing myth interpretation when the scientific study of myth began. As far as I can tell, it left few traces in North American Indian mythog-

---

1. It is however possible that the "new ethnography" will mean a turning point. Scholars working in this vein attempt to place ethnographical traits in their proper setting, the cognitive world of the peoples concerned. Religion is part of that world.

raphy except for Brinton's obsession with solar and Kunike's with lunar mythology (Brinton 1882; Kunike 1926). The historico-geographical schools started by Boas in anthropology and Krohn in folklore have far more important repercussions. Most myths and tales were analyzed according to the diffusionistic key provided by Boas. The latter's *Tsimshian Mythology* and Reichard's study of Plateau Indian myths are good examples of the method (Boas 1916; Reichard 1947), while Krohn's influence may be traced in Thompson's famous study of the Star Husband tale, for example (Thompson 1953). As Dundes has shown, the preoccupation of the same Finnish school with tale types and motif indexes had a precursor in Swanton's call for a concordance of North American myths and Kroeber's and Lowie's listing of mythological catchwords (Dundes 1967: 63). This was a line that Thompson took up later on; his survey of North American Indian tales from 1929 remains a source of comparative information (Thompson 1929). Tale type and motif index mean to a historical interpretation what genre analysis means to a religio-scientific interpretation: they are both necessary methodological tools.

In the time between the two world wars, Malinowski's functionalism had a great following among students of myths. Its impact on North American scholars was less remarkable, however, due to the predomination of the Boas school and its, as it were, submerged functionalism. (As Kroeber has demonstrated, Boas was more interested in function and process than in history.) Malinowski's genre analysis of Trobriand tales is well known; it had apparently little effect on American anthropologists and folklorists. This was unfortunate, for in this way the religious factor in mythology continued to be bypassed. Indeed, Waterman's analysis of explanatory tales had demonstrated the nonessential import of religious *aitia* in such tales (Waterman 1914).

Another trend from the same time, the psychoanalytic approach (also present in Malinowski's writings), had a stronger and more lasting impact on the interpretation of North American myths. A mythical key figure like the culture hero (or, as American students of myth prefer to see him, the trickster) attracted because of its janus-character, the attention of both professional psychoanalysts (Róheim; Jung) and anthropologists (Radin; La Barre) (Róheim 1952; Radin 1956; La Barre 1970). The center of the interest was and is irrational man, in particular his *id* and its sublimations. Religion comes in as an illustration of the sway of the subconscious forces. This reductionistic attitude, clearly demonstrated in La Barre's work, has unfortunately meant that, for instance, the solutions to the trickster problem residing in the religious context have been overlooked.

A most important way of understanding myth was introduced by sociological students. Two main approaches may be distinguished, originating with Robertson Smith and Durkheim, respectively. The former stated that mythology on the whole constituted a
description of ritual. He is therefore held as the progenitor of the
British myth-and-ritual school, later called the Cambridge school
(after Jane Harrison and others). The Near Eastern mythology investigated by this group (and like-minded Scandinavian historians of
religions) yielded a good harvest of confirmations of the theory. However, the close-knit societies in the Near East have few counterparts
in North America, and although a case might have been made for
Zuni and Winnebago myths, North American Indian myths were
not investigated from this perspective.[2] Here, again, the lack of
concern for religion among most American anthropologists may
have played a role.

Durkheim's position, subsequently heralded by a majority of
French sociologists and, in Britain, by Radcliffe-Brown and his pupils,
was simple enough: religion, including myth, is modelled on and
integrated with society. It will remain a problem whether the American studies of cultural reflections in mythology, initiated by Boas (on
the Tsimshian and Kwakiutl) and followed up by, for instance, Ehrlich
(on the Crow), Spencer (on the Navajo) and Stern (on the Klamath),
were stimulated by the sociological school (cf. Hultkrantz 1956: 24;
Dundes 1967: 66 f.). In any case, these studies are the closest counterparts from the North American field to this kind of mythological
research. Common to both approaches was a deficient interest in
religious aspects of myth and, in the French-British social anthropology, a tendency toward reductionism in dealing with religion and
myth. These reservations on my part should not conceal the fact,
however, that the sociological school has contributed greatly to our
understanding of religious oral traditions in their socio-cultural setting. Likewise, the students of this school have shown in what important ways a myth can serve as a *charta*, or sanction, of both ritual and
profane institutions.

The latest fashion in mythological research is, as we know,
structuralism. It has greatly affected North American Indian mythology. The culture hero behind this approach, Lévi-Strauss, used Tsim-

2. American scholars have not been immune to such studies in other fields
(cf. Hyman 1955). The intimate relation between myth and rite in North America
was observed by Matthews, but he meant that myth had priority over ritual (see
Matthews 1902).

shian materials from Boas' already mentioned monograph in his classic essay on *Asdiwal*, and North American myths have been used extensively in his later volumes, known under the collective name of *Mythologiques* (Lévi-Strauss 1958, 1967). There is no need to recapitulate more closely the French scholar's ideas here. His main target is the operations of the human mind, not the myth as such. By structural analysis he finds that all myths aim at resolving conflicts that haunt human existence. In coded messages the myths hide their ulterior meanings, which may be found out through dialectic logic and different kinds of transformal procedures. The manifest, religious contents of myths are never discussed. Such questions have to give in to the deeper problem of the structure of the human mind. Indeed, Lévi-Strauss confesses that he does not understand what religion is (Lévi-Strauss 1969: 43).

This is not the place to launch a full-scale criticism of this scholar's program. Some scholars are satisfied with it, while others, like myself, are not. His analysis is both arbitrary and, with respect to the results, monotonous; that it evinces the brilliancy of a creative thinker is another matter. What cannot be disputed is that this structuralism reveals the inherent logic of a myth, its rhythm, its style. Questions of style have been an enduring theme in studies of American tales (cf. Reichard; Jacobs), and no doubt Lévi-Strauss has contributed to the genre.

Nevertheless, some students of religion have approached the structuralism of Lévi-Strauss in a positive way. There is thus an analysis of the Sedna myth among the Central Eskimo in which the author, J. F. Fisher, finds "that Sedna mediates between several sets of oppositions in Eskimo culture." He also concludes that Sedna provides a means of dealing with oppositions that are inherent in the Eskimo world-view (Fisher 1975: 36 f., 38). This is a trivial conclusion. The main fact is that Sedna, mistress of the sea animals, is such a central person in the Eskimo world that she has attracted a set of myths, well analyzed by Fisher. As we shall see, it is dangerous to infer from myth what belongs to religion.

A structural approach also underlies Dundes' analysis of North American folktales. However, it concerns the narrative rather than its contents. It is in many respects a scholarly work. Unfortunately, the author commits the sin of identifying tales on the basis of their structures as outlined by him. The outcome is that, for example, the North American Orpheus tradition is identified with a completely different abduction tale (Dundes 1964: 77). This example shows that formal structures are too general to define a tale. Only analyses of contents can lead to constructive definitions. If we are dealing with religious tales—and the Orpheus tradition belongs to this category— the functional setting of the tale is also important.

This short review of research on North American myths and tales shows that scholars have avoided denoting myth as a religious category. Only one American, the philosopher Alexander, endeavored to identify the religious contents of American Indian myths after Brinton (Alexander 1916). It is remarkable that the editors of the series *Mythology of All Races* designated a philosopher, not an anthropologist or folklorist, to compose the North American volume of the set. Scholars like Lowie, Radin, and Speck occasionally subjected myths to religious analysis, but halfheartedly (cf. Hultkrantz 1966–67: 192, 194 f.). European Americanists with their background in comparative religion did more, but they were few, and their ideas were ruled by fashionable theories of perishable nature.

This is no condemnation of the approaches and methods that have been used so far in studies of North American myths. The field of mythic creations is a wide one, in which many disciplines are involved, and many facets are explored. However, myth is more than just a tale. It is a myth because it has religious relevance. As myth it should therefore be primarily investigated with an eye to its religious value. Thus the necessity to perform such research seems urgent, indeed, compelling here.

The Definition of Myth

This approach presupposes, of course, that we know what a myth is. Here again there is much confusion, not least in the ranks of North American mythologists.

Let us return to the source of our systematization, Jacob Grimm himself. In his *Teutonic Mythology,* first published in 1835, Grimm laid down the essential differences between myth, legend, and fictional folktale, or fairytale (*Märchen*). He observed that the folktale is flighty, fantastic, migratory, and the legend local bound, close to history, whereas the myth portrays gods and supernatural animals and all kinds of metamorphoses (Grimm 1966, 3: xv ff.). This scheme, admittedly inspired by the specific conditions in continental Europe, was widely accepted in its general outlines (whereas the criteria for the respective categories were soon refined). For instance, it was adopted by British folklorists and students of comparative religion (Hartland 1914; Harrison 1912: 330). When, at the turn of the century, American anthropologists published collections of epical narratives under the heading "myths and folktales" this was an echo of Grimm's classification (see, e.g., Boas 1915). At the same time, American folktales were never systematized in a rigorous way; anthropologists speak indifferently about myths and folktales even today. Indeed, Boas was opposed to a classification if it was not supported by native terms (Boas 1915: 310). It is true that few American Indian collections of traditions can be categorized according to Grimm's system; Bascom lists a few, however (Bascom 1965: 9 f.).

This is scarcely surprising. The Oriental "wonder tale" that invaded Europe in the eighteenth century gave rise to fictional tales. Among American Indians this type of tale is not unknown, but there is no doubt that it was introduced at a rather late date by Europeans (cf. Thompson 1919). The original situation in both Europe and North America was, then, that two types of narrative could be distinguished, both of them objects of belief: myths and legends (traditions). It is necessary to stress the word "could" here. If we go back in European cultural history, we find that the Greek word *mythos* originally meant tale in a very general sense. Since most of these tales concerned the gods, the genre was soon settled (cf. Kirk 1970). Similarly, many American Indian tribes know only one word, tale. There are, however, quite a few tribes that distinguish between two categories which we could label "myths" and "legends" (cf. Beckwith 1938: xvi f.). As Boas has pointed out, the two classes refer mostly to a distance in time. Among the Winnebago, for instance the *waika* refer to divine actors in a distant mythical era, while the *worak* refer to human actors within the memory of man (Boas 1915: 310 f.; Radin 1948: 11 f.).[3]

Even in those cases where only one native (linguistic) category can be identified, an analysis may show a covert categorization. Thus in my interpretation of Shoshoni religious narratives, I found the term for narrative stands for two main types of religious epic accounts, myths and legends. Not only the distance in time but also the attitude of veneration and sacredness were criteria for my judgment. A third category, fictional tales, has apparently developed in more recent times but plays a minor role (Hultkrantz 1960b). Some may object, as Boas did once, that an analysis which is not supported by the overt categorization of the aborigines themselves should not be permissible. My answer is that modern cultural research is acknowl-

---

3. Like Bascom, I am inclined to identify the second category with legends.

edged to operate on two levels: we may see things as the natives see them, or we may systematize them according to guiding principles which we perceive to be basic. Anthropologists talk about emic and etic units (Pike), or unconscious and conscious models (Lévi-Strauss). Certainly, Bascom is in agreement with my views when he says: "Despite the incompleteness of the evidence, and despite these variations in native categories, the definitions of myth, legend and folktale offered here are analytically useful. They can be meaningfully applied even to societies in which somewhat different distinctions between prose narratives are recognized" (Bascom 1965: 15).

With his article on the genres of folk narratives, Bascom has reintroduced the Grimm classification as a legitimate tool in American folkloristics. It would be advantageous if also American Indian traditions could be subjected to the same kind of analysis. In that way we would arrive at a clearer understanding of the religious contents of North American tales and could compare them with Old World myths in a more relevant way.

With this discussion in mind the genres should be defined. A thorough definition should contain all those criteria which have been laid down as essential by Honko in an important paper (Honko 1968). However, most of our North American materials were collected during the first fifty years of this century, without the collectors transmitting to us information on all the circumstances that we need to know for a classification in Honko's spirit. If we use a few basic criteria, it should be possible to identify, as I have tried to demonstrate in my book on the North American Orpheus tale, a good number of texts in archives and printed publications as myths, legends, and fictions (Hultkrantz 1957: 274 ff.).[4] I suggest that our criteria will include the time and scene for the action, the character of the personages, and, as far as it goes, the form of tradition. We arrive then at the following classification:

1. The myth. It takes place at the beginning of time, its acting personages are gods and mythic beings like the culture hero, primeval man, and the prototypes of animals, and the scene for action is the supernatural world. The myth has a fixed pattern of events, and actions are often repeated four times in North American texts.

2. The legend. It takes place in historical and recent times, its acting personages are human beings in their encounters with repre-

---

4. I am aware that misjudgments may be caused since we do not know one of the most essential details, the attitude of the listeners, the situation of story-telling.

sentatives of a supernatural world—spirits, ghosts, monsters—and the scene for action is this world or the supernatural world.

Both these categories are considered to be true. The myth depicts events in a far off time "when animals were human beings," as it is often said in North American myths. Furthermore, the myth has been passed down through the generations as a sacred tale, or as a contribution to knowledge about the world. The legend, again, with its supposed roots in a later, historical reality can often be traced back to a memorate, that is, a narrative of a certain person's meeting with a supernatural in a vision or a dream. It stands to reason that North American Indians with their vision-quest pattern have a rich store of such legends.

3. The fictional tale. It belongs to any time and any place, but it is always framed in a world of wonder. Its characters are fictive persons, in North America mostly supernaturals from European tales. The form of the tale may reveal the same European provenience.

Strictly speaking, the fictional tale is not at home in North America. Hallowell mentions that the Saulteaux of Manitoba believe all their tales to be true (Hallowell 1947: 547). It seems the same rule prevailed all over North America. Only where a disintegration of old cultures has taken place, or where European fairy tales have been accepted, the genre of fictional narratives for entertainment has spread. Many would perhaps refer the adventures of the trickster to the fictional tales, but they are indeed basically myths (see below).

The Sanctioning Power of Myths and Legends

Our genre classification means, of course, that the range of folktales that may pass as myths becomes much more narrow than it generally is in the opinion of most of my American colleagues. It becomes even smaller if we separate sacred myths from other, less functional myths. On the other hand, there is an affinity between sacred foundation myths and certain legends having the same general function. This complicates our picture. However, in the interest of comparative research, the line we have drawn between myth and legend ought to be upheld.

In principle every bonafide myth serves as a model, a *charta*, of the world and of human institutions. As I have expressed it in another connection, "the myth gives instruction concerning the world of the gods, and therewith concerning the cosmic order; it confirms the social order and the cultural values obtaining and it is in itself sacred" (Hultkrantz 1957: 13). Modern scholars of religion, in particular Eliade, have emphatically asserted that this is the real importance of myth; they have thus expanded the view put forth by Malinowski that the myth "expresses, enhances, and codifies belief" (cf., e.g., Eliade 1949). (The latter statement is, as we shall see, not entirely acceptable regarding North American material.) If the myth allows us to experience a drama *in illo tempore* (Eliade), in a "dream-time," to quote Australian aborigines, which is present even today, this mystery is facilitated by the tense constructions of Indian verbs (Brown 1976: 28). At the same time there is the deep meaning behind it all that the mythical events form the prototype for things today: not only the world-view but also the daily occupations and events have their model—and of course, their origins—in the mythical world. In a way the perspective is etiological, but this concept does not include the model and sanction functions of the myth and is therefore insufficient.

This is the ideal myth, as we meet it in Eliade's writings. I suppose it is the same type of myth Kluckhohn seeks when he points at "the connotation of the sacred as that which differentiates 'myth' from the rest of folklore" (Kluckhohn 1942: 47). However, North American myths are not always sacred, as will soon be demonstrated. Furthermore, there are legends that have mythical functions; we are here reminded of Boas' general view that in North America myths may turn into legends and vice versa (cf. Boas 1915: 310 f.). These reservations are justified, if we proceed from a general idea that myths and legends always keep clear of each other. But in fact, all I want to do here is to insist upon a correct *classification*. Myths, or at least mythical patterns, may be integrated with legends, just as legends may be reinterpreted into myths. Both processes may be illustrated with the North American Orpheus tradition. As I have tried to show, it is basically a tale of a shaman bringing back a sick person's free-soul from the realm of the dead, a soul-loss cure through the shaman's soul-flight (Hultkrantz 1957: 259, 261). In most North American cases it appears as a legend, but in a few societies it is told as a myth. It is a real myth among the Modoc, Nisenan, Navajo, and Taos Indians in California and the Southwest, and among the Cherokee of the Southeast (Hultkrantz 1957: 279). The actors are here exalted supernatural beings. Among the Winnebago the legend has been endowed with mythic details so that Radin classifies it as a "myth-tale": it includes "motifs and incidents from the mythological background" (Radin 1926: 22). Surely, the demarcation line between myth and legend is not absolute in this material.

Whether the same situation obtains or not in other areas of the world, there is no doubt that the importance of the vision-quest in North America has determined the ease with which genres overlap. The vision paves the way for the mythical integration of the legend or the legend's transformation into a myth. Indeed, the vision is so powerful that it even creates myths. This is the situation among the Mohave Indians of California. Their medicine-men receive whole myths in their dreams (see on this matter, e.g., Kroeber 1948: 1 ff.). In practice it means of course that dream contents are worked into a prefigured mythic pattern. Above all, visions have produced many legends which have the same sanctioning power as sacred myths.

Some examples. The Orpheus tradition in North America which is mostly a legend reinforces and gives authority to beliefs in the afterworld (Gayton 1935: 285; Hultkrantz 1957: 290). There is positive information that it even forms eschatological ideas (Hultkrantz 1957: 282). In the last century the Orpheus tradition, probably on account of its shamanistic background, functioned as an "institution legend" for the Ghost Dance (Hultkrantz 1957: 145 f., 263, 307, 311 f.). Another legend with similar functions tells of a warrior who, resting on a hill distant from his camp, received a vision. A buffalo spirit appeared to him, gave him instructions on how to set up and perform a Sun Dance, and ordered him back to his camp to realize the vision. The Indian did so, and that was the beginning of the Sun Dance. This tale is told by Shoshoni and Ute.[5] Finally, there is the well-known legend of the two Dakota men who met a buffalo maiden out on the Plains. One of them wanted to seduce the beautiful girl and turned into a skeleton; the other had decent thoughts and was endowed with the sacred pipe by the buffalo maiden. This is the origin legend of the sacred pipe and the ceremonies surrounding it.[6]

These legends all show that supernatural actions in legends in which humans take part may receive the same binding force as such actions in myths on two counts, namely (1) if the course of events is supposed to have happened long ago, and (2) if the events have proved to have importance for a whole group of human beings.

5. The version given here was told me by the Wind River Shoshoni. For a Southern Ute variant, see Jorgensen 1972: 26.

6. There are many versions of this legend. See, for instance, Brown 1953: 3ff.; Dorsey 1906a; and compare the ritual in Fletcher 1883.

Classification of Myths in North America

The North American Indian myths may conveniently be divided into sacred myths and myths of entertainment or—if that term is preferred—mythological tales. By the latter term I do not mean what Boas had in mind (or Radin, when speaking of myth-tales), but tales which have the status of myths but have no serious function. The sacred myths, which all have a sanctioning purpose, may be divided into cosmological myths, institutional myths, and ritual myths.

We arrive at the following four groupings:

1. Cosmological myths are sacred myths that describe the cosmos and the interrelations of its phenomena by anchoring them in a series of supernatural events in primordial time. The cosmic phenomena are thus seen as products of an *Urdrama*, a cosmogony. Cosmological myths may be connected with a ritual, but this is not always the case, particularly not among the hunting and gathering peoples. Cosmological myths procure for a man a world-view but not necessarily a religion (cf. below). The people that appear in these myths are not necessarily the deities and spirits of practical religion.

Among cosmological myths proper we may primarily count the creation myths and the astral myths. The former exist in many different types (Rooth 1957). There is the North Central Californian myth according to which the world came about through the power of the Creator's word (cf., e.g., de Angulo and Benson 1932). There is the South Californian myth that describes the emanation of the world as a result of the cohabitation between the sky god and Mother Earth. As Kroeber remarked, it recalls Polynesian creation myths (Kroeber 1925: 677). And there is, last but not least, the myth of the Earth-diver, in which the Creator orders animals to dive for mud in the primeval sea, or dives himself; out of the mud he creates the earth. This myth is associated with a widespread mythological theme, the rival twins (Count 1952). This is not the place to discuss this interesting relationship. However, there is clear evidence that both the myth and the idea of dual creators have disseminated from the Old World (Hultkrantz 1963: 33 f., 44 f.).

The position of astral myths is somewhat enigmatic in North America. Usually a myth is not astral all through, but it ends with an astral motif, or the final episode in the narrative has astral symbolism. Among the Wind River Shoshoni, for instance, many tales of Coyote's adventures have astral motifs appended at the end. When Coyote tries to seduce his daughters they flee to the sky where they become a star constellation, or three mountain bucks pursued by hunters finally flee up to the sky and turn into stars (cf. Hultkrantz 1960b: 567). These endings remind us of Waterman's discussion of explanatory tales. It is difficult to judge how they once came about. However, knowing the development of the trickster tales (cf. below) it is possible to see them as remnants of old myths, perhaps attached to other tales (cf. Hultkrantz 1972a: 343).

There are, namely, astral myths in a true sense, myths that connect the star-spangled sky with primordial times. The Pawnee and Blackfoot possess such myths. Indeed, the former identify their gods with stars (cf. Dorsey 1904, 1906b). Many tribes in the Southwest, Southeast, and on the Plains connect the Supreme Being with the sun. Among them, the sun figures in a few myths but shows little of the religious dignity and kindness that is the stamp of the Supreme Being. Most widespread is the myth of the cottontail and the sun. In some versions we are told that the sun burned the earth, killing people, because she (observe the sex) was not as much loved by them as her sister, the moon. The tension between stars is a dominant theme in many star myths. The San Juan tale of two stars, man and wife, who follow each other through the skies, is an example of the genre (Parsons 1926: 22 ff.).

To the cosmological myths we may also refer the transformer myths and the myths about human origins. The former are associated with the assistant creator, who is often also the culture hero. Raven of the Northwest Coast Indians and Glooscap of the northeastern Algonkian belong to this category of divine beings, vigorous in primordial times but not active in the present. The myths of Raven, for instance, describe how, among other things, he stole the fire (or the sun) and the salmon from the mysterious beings who kept these treasures and delivered them to mankind. Among the myths about human origins the emergence myth deserves particular mention (Wheeler-Voegelin and Moore 1957). This myth that is disseminated in the southern parts of the continent (and quite clearly related to agricultural ideology) tells us how the first human beings ascended from the underworlds where they had lived before. Most Navajo regard this myth as their most sacred, but, if we may believe Kluckhohn, it is not held by them to be the basis for any single ceremony (Kluckhohn 1942: 60 n. 61; cf., however, Haile 1942).

There are many other myths associated with the beginning of times which could be mentioned here, for instance myths about the origin of night and day, the change of the first beings into animals, and the dispersion of the animals, etc. Of particular interest are the myths of the origin of death. They tell how the human fate was determined by two divine beings through an agreement or by divination (Boas 1917).

2. Institutional myths relate how cultural and religious institutions were established in primordial times. The way the mythic beings arranged it has to be followed today by the people. The ancients gave the pattern, the people repeat it, but there is no ritual identification. All those myths belong here in which the culture hero instructed the ancestors how to make houses, canoes, how to regulate the laws, how to deal with menstruation and death—although these myths may often also be catalogued as myths of entertainment.

As we have observed, many of the institutional myths tend to merge with sacred legends. We have seen how the Shoshoni and Ute had their Sun Dance presented to them by a buffalo spirit that appeared to one of their warriors. In the Cheyenne origin myth of the Sun Dance, the warrior has turned into the culture hero Erect Horns who, with his woman, receives the ritual in the mythical mountain of Roaring Thunder (Dorsey 1905a: 46 ff., Powell 1969, 2: 467 ff.).

Very prominent is the place taken by institutional myths in the celebration of sacred bundles. For instance, the opening of the Arapaho flatpipe bundle is accompanied by four nights of telling the myth that belongs to it (Carter 1938).

3. Ritual myths are cosmological myths which serve as "texts" for ritual performances. The ritual procedure is identified with the incidents of the myth, the officiants of the ritual represent the mythic personages. Not all cosmological myths are, or are used as, ritual myths. Students of religion who deal with Near Eastern mythology tend to consider all myths as ritual myths, and they consequently conclude that every myth has taken form in a ritual setting (cf. Widengren 1968: 130). The North American materials show that such ideas are unwarranted (cf., in particular, Kluckhohn 1942: 61). Although no exhaustive investigation of the occurrence of ritual myths in North America has been done, it is my impression from my own reading, that cosmological myths occasionally are integrated with rituals, particularly in more complex and agricultural native societies. (This statement needs, of course, empirical corroboration.)

Let us adduce an example. The Sun Dance is, at least among the Plains Algonkian tribes (Cheyenne, Arapaho above all), a reproduction of the primeval creation. It is a dramatization of the myth of the Earth-diver: pieces of mud that are placed on the ground of the Medicine Lodge should represent the solid ground that grew from the sods picked up out of the primeval sea. Furthermore, the Sun Dance pole is held to be a ritual replica of the cottonwood tree on which the woman of the Star Husband myth climbed to heaven (Hultkrantz 1973b: 10, 15). Thus two migratory myths, one of them—the Earth-diver—of Asiatic provenience, have in this instance become ritual myths. It would not be possible to prove the other way round.

The impersonation of mythic beings (not necessarily divinities in religion) may be illustrated with details from the Great Medicine Society (*midewiwin*) among the Ojibway. The person to be initiated into the society is identified with the culture hero, Minabozho, and his actions in the sacred lodge imitate, for example, the journey of the culture hero to the realm of the dead as described in the foundation myth of the ceremony (see Hoffman 1891: 280).

Ritual myths, as I said, seem primarily at home in the fertility rituals of agrarian societies. This does not imply that all myths from these societies are ritual myths, particularly not in the East. In a Seneca myth the corn goddess, who is the daughter of the earth goddess (cf. Demeter—Kore in Greece), becomes a captive of the bad twin under the earth. However, she is found by a sunbeam and returns to her fields (Converse 1908: 64). This is an accurate description of the life of the grain during the agrarian year and a close counterpart to a well-known theme in Near Eastern and Mediterranean mythology connected with a ritual. However, we do not know if the American myth was part of a ritual. There is greater probability that the Pawnee sacrifice of a captive girl to the Morning Star was connected with the so-called immolation myth. The latter (which has a wide diffusion in eastern North America, Mexico, and South America) describes how the corn mother is killed and her body dragged around on the ground, thus giving rise to corn and other crops (Hatt 1951: 854 ff.). In the Pawnee ritual drama the body of the sacrificed girl was cut in pieces, the blood of which was poured over the soil to enhance fertility (cf. Dorsey 1907).

The evidence from the Southwest is less controversial, and less spectacular. Zuni creation myths are recited during ritual performances (cf. Bunzel 1932c and d), and the Flute Ceremony of the Hopi may be seen as a dramatization of their emergency myth (Parsons 1939, 2: 1042).

4. Myths of entertainment, or mythological tales, are myths that have been elaborated by the raconteur and thus lost their sacredness but are nevertheless considered as basically true. Their counterparts in literate cultures are the literary myths (Homer's books, Snorri's Edda). The whole series of so-called trickster tales belong here. However, the trickster is just one side of a mythic being that also appears in the sacred myths, the culture hero. What seems to have

happened is that this ambiguous personality, at once both adversary and helper of the Creator, because of his ludicrous shortcomings has become a favorite object of the raconteur's imagination (Hultkrantz 1963: 35 ff.). In particular, his sexual appetite, his greediness, and anal capacity have been embroidered upon in these myths, but also his buffoonery, stupidity, and treachery. On the Plains this category of myths is the most beloved, the most told, and the most widespread.

Two questions naturally arise here: why do we call such stories "myths," and why did not the raconteur also manipulate other myths?

A perusal of all these tales (as far as they have been available to me) has convinced me that they are basically sacred myths that have developed into plain folktales. They have lost their sacred cosmological character but have kept two original qualities: they are considered true (at least by old-timers), and their main character is a true mythic being (cf. Hultkrantz 1960b: 559 ff.). They are consequently not fictional tales, even if the listeners know that some episodes have been added to the general pattern. "Truth" is, of course, a relative concept here. What is true to some is not true to others, and the degree of truth can vary in one and the same individual. But the tendency is clear enough.

The role of the raconteur has been particularly stressed by Radin (Radin 1926). There is certainly always a raconteur's talent at work in oral tradition. However, its influence is restricted in the recounting of a sacred myth,[7] unless the actions and character of one outstanding personage invites to diffusive narration—and the Coyote of the western Plains and Basin folktales is such a personage. The composition of an original sacred myth has a firm structure, whereas Coyote myths offer a chain of unrelated incidents that betray their origins in the raconteur's art.

Myth and Religion

Myth has thus a religious value, but is myth religion, as many anthropologists and historians of religions tend to think? The foregoing account, with its differentiation between cosmogonic and religious figures, between gods and mythic personages, should have given the

---

7. Informants are particularly keen to point out that they have memorized the right words of the sacred myth.

answer. Myth deals with primordial times, religion with the present day; myth is epic, religion symbolic. There is thus a natural separation between myth and religion. However, ritual myths create a link between myth and ritual and thereby afford an identification between mythic beings and the gods of religion.[8]

The situation is different in different places. In the Pueblo area myth and religion go together to some extent. In the Great Basin the reverse rule holds (Hultkrantz n.d.). The Wind River Shoshoni believe in different sets of supernatural beings, one belonging to mythology, the other to religion. There is almost a wall between these "configurations of religious belief" (Hultkrantz 1972a). The Winnebago clans have each one a separate creation myth. Nobody finds this peculiar: the recitation of the origin myth is a kind of clan identification (Radin 1923: 207 ff.). Also subdivisions of the Cheyenne tribe have different creation myths that legitimized the political existence of these divisions. The consequence is, however, that group conflicts arise (Moore 1974: 355).

The religious import of myths is thus highly variable. It is to be hoped that more research will be done on this interesting but much neglected subject which, in my estimation, is the most important aspect of myth.

8. Some Papago rites have a vague connection with myths which, according to Ruth Underhill, is "a rationalization made for the sake of unity" (Kluckhohn 1942: 49).

2

The Structure of Theistic Beliefs
among North American Plains Indians

For A LONG TIME the religio-scientific debate has paid particular attention to certain theistic concepts of the North American Indians, such
as the Algonkian *Manitou*, the Siouan *Wakanda* and some central
Californian creator ideas (see Hultkrantz 1963: 16 f., 18 f., 24 ff.). Originally, the reason for this interest was the desire to find out whether a
concept such as a single high god existed among so-called primitive
peoples, and whether it was represented by the above notions—an
alternative which was impossible for the evolutionists to accept but a
matter of course to the defenders of primeval monotheism. The gap
between these two views has since then been spanned, for overwhelming materials from different "primitive" peoples, including the
North American Indians, have demonstrated the presence of a high
god who, however, does not stand alone.

The conclusion we can draw is that theistic beliefs among the
really "primitive" peoples, hunters and collectors, rarely fit such
labels as monotheism or polytheism. Polytheism is, as for instance
Swanson and Pallis have stressed, the religious belief pattern in an
advanced society like that of, say, the Near Eastern city-states or the
New World florescent and classic kingdoms (Swanson 1960: 82 ff.;

20

Pallis 1944: 415). Monotheism is, to quote Pettazzoni, the reaction to polytheism (in an advanced society), as we can see from the monotheistic systems created by Achn-aton of Egypt, Nezahualcoyotl of Texcoco (Mexico) or Mohammed from Mecca (Pettazzoni 1954: 9).[1] Hunters and collectors do not share such religious systems, the products of priest speculation, dynastic ambitions, and historical impact. They evince rather an unqualified "theism" where different vaguely delimited concepts exist side by side. Very common is a pattern characterized by a belief in a high god and a host of lesser spirits.

This is a pattern which is known from Africa, for example from the Nuer (cf. Evans-Pritchard 1956),[2] and from Siberia and North America. It occurs among several Plains Indian tribes, such as the Shoshoni and the Dakota (Sioux). In the following we shall study the structure of this theism among these two tribes, in order to illuminate the relations which exist—or at least may exist—between the high god and the spirits. These relations have been variously interpreted by scholars, particularly concerning the Dakota (see Hultkrantz 1966–67b: 14 ff.). Some have conceived of a vertical structure where the spirits are subordinated under the high god, others a horizontal structure where the spirits cooperate with the high god on an almost equal level, or where together they constitute the divine essence of a high god. The theistic structure is thus rather disputed among scholars.

Let us first consider the Plains Shoshoni, or Wind River Shoshoni, as they are called today after their reservation in western Wyoming. I draw here upon my own field material gathered during repeated visits to these Shoshoni in the 1940s and 1950s. The Plains Shoshoni believe in an undetermined number of spirits and a Supreme Being, *Tam Apö*. The spirits are mostly conceived of in animal disguise, a heritage of the long hunting existence (cf. Hultkrantz 1970a: 70 ff.). If we disregard those spirits which only fulfill a part in mythology, such as the trickster (culture hero) and certain primeval animal characters (Hultkrantz 1962b: 546 ff.), we receive the following series of believed-in spirits and divinities in Shoshoni religion:

1. The monotheistic exclusivity of the early Hebrews constitutes, in my opinion, a remarkable case apart, although Pettazzoni did not see the matter thus.

2. It should be noted, however, that Evans-Pritchard tries to prove (less convincingly, I think) that the lesser spirits are just different aspects of the Supreme Being, corresponding to different social structures. He seems to confuse the observer's and the native's points of view. For the alternation between monotheism and polytheism in African religions, with particular attention paid to Lienhardt's interpretations of the Dinka concepts of God, see Pettersson 1966.

1. *Tam Apö* ("Our Father"), Supreme Being, sustainer of the universe, the utmost resource of all things. He is represented by the sun and (possibly) the moon.

2. Thunder, lightning, and wind spirits, all very powerful.

3. Spirits of nature which are and give *puha* or supernatural power both to the medicine-men and to young men and warriors who seek this power at rock-drawings. These spirits almost always appear as animals and birds.

4. *Tam mbia*, Mother Earth, who makes the earth green and gives her human children plants and water.

5. Diverse uncanny spirits such as the water buffaloes, the man-eating ogre (*pa:ndzoaBits*), the disease-giving dwarf (*ninimbi*) and the wandering ghost (*dzoap*). These are avoided as far as possible.

6. The spirits of the dead in the land of the dead. They can be approached only by outstanding, very gifted medicine-men who put themselves in a trance and travel in a nonphysical form to the realm of the dead. Such medicine-men no longer exist. Severely ill people who have arrived in a coma sometimes also enter this realm.

Admittedly, this formal division of the spirits does not correspond to any general Shoshoni opinion; it is entirely the construct of the observer. Some exceptional medicine-men do, indeed, try to discern a hierarchy among the spirits. However, their interest as medicine-men is only to arrange the *puha,* and these may, of course, be grouped in descending order with such spirits as the mighty buffalo and the clean eagle at the apex (Hultkrantz 1956a: 200). Nevertheless, the model offered here represents the actual categories of spiritual beings and would, I think, scarcely be disputed by the Shoshoni Indians.

With the exception of the two last-mentioned groups of spirits, the uncanny spirits (5) and the dead (6), all categories perform some function in the lives of the Shoshoni. Their main functions correspond to specific situations. Thus the *puha* are approached when a person's mental or physical capacity needs to be improved; that is, when he needs luck in hunting, in war, in love, in overcoming his own or somebody else's sickness. The Supreme Being is prayed to in situations of extreme need or, collectively, in the yearly Sun Dance. The Earth Mother is marginally appealed to at the Sun Dance and in some other connections. She figures more prominently in the newly acquired peyote cult. The spirits of the atmosphere (thunder, etc.) are partly included in the *puha* complex but play a more independent role as providers of rain, thunder, and wind. When the elements of nature are adverse to man these spirits have to be propitiated.

All this is to be expected. However, keeping in mind Max Müller's idea of *kathenotheism,* we can observe that just as a situation is complete in itself, the spiritual agencies which operate within its confines constitute the whole supernatural world—at that moment. This is the case at least with the Shoshoni. When prayers are directed at the rock-drawings they concern only the *puha,* never the Supreme Being. He does not exist in this connection, although at least some Shoshoni thinkers consider that theoretically the powers of the spirits derive from him. On the other hand, when *Tam Apö* is called upon in situations of great need and distress the spirits do not enter the picture; they are lesser powers, and there is no reason why they should appear on the scene. Here we have a system of what I have called alternating configurations of religious belief (Hultkrantz 1956a: 194 ff.). What is important to observe in this connection is that the Supreme Being and the *puha* spirits belong to different belief structures which usually alternate with each other. God and the spirits are theoretically coexisting, but in practice they substitute each other. As to thunder, lightning, and wind spirits, they appear without associations to God; but God can assume the functions which these spirits express and thus supplant them. This, however, happens very rarely. It is perhaps less surprising that different sets of spirits operate in alternating configurations, for instance, the guardian spirits and the "uncanny" spirits.

These belief structures certainly reflect, in their very organization, the ancient social and political structure of the tribe: the prevalent socio-political pattern in the old days was one of a semi-independent band-organization interacting with an emergent centralized authority (Chief Washakie). At the same time these structures corresponded to specific cultural, social and ecological situations which challenged the balance of man and released culturally determined responses in him: the desire for success in hunting or on the war-path induced him to guardian spirit quests at rock-drawings, the longing for safety in thunderstorms made him appeal to the thunderers, and the immediate need to escape from great danger forced him to call on the high god himself for help. The social and political, and partly also the ecological motivations have disappeared with the breakdown of traditional Plains culture at the end of the last century, but the religious patterns are largely intact to this day.

We now turn to the Teton Dakota, a branch of the great Sioux nation, who nowadays reside in the Dakotas but used to roam as nomads from the Missouri River to the Bighorn Mountains. There are several, sometimes very conflicting sources to their religion (see Dorsey 1894; Walker 1917; Densmore 1918; Deloria 1944; Brown 1953. Cf. for Eastern Dakotas, Lynd 1889; Pond 1889; Pond 1908). It is quite difficult today to create a true picture of traditional Western Dakota religion. Says Ella Deloria, herself a Dakota by birth, "The Dakota people of the past were not asked to analyze for posterity their beliefs about God. We cannot really know, therefore, in so many words by them uttered, exactly what they believed and how they expressed that belief" (Deloria 1944: 49). If, however, we rely on the information we have the Dakota supernatural beings may be classified as follows (another classification in Dorsey 1894: 434):

1. *Wakan Tanka* ("Great Holy"), also called *Taku Wakan* ("Something Holy") or *Taku Skanskan* ("Something in Movement"), is the Supreme Being. Although Gideon Pond, and after him Dorsey, did not find the idea of a Supreme Being represented among the (Eastern) Dakota (Pond 1889: 217; Dorsey 1894: 431), both Lynd and Densmore and later writers testify to its existence and pre-Christian origin (Lynd 1889: 151, 152 n.; Densmore 1918: 85 n. 2).[3] It is significant that whereas Gideon Pond interprets *Taku Wakan* as a collective name for the gods (Pond 1889: 217, 251), Samuel Pond says it "had such a meaning in the minds of the Indians that none of us hesitated to use it when speaking of the providence of God" (Pond 1908: 242 f.). It is obvious that the concept of the high god was difficult to grasp for foreigners, certainly partly due—as Deloria points out—to the structure of the Dakota language. Densmore, who also stresses the difficulty of formulating "the exact significance of the term in the mind of the Sioux" (Densmore 1918: 85 n. 2) quotes one of her informants, Chased-by-Bears, who, speaking about prayers to *Wakan Tanka*, says, " . . . we are sure that he hears us, and yet it is hard to explain what we believe about this. . . . We believe that he is everywhere, yet he is to us as the spirits of our [dead] friends, whose voices we can not hear" (Densmore 1918: 96). Personal and impersonal aspects seem to be interchangeable in this concept of God.

Like the Shoshoni, the Teton Dakota believed that the sun represented the high god (Densmore 1918: 86). (The moon, on the other hand, was supposed to be a goddess.) The name *Taku Skanskan* indicates that the high god was also identical with the sky.

2. The divinities of the atmosphere, including *wakinyan* (the thunderbird), the four winds, and the whirlwind.

3. The rulers of the animal species, which among the Dakota

---

3. Also an early writer like Riggs postulates that *Wakan Tanka* should be translated as "Great Spirit." See Riggs 1893: 105 ff., 108.

means the master spirit of the buffalo and possibly the bear (cf. Brown 1970).

4. The guardian spirits which revealed themselves in visions—the culmination of the vision-quest—and generally manifested themselves through natural phenomena such as birds and animals. "They are not themselves Wakan [holy, or supernatural], but the Wakan is in all things" (Deloria 1944: 52). Other natural objects became *wakan* by being colored red and prayed to, as were rocks and trees, for instance. The rock, *inyan*, was supposed to be the oldest manifestation of the divine (cf. Lynd 1889: 168 f.; Walker 1917: 82).

5. *Maka*, the Earth Mother, and "The Beautiful One" or *Wophe*, the patron of chastity and children. The latter is also the buffalo-woman who entrusted the sacred pipe to the Dakota (Brown 1953: 3 ff.; Dorsey 1906a: 326 ff.).[4]

6. Dangerous spirits of different kinds, such as the horned water monsters (*miniwatu* or *unktehi*, among the Eastern Dakota) which were at war with the thunderbirds, man-eating giants, elves (deer women) who led people astray and various goblins.

7. The spirits of the dead in the land of the dead.

Finally there were principally mythological figures who were considered to be capricious, such as the culture hero and trickster *Iktomi* ("Spider"), the wizard *Waziya*, and the latter's two-faced daughter. With few exceptions these beings do not seem to have figured in ordinary religious beliefs and cult practices.

The above categorization is the author's and is not entirely exhaustive. It gives, however, a general idea of the range of supernatural beings among the Teton Dakota. Furthermore, it reflects, as far as I can see, the ideas on the subject which are held by the common man. The same tendency to compartmentalization that we observed among the Plains Shoshoni seems to be present here as well, but the deficiency of our sources does not allow us to draw decisive conclusions. What we definitely do know, however, is that there is the same characteristic interplay between the high god and the spirits as exists among the Shoshoni.

This interplay is facilitated by a most inclusive concept of God. "*Wakan Tanka*, you are everything, and yet above everything," says Black Elk, the Oglala Sioux medicine-man.[5] And Red Bird assures us, "We believed that there is a mysterious power greater than

4. *Wohpe* is exclusively the medicine-men's name for this divinity.
5. A Swedish scholar has tried to penetrate the consequences of the Dakota high-god concept for their view of the relation between God and his creation. See Almqvist 1966.

all others, which is represented by nature, one form of representation being the sun" (Densmore 1918: 86). Deloria even equates *Wakan Tanka* and *wakan*, thereby subsuming our above categories (2)–(4) under the first-mentioned concept (Deloria 1944: 51). This expansion of the main theistic concept explains why Gideon Pond could mistake *Taku Wakan* for meaning "the gods." The traditional material at our disposal shows that the high god is called upon when the unifying force of the universe is implied, whereas individual spirits are needed when special supernatural actions are inferred. Unity and diversity in religious theism are thus expressed in a simple way. The consciousness of the inclusive character of *Wakan Tanka* represents an epistemological conclusion of this world-view.

These alternating structures of theistic beliefs also reflect, as among the Shoshoni, socio-political patterns and ecological conditions. What has been said above concerning the Plains Shoshoni in this respect also holds good for the Teton Dakota.

It was pointed out that among the Shoshoni certain "religious formulators," as Radin called them, tried to arrange the spirits into a ranking system. A similar development has taken place among the Teton Dakota but resulted here in a more elaborate theological system. In other words, among the Teton Dakota we find an esoteric tradition administered by medicine-men who spoke a secret, old-fashioned language.[6] In this shamanistic speculation, *Wakan Tanka* is identified with all the positive spirits, categories (1)–(5), and with certain soul concepts as well. They are united in a system based on the sacred number four and with the implication that four may be reduced to one. Thus according to Walker's informants, *Wakan Tanka* is one but consists nevertheless of four: the chief god, the great spirit, the creator god, and the executive god. Each of these in turn comprises four individuals: the chief god, for instance, the sun, the moon, the buffalo, and the spirit (= free-soul). Vertical and horizontal combinations of four cross each other and may all be reduced to one, *Wakan Tanka* (Walker 1917: 78 ff., 152 ff.). In this way the gap between extant belief structures is partially bridged. It is important to note,

---

6. On this secret language, see Walker 1917: 56, 78 f.; and Densmore, 1918: 120 n. 1. The secrecy may have to do with the taboo nature of certain religious concepts, such as *Wakan Tanka*. See Densmore 1918: 85 n. 2. Certainly, Lynd states that prayers were never directed to *Wakan Tanka*, who—after having created the world—had lost interest in his creation (Lynd 1889: 151). This, then, would indicate that he was a *deus otiosus* rather than a tabooed concept. However, Lynd seems to have overstated the case, as Dakota prayer texts clearly show.

however, that this theological system is not part of the creed of the common man.

Basic structures of theistic beliefs, similar to the ones outlined above as part of the religion of the common man in some Plains societies, can also be identified among other American Indian groups as well, for instance, among the Ojibway (Chippewa) of the Northern Woodland.[7] On the whole it may be stated that many so-called primitive religions are characterized by such alternating structures. Where shamanistic speculation has not arranged the high god and the spirits in a hierarchical order, the relation between them is one of alternation and interplay. The reasons for this may be sought in the demands of the cultural, ecological, and psychological situations and in the experience of cosmos as one and united or pluralistic and divided.

7. In his stimulating account from 1855, the German explorer Kohl says that the word for the Great Spirit, *Kitsche Manitou*, sometimes ("zuweilen") was no *nomen proprium* of a single being but an appellation of a whole class of great spirits (Kohl 1859a, 1: 86).

3

Configurations of Religious Belief
among the Wind River Shoshoni

MANY OF THE EARLIER WRITERS in the fields of ethnology and religion described the religions of primitive peoples as unified systems of belief, admitting, however, that they contained many contradictions. Although they presumed that such systems were better understood by the medicine-men and the secret societies, they considered them common to all individuals and social groups within an ethnical unit, a tribe, or a people. Naturally, such oversimplified representations had an unfortunate effect on the comparative study of religious conceptions and customs which was then carried out more intensively than it is now. As a result, research lost contact with the psychological and sociological truths behind the different types of religious representation.

Of course, there were talented researchers and observers who, more of less consciously, applied sounder principles to the study of primitive religion. Thus as early as 1709, Antoine Denis Raudot said of the Eastern Canadian Indians that "the religion of the savages ... is nothing but an idea; each has his own notion of the divinity according to his caprice, although there are nations which recognize gods for all the people in general" (in Kinietz 1940: 353).

Indeed, it seems possible that the very individualism inherent in the religions of the North American Indians, particularly among the hunting tribes, quite naturally leads field researchers to a realization of the internal differentiations within the religion of a primitive tribe. In any case, it is readily perceivable that it was the American ethnologists, such as Boas, Lowie, and Radin who, at the beginning of this century, paved the way for a more thorough comprehension of the nature of primitive religions, their connection with the forms of social organization, and personal, individual creation.

　　Investigations of the religious conceptions of specific groups and individuals among primitive peoples are fairly common nowadays. However, there is still another dimension of religious differentiation which, at least as regards primitive peoples, has not, as yet, been given much attention. The field researcher has observed that the religious belief of one and the same person can vary over a period of time. But he has not paid sufficient attention to the fact that these religious conceptions are able to change from one situation to another so that a religious person is capable of exhibiting several religious systems which, in their relationships to one another, are fairly incompatible. It is my intention in the following study to try to elucidate a religious differentiation of this type. My material is taken from the Wind River Shoshoni (that is, the Plains Shoshoni) whose culture and religion I studied in the field during 1948 and again in 1955.

Alternative Patterns of Religion among the Shoshoni

Every religion is characterized, as Goode states, by "variation in religious beliefs" (Goode 1951: 237). Belief is concentrated upon certain main religious categories, such as gods, eschatology, and rites. However, it is impossible for one and the same individual to pay attention to all of these categories at the same time. Circumstances determine which of the chief categories will arise—to quote Freud—from the "foreconscious" (das Vorbewusste) into the conscious mind. The life of a Shoshoni Indian has always been bound by religious conceptions and customs which changed character according to the situation. For example, in earlier times, he strove during his childhood and early manhood for contact with guardian spirits which could ameliorate his existence. In the Sun Dance he prayed for the blessings of the Supreme Being. If he became ill, his thoughts centered on the dangerous being which brought about his illness—perhaps the dwarf

spirit *ninimbi*, or a malign sorcerer. If someone in his immediate environment died, he thought of the ghosts which haunted the burial
places and former scenes of battle. The religious picture is a constantly shifting one; the dominating personages in it change, the hue
glides from light to dark.

All this is not particularly remarkable, being more or less
what one expects. The interesting thing is, however, that in certain
situations, the religious reality is given such a form that certain other
temporarily nonrelevant religious conceptions are logically impossible or, at least, practically out of the question. Let us now critically
examine three such situations which originated in olden times but
exist in their essentials even today; namely, the vision-quest, the Sun
Dance and the telling of stories on winter evenings.[1]

In a community of primitive hunters, success in life depends
to a very great extent on the ability of the individual to procure supernatural help. Like other Plains tribes, the Shoshoni originally had an
individualistic hunting culture. This characteristic individualism did
not disappear even when, after the introduction of the horse, the
social groups were more closely welded together to make possible the
hunting of the buffalo. For, to be truly effective, such an enterprise
must necessarily be a collective rather than an individual one. However, individual initiative, the contribution of each person, was still
essential. This fact was most apparent in the economic activity of the
Shoshoni in the summertime, for then the tribe was split into small
family groups which hunted the elk and smaller game, and gathered
roots, berries, and wild seeds in the lower mountain regions. Similarly, the central importance of individual initiative was evident in
warefare in which personal feats and distinctions played a decisive
role. The guarantors of these economic and military enterprises, in
which the happiness and prosperity of each and every individual
were at stake, were the *puha*, the supernatural powers or spirits. Or,
more correctly: the spirits who were able to transfer some of their
power to human beings—for all spirits were not *puha*, power-
endowing beings. Since this transfer of power took place during the
experience of visions (*puhanavuzieip*, "power-dream"), these supernatural beings can reasonably be called vision-spirits.

Just how closely the gifts of the spirits coincide with the needs
of the individual Shoshoni in his struggle for existence and against
external misfortune, illness, and enemies, appears perhaps most

1. The vision-quest now belongs almost entirely to a bygone age as only a
very few medicine-men still receive visions.

An island of prayers, Dinwoody Lake, Wind River Mountains. The supplicant prostrates himself on this little rocky island, and here receives, during a
night's dream, his vision, his power.

clearly in the following specification of the beneficial powers of the
various supernatural beings, information which was given to me by
one of the Shoshoni medicine-men.[2] It should be kept in mind that
the spirits usually appeared in the shape of animals and that, consequently, their gifts had a direct connection with the appearance,

2. The medicine-man, J. T., was born in 1884, and in 1956, was one of the
more active bearers of culture among the Shoshoni.

characteristics, and abilities of the animal in question. That the conception of just what these abilities included varies from medicine-man to medicine-man is another question.

The following *puha* bring happiness and prestige in family relations and in economic and military enterprises: the elk (wapiti) protects his ward from wounds and injuries; the famous chieftain, Washakie, was protected by his wapiti-*puha* "so he did not die when they stabbed him with a spear." The antelope not only gives "running-medicine," the ability to run swiftly, but is furthermore an excellent scouting-*puha*. The *puha* of the horse gives renewed energy and a reliable sense of location to the tired wanderer in the desert; "you can trail a person with him." The wolf and coyote are of priceless value to those wishing to steal horses from another tribe, besides being the best scouting-medicine, "they can't beat them." Even the badger is "good for stealing" while at the same time being, like the dog, an excellent *puha* for those desiring a successful coition and many children. The beaver is a good builder of dams; "because of that I can dam water," my informant, who had beaver-medicine himself, told me. The weasel gives one the ability to locate a horse one has lost and "helps you to kill persons without anybody knowing anything about it." The ground squirrel gives its ward the ability to perform black magic; that is, the ability to send illness-bringing things into the body of a person he wants to get rid of. The jack-rabbit gives more harmless gifts: "you can run fast, and you can run on top of the snow." The rattlesnake brings rain when the heat of the day becomes too trying. The lizard, like the coyote, can be sent out to kill enemies. Of the *puha* spirits which appear as birds, the eagle is the most noteworthy as it can give the medicine of invulnerability. The crane gives "travelling-medicine." The magpie, raven, and crow (the two latter being seldom distinguished between[3]) are good guardian spirits for those wishing to look for, and find, distant and hidden things. During the Sun Dance I witnessed in 1955, one of the medicine-men appeared with two magpie feathers standing upright in his hair. This was a sign of his investigatory activities—whether they were directed toward people or the secrets of the future. Even the hawk is useful for those wanting to gain information about diverse things; for example, he warns his ward in dreams of threatening dangers and tells him the best way of escaping them.

Almost all of the guardian spirits mentioned above, except for those which have a directly negative function, are also good healers.

3. Both the raven and the crow are called *ha:i,* and their nickname is *ka:kh.*

The thunderbird depicted on a rock wall at Dinwoody Lake, Wind River Mountains. Observe the zig-zag lines which represent lightning.

Indeed, it is mainly in their healing function that they appear to those granted the honor of being medicine-men. Naturally enough, my informant was particularly anxious to emphasize this aspect of their activities. Among healing powers not already mentioned above, are the buffalo which helps protect one from measles and small pox, the black bear which protects one from fevers and measles, the otter, and the mink.

However, it should not surprise us that certain guardian spirits, such as the grizzly bear, mountain lion, porcupine, and skunk, are considered harmful to their owner. On the other hand, this fact cannot nullify our impression that by far the majority of the *puha* have been, and are, positive spirit powers which satisfy the needs of the individuals in a nomadic hunting and warring culture.

For the present study, it is of some importance that the internal hierarchy among the spirits is made clear. It is more than natural that certain guardian spirits are able to give greater capacities than others, or a more important ability. The person who wants to acquire a whole set of *puha* is wise if he begins with the least and most easily obtained, for the really powerful *puha* are extremely dangerous if treated incorrectly, as the informant I have referred to above assured me. He also furnished me with the following order of hierarchy among the spirits. The most powerful is lightning whose force is the very essence of every vision. Next comes the thunderbird and then the eagle—the former is sometimes represented as an eagle, but most commonly as a hummingbird. A high level of effectiveness is also attributed to several other *puha;* namely, the bear, beaver, weasel and, in second place, the buffalo, otter, and antelope. Apparently, there was no definitely fixed order as two *puha* could quite easily change places. But, in general, it can be said that the groups of animals listed above possessed the highest *puha* in order of decreasing importance. Of greatest significance to the present discussion, however, is the fact that the Supreme Being, *Tam Apö*, is not included among them. When I made a point of asking my informant about this, he explained that "he is over the *puha*," but at the same time, he was uncertain of the actual relationship between the highest being and *puha*, if *Tam Apö* gave power to the *puha*, or not. Only after lengthy deliberation did he arrive at the conclusion that *Tam Apö* is the source and origin of all *puha*.

This grading of the spirit powers and the idea of their relationship to the Supreme Being turned out to be common to the more religiously initiated of the Shoshoni; mainly, of course, to the group of medicine-men.

The procuration of *puha* demands careful preparations. Except for certain great medicine-men especially chosen by the spirits all who desire *puha* must themselves seek the spirits. Alone and unarmed, the Indian has to set out for the wide open spaces, to the regions known from legends and tradition to be the abodes of the spirits. Sometimes he turns his steps towards hillocks or solitary rocks out on the prairie where the desert *puha* generally appear. At other times, he travels to the water where the fish *puha* may manifest themselves. But most often, he makes his way to the mountains, to those places where the rock-carvings are to be found, for there the animal *puha*, the most powerful but also the most dangerous of all spirits have their haunts.

After fasting for three days and nights, the Shoshoni Indian prepares himself to meet the spirits. As it draws toward twilight, he throws off his blanket and takes a cleansing bath in a nearby lake or stream. Next, he seeks out a place immediately below the rock-carvings, spreads out his blanket on the ground and sits on it, wearing only a simple breechcloth. He smears his chest and forehead with red paint, smokes his pipe and burns incense—"smokes cedar." At the same time, he prays to the spirit, reproduced in the rock-carving, whose particular favor he seeks. When night falls, he sinks down on to his blanket. Although his body remains uncovered and the nights are cold up in the mountains even during the hottest summer, he is soon able to devote himself to what the Shoshoni call *puhawido?* ("sleep at medicine rock"). If he has fulfilled all the requirements expected of him by the spirits, they will appear to him in his dream. This meeting with the spirit world occurs in an unusually dramatic way as I have explained elsewhere (Hultkrantz, ed. 1955: 65 ff.). The dreamer obtains *puha*, instructions about its correct use, and a holy song.

Here, however, we are not so much interested in the supernatural experience as such as in the prayers which form part of the methodical preparations for the experience. To whom are these prayers directed? All of my informants have explained that, in his prayers, the Indian appeals to the spirits; that is, to that particular spirit whose power and favor is sought. However, it is far from certain that the spirit chosen by the Indian will become his possession—the spirit can send another in his stead. But one thing *is* certain: the prayers have not been directed to *Tam Apö*, since the Supreme Being does not belong to the vision complex. He stands outside it. In front of the rock-carvings, an Indian dreams of different kinds of spirits but never of *Tam Apö*. On the other hand, the Creator has been theoretically introduced into the picture, at least in more recent times. Every elderly believing Shoshoni desires, on second thoughts, to give *Tam Apö* the highest formal control over the *puha*. But functionally, he is of no importance. Perhaps one or other more modern Indian—as an old Indian woman supposed—prays to the Supreme Being at the rock-carvings. But, she assured me, that is a new custom. Older Indians never prayed to *Tam Apö* under those circumstances but only to the spirits. It is also typical that when, in the nineteenth century, the vision complex was moved into the Sun Dance lodge, the visionary

The Shoshoni Sun Dance lodge in 1955.

received instructions in his trance to pray to the spirits, not to the Supreme Being who was associated with the Sun Dance cult.

It would be too much to say that the concept of the Supreme Being is incompatible with the vision complex. The situation is not so simple as that. A vaguely comprehended Supreme Creator can always be made a theoretical source of most things in the world of religion. But as far as I can understand, the Creator has not naturally been associated by the Shoshoni with the vision-quest. The spirits appealed to during the fast were able to guarantee all the values associated with the life of the Shoshoni Indians. The powerful, dramatic effect of his visionary experience gave the Indian an emphatic confirmation of his belief. And *Tam Apö*, who never manifested him-self in dreams has, to all intents and purposes, been a *deus otiosus*. An old Shoshoni woman, who has since died, told me in 1948 that her parents had told her that in ancient times one never prayed to the Supreme God.

At the same time, there is no doubt that this creator god is an ancient indigenous conception among the Shoshoni. Above all, in more recent times—namely, after the Shoshoni became a mounted, buffalo-hunting tribe—he has played an active role through his associ-ation with the Sun Dance. Thus we have arrived at the second type of religious situation which ought to be studied in this connection.

Just as the guardian spirit complex constitutes a response to the needs of the individualistic hunting life, the Sun Dance (*táguwune nĭkaβo:n*, "dry-standing-dance") comprises an ideological comple-ment to the collective group cooperation in the buffalo hunt and the tightly organized tribal system which that necessitated. The social organization established by these Shoshoni Indians and which so strikingly violated the economic pattern (Hultkrantz 1949: 153 f.; Hultkrantz 1956c: 184), was a natural consequence of the require-ments of the seasonal buffalo hunting. In itself, this hunting de-manded the mobilization of a considerable number of people. At the same time, one faced the ever-present risk of running into other Plains people who were also out hunting the buffalo. For a mounted group of people, spread out over a wide area and in constant fear of such competition, a strict military organization was an absolute necessity. The Shoshoni, who otherwise were noted for their intract-able individualism, were forced by such circumstances to unite them-selves together under a competent leader. They established a warrior society, inaugurated the military point system of the Plains Indians (with "coups," scalps, etc.) and developed fixed standards for hunt-ing, marching, and battle. In fact, their military discipline has aroused admiration.[4]

It is completely natural that the Sun Dance of the Plains Indians was introduced simultaneously with their new social organi-zation. For the Sun Dance presupposes tribal organization and a camp circle. It also fulfills extremely important religious needs in an extensive, militarily organized group of buffalo hunters, since it guarantees the existence of the tribe, its solidarity, its ability to resist enemies, its supply of food. Now, the main emphasis was placed on

4. Cf., for example, the behavior of the Shoshoni at the Laramie Conference in 1851 (see Hebard 1930: 68 ff.).

the collective unit and not on the individual. Nevertheless, individual performance still played an important role. The Indian who was able to keep on dancing for the three days and nights of the Sun Dance, his bare feet on the rough, sandy ground, without eating or quenching his thirst with water, and without faltering in his belief, contributed not only to the happiness of the entire tribe during the coming year but also assisted his sick relations in regaining life and health.

The Sun Dance, which has always been celebrated in the summertime—nowadays at the end of July and in August, but formerly at the beginning of June—is without doubt an annual renewal rite of Algonkian origin (cf. Schmidt 1929: 811 ff.; Müller 1954: 134 ff.; Spier 1921: 498 f., 503). It is thus an eastern trait in Shoshoni religion (see Shimkin 1953). In the entire Plains region, the Sun Dance is associated with a belief in a creating god, or a god which controls the weal and woe of the tribe and nation. At the same time, the Sun Dance comprises a sacrifice and an act of gratitude to this god: the personal, individual suffering arouses his compassion, the prayers directed to him under the guidance of the medicine-men thank him for past blessings and solicit his mercy and blessing during the dance itself as well as during the coming year.

The Shoshoni, too, pray to the Supreme Being during the Sun Dance. Admittedly, they do not pray solely to him for, as with the other Plains tribes, other supernatural beings, such as Mother Earth and the buffalo, also occur as protective spirits in the Sun Dance. It is typical that both of the two last-mentioned divinities are intimately connected with the economic aspects of the Shoshoni's life. *Tamsó:gobia*, "Our Mother Earth," is an animatistic being identical with the earth itself, the earth which nourishes berries and plants. *Ku'c*, the buffalo, whose head is bound to the center pole of the dance lodge, is a representative of the very important buffalo herd which was of great significance in earlier times when it fed and clothed the Indians. The Indians, therefore, direct prayers to both of these beings during the dance, although, first and foremost, they pray to *Tam Apö*. This creator god, once a passive, reposing Supreme Being, has regained an active significance through the Sun Dance in which he appears as a dynamic power. To a certain extent, this development has been inspired by the high god cult which, in its integration with the Sun Dance, existed among the other Plains tribes. However, the most decisive factor of all was that, in the Shoshoni pantheon, *Tam Apö* represented the only supernatural being with a personal profile and was, therefore, the only one capable of fulfilling the demand of the Sun Dance for a cosmic deity, a protector of the tribe as a whole.

One of my informants, who is now dead, gave me the following description of *Tam Apö* and of the cult associated with him: "We think about him as the whole sky, he covers the whole world. He is a human being above the sky. His power extends over the whole earth. In ancient times we did not pray to him, but we prayed to different spirits. Still, we believed in God. Only in the Sun Dance did we pray directly to God."

Here follows a prayer to the Supreme Being, used at the sunrise ceremony by a leader of the Sun Dance in 1948: "*Tam Apö*, here we are, standing up and facing towards the sunrise. I am offering a prayer again, asking your blessing. The sun you made has come up, it is shining towards us, all over; and it is the light from you and we like to have this every day of our life, and we want to live a long time. Because we are suffering for our homes, families, friends, and all kinds of nations, I want you to bless us. And I ask you to bless the service boys[5] so that they will be safe and nothing will happen to them. ... I ask you to see to it that there will be no war, make it that way through your willpower. And when we get to the end of these three days, when we get out, give us our water and our food. The powerful water will give us good strength, and so will the food— what we eat will give us good strength. For we want to live as long as we possibly can."

The Supreme Being and the powers associated with him, especially Mother Earth, completely dominate the Shoshoni's Sun Dance. In fact, the dance would be meaningless without them. The usual spirits, the *puha,* are only to be glimpsed in the background. The Indians who have received supernatural medicine, paint themselves during the Sun Dance according to the instructions given by the guardian spirits. Moreover, the Sun Dance lodge is theoretically full of *puha.* Functionally significant is the fact that those who become exhausted from the dancing and fasting sometimes faint and experience a meeting with *puha* in their coma. Many Indians consider that *puha* obtained in this way is of greater value and more effective than that received from the visions at the rock-carvings—a point of view which appears to be influenced by the ideology of life on the plains.[6] Nevertheless, it is obvious that *puha* does not belong to the Sun Dance as such. The same medicine-man who prays to the spirits at

5. Reference is here made to the young Shoshoni who, at the time, were serving in the American forces in Europe and Asia.
6. One of the most prominent medicine-men felt definite aversion to places with rock-carvings and, indeed, feared their spirits.

Shoshoni medicine-man Tilton West making smoke sacrifice to Mother Earth in the Sun Dance.

the rock-carvings and would never consider praying there to the Creator, directs his prayers during the Sun Dance to this Creator, but only in exceptional cases to the *puha*.

Thus the religions of the rock-carvings and of the Sun Dance lodge practically, but not theoretically, exclude each other. Now that we continue on to a consideration of the storytelling on winter evenings in the family teepee, we come face to face with a mythological complex which completely violates the circles of conceptions we have spoken about so far and which is theoretically incompatible with them.

In former days, summer was the active season among the Plains Shoshoni, the time of hunting and warfare. Winter was the time of passivity and rest. They lived on dried buffalo and elk meat, made occasional hunting expeditions, played the hand-game, and narrated stories. These stories, *náreguyap*, served an important purpose during the cold winter evenings. From the point of view of entertainment, they corresponded to the dances and ceremonies of the summer. The storytellers were usually older men and women who enjoyed renown for their talents and thus attracted many listeners. A good storyteller has learned the story thoroughly. He knows how the various motifs succeed one another, how the events should be described. But he must also be good actor with a feeling for a dramatic effects and humourous points. His public was mainly composed of children and young people, but even adults and elderly people frequently liked to listen.

To a certain extent, it is true to say that the expectations of the listeners determined the plot of the stories. Most of the stories were narrated to entertain; but there was always some implied pedagogical meaning, particularly if the listeners were children. The stories helped to keep the children quiet, to dampen their playfulness and constant activity when the grown-ups wanted peace and quiet. Many of the stories about dangerous beings that kidnap small children were intended to frighten the youngsters into obedience to their elders. But these stories were not only didactic tales or "ficts." They were also the objects of religious belief—and this immediately complicates the picture.

The majority of the storytellers today—among them, medicine-men who believe *puha* at the rock-carvings and *Tam Apö* in the Sun Dance—maintain positively that the stories they tell are mostly true; this is particularly so of the legends about the heroic, military feats of the Shoshoni in past times, traditions concerning meetings with supernatural beings, and stories about Wolf, Coyote, and other powerful beings. All of these are regarded as "true stories," as the Indians call them, and some of them—those dealing with events in primeval times and which tell about supreme powers and spirits that lived then—could be called myths.[7] these myths sometimes contain a humorous element, shocking to the outsider. Here we meet a mythological pattern which is to be found in large areas of the

7. "Myth" in the meaning of "true narration" about divine beings that one believes in, with their action set in the days of yore.

Shoshoni medicine-man John Brown praying to the Creator in the Sun Dance.

western part of North America and which, in many respects, has parallels in the eastern part of North America.

It can be of particular interest to give a more detailed presentation of some of those mythological beings which the Shoshoni have believed in even up to our time.

The best-known myths and legends group themselves around, on one side, Wolf and Coyote and, on the other, certain man-eating beings called *pa:ndzoaBits, nimirika,* and *wo:kaimumbic.* Of these, by far the most popular are the stories about Wolf and Coyote, the so-called coyote-stories (*ižapönareguyap*). They carry us back to a far distant time when animals were people, when Wolf was chieftain, and Coyote, his younger brother, was his herald, the camp crier. Many stories describe how, together, they led all the animals on hunting and warring expeditions. Other stories portray Coyote as an unreliable trickster, an obscene joker who cheated his fellow human beings and enjoyed coition with both his mother-in-law and his daughters. Occasionally, even Wolf assumed the role of a trickster, although usually he attempted to check Coyote's reckless plans and correct his mistakes. But, unfortunately, Wolf was not so shrewd and intelligent as his younger brother. He often got into trouble as a result of Coyote's tricks. However, Wolf and Coyote are not only humanlike beings, they are also divine. The creation of human beings and animals, the changing of the seasons, the institution of death, all these are their work (see, e.g., Hultkrantz 1955). Wolf is represented in mythology as the Creator, Coyote as an assistant creator, but one who was definitely unsuccessful.

This brings us to several difficult problems as seen from the points of view of ethnology, social psychology, and comparative religion. In this present study, we can merely touch upon one of them; namely, the relationship between the pair of creators in mythology and the divinities of the cult.

The most striking aspect is certainly the fact that the Creator in mythology and in the Sun Dance are not identical, although both are objects of religious belief. Or are they perhaps fundmentally variations of the same idea of God? When I demanded a definite answer to this question, my informants were placed in a particularly embarrassing situation. The most varying answers were presented to me, often by one and the same person (Hultkrantz 1955: 134). At one minute, Wolf was thought to be identical with *Tam Apö*, at another, he was represented as a spirit created by him and intended to assist at the shaping of the world, and again, he was converted into an evil spirit. Behind all these answers, one can glimpse an uncertainty, a feeling of insecurity which suggested that my question could not be asked. The gods of the cult were true, but those of mythology were also true. Few had bothered to try and figure out how they could be reconciled.

In this connection, it is important to remember that the conceptions of Wolf and Coyote as creators do not fit into the belief in spirits connected with the visionary experiences. We have seen the limited resources granted to the wolf and the coyote as *puha:* they are good scouts and thieves, the coyote is also a murderer. More positive abilities are apparently not considered suitable to them. In the hierarchy of spirits, they also rank low, being unable to compete in any respect with the eagle or the beaver, for example. Even other mythological beings, for example the above-mentioned man-eaters, lack importance in the *puha* "theology." However, an essential exception here is the weasel which has a fairly prominent place both in the vision complex and in mythology. Such an exception, on the other hand, can scarcely alter the principle impression of this comparison.

In this chapter, we shall not attempt to solve the difficult problem of the psychological and historical origin of the mythological conceptual complex. It is sufficient to state that it constitutes a circumscribed unit, an isolated segment within the Shoshoni religion. In the Sun Dance, people believe unconditionally in *Tam Apö* as the Creator; but around the fire in the teepee, they may accept for the moment another creator, Wolf, *pia izapö* ("big coyote"). The distance between these two conceptions is so great nowadays that it would be practically impossible to reconcile them.[8]

It is tempting to cite examples of a fourth contrast within the religion of the Shoshoni; namely, the modern dichotomy between the traditional, indigenous cult and recently introduced Christian belief. Since the latter, however, does not give a spontaneous expression of the Shoshoni's own religious activity, it falls beyond the limits of this discussion. As regards the Christian religious conceptions, they have been attached on to the already existent patterns of belief and thus do not alternate with these, but rather reinforce them.[9] Finally, the peyote religion which is mixed with Christian elements forms a sect within the Shoshoni community which reinterprets the old religion from its own point of view. Thus it, too, is irrelevant in this connection.

The Configurations of Religious Belief

We are now able to obtain a clearer idea of the psychological "levels" we have here described. The above presentation should have demon-

---

8. The possibility that *Tam Apö* and Wolf were one and the same person in the beginning—as comparative material from the more western Shoshoni suggests—must not be overlooked. However, this possibility lacks relevance to the present discussion.

9. This is not so among the Klamath Indians, however. Cf. below. Cf. also Rousseau and Rousseau 1952: 118: Christianity and paganism among the Mistassini-Montagnais "cheminent parallèlement sans se compénétrer, chez le même individu." The two religions are not incompatible antitheses to each other, they supplement each other but are active in quite different situations.

strated that the Shoshoni in Wyoming, regardless of all differences between individuals and groups, have not had a uniform, coherent system of religious belief. In different situations, they have applied for the protection of different types of supernatural beings or believed in completely heterogeneously shaped powers that appeared alternatively in the same function.

In order to characterize these circles of religious beliefs, which constitute in such a remarkable way units that exclude one another, I should like to use the expression *configurations of religious belief.* A configuration of religious belief implies that one complex of religious conceptions which occurs beside other complexes of religious conceptions, dominates and momentarily displaces these in the area of active belief. The decisive factor for this domination is its functional association with a dominant social situation.

The concept of "configuration" has been taken from the ethnological (anthropological) debate in which it is often used to name an integral cultural unit, a coherent system of cultural elements.[10] A configuration of religious belief is, in the same way, an arrangement of religious conceptions which are integrated the one with the other. Among the Shoshoni, the series Wolf-Coyote-primeval animals, is such an arrangement, the series *Tam Apö*-Mother Earth-buffalo, is another.

How, then, can one explain that different configurations of religious belief are able to replace one another? Here one can partly cite the experiences of "Gestalt" psychology: the situation is experienced, momentarily, as a whole. Under the influence of a given mood, a given environmental situation, a definite religious picture ensues, and it persists for as long as this situation lasts. In this connection, the sociological field theory of Kurt Lewin can be quoted: a given social (cultural) situation forms, together with the corresponding religious milieu, a dynamic field. A third, and complementing explanation is that the expression "religious belief," as we customarily use it, is too undifferentiated. There are various kinds of belief: there is a definite and obvious difference between absolute conviction and the ability to enter into an imaginative experience. Different configurations of religious belief should, consequently, be given different values.

---

10. It should be observed that my use of the expression "configuration" is not the exact equivalent of the configurations of culture which Benedict, Kroeber, etc., speak of.

Some Comparisons

In order to clarify even more the opinion expressed in this chapter, I shall conclude by briefly presenting some other proof of the occurrence of configurations of religious belief. All of them have been taken from native North America.

Among the Coast Algonkian, W. Müller has found traces of a religious dichotomy which very closely resembles that we have just found among the Shoshoni. He constates that Iroquoian influences in the seventeenth century made themselves felt in the Algonkian region. "Doch," he writes, "diese Einflüsse wurden nicht verarbeitet, auch nicht die geistigen, die auf mythischem Gebiet lagen. Das unverkennbare irokesische Mythenmuster schob sich in die Mythologien der Küstenstämme hinein ohne eine Amalgamierung, ja ohne das originale atlantische Schema auch nur zu berühren." Thus "können diese mythischen Einflüsse unmöglich auf die angeblichen Hochgötter gewirkt haben, da sie auf einer anderen Ebene spielen. Diese höchsten Wesen werden nämlich stets der Praxis, der lebendigen Religion der Stämme zugewiesen, während die nachweisbaren irokesischen Schübe bei der mythischen Urgeschichte der Welt ansetzen und in der Sphäre der Texte gewisse Anreicherungen nach sich ziehen" (Müller 1956: 37). This means that among these Coast Algonkian we find, partly an older belief in a Creator, partly the Iroquois myth of the creating twins. They represent two different configurations of belief which practically and theoretically exclude each other.

A similar division between the practical religious belief of everyday life and the mythological comprehension of reality occurs, according to Stern, among the Klamath. "Even today, elderly informants who are practicing Christians are by no means ready to abandon the old Klamath myths. They are, of course, mystified by the ambivalence of the chief culture hero-trickster, whom the Klamath originally identified with the Christian God, and they evince some uncertainty as to the duality of the nature, half-human, half-animal, of some of the mythic beings. As they become more absorbed in the recounting of the old myths, doubts vanish, affirmations become clearer" (Stern 1956: 8).[11]

The division into various configurations of belief is perhaps most striking in the field of eschatological belief. In another, and earlier connection, the present writer has emphasized that belief in

---

11. As among the Shoshoni, the relationship of the culture hero to God is a problem (see Spencer 1952: 223 ff.).

numerous realms of the dead can generally be traced back to divergent traditions (for example, in a stratified society) while the actual belief by one and the same individual in a dead person's simultaneous existence as a grave ghost and inhabitant of the realm of death—two totally incompatible representations!—must be explained as "practical, unreflecting experiences," or better, as manifestations of two varying lines of religious conceptions which alternate in the conscious mind (Hultkrantz 1953: 32 f., 473 f.). Proof of this are legion in North America and, indeed, could easily be exemplified from our own culture.

In connection with the abandonment of the old belief, eschatology naturally enough, has in many places been lost. But the conceptions associated with it have been kept intact and survive in the material of oral tradition. The Serrano, for instance, do not believe any longer in the realm of the dead of their forefathers, but the details of this belief have been incorporated into the still popular Orpheus tradition (Benedict 1923a: 104). In this case, however, it is not a question of two configurations of belief, an agnostic (or Christian) and a mythological—as the Orpheus tradition is here not a myth but a fairy tale.

However, if the theory put forth here is correct, great possibilities are opened up for research within the field of religion. Likewise, it helps us to understand many of the discrepancies in the ethnographical reports about the religions of primitive peoples.

WORSHIP AND RITUAL

4

Ritual in Native North American Religions

I<small>T HAS OFTEN BEEN SAID</small> that the North American Indians "dance out" their religions. Their religious convictions are expressed through the medium of dances, songs, repetitive movements. Lowie pointed at the central place of what he called "ceremonialism" in Amerindian culture (Lowie 1915a: 229 ff.). Perhaps we should remember that at the time he wrote his article on the subject the ritualism of more complex societies on the Plains, in the Southwest, and on the North Pacific Coast had just been investigated. The cultures of technologically more "simple" tribes were as yet less well known (particularly in the Great Basin and western Canada [interior] and Alaska). These cultures have later proved to lack the intricate ceremonialism of the more complex societies. Nevertheless, the recent westward expansion of Plains Indian cultural traits gradually changed the picture in the Great Basin, and the attraction of Northwest Coast cultural features has, to some extent, had a similar effect among Athapascan Indians of the Mackenzie (cf. Gunther 1950; and Swanton 1904).

Ritual is thus a prominent part of North American aboriginal religion, and to behaviorists (like most American anthropologists) it is the foremost religious document of a primal people. This is not the place to challenge this view, although I do not share it: personal

51

confessions, beliefs, and legends are in my eyes important records of what people really hold. A ritual is a system of fixed behavior, and it sometimes tends to move away from the belief system that once motivated it. We know this to be the case in stratified societies where the official cult may have very little relation to the living beliefs. We also know that members of tribal societies act ritually in a certain way because this was the way their forefathers did it. In North America many strange ritual actions cannot be explained symbolically by the Indians, because they had simply been taught in dreams by their guardian spirits (or the guardian spirit of the first owner of the ritual) to enact the ritual in just that manner. The ritual has always an ulterior background in religious experiences and religious beliefs, something that is rather easily observed in Indian North America.

At the same time ritual forms follow a well-established pattern and, as socio-cultural phenomena, they take part of the same dynamics as other institutional forms of society. This is why they have become favorite objects of social-anthropological studies: kinship systems, political systems, and other structural forms of society are reflected in and models for a ritual organization, ritual expressions, and ritual values. Of late, however, anthropologists interested in cognition and symbolism have approached the ritual in a new spirit. I think particularly of such scholars as Victor W. Turner, Mary Douglas, and Melford Spiro. Their analyses come close to what could be wished for by scholars of religion, with the additional caveat that the "symbolism" may have been more easily revealed had more references to religious problems been evident (cf., for instance, Turner 1967, 1969).

In contrast to anthropologists, students of comparative religion have for a long time been absorbed by the problems of interrelationships between myth and ritual. If only they had taken seriously native North American materials, their one-sided interpretation of one with the other would never have occurred. Regrettably, students of religion have been interested in native American religions only marginally. There is now a more positive trend in this respect. Perhaps this will lead up to a more modulated opinion on rituals.

In this chapter I shall try to see the North American Indian rituals from the point of view of religion, that is, as an expression of religious beliefs. In that connection a succinct survey of prominent types of ritual in North America will be supplied. The theme I have chosen is, of course, enormous in scope, and only some very general observations can be presented. To a large extent they also hold, I presume, for rituals in other parts of the world.

Types of Ritual

Ritual is, then, a fixed, usually solemn behavior that is repeated in certain situations. Anthropologists like to call the latter "crisis situations," but there is not always any crisis involved. It would be better to speak of "sacred situations," in Durkheim's spirit. Although not all rituals occur in a religious setting (e.g., receptions to secular order societies in Europe or American Indian rites of greeting), most rituals in tribal cultures are symbolic expressions of religious thought, feeling, and will. They usually correspond to human needs and desires, and they are instrumental in carrying them out. There is no reason why we should discuss here the problem then arising as to what extent a ritual is either religious or magical. This is a major problem in itself. I shall avoid it in this presentation.

There are rituals that consist in prayers, harangues, and songs, as for instance, many of those found among the Navajo. However, the characteristic thing about most North American Indian rituals is that action reinforces the word, thereby giving more palpability to religion. The word is a poor symbol of all the individual thinks and feels when confronted with the supernatural. By dancing it out he is relieved of the tension caused by verbal deficiency. At the same time, the action is palpable and concrete with the number of participants enhancing his feeling of reality and realization. The ritual may have its origin in a visionary dream, in a dictate by a culture hero or a mythic event in cosmogonic time, or it may stem from a neighboring tribe to serve as an institution that makes "good medicine." The important thing is that ritual, if truly integrated in a living culture, does not exist as an independent phenomenon. It is always a vehicle of religious aims which alone can legitimize its occurrence.

Rituals may be systematized according to various scales (see, e.g., Wach 1947: 55 ff.). Here are some examples.

1. Quantitative scale: observance—rite—ceremony. The observance is the smallest unit. It is an observance, for instance, to avoid visiting a tabooed place, like the spouting geysers of the Yellowstone Park (Hultkrantz 1954b). A ritual is a simple ritual, or a part of a complex ceremony. For instance, the actual sandpainting is part of the lengthy Navajo ceremony of two to nine nights (see, e.g., Matthews 1897: 43 ff.).

2. Sociological scale: there is a difference between a personal, private ritual and collective, institutional ritual. In complex societies the latter may be divided into folk, official, and secret ritual. A clan ritual may belong to either of these three categories.

3. Psychological scale: attitudes of veneration contrast with attitudes of self-assertion. To many this is the difference between religion and magic. It would, in this connection, be more advantageous to emphasize the line between rituals that are the gift of gods and rituals that are acquired through training. To the former belong most cultic acts that seek divine or spiritual help; to the latter rituals of shamanism.

4. Temporal scale: rites of transition, calendar rites, crisis rites. This is Honko's classification, presented at the methodological congress for the study of religion in 1973, and it comes close to Spiro's classification from 1970 (Honko 1975; Spiro 1970: 206 f.). The rites of transition are van Gennep's well-known *rites de passage*, with their three phases (van Gennep 1909). Calendar rites are, I think, primarily typical of agricultural societies. In North America the Iroquois and Pueblo calendars regulate the rhythm and the rites of the vegetational year (Fenton 1936; Hale 1883; Parsons 1922, 1933; Fay 1950). On the other hand, there is archeological evidence that hunting societies might have observed solstices and the exact yearly cycle, probably for ritual purposes (Kehoe and Kehoe 1977). The appearance of salmon on the Northwest Coast and in the Plateau rivers, and the growth of luscious grass on the Plains were in a way calendrical marks for festive religious occasions among the hunters and gatherers living there. Crisis rites, finally, are arranged when an unforeseen crisis jeopardizes the welfare of the individual or the people.

There is no doubt that this scheme is of great value to our interpretation of rituals. It is certainly the best one among those here proposed. At the same time it tends to disregard certain categories of ritual action, such as ancestor rites. These may belong to all three types of ritual but are at home in none of them.

5. Structural scale: ritual drama—ritual address—ritual meditation. The ritual drama has two different faces. Firstly, it may be an imitation of the cosmological primeval events, with the partakers impersonating (with or without masks) the mythic beings. The Pueblo Kachina dances are a good example (Anderson 1955). Ritual myths usually serve as texts for such dramas. Secondly, the ritual may be an actual ride into the unseen world, performed by the shaman, and watched by a number of observers. This is a real, in some details, unforeseen drama; the imitation is limited to the shaman's symbolic references to the course of events during the act. The ritual address takes the form of a prayer, an offering, or other divine service. It presupposes a direct mutual interaction between the god and his devotees. Ritual meditation is characteristic of the vision-quest, for

instance. It may be defined as wordless prayer within a ritual frame.

The ritual drama and ritual address have a vague likeness to Spiro's commemorative and expressive rites, but there is certainly no exact affinity. Apotropaic or preventive rites may be subsumed under all the three categories here suggested. For instance, the Navajo have detailed apotropaic rituals which may be termed ritual drama (cf. Haile 1938). (They also convey a positive identification with the universe, and are thus only indirectly apotropaic.)

We could also classify rites according to their contents, but such classifications will remain unsystematic if they are not correlated with a typology of the kind presented above.

One term has been avoided here quite consciously: cult. There is an unfortunate habit among American anthropologists to use the words cult and cultic as equivalents for religion and religious. It seems that Kroeber was the first to introduce this linguistic designation when, in his *Handbook on California Indians*, he discussed the "Kuksu cult" (Kroeber 1925: 364 ff.). Later new religious movements, such as the peyote religion, have been acclaimed as cults. Even archeological complexes have been designated as cult: we could mention the so-called Southern Cult in the Southeast, presumably the predecessor of the harvest feast, the *busk* ritual, among the Creek and their neighbors (cf. Howard 1968). A cult is indeed not a religion but a ritual of supplication directed to a divinity. We should therefore be cautious in our use of the term. Many rituals are cults, but not all.

The Belief System of the Sun Dance

If a ritual expresses religious beliefs, it cannot be reduced to a collection of ritual traits. Certainly, there is, as Jensen has pointed out, a development between spontaneous rites and an intricate pattern of traditional rites handed down through the generations (Jensen 1963). The latter may have little in common with the beliefs that once energized it.

Still, the rites give a general response to the particular beliefs held, and a ritual has a motivation that keeps it going.

This was overlooked when at the beginning of this century Clark Wissler organized the field collection of Sun Dance rituals for the publication department of the American Museum of Natural History in New York. Scholars like Goddard, Lowie, Spier, and Wissler himself assembled all information they could among the different Plains tribes (see the papers in the museum's anthropological series, Vol. 16). Spier made a meticulous distributional study of the traits and trait complexes (Spier 1921). However, the import communicated by the ritual was lost behind all the details. Writes Fred Eggan many decades later, "despite all the studies of the Sun Dance we still do not have an adequate account giving us the meaning and significance of the rituals for the participants and for the tribe. One such account would enable us to revalue the whole literature of the Sun Dance" (Eggan 1954: 757. Cf. also Hultkrantz 1976a: 90). This was written in 1954. Since that date some more congenial works on the Sun Dance have appeared like Peter Powell's study of the Cheyenne ceremonial and Joseph Jorgensen's of the Shoshoni-Ute rituals (Powell 1969; Jorgensen 1972). Still, the Sun Dance is mostly seen as a ritual with a compound of aims, like fulfilling a vow, healing the sick, gaining a particular favor, making good war or hunting-medicine, and so on. In other words, the fixed point is the ritual, whereas the motivations differ. I think that the basis of this attitude is, beside the general behavioristic approach, the ahistorical, "flat" perspective that domineered when Wissler and his colleagues were writing about the dance (Hultkrantz 1967a: 102). The fact is that archeology, documentary research, and comparative investigations— in short, "ethnohistory"—could lend us support for deeper penetrations into the historical past. In this way the original ideological complex of the Sun Dance could be revealed.

Thus there are indications that the Sun Dance ritual is an instance of the North American Indian new year rituals, best known from Northwest California as world renewal ceremonies and the Lenape or Delaware Indians as the Big House Ritual (Kroeber and Gifford 1949; Speck 1931). Additionally, the Plains ritual has its close counterpart in the new year festival of the Siberian Tungus. This festival was a celebration of the renewal of nature, but it also included, like the Sun Dance, the initiation of new shamans. The central ritual attribute was the offerings pole, decorated with skins of sacrificed animals, and with two colored pieces of cloth at the top. This pole, symbolizing the world-tree, resembles the center post of the Sun Dance lodge (Anisimov 1963: 92, 93, 116). There must be some connection here between the Plains and the Tungus ceremonies, perhaps even a common heritage.

These comparisons, if accepted, suggest that the new year, or new creation, is the central feature of the Plains ceremony. Of course, if we consider the motivations given by the different Sun-Dancing tribes they are most diverse. However, through his distributional tabulations Spier suggested that the Cheyenne and Arapaho were the originators of the dance. Precisely among these two tribes the Sun Dance is a ceremony of new creation, the lodge is the world, and its center post the world-tree, the communications channel between man and the powers above (see Hultkrantz 1973b: 8 f.). This central idea practically explains the whole Sun Dance ritual in all its variations. With the dissemination of the dance to tribes with other cultural traditions a variety of other motives came to the fore. Among the Dakota, for instance, the Sun Dance has turned into a shamanic ritual, an initiation ceremony for young candidates of the shamanic profession and for other visionaries, while the self-torture so conspicuous in the Dakota and Blackfoot dance seems to have been in harmony with their military ethos.

This kind of analysis, focusing on the ideological premises of the rituals, opens up these rituals to us and makes them meaningful. So many American Indian rituals are just a jumble of ritual elements and ritual movements to the spectators (and the scientific observers among them). It is time for us to try to discover their real import, their message.

Survey of Major North American Indian Rituals

It is now time to present a short descriptive survey of some historical ritual forms in Indian North America. What follows is thus no classification but an enumeration and characterization of rituals that have played a major role in North America. It is a representative selection, for the rituals among the North American aborigines have been legion. Those mentioned here are all traditional rituals, that is, they have not as such been influenced by white American culture.

1. New year rituals. These may also be called thanksgiving rituals. They reiterate the cosmic creation and are thus dramatic performances of the mythic events at the beginning of time. The lodge or house where they are held is a replica of the universe, and the length of the celebration corresponds to the progress of the cosmic creation. Thus the Sun Dance is a creation drama during four successive days, and the Lenape Big House ceremony lasts twelve days. In this case also another interpretation is current: "The belief that each day's performance lifts the worship a stage higher in the series of twelve successive sky levels until on the final day it reaches the Great Spirit himself" (Speck 1931: 61). The Hupa Indians and Karok Indians of northern California have a sweat house as their cosmic building, and its construction symbolizes the creation of the world (Kroeber and Gifford 1949).

2. Hunting rites. The northern Californian new year ritual is combined with the custom of honoring the first salmon that has been caught in the season. This ritual exists independently among many tribes on the North Pacific Coast and the Plateau (Gunther 1928). Veneration of the killed game, called animal ceremonialism, is known all over North America (see, e.g., Paulson 1959; Heizer and Hewes 1940). Best known of the hunting rituals is the historically connected bear ceremonialism in northern North America (Hallowell 1926). Rituals promoting the growth and access of animals have been rather general and occur even in agricultural regions like the Pueblo area (Underhill 1948).

3. Fertility rites. These belong to the agrarian cultures in the Southwest, some Plains tribes and Eastern Woodlands populations from the Iroquois to the Creek. The rituals are determined by a calendar, resulting in a cycle of ceremonies. The Zuni, for instance, have dances in the summer to please the rain gods, while the winter dances are held by societies specialized in promoting fecundity and in curing diseases (Bunzel 1932a). Also the Iroquois year was divided into a series of rituals, the most important of them being the Midwinter ritual which, like the Creek harvest festival, was associated with a rite of new fire—the token that it may derive from a new year ritual (Speck 1949).

4. Moiety rituals. The idea that there is a dual cosmos, divided between the powers above and the powers beneath, or two sacred world halves, has generated the moiety systems. The moieties of the tribes perform rituals for collective aims in such a reciprocal way that the cosmic unity is secured. Moiety rituals occur in the Southwest, Southeast, and on the Prairies (see, for instance, Fletcher and La Flesche 1911).

5. Initiation rituals. There are tribal initiations, as in California, initiations into clans, as among the Prairie tribes, and into secret societies, as among the Kwakiutl and Ojibway. The Apache of the Southwest arrange great puberty rituals for girls that refer to the creation. We even find adoptions of foreign groups into a relationship of friendship through rituals, called the *hako* among the Pawnee, *hunka* among the Sioux. This ritual includes the famous calumet dance, once distributed from the Plains to the Iroquois area (Fenton 1953). Finally we have the initiations into sacred professions, for instance, shamanhood.

6. Bundle rituals. Rituals around sacred bundles are common in the Plains-Prairie area. They may involve the whole tribe, as the ritual of the sacred arrows of the Cheyenne (Powell 1969), or segments of the tribe, as the opening rituals of most inherited family bundles

and the rituals that have been formed in clubs joined by visionaries who have procured visions and bundles from the same spirits (e.g., Ewers 1955a).

7. Shamanic rituals. These may be roughly divided into vision rituals, associated with the quest for guardian spirits, which are common in North America outside the Pueblo area and concern most men (Benedict 1923b), and the divination and healing rituals which are performed by the recipients of specific powers, the medicine-men and shamans. The most widely known divination ritual is the Shaking Tent ceremony, in its Sioux form called *yuwipi* (Hultkrantz 1967b). The healing rituals vary from ecstatic pantomimes of the shaman's soul-flight to the nine-night curing ceremonies of the Navajo. (The idea of a ceremony of nine nights has been taken over from the Pueblo Indians.)

8. Death rites. These include mourning rites (blackening of face, mutilations, various taboos) and burial rituals. So-called secondary burials (in which the bones were cleaned from flesh and deposited in a new grave) at one time occurred in the East, for instance, among the Huron. Proper ancestor rites are lacking in North America, unless the Pueblo *kachina* rituals should be named thus: the *kachina* are supernatural beings recruited, at least partly, among the dead.

The North American Indian ceremonials are often preceded by ritual cleaning, either through induced vomiting (the Southeast), or through sweat baths (for instance, on the Plains). Ceremonies are usually ended by general feasting.

All these rituals have one thing in common: they serve religious ends.

Ritual Persistence and Ritual Change

Finally, some words should be said about the dynamics of rituals from the point of view of religion. It was said before that although rituals are provoked by religious experiences, they tend to become self-operative, cultural mechanisms. Disregarding influences from outside there are two possibilities for their development: either they remain integrated with the goals and values of the society, or they show the inclination of becoming rigid systems indifferent to, indeed, conflicting with tribal ideology. For instance, among the Wind River Shoshoni there are some doubts whether the old vision-quest should be upheld when "spontaneous" visions may be acquired through the Sun Dance (Hultkrantz 1969: 30). The rule is, however, that a ritual endures as long as it is serving the prevalent religious ideology.

Since Robertson-Smith's days it has been taken for granted in some circles that of the three genres of religious materials, myths, rituals, and beliefs, only the first two resist the change of time whereas beliefs are too vague and too brittle to remain for a longer time. This view, still held by many scholars, is actually without foundation. The state of affairs is more complicated.

While beliefs may concern peripheral things such as diverse "superstitions," they often mediate value judgments and basic convictions at the very core of religion (cf. Hultkrantz 1968a). It is therefore exceedingly difficult to measure their rate of change. Probably most beliefs partake in the fate of the rituals: at least among the Eastern Shoshoni they have changed with the cultural premises (Hultkrantz 1962b: 551 f.). In contradistinction to rituals, however, they seem to linger on for some time.

Myths may give the impression of being less tenacious, in particular in preliterate societies such as found in North America. Indeed, migratory myths may have only a weak hold if they do not refer to fundamental issues. However, in comparison with rituals, myths seem more permanent. Or, as Kluckhohn put it, "taking a very broad view of the matter, it does seem that behavioral patterns more frequently alter first" (Kluckhohn 1942: 53). There are reasons to suppose that a mythology that is not built around central cultural values, and thus is less submitted to change, is more conservative than other parts of religion (Hultkrantz 1962: 552).

Rituals, on the other hand, change with their cultural premises. When the eastern Plains Indian technology, value pattern, and ceremonial complex were imprinted upon Shoshoni culture, their old thanksgiving ritual, in a round dance, was supplanted by the Sun Dance (Hultkrantz in press). On the other hand, the Navajo did not accept the Ghost Dance because their old value pattern with its outstanding fear of the dead had remained intact (Hill 1944). Hence, ritual change is another indication of the links that exist between ritual and basic religious tenets.

5

Spirit Lodge, a North American Shamanistic Séance

General Remarks on North American Shamanism

IN ITS MORE LIMITED SENSE shamanism is a phenomenon characteristic of the North Eurasian peoples. We may then define it as a religious and magic complex centered on the ecstatic magician, the shaman.[1] In a more general sense, however, shamanism is supposed to include all activities peculiar to the medicine-man. Anglo-Saxon and French scholars in particular interpret shamanism in this broader aspect. The result is that all manifestations of the American medicine-men may be called shamanism, and shamanistic (cf. Hultkrantz 1963: 84 ff.).

If the word shamanism seems ambiguous, the word shaman is less so. Most scholars agree that the activities of the shaman presuppose some form of ecstasy. Eliade, for instance, finds that the shaman is distinguished from the medicine-man, the magician, and the sorcerer "by a magico-religious technique which is in a way exclusive to him and which may be called: the ecstatic trip to Heaven, to the Lower World, or to the depths of the ocean" (Eliade 1950: 299). It

1. Some scholars consider shamanism to be a religion; Findeisen, for instance, thinks that it is a "spiritualistic religion" (Findeisen 1960: 192 ff.). As pointed out by Stiglmayr this interpretation is incorrect (Stiglmayr 1962: 47 f.).

seems to me, however, that this definition is too limited; it is at least as characteristic for the shaman to operate without any extracorporeal journey to the other world, provided he is in an ecstatic state. A shaman is, according to this definition, a practitioner who, with the help of spirits, cures the sick or reveals hidden things, etc., while being in an ecstasy. During the trance he may leave his own body, or he may simply summon the spirits to him and ask them to help him (cf. Haekel 1958: 62 f.). This extension of the meaning of the term "shaman" is important, for it allows for the inclusion of the Spirit Lodge to be described in the following among the true shamanistic rites.

There are many references to shamans or "jugglers" in the early sources on North American religion, for instance in the Jesuit relations, and the material on shamanism has accumulated in the course of the centuries. Nevertheless, research on shamanism has scarcely more than begun, and we still lack a general treatise on the North American medicine-man and shaman which absorbs the whole complex of shamanism in its manifold morphology. A good start was made shortly after the turn of the century when Roland Dixon wrote his famous article on the American "shaman" (by which term he understood the medicine-man in general). Dixon has here outlined the North American shamanistic complex and mentions, among other things, the Spirit Lodge phenomenon (Dixon 1908: 9). He also makes the important statement that "the spiritual flight of the shaman himself, in search of information, so characteristic of the shamans in northeastern Siberia, seems on the whole rare" (Dixon 1908: 9). Here lies indeed the greatest difference between North American and Siberian shamanism, the latter term used in its more restricted sense.

Dixon's good initiative had unfortunately no immediate following. Instead, attention was concentrated on the characteristically North American vision quest, particularly after Benedict had published her famous work on the guardian spirit (Benedict 1923b; Benedict 1922: 1 ff.; Blumensohn 1933: 451 ff.; Haekel 1938: 35 ff. Cf. Hultkrantz 1963: 77 ff.).[2] This vision-seeking was named "democratized shamanism" by Lowie, and undoubtedly represents a heritage from an older shamanistic practice (cf. Lowie 1940: 312; Hultkrantz 1963: 74 ff.; 77. But see Schuster 1960: 36 ff.). Shamanistic studies were, however, resumed in the late twenties and early thirties with

---

2. It should be observed that Benedict presents a subchapter on shamanism in which she discusses the position of the medicine-man and shaman in relation to the common visionary (Benedict 1923b: 67 ff.).

extensive monographs on North American Indian shamanism by Leh and Corlett (Leh 1934: 199 ff.; Corlett 1935. See also Parker 1928: 9 ff.). These are not, however, exhaustive, nor do they treat the really essential features of the shaman and his art. Later works by Ohlmarks, Bouteiller, and Eliade stress the parallels between North American shamanism and shamanism in the Old World from psychological, phenomenological, and "religiously interpretative" points of view (Ohlmarks 1939; Bouteiller 1950; Eliade 1951: particularly 261 ff.). Finally, a German doctoral dissertation, unpublished and inaccessible to the present writer, discusses the Subarctic forms of North American shamanism (Bechmann 1958).

Besides these general works on North American shamanism there are numerous others dealing with selected aspects of shamanism, as Stewart's investigations of possession (Stewart 1946: 323 ff.; Stewart 1956: 41 ff.), or with shamanism in particular tribes, as Park's treatises of Paviotso shamanism (Park 1938; Park 1934: 98 ff.). There are also many studies of the integration of shamanism in modern American Indian cults, such as shakerism (Waterman 1924: 499 ff.; Gunther 1949: 37 ff.; Collins 1950: 399 ff.; Smith 1954: 119 ff.; Barnett 1957). Strangely enough, the shamanistic background of the Ghost Dance movement has not as yet received an adequate and thorough investigation (cf., however, Hultkrantz 1957: 306 f., 311 f.).

It is well known even among scholars who are not Americanists that shamanism in North America sometimes appears in very specific forms, particularly where shamanistic societies have developed; it is sufficient to remind the reader of the Medicine Lodge society among the Central Algonkian tribes and the cannibal society among the Kwakiutl (see Hultkrantz 1963: 114 ff.). In the present chapter, however, interest is concentrated on the more original, individualistic forms of shamanism, and whenever shamanism is mentioned it is the activities of the lone practitioners which are referred to. It is less well known but nevertheless a fact that also this individualistic shamanism appeared and continues to appear in several different forms.

The regional typology of North American shamanism is rather complicated and still needs a thorough analysis, although the authors mentioned above have made some progress in trying to reveal the pattern. If, however, we apply broad historical-phenomenological perspectives, we may observe a major difference between two main forms: first, a type of shamanism which is very common also in other parts of the world, and is characterized by considerable variation but (usually) low intensity in its forms of expressions; and, secondly, a more limited shamanism which is characterized by its uniformity and intensity. In this chapter, I shall call the former type "general shamanism," the second, "Arctic shamanism," since it dominates the Arctic areas (the Eskimo) and parts of the Northwest Coast area and most probably has direct connections with similar shamanistic manifestations in the Arctic areas west of Bering Strait. There is no doubt that Arctic shamanism has developed on the foundations of general shamanism. It may be defined as an ecologically conditioned special form of the latter. This does not exclude, however, that also a common circumpolar historical tradition has contributed to its growth (Hultkrantz 1965b: 265 ff.).

In general shamanism, ecstasy does not function as a constantly prevailing factor. The medicine-man has, perhaps, attained his profession through an ecstatic experience in which the guardian spirits have appeared and delegated their power to him; in his shamanistic activity, however, he can operate without falling into a trance—in some cases he is even unable to enter into ecstasy. Since his activities are mostly directed to the curing of diseases (every shaman and medicine-man is first and foremost a healer), he has recourse to healing methods which do not demand a higher degree of meditation: extraction and sucking of disease spirits and objects from the inflicted person's body are primarily resorted to, less often extraphysical journeys to catch a strayed or stolen soul. If the diagnosis of soul loss is inescapable—which it usually is when the consciousness of the sick person is darkened—the medicine-man has several ways of retrieving the lost soul. He can, for instance, show in a pantomime how he seeks it in the environment or how he catches it in the realm of the dead. There are also occasions, at least in some places, when, during an ecstasy, he dispatches his own free-soul to overtake the forlorn soul of his patient. In most cases, however, the shaman's trance is reserved for the summoning of his assistant spirits. These are called on for consultation or active intervention, be it the curing of the sick, the finding of lost articles or the discovery of secrets and of future events.

In Arctic shamanism the trance is an integral part of the shamanistic procedure. The shaman resorts to ecstasy, either to recall the sick person's soul, to remove a disease-object from the patient's body, or to gather information concerning human beings and fateful events. During the ecstasy he usually sends out his free-soul, or his guardian spirits—the boundary line between these spiritual agents often tends to be effaced, the shaman being able to journey in the figure of his guardian spirit. When the shaman cures a patient whose disease is caused by the intrusion of an inanimate object or a spirit (a diagnosis which somehow is forced aside in Arctic shamanism), he usually lives in a kind of half trance and is assisted by his helping spirits. The notion exists sometimes that the latter, and not the shaman, remove the disease agent.

This summarily sketched outline of the two most prominent forms of shamanism in North America will serve as a background and help us to put in its right place the shamanistic performance which will be described in what follows. In the bordering area between general and Arctic shamanism we find a ritually elaborated shamanistic séance characterized by the summoning of spirits for information (divination, etc.) and, in some cases, healing. It is held in a dark place, and the medicine-man is not infrequently practicing in a cylindrical tent erected for the purpose. This may be placed outdoors or in a largish lodge or house. Sudden confusion of spirit voices, shaking of the tent and the medicine-man's mysterious disentangling of ropes and thongs are some of the most conspicuous features of the performance. It is known under the denominations "Shaking Tent" and "Spirit Lodge," or is simply described as "conjuring ceremony" or "jugglery." Since the feature of the shaking tent is not present everywhere in this ceremony, particularly not in the Arapaho séance to be described here, the term "Spirit Lodge" is preferred in this chapter. The ceremony has been dealt with from different points of view by authors like Cooper, Hallowell, Lambert, and Ray (Cooper 1944: 60 ff.; Hallowell 1942; Lambert 1956: 113 ff.; Ray 1941: 204 ff.). Its religio-historical position has, however, never been made the object of a closer investigation.

A Spirit Lodge Ceremony among the Arapaho Indians

In August 1955, the author attended a medicine ceremony among the Arapaho Indians on the Wind River reservation, Wyoming. The Arapaho constitute a branch of the great Algonkian linguistic stock; their nearest kinsmen are the Atsina or Gros Ventre (of the Plains) who broke away from them several hundred years ago. They were, until the end of the last century, typical Plains Indians equipped with horses and teepees (i.e., conical tents of buffalo hides), living on buffaloes, organized with military societies, and having the famous Sun Dance as their foremost religious expression. With their well-known neighbors and linguistic kin, the Cheyenne, and the likewise well-known northern Sioux (Dakota) Indians, they were until late times among the most warlike tribes on the Northern Plains. It was a close common interest, viz., the opposition to the white invaders, which brought them and the Sioux together; and the bands between the two tribes are still rather strong, as will appear from the following account. It is also important to note that the Arapaho have always been known as devotedly religious; their inclination to religious mysticism distinguished them from most other Plains tribes. In 1878 they were removed by force from their old hunting grounds in eastern Wyoming and western Colorado to their present home in western Wyoming (cf. Mooney 1896: 953 ff.; Mooney 1907: 72f.; Kroeber 1902: 1 ff.; Clark 1885: 38 ff.; Hilger 1952: 1 ff.; Elkin 1940: 207 ff.; Wright 1951: 42 ff.).

Anyone who knows the Arapaho's strong dedication to religion would expect the medicine ceremony to be performed by some of their old medicine-men. This strangely enough was not the case. The acting medicine-man was an Oglala Sioux from the Pine Ridge Reservation in South Dakota by the name of Mark Big Road. Although a very silent and reticent man—he did not like to discuss the ceremony with me—he nevertheless disclosed certain particulars about himself and his calling. Mark Big Road, a tall and strongly built man in his forties, told me that he practiced the same type of séance as his father and grandfather had done before him. They were medicine-men like him, and Mark had inherited their guardian spirits. In spite of this, however, he had not acquired them automatically but had like other medicine-men to go through an ordeal of fasting and waking, whereupon the spirits had appeared in visions. His foremost helping spirit was Skadi, the ghost of a white man who had become so "Indianized" that he now spoke the Sioux language. Mark had met Skadi in his first vision, and then after Skadi's instructions he had received many other guardian spirits, he did not say how many. An Arapaho woman who considered herself initiated told me they were 427 all in all, other participants in the ceremony thought they were many but would not say how many. One spirit is supposed to be 7,000 years old. Mark counts among his guardian spirits also the mighty spirit of the thunder (*wakinyan*).

Mark Big Road had been called to Wind River by Arapaho Indians who had witnessed his magical performances on the Sioux reservation and among white men in Rapid City. Older Arapaho remembered that similar remarkable feats had been achieved amongst them fifty years earlier, or around that time. However, no present-day medicine-man among them mastered the art any longer. Therefore,

Mark was called upon to reintroduce the medicine ceremony during a series of performances. Admittedly, this meant that the Oglala version of the ritual had to be accepted, but the difference between this and the earlier indigenous ceremony was apparently very slight. Anyway, this reintroduction of an old shamanistic rite must be considered to be a remarkable event, particularly if we keep in mind that seventy-five years earlier the Indian agent at Fort Washakie (Wind River Reservation) thought he could report that the Arapaho medicine-men had finally ceased with their jugglery (*Report of the Commissioner of Indian Affairs* 1881: 242). In other words, the revitalized medicine ceremony among the Arapaho in the 1950s ought to be conceived as a "nativistic" rite, according to Linton's definition of the concept (Linton 1943: 230). It thus represents a new trend in the tribal life, a renaissance and renewal of the best values in the old religion. In this connection it is important to note the role and functions of the medicine ceremony. It does not only help human beings to have their health restored, or their lost and hidden things regained. It also creates for them the contact with the reassuring world of spirits which is the heritage of the Indian religions since time immemorial.

The medicine ceremony on the eve of August 23, 1955, was arranged by one of the most active promoters of a religious renewal among the Arapaho, Buster Crispin, and was given for the benefit of his kinsman Steve Duran, who for many years had felt pains each time he had a meal. The ceremony was held in a primitive log cabin close to the Little Wind River, ordinarily occupied by a middle-aged Arapaho Indian. In the course of the evening many Arapaho arrived at the house, until finally its large room was filled up by some sixty persons, mostly women and children. They sat down on blankets spread out on the floor along the walls, the men being seated in the western and the women in the eastern parts of the room. Four drummers placed themselves on two mattresses in front of the men's row. Mark, appearing in the usual modern Indian apparel of "cowboy fashion," took his seat at a place where the men's and the women's sides joined each other. The windows were covered by sackcloth. It was now ten o'clock. The séance could begin.

The hostess, Helen Crispin, hands over in a dignified way a big ceremonial pipe to the medicine-man, asking him at the same time, with tears glittering in her eyes, to cure her sick relatives.[3] Mark accepts the pipe, lights it and starts smoking. This is a sure sign that

3. All conversation during the performance was held in English, since Mark, being a Sioux, does not understand the Arapaho language.

he has decided to accede to Helen's wishes. Helen's husband now rises from his seat and admonishes those present to try to believe, not to doubt, not to wonder; they must pray incessantly to the ninety-six spirits who will be present during the performance.[4] "And," he surprisingly finishes his speech, "I ask for the blessings of God and the Holy Ghost." Hot stones are now carried in a tub to the middle of the room, water is poured over them, and the room is filled with steam and strong heat. Men and women rise and, passing slowly the heated place, they fan the steam up toward face and breast. This being done everybody receives small seeds of sweetsage which they rub into their heads and arms. This rubbing procedure as well as the steam bath are preparatory cleaning rites.[5]

The medicine-man now takes his seat in the center of the room on a carpet which is covered by long straws of sagebrush. Around him are placed small flags and a rectangular enclosure, consisting of a string which is bound to a series of jars standing on a line. The string is stretched between them some few inches above the ground and carries 147 small red bags filled with tobacco. Beside his blanket, but inside the enclosure, the medicine-man arranges a little altar, provided with, *inter alia*, feathers, sacred pipes, tobacco, and gourds. He thereafter sets a piece of sagebrush on fire and makes the incense pass over the sacred objects of the altar, at the same time as the thundering sounds of the drum fill the room and the harsh voices of the drummers reach the ceiling. Mark fetches his two ceremonial pipes and points first one, then the other in the direction of the four cardinal points and over the heads of the assembly, making blessing hand movements.

After these preliminary rites there takes place a sacrificial ceremony of a type which occurred in the Sun Dance in the old days. A young daughter of Buster and Helen Crispin, Helena, steps forward, withdraws her moccasins and places her feet on the blanket, at the same time looking towards the west. The medicine-man comes closer, strokes her left arm with sagebrush, raises his hand and prays over her. Thereafter he brings out a razor, and under the deafening

4. Already before the ceremony began Buster Crispin tried to dissuade me and the white lady I brought along from attending it. He pointed out to us that curiosity in this connection was no good, and that the spirits would not appear if the whole audience did not join in prayers to them. Cf. also Hurt 1960: 52.

5. It is interesting to observe that the sweat-bath rite which was formerly performed in a separate hut outside the Spirit Lodge has now been incorporated in the main ceremonies. Concerning the sweetsage, this was probably *Artemisia ludoviciana*, an herb that often serves as incense among Northern Plains Indians.

roar of the drums he cuts thin slices of skin and flesh from the girl's upper arm. She makes faces, but apparently does not utter a sound; her blood pours out of the wounds, while the assembled, still seated, pray with lowered heads. After a while Mark nods as a sign that her torture is over. She returns to her seat, and is relieved by Mark's wife who now steps forward to suffer the same painful procedure. The sacrificial flesh of the two women is then collected and placed in a little gourd that has its place on the altar. The spirits have received their tribute.

It is now time for the main performance, the shamanizing. The medicine-man who is stripped to the waist stands up on his carpet, whereupon two men approach him and wrap him up very tightly in a blanket. Then they bind him with ropes all over the body, and his hands are tied together behind his back so tightly that they become red. At the same time Mark starts calling on his guardian spirits in a tense, strained voice. Now and then he disrupts his singing with the voice of the owl: "hu, hu." The assistants cover up his face, but his singing continues, although with a partly stifled voice. Finally, the medicine-man is placed on the floor, lying on his face. And then the light in the ceiling is extinguished.

There follow four steady beats on the drums, then the tempo becomes faster and faster working up to a fenzy, and the room resounds with the intense singing of those present. After a few minutes have elapsed in the dark something seems to happen,[6] and suddenly one can hear a rattle jingle in the midst of the turmoil. It seems to move around the room at the level of a man's height. The drums and the singing cease, and the only thing that may be perceived by the ear is the quiet moaning of the medicine-man, still, as far as I can judge, emanating from the level of the floor. The spirits have arrived.

Helen Crispin's voice breaks the weird silence. "Oh, Skadi and you other spirits, please, pity us. We are here to ask you to take care of and to cure Steve, my brother-in-law, who is very ill. Help him to get well. We believe in you, Skadi. Please cure him, allow him to be with us, let him take care of his family. Skadi and you other spirits, we ask you from all our heart to make him well." One can hear agreeing mutterings from the assembled, even an "amen" here and there. Helen prays again: "Skadi, take away the evil from Steve, place it somewhere out in space where there are no people and where

6. According to what Crispin and others said, one can see blue and green sparks when the spirits enter (cf. Hurt 1960: 51). My own experiences—however they may be explained—were restricted to feeling a strange draught along the wall and shivers running up and down my spine.

nobody may be hurt by this evil. And think, Skadi, of my niece who is sick and weak, and cure her." Other persons also send up similar prayers, asking for the cure of their sick kinsmen. They ask Skadi if he will make them well, and beseech him to give counsel whether or not they should send their sick youths to school.

Suddenly, Mark says something under his blanket. Those seated very close to him apprehend that the thunder spirit has arrived, not, on the other hand, the longed-for Skadi. The latter is expected from Rapid City in the Black Hills, and because of his distant abode it takes time for him to arrive. Some minutes are spent in eager expectation. Then Mark starts singing, the drums are sounded again, but more violently than before, and men and women sing with all their voices—indeed, the noise is deafening. Now the cry of an owl breaks through the turmoil. It is Skadi who has arrived; being a ghost he chooses the apparition of the owl. Heavy steps resound from the boards of the floor. Sighs are perceived from the center of the room where the medicine-man is supposed to be lying. All the rest is now silence.

At the request of Buster Crispin the assembled move away some inches from the walls in order to make it possible for the spirits to pass freely in and out. Mark's voice is again heard all over the room. He announces what he has been told (not audible to the rest of us) by Skadi. The girl N. N. will have a baby. "Ugh," the listening crowd comments. Skadi promises to see to the patients who have been prayed for, but he will first treat Steve. The latter is ordered by Crispin to rise to his full length against the wall. Again there is singing and drumming, until Mark announces that Steve has been cured and that Skadi has left to visit the sick ones at the hospitals. The sound of an airplane can be vaguely perceived by all present. Mark bursts into laughter: "Skadi regrets that he can't take the airplane, he missed it." There is mirth everywhere, a sort of release from all the preceding tensions.[7] Mark adds that the séance may be adjourned for some minutes, since Skadi is not present any longer and will be away for a while.

When the light is turned on Mark is found seated on his carpet which he has rolled up. Drops of perspiration fall from his naked back. The rope that had fettered him is lying neatly coiled at his feet, the blanket is away, it had been thrown out in the dark and had

---

7. The occasional outbursts of laughter during the conjuring ceremony have also been observed by other authors (cf. for instance Hallowell 1942: 44 f.).

landed among the audience.[8] Crispin is satisfied: this is how it should be done, he says, this is how the old-timers did it. "The Whites don't catch anything when they take photographs, and therefore it is meaningless to photograph."[9]

It is now past midnight. Soon, the light is put out again. There is, once more, singing and drumming, thereafter the rattle is sounded again. Skadi announces through Mark that he has helped the sick and cured them. Steve will get well, but in future he must think of Skadi and take care of himself. This information from the spirit is followed by happy cries of delight from those present, and above all the humming sounds Helen's quiet voice: "Thank you, thank you, Skadi."

Mark announces that Skadi is now leaving us. After some minutes the light is turned on again. The séance is at an end. What remains pertains to the common Indian feast traditions: the feathered ceremonial pipes pass around among the assembled, and a feast is served by Crispin's daughters. It was 2:45 o'clock in the morning when the meeting was dissolved.

As far as I know, Steve Duran kept fairly well henceforth; at lest he did not get worse. The believers said, of course, that he had become better, and it is certainly not impossible that this was so.[10] Throughout the autumn and winter Mark remained among the Arapaho, and he was very popular since he never charged his clients for the services he rendered them, thereby differing from other medicine-men among the Dakota Sioux.[11] I was informed that the spirits had imposed many taboos on him, amongst other things, the prohibition to make money in his work as *wapiye,* medicine-man.

During the years which have since elapsed the type of medicine ceremony here described has gained a secure position among the Arapaho, and according to the latest information at my disposal it is now performed by a young Arapaho Indian whose repu-

8. The blanket, in fact, hit the white lady whom the author had in his company. It is known from other similar ceremonies that it sometimes falls down on somebody who is unbelieving (see Hurt and Howard 1952: 292 f.).

9. He is referring to photographic experiments during spiritualistic séances in Rapid City.

10. On the other hand, Buster Crispin, the host of the ceremony, passed away during the Sun Dance the following year.

11. In most conjuring séances of this type it is a common thing that the medicine-man abstains from fees.

ted capacity to work miracles has induced Indians from many tribes to visit the Wind River Reservation (see Dusenberry 1962: 172).[12]

Old and New Forms of the Spirit Lodge Ceremony

The ceremony described above is a variant of the great ceremonial complex Spirit Lodge. This variant is called *yuwipi* in the Dakota language, a word which denotes the binding and wrapping up of the medicine-man, and it is performed among the Dakota Sioux, in particular the Oglala branch (Hurt and Howard 1952: 286 ff.; Hurt 1960: 48 ff.; Hurt 1961: 43; Feraca 1961: 155 ff.; Feraca 1963: 26 ff.). What differentiates the *yuwipi* from other Spirit Lodge performances is, above all, the intricate ritualism with much ceremonial paraphernalia and—in modern times—the location of the ceremony in the quadrangular room of a cottage. To these elements may also be added the blood sacrifices.

The exhibition of ritual objects within a square, mentioned above, seems to be an item of the common ritualistic pattern in the Northern Plains. It is possibly related to the Sun Dance altar and other similar ceremonial structures among the Plains Indians (Lowie 1954: 170; Wissler 1941: 129 f.; Spier 1921: 471 ff. See also the illustration in Dorsey 1903: 118, Pl. LXI.) and may, as in the Cheyenne Sun Dance, represent the earth or the universe (Dorsey 1905b: 146). From the formal point of view the *yuwipi* altar reminds one of the sacred shrines of the Pueblo Indians and may, indeed, be related to these (cf. Parsons 1939, 1: 353, 2: 956 f.). A different opinion has been developed by the anthropologist S. E. Feraca who thinks that the earthen altars are variations of the fireplaces among the Indians of the Southeast (Feraca 1961: 155).

The blood sacrifice was formerly common in the Plains Sun Dance and in the vision-quests in this area (Spier 1921: 492 f. Cf. MacLeod 1938: 349 ff.). It is of great interest to note that the sacrifice made in the Arapaho-Dakota rite which has been described in this chapter corresponds completely with the famous Sioux (Hunkpapa) Chief Sitting Bull's self-sacrifice in the Sun Dance of 1876: also in

---

12. The reader is reminded of what was said above concerning this medicine rite as a nativistic ceremony. According to Dusenberry, the interest in the Spirit Lodge is growing among all the northwestern Plains tribes. The Cree in Montana who gave up the ceremony in 1904 or perhaps a little later, reintroduced it in 1945 (Dusenberry 1962: 167 f.). Cf. below concerning the spread of the rite in its modern Dakota form.

this case, slices of flesh and skin were cut out of the arms (Vestal 1957: 149 f.).

The present habit of arranging the rite in the room of a wooden building, the most common dwelling among the Arapaho of today, is of rather recent origin. In the old days the performance took place in a lodge (teepee), and it could frequently happen that the tent shook in a mysterious way when the spirits entered and departed, or even during the whole ceremony (see Pond 1889: 249 f.). These agitations were formerly common in most places where the ceremony occurred. They motivate its most popular name, the "Shaking Tent."

The Arapaho, too, have once known the rite in this form. Bruce Grosbeak, an elderly Arapaho, who died in 1956 and who had a good knowledge of the old traditions of his tribe, told me that before the turn of the century the Spirit Lodge ceremony was arranged in a tent. The medicine-man was tightly tied to the base of a lodge pole, and the spirits entered through the smoke hole; the audience could hear their voices from the top of the tent.

Such séances were reported already in the beginning of the seventeenth century by Samuel de Champlain and Father Le Jeune who had found them in the territories of the Algonkian Indians (Biggar, ed. 1925: 86 ff., 1932: 85 ff.; Thwaites, ed. 1896–1901, 6: 163 ff., 12: 17 ff. (Le Jeune).[13] They still occurred in this area until very recent times, and most probably exist there even today. The Shaking Tent was, as we shall see, also common in the northern Plains and Plateau areas farther west. In most cases the ceremony was held in a tent which had been raised for the purpose, and not infrequently we are informed that the medicine-man performed his magic tricks in a small, closed tent which was put up inside a large lodge. Sometimes the medicine-man was not tied up. Otherwise, the similarities between the oldest known Spirit Lodge performances and the *yuwipi* rite which has just been described were so great that it must be taken for granted that both of them belong to a very old, fixed shamanistic tradition. It is possible to say that the *yuwipi* today supplies the form in which this tradition can survive; it has, so to speak, transferred shamanism from the tent milieu of the nomad to the modern, urbanized milieu.[14] The *yuwipi* rite has recently expanded and not only

13. Champlain's experience is from 1609, Le Jeune's from 1634. The first picture of a Spirit Lodge rite appears in Schoolcraft 1860, 5: Pl. 32. It shows a cylindrical Medicine Lodge in which the spirits are conjured up and probably refers to the Ojibway; cf. the text, 421 ff.

14. Cf. Hurt and Howard 1952: 294. The architectural structure motivates the absence of the shaking trait in the modern *yuwipi*.

among the Arapaho. At present it is on its way to penetrate Sioux reservations where the secret of the Shaking Tent was forgotten many years ago (Feraca 1961: 162; Hurt and Howard 1952: 288 n. 2). It seems that nowadays the *yuwipi* performance is the most vital element of the old pagan religion among the Dakota (Macgregor 1946: 98 f.; cf. Feraca 1961: 162).

In this connection we must abolish the suspicion that this medicine ceremony, in any case in its *yuwipi* form, has received a decisive influence from modern spiritualistic séances. There are, certainly, reasons for assuming such influence, as when, for example, the medium in both ceremonies keeps in contact with a spirit control who is the ghost of a deceased person—in the Arapaho ceremony even the ghost of a white person.[15] On the other hand, the presumed connection is impossible in view of the fact that right since the beginning of the seventeenth century the Spirit Lodge ceremony has preserved its tight molding and has been diffused over a considerable area, as we shall soon see. It is more likely that modern occidental spiritualism has been influenced by American shamanism as this appears in the Spirit Lodge (cf. in this connection the comparisions between modern spiritualism and Siberian shamanism in Findeisen 1960; Stiglmayr 1962). This is also the opinion of Richard Lambert who points out that both the trick of escaping when being bound up and the custom of giving the controls Indian names have been passed over from American Indian shamanism to modern spiritualism (Lambert 1956: 128).[16] It is appropriate to mention in this connection that the well-known Swedish author and spiritualist Jan Fridegård claims that he has an Indian guardian spirit, the ghost of a medicine-man (Fridegård 1963: 87).[17]

---

15. Several parallels between the Spirit Lodge and the spiritualistic séances were already pointed out by J. G. Kohl who studied the Ojibway ceremony in the 1850s (cf. below).

16. Another writer goes even further when he claims that the séance cabinet of modern spiritualism is directly derived from the North American Indian conjuring lodge (Rawcliffe 1959: 302). The impact of the Spirit Lodge on spiritualistic literature has been discussed by Hallowell (1942: 2).

17. Fridegård does not know the name of this spirit. He mentions, however, the names of some other spirits of American Indian origin appearing in the séances he partakes in: Chief Black Eagle, who is a control, and "Kockum," a trickster playing practical jokes during the séance (Fridegård 1963: 40, 87).

The Diffusion of the Spirit Lodge Complex

From the phenomenological point of view the religious beliefs and rites making up the Spirit Lodge constitute a unitary, complex whole. The different elements pertaining to it occur to a surprising extent in a fixed order and clearly delimited from other shamanistic performances. The area of diffusion is, moreover, restricted, or mainly so, to a continuous east-western belt in Canada and the United States. It is thus evident that the Spirit Lodge ceremonies have a common historical origin (Ray 1941: 204; Collier 1944: 45). The efforts made by American anthropologists to establish the roads of diffusion must, however, be considered only partly successful. Not only does every new discovery of the conjuring practice change the earlier historical reconstruction, but also the information available from times past is too scattered to support more than a tentative analysis of this kind.

This does not rule out the possibility that a study of the distribution of the Spirit Lodge may reveal to us where this ceremony had its center of gravity and, in all probability, its center of diffusion. Its main area takes in three important cultural regions, the Northeastern Woodland, the Plains, and—less intensely, it is true—the Plateau. A separate but major field of distribution is the Eskimo area. Within the main area the ceremonial complex seems to be concentrated to ethnic groups of Algonkian affiliation. It is preferably these tribes who have used the particular, shaking conjuring tent (Hallowell 1942: 14; Flannery 1939b: 14 ["an exclusive Woodland Algonquian usage"]). The rectangular enclosure of strings and flags in the Arapaho ceremony and in the conjuring performances of other Plains tribes is to all appearances a substitute for the shaman's tent among the Algonkian tribes. These and other facts seem to point to the main role played by Algonkian Indians in the dissemination of the complex phenomenon.

In the Northeastern Woodland the Spirit Lodge ceremony is known from a series of Algonkian tribes and ethnic groups: the Cree, Mistassini, Naskapi-Montagnais, Ojibway (see Cooper 1944: 78 ff.; Hallowell 1942: 14 ff., 35 ff.; Ray 1941: 205 f., 208 n. 2. Cf. Hilger 1951: 75 ff. See Rousseau and Rousseau 1948: 307 ff.; Rousseau 1955: 129 ff.; Burgesse 1944: 50 ff.). From the seventeenth century onward the evidence is rich from these groups, so rich that it is possible to consider the Northern Algonkian Spirit Lodge as the high mark of the ceremonial complex. In later times it appears that almost every small band had the séance (Cooper 1944: 79). In the periphery of the area the ceremony, strange to say, is missing among the Coast Algonkian Indians (Hallowell 1942: 14 n. 21; Cooper 1944: 82; Flannery 1946:

264 f.), whereas we find it among the Menomini (Central Algonkian) (Hoffman 1896: 142 ff.).[18] It is not improbable that it has reached the latter from the Northern Algonkian tribes. The existence of a shaking-tent rite to the south of this area, among the Creek, seems rather enigmatic (Cooper 1944: 83). One could possibly expect that the Southern Algonkian tribes, in particular the Shawnee, should have brought the ceremony to some southern peoples. But this is not the case, for the Shawnee and their neighbors do not know it. We shall return to this problem later on.

It is quite probable that the Spirit Lodge was spread over the Plains by stimulus from the Algonkian tribes in this area, the Plains Cree, the Cheyenne, Arapaho, Gros Ventre, and Blackfoot (Collier 1944: 47 f.; Ray 1941; cf. Dusenberry 1962: 166 ff.; Cooper 1944: 60 ff.; Flannery 1944: 54 ff.; cf. also Kroeber 1908: 276; Cooper 1944: 77 f.; Long Lance 1928: 51 ff.).[19] It gained a firm footing among the Northern Sioux Indians, that is, several Dakota groups—the Wahpeton, Sisseton, Mdewakanton, Yankton, Yanktonai, Teton (to whom the Oglala belong)—and the Assiniboin, Mandan, and Crow (see Hurt and Howard 1952: 287; Wallis 1947: 102 f.; Collier 1944: 47 n. 5; Cooper 1944: 78; Long 1961: 162 ff.; Bowers 1950: 179 f.; Lowie 1922b: 380 f.; Lowie 1935: 70 f.). Finally, the ceremony reached the Arikara at the Upper Missouri and the Kiowa on the southern Plains (Chittenden and Richardson, eds. 1905, 1: 250 f.; Collier 1944). The latter, isolated case may seem surprising. It should, however, be observed that the Kiowa some centuries ago probably maintained their existence in the northern Plains (Wedel 1959: 78 f.; Hyde 1959: 137 ff.). Lowie has noted down some few cultural elements joining the Kiowa with the Crow (Lowie 1953a: 357 ff.; Lowie 1953b: 1 ff.). It is now possible to add to them the Spirit Lodge.

Some Plains tribes, perhaps the Blackfoot in the first instance, were probably responsible for the diffusion of the conjuring lodge to two eastern Plateau tribes, the Kutenai in British Columbia, and the Salish-speaking Colville in Washington (cf. Ray 1941; and see Chamberlain 1901: 95 ff.; Turney-High 1941: 174 ff.; Cline et al. 1938: 152 f.). There are no traces of the ceremony farther west, unless we include the shaking post in the Cannibal dancing rites of the central and northern Kwakiutl (Wikeno, Bella Bella, and Haisla). It was common

18. The forms taken by Huron and Iroquois shamanism resemble certain aspects of Algonkian shamanism but lack the Spirit Lodge features (see Kurath 1961: 183).
19. There is no earlier information on Arapaho jugglery in the ethnographic literature.

usage here to tie the future shaman to the loosely set pole during the initiation rite (Drucker 1940: 204, 208 f., 216). The parallel with the Spirit Lodge is, however, very far-fetched and certainly does not prove any immediate connections.

Against the distributional background as drawn up above it may seem surprising to instance the occurrence of a Spirit Lodge ceremony among the Eskimo, particularly the Central Eskimo (see e.g., Boas 1888: 593 f.; Rasmussen 1929: 123 ff.; Holm 1914: 90 ff. Cf. also Hultkrantz 1962a: 405). It is, however, possible to find evidence for a direct communication between the Eskimo and the conjuring tribes to the south. Theoretically, there may have existed two channels of diffusion, via the Naskapi or via the Cree. As concerns the Naskapi, they are in touch with the Eskimo on their northern boundary (Turner 1894: 184). Cree shamans have performed Spirit Lodge séances as far north as the White Sands at the Mackenzie River, Lake Athabaska, and the Athabaska River (Cooper 1944: 79, 82; Black 1934). It is doubtful, however, whether they have come in closer contact with the Eskimo, from whom they were separated by the Athapascan tribes to the north and east. The evidence is contradictory where the dedication of the latter to the Spirit Lodge practice is concerned. Cooper assures us that the Chipewyan lacked the ceremony, even where they bordered on the Cree (Cooper 1944: 82 f. Cf., however, a similar shamanistic rite in Birket-Smith 1930: 82). Regina Flannery also denies its existence among the Chipewyan and adds that, although it does occur among the Beaver, it has only been observed among those Beaver Indians who have been strongly influenced by the Cree (Flannery 1939b: 14). On the other hand, a traveller in the Great Bear Lake area in the middle of last century, W. H. Hooper, saw there a conjuring lodge, probably belonging to the Satudene (Osgood 1932: 48). Furthermore, the medicine-men among the Hare and Loucheux (Kutchin, or rather a band of mingled Hare and Kutchin) are reported to have been suspended in the air to promote their communion with the spirits—something which could be interpreted as a Spirit Lodge séance (Jenness 1934: 395; cf. also Wissler 1950: 203). It is, of course, possible that they as well as the Satudene had been influenced by their close neighbors, the Mackenzie Eskimo. In this connection it should also be pointed out that the "rope-trick," i.e., the shaman's mysterious release from the mat and the ropes in which he is entangled, was once known to the Tlingit of Sitka (Krause 1885: 286 f., 1956: 196).

Although the link through the Athapascan tribes cannot be proved, it seems probable that the Eskimo and Algonkian-Plains-

Plateau conjuring practices once belonged together; they may be considered branches of the same fundamental conjuring complex. From all the evidence the Algonkian groups and the Eskimo must be the originators of the complex in North America. Since it shows a remarkable uniformity over a vast area, despite important variations in certain details, the hypothesis of a rapid dissemination and a single origin is justified. There is, however, no clue to its age which may be quite considerable. The theory has been developed that the Spirit Lodge was created by the Central Algonkian tribes together with their well-known Medicine Society and the vision-quests of children (Müller 1956: 206 f.). This is not convincing, partly because it does not account for the Eskimo cases and partly because the Spirit Lodge is intrinsically a ritually fixed form of a more general conjuring practice.

It is possible that both the Creek and the Kwakiutl performances mentioned in the foregoing represent this more general form. Further examples of the latter may be found in the Southwest and in South America. Clairvoyant medicine-men among the Maricopa and other Yuman tribes in the Southwest (Yavapai, Walapai, and Mohave) went into a trance in a special hut, among the Maricopa built inside the meeting house, and were possessed by spirits who prophesied the future or revealed some sickness (see especially Spier 1933: 292 f.; Kroeber 1957: 226 ff.). Among the Cuna, Isthmus of Panama, the medicine-man was formerly seated behind a partition when he had his nightly séances with the spirits, and similar performances occurred also among the Cágaba in northern Colombia and the Caribs in the northern parts of South America (Wassén 1961: 19). The Manasí in Bolivia arrange divining ceremonies in the chief's large assembly hall. A ceremonial leader, *mapono,* takes his seat behind a curtain, calls on the gods and consults them concerning rain, harvest, hunting luck, etc. His questions and the answers of the supernatural beings form a quick dialog completely audible to the audience on the other side of the curtain. The big building is shaking both at the arrival and the departure of the spirits (Métraux 1943: 22 f.). There are other South American instances of the same general type (Steward et al. 1946: 302 ff.: "Inca"; 1949: 594: "Tupinambá").

We also find similar examples outside of the American continent. Hallowell mentions a conjuring performance among the Semang of the Malay Peninsula, quoting Schebesta and Evans (Schebesta 1927; Evans 1937). The construction of the conjuring hut, the turmoil of the spirits, and the curative and clairvoyant functions of the medicine-man in action remind him of the Saulteaux Spirit Lodge. He continues, however, "I am not citing these analogies in order to raise the question of any possible historical connection, but they do seem interesting because, so far as I know, similar parallels *do not* occur in boreal regions of Asia. If they did, it would be difficult to dismiss the possibility of historical connections with North America" (Hallowell 1942: 14 n. 20. Cf. also Fraser 1963: 400 ff.). But indeed, North Asiatic parallels do exist! A very interesting conjuring performance from the Yakut was described at the turn of the century by Sieroszewski. It is true that both the conjuring booth and the shaking are missing, but we find the binding of the shaman ("pour le retenir dans les cas où les esprits tenteraient de l'enlever"), the dramatic entrance of the spirits with much noise, curing and prophesying, etc. (Sieroszewski 1902: 325 ff. Cf. also Anisimov 1963: 100 ff., description of a Tungus shamanistic performance). Moreover, the leading guardian spirit is here as in many cases in the American conjuring lodge a deceased person, usually a shaman (Sieroszewski 1902: 312, 314). A ghost is also the chief spirit in a Chukchee séance that shows many features of the Spirit Lodge: the sudden sounds of the voices of the spirits all over the dark room, the shaking of the lodge, throwing of articles, etc. (Bogoras 1907: 434 ff.). It is important to note that Lowie presumed ancient historical connections between northern Asia and North America, *inter alia* by uniting the Chukchee performance with the Spirit Lodge performance (Lowie 1934b: 188). The Eskimo jugglery should, then, be considered the connecting link.

This reconstruction seems most probable. We can go even further. The North American séances should in my opinion be judged as ritually patterned specific forms of a jugglering complex spread not only in the northern parts of Asia and America, but also in South America and Southeast Asia. The reiteration of certain conspicuous elements, for instance the violent entrance of a crowd of spirits, the shaking of the tent and the binding of the medicine-man, make a common origin probable. It is, of course, useless to speculate about the place of this origin. In view of the data collected here one could think of a circumpacific rite complex, but the question cannot be settled until further research work on its distribution in the Old World has been done.

It is as difficult to decide the age of this wide complex. Discussing the Chukchee ceremony, Eliade asserts that it has no original touch. "On a l'impression," he says, "que la technique extatique est en décadence, les séances chamaniques se réduisant la plupart du temps à l'évocation des esprits et à des prouesses fakiriques" (Eliade 1951: 231, cf. 232 f.). This would mean that the conjuring ceremony should be judged as a later development of the great ecstatic séance with imaginary extracorporeal soul-journeys. Eliade is here, of course, proceeding from his general theory concerning the character of the original, genuine shamanistic trance. He is quite right in his opinion as far as the great shamanistic ecstasy is concerned, for, as Miss Czaplicka testifies, "The modern shamans actually 'sink' very seldom, but they know that it was done in the old days" (Czaplicka 1914: 232). It is, however, important to note that the Spirit Lodge ceremony is an altogether different complex, a particular form of shamanism where (usually) the intense ecstasy has no necessary function. Therefore, a comparison between the two forms of shamanistic expression cannot give us any clue as to the age of one or the other.

The Position of the Spirit Lodge in American Shamanism

In order to establish the place of the Spirit Lodge within the North American shamanism it is necessary to discuss some of the more diagnostic traits of the former. This can only be done very summarily since space prohibits a more comprehensive analysis; I hope, however, to be able to revert to the subject more closely in a future treatise.

The following points seem to be of particular interest in the present connection: the ecstasy; the shaking of the tent and other shamanistic tricks; the nature of the spirits; the suspension of the medicine-man; the occurrence of soul-flight; and the way of curing.

1. The ecstasy. Opinion is divided whether the conjuring medicine-man[20] is in a state of ecstasy or not. Quoting Shirikogoroff's pronouncement that the Tungus shaman falls into ecstasy, Hallowell says, "So far as I know, nothing of this sort is believed to happen to Saulteaux conjurers, nor do I think that trance actually takes place" (Hallowell 1942: 13). It is more than probable that Hallowell has been influenced in his judgment by the rather frank statement of an occasional conjurer (he had tried only once) that he himself had made the lodge shake and the voices sound (Hallowell 1942: 76 ff.). This statement is, however, definitely an exception; most conjurers believe that

---

20. It is as a rule a medicine-man who performs the jugglery. Among the Kutenai, however, anyone possessing a guardian spirit could be a conjurer, and among the Cheyenne the latter had to be a layman (Ray 1941: 207, 209). It must be recalled, however, that the boundary line between a medicine-man and other visionaries is very slight and sometimes completely disappears, particularly on the Plains.

the spirits act without their interference (Hallowell 1942: 73 ff.). Hallowell also refers to the normal mental make-up of the conjurers, as also other investigators do, apparently in the belief that ecstatic shamanism is combined with an abnormal, pathogenic personality structure (Hallowell 1942: 13; Cooper 1944: 81; Hurt and Howard 1952: 295). The absence of the trance is also taken for granted by other researchers, e.g., Cooper for the Algonkian tribes and Hurt and Howard for the Dakota (Cooper 1944: 81; Hurt and Howard 1952: 295).

Other observers testify, however, that ecstasy has been part of the ritual. Champlain noted how the conjurer works himself up into a frenzy, then "se leve sur les pieds, en parlant & se tourmentant d'une telle façon, qu'il est tout en eau, bien qu'il soit nud" (Biggar, ed., 1925). Le Jeune tells us how the medicine-man became more and more animated and "fell into so violent an ecstasy that I thought he would break everything to pieces" (Thwaites, ed., 1896–1901). Speaking about the Mistassini ceremony during the 1930s, Burgesse says that "the chant begins slowly and softly, increasing in tempo and pitch to reach a climax when Mictabio [=the control] manifests himself and the shaman is entranced" (Burgesse 1944: 51). The descriptions of the Eskimo performance leave no doubt concerning its ecstatic nature. Ohlmarks, referring to the Menomini rite as described by Hoffman, talks about a modified ecstasy. "Von einer wirklich grossen Schamanenextase ist ja hier nicht die Rede," he says, "wohl aber von einer gewissen Ekstase und Erregtheit, wo die Geister den 'Juggler' inspirieren und ihm die Zukunft entschleiern" (Ohlmarks 1939: 98). Lambert, on the other hand, is less inhibited in his general assessment of the Spirit Lodge phenomena. He states that the medicine-man employs a rattle and drum as he chants and howls "in preparation for going into a trance" (Lambert 1956: 126).

It depends, of course, on our definition of ecstasy whether we can characterize the Spirit Lodge shamanism as ecstatic. Ernst Arbman, our foremost authority on the subject, describes ecstasy as a "total suggestive absorption in the object of belief," an absorption which reveals itself in "a peculiar, strictly organized and intensively clear, conscious and realistic visionary state of dream" (Arbman 1963: xv. Cf. Hultkrantz 1957: 236 f.). The visions have in certain cases an "almost dazzling inner clairvoyance or illumination," with "actual perceptions of light of a purely hallucinatory or physically sensuous nature" (Arbman 1963: 297). It is of interest to note that Arbman shows after lengthy investigations that religious ecstasy, although anormal, can in no way be said to presuppose a pathological state of mind or a psychically disintegrated personality system (Arbman 1963:

215 ff.). This conclusion eliminates the apprehensions of certain anthropologists, referred to above, against associating the conjuring with states of trance.

In view of these definitions it seems justified to consider the Spirit Lodge shamanism an ecstatic performance (cf. also Hultkrantz 1963: 90, 98 f.). We know for sure that the conjurer, who is certainly no fraud, believes that the mysterious things that happen are the result of the spirits' own activity; it should be impossible for him to maintain this if he is not himself entranced, i.e., absorbed in this belief. Drumming, shaking of rattles, singing, and other suggestive acts produce the preparation for ecstasy. Obvious proofs of the presence of ecstasy are the light visions, the automatic speech, and, where they have possibly occurred, the states of possession.

The light visions are, as mentioned above, a typically ecstatic symptom. They are mentioned in several sources as belonging to the experiences of both the conjurer and his audience—for instance, already in Champlain's description, and as late as in the notes on the Arapaho rite in the present article. It is probable that the audience's visions reflect the suggestive influence of the conjurer who sees the light within the frame of his ecstatic state.[21] An excellent case of the conjurer's light perceptions is found in Kohl's description of an Ojibway séance (the disadvantage however being that the author received his information second-hand). The medicine-man told Kohl's informant that the top of the lodge in which he made his performance was filled with the voices of the spirits and lit up by a shining light, and the whole universe, heaven and earth, lay open before his eyes (Kohl 1859a, 2: 78). Arbman, who quotes this passage (Arbman 1963: 303 f.), states that what is here described is "the very ordinary hallucinated light that must be supposed to be present in every really ecstatic vision or inner visionary scenery in the same way as in the natural dream," although the rapid transition from inner darkness to vision makes the light perception more intense in the ecstatic vision than in the natural dream (Arbman 1963: 332 f.).

The automatic speech functions sometimes in the messages which the spirits give to the public through the medicine-man. It is true that these messages can be delivered in a quiet, natural way and with a voice that sounds normal and talks the same language as the audience (cf. the Gros Ventre, Cooper 1944: 67; and the Saulteaux,

<hr>

21. Even Le Jeune saw fiery sparks emerging from the top of the lodge (cf. Thwaites, ed. 1896–1901, 6: 173). A recent observer, Hurt, noted the same thing (see Hurt 1960: 51).

Hallowell 1942: 44 ff.). But in other cases the language of the spirits is unintelligible and has to be translated by the control or the medicine-man (Flannery 1940: 16).[22] It is difficult to avoid the conclusion that we have here to do with verbal automatisms on the part of the medicine-man, and such phenomena belong, of course, to ecstasy.

Neither the light vision nor the automatic speech do as such necessarily presuppose a deeper trance.[23] It is different when the ecstasy also includes a soul-journey or a possessional state. North Asiatic and Eskimo conjuring séances contain in any case the former of these traits (see below), perhaps also the latter although this is difficult to decide. Possession is an ambiguous concept in most ethnographic texts, sometimes referring to the intrusion of a spirit in the body, at other times referring to the domination of the personality by a foreign spirit which has usurped the place of the ego. From the psychological point of view only the latter definition is important, and it will therefore be used here.

States of possession are, as we know, rather rare in North American shamanism (Hultkrantz 1963: 96 ff.). The cases which could be adduced in connection with the conjuring ceremony are not very convincing. In the Kutenai and Colville rites, the medicine-man is supposed to be carried away by the spirits and replaced by them; it is doubtful whether this means a case of possession, since the conjurer's body and not only his soul are said to disappear. In a Montagnais séance described by Burgesse the medicine-man was lying unconscious, or seemingly so, while the spirits answered the questions put by the audience. "Replies to the hunters' questions are always given in the voice of the shaman but Moar [=the informant who had witnessed the séance] explained that it is really Mictabio [=the control] who speaks" (Burgesse 1944: 52). We are after all not told that the medium had been possessed by the spirit, although the situation may be interpreted that way. Le Jeune and several observers after him have noted that the medicine-man, when personifying the spirits, talks in a harsh or nasal voice which is otherwise foreign to him. It is obvious that in many cases the medicine-man practices ventriloquism. Kohl, Black, Hallowell, and others reveal that there is a dialog going on, the medicine-man speaking from the ground, the spirits, with the medicine-man's twisted voice, speaking from the top

22. These Indians are Ojibway (or Ojibway-Algonkian).
23. Eliade's pronouncement that the shaman's trance always has the same intensity (Eliade 1950: 302) is scarcely correct (see Hultkrantz 1953: 277 ff.; cf. also Findeisen 1960: 202).

of the lodge (see, e.g., Kohl 1859a: 77). Possession is here no necessary inference, but it cannot be entirely ruled out that it has occurred in some cases.[24]

Possession or no possession, we are satisfied to know that the conjurer is entranced. The trance is produced by different means. Besides drum and rattle, already mentioned, some shamans have resorted to drugs, as for example the old conjurer referred to by Kohl.

2. The shaking of the tent and other shamanistic tricks. The shaking feature seems to be fundamental in most rites in the Woodland and Plains areas, and it also occurs among the Arctic groups (Eskimo, Chukchee) and in South American conjuring (cf. Cooper 1944: 81; Collier 1944: 49). Its absence in the modern *yuwipi* form has here been explained with reference to the construction of the conjuring building; the same explanation applies to its absence among the Mandan and Colville (cf. Ray 1941: 208 f.; Hurt and Howard 1952: 294). From a superficial point of view the shaking is the most impressive feature in the Spirit Lodge; from a functionalistic point of view it is only one of the signs that spirits are present.

Other phenomena testifying to the presence of the spirits are the light visions, the confusion of voices, sounds of tapping and steps on the ground, the throwing around of articles, the liberation of the medicine-man from his bonds, and the magical removal of the medicine-man. In this connection only the rope-binding trick will be discussed.

It is usually called the "Houdini trick." It is not always present in the Woodland (Algonkian) performances—indeed, Cooper considers its absence characteristic of the Montagnais and Eastern Cree (Cooper 1944: 81). Otherwise, there is information about its occurrence among all the Algonkian groups having the Spirit Lodge, the Eskimo, and the Plains and Plateau tribes. Some sources underline that the Houdini trick is a secondary feature, and unnecessary (Hurt and Howard 1952: 292; Dusenberry 1962: 170; Cooper 1944: 66). Cooper suggests that it "had the purpose, overt or covert, of creating or confirming faith in the authenticity of the ghostly visitation" (Cooper 1944: 66). As we remember, the binding of the shaman also occurs among the Yakut in Siberia. Its motivation was there that the spirits might carry off the shaman if he were not bound. The same explanation is given by the Central Eskimo; their shaman is bound so

24. Possession has been emphatically denied by some observers (see Rousseau 1955: 136, Cooper 1944: 81). The Arapaho rite described in this article was not associated with the medicine-man's being possessed. As we have seen, possession occurred in the more general conjuring form represented by the Maricopa.

that only his soul can move away from the place. This motivation is, however, not sufficient to account for all the American cases in which the medicine-man is untied by the spirits. Although no explicit explanation can be laid forward here it seems fairly certain that the Houdini trick, besides showing the cleverness of the medicine-man and thus strengthening the belief in him and in the rite, demonstrates the presence and interference of the spirits.

The interpretation of the reality behind these shamanistic acts cannot concern us here. The judgments of the observers and writers are very contradictory. Paul Kane, the artist, who witnessed a conjuring ceremony among the Saulteaux in 1848, was amazed to find that the enclosed shaman could feel the presence of a white man in the dark, and he assures us that the detailed and clear prophecies the medicine-man had told him all came true (Kane 1925: 311 f.). Similar statements have been given by, i.e., Densmore, Hallowell, and Dusenberry (Densmore 1932: 311; Hallowell 1942: 16 n. 27; Dusenberry 1962: 168). Eliade considers that the confusion of voices and the liberation of the medicine-man from his bonds are enigmatic phenomena which should if possible be revealed by psychical research (Eliade 1951: 231 n. 1, 265 n. 1). On the other hand, the most spectacular feature of the conjuring act, the shaking of the lodge, can, according to several observers, be explained with reference to the construction of the lodge (Densmore 1932: 313 f.; Hallowell 1942: 73 ff.; Rousseau 1955: 145). These authors do not agree, however, on how the mechanism functioned, and one modern observer can find no clue in the construction of the lodge (Black 1934).[25] The medicine-men themselves and even the conjurer mentioned by Kohl who made his statement after he had been converted to the Christian faith, assert that they do not move the top of the lodge (Kohl 1859a: 78. See also Hallowell 1942: 74 f.; and the quotation from Schoolcraft in Mead and Bunzel, eds. 1960: 166). The value of such pronouncements can of course be contested. As Andrae says, spontaneous experience and simulation go together in religious practitioners with a hysterical—or rather, hysteroform—nature (Andrae 1926: 139, 171).[26] At the same time they identify themselves with a role set by their society (Hallowell 1942: 75 f.).

25. Cf. also Le Jeune's observations on the solidity of the tent in Thwaites, ed. 1896–1901, 12: 17 ff. See further the criticism of Densmore's hypothesis in Flannery 1939: 15 f., and Hallowell 1942: 83 n. 129. See also Lambert 1956: 127 f.

26. An example of a conscious manipulation on the part of the medicine-man may be found in Feraca 1961: 161.

3. The nature of the spirits. The spirits appearing in the conjuring lodge are of very varying types, but two kinds stand out as
being the most common: the spirits of nature, prevailingly called
upon in the eastern part of the conjuring area in North America, and
the ghosts, common on the Plains (Cooper 1944: 81). In the East, i.e.,
among the Forest Algonkian groups, thunder, turtle, and a crowd of
animal spirits dominate the scene. Most of the latter belong to the
category of "owners" or "masters," each group of animals having a
chief (cf. Hultkrantz 1961b: 53 ff.). This is a very general idea among
North American Indians, but it has particularly developed among the
Algonkian tribes. The Saulteaux, for instance, apply the concept of
"owners" first and foremost to the natural phenomena, the animal
and plant species, but they also extend it at the same time to the
spirits of the dead (Hallowell 1942: 6 f., 10; Hallowell 1940: 39). Thus,
in their Spirit Lodge both the masters of the animals and the masters of
the dead are invoked. Hallowell gives an interesting sketch of a conjuring performance in which the spirits of deceased relatives were
present, their "boss" acting as the control (Hallowell 1940: 42 ff.).

Séances where the dead appear are, however, more characteristic of the performances on the Plains. The crowd of spirits consists of both spirits of nature, more or less unidentified, and spirits of
the dead, often close relatives recently deceased. The control spirit is
always, or nearly always, a ghost helper; the Algonkian Cheyenne
have, however, the badger in this role (Grinnell 1923: 114 f.). Cooper
stresses emphatically that no one lacking a ghost helper could conduct the shaking tent rite among the Gros Ventre, no matter how
much power he had received by fasting and crying. Most people have
guardian spirits representing the realm of nature, fewer individuals
have ghost helpers; and only the latter spirits enter into the Gros
Ventre rite (Cooper 1944: 61 ff.; cf. Flannery 1944: 54, 58). All over the
Plains it seems that the owl could act as a substitute for the ghost
helper (cf. Collier 1944: 48, 49).[27] Actually, here as everywhere in
North America—and, for that matter, all over the world—the owl is
the form of manifestation of a dead person.

This association between ghosts and shamans is particularly
interesting since, as pointed out by Benedict, "in North America the
idea that one may seek tutelaries among the dead is very nearly
absent" (Benedict 1923b: 47). There is undeniably a certain difference
in the functions of the ghost helper and those of the other guardian

27. Note that in the Arapaho rite as described in this article the medicine-man
hooted like an owl.

spirits: the former gives "knowledge about past, present, future, or distant happenings, and counsel and direction in illness or danger." In short, he imparts information but does not as such grant power (Cooper 1944: 64, referring to the Gros Ventre). The idea of the ghost helper recurs in the Yakut and Chukchee ceremonies, mentioned above. It is tempting to see here an original trait in the conjuring complex, overshadowed by the common guardian spirit idea among the otherwise so conservative Algonkian groups in the East.

4. The suspension of the medicine-man. In some instances we are told that the medicine-man when freed from his bonds is found suspended at the top of the conjuring hut. According to a Blackfoot statement, the onlookers can see the shaman "hanging precariously by one foot at the top of the Lodge, stripped as naked as the day he was born" (Long Lance 1928: 57). A similar occurrence is reported from the Teton Dakota (Densmore 1918: 346. Cf. also Chamberlain 1901, Kutenai). As far as I know there are no examples from the Woodland distribution area. It is true that the Indians told Le Jeune that the medicine-man's soul left the body and mounted upwards, but this information is probably only a reference to the shaman's amazing ability to throw his voice.[28] We are, for instance, reminded here of the way in which Kohl's Ojibway conjuror could make a conversation between himself, lying on the ground, and the spirits entering on top of the tent (Kohl 1859a: 77); or of the Ojibway performance described by Jenness in which Thunder "is at the top, covering it like a lid" (Jenness 1935: 66).

The Kwakiutl custom of tethering the shaman-to-be to the pillar of the world has been mentioned earlier. It belongs most probably to a larger cultural connection obtaining in North and South America and in Siberia and characterized by the belief that the center post of the world as pictured in the cult may serve as a vehicle for the communication between the medicine-man and the spirits in the world above. The spirits may come to the post, or the medicine-man may climb the pole to reach them (Haekel 1955: 229). As we have seen, both acts occur, or are supposed to occur, in the conjuring lodge. The spirits enter on top of it, and—on the Plains—the medicine-man climbs up there. There is evidently a liaison here between the climbing-shaman complex and the Spirit Lodge. The

28. "Some of these Barbarians imagined that this juggler was not inside, that he had been carried away, without knowing where or how. Others said that his body was lying on the ground, and that his soul was up above the tent, where it spoke at first, calling these Genii, and throwing from time to time sparks of fire" (Thwaites, ed. 1896–1901, 6: 167).

Dakota and Blackfoot climbing acts in the Spirit Lodge have their close counterparts in the medicine-man's climbing of the center pole in the Crow and Kutenai Sun Dances. It would be most convenient to see the climbing feature in the Spirit Lodge as a local adaptation on the Plains to the shamanistic climbing complex. Of course, the possibility that the Spirit Lodge as such has its roots in ceremonies connected with this complex cannot be ruled out.[29]

5. The occurrence of soul-flight. The two Plateau instances of the conjuring complex, Kutenai and Colville, contain a phase in which the medicine-man is said to be carried away to a distant place by the spirits (Ray 1941: 208). It is indeed difficult to form an opinion about the beliefs involved, but from all appearances it was the medicine-man in body, and not his soul, who departed. The difference is, however, not very substantial in this connection, since the free-soul from a psychological point of view is identical with the image of the person (Hultkrantz 1953: 242 ff.; the Kutenai soul beliefs are discussed on 72 f.). (It is, of course, quite another matter what really happened to the medicine-man.)

As just mentioned, above, the conjuror observed by Le Jeune was supposed to have dispatched his soul to the top of the lodge.[30] This was at least the interpretation of Le Jeune's Indian companion, Manitou-Chat-Ché. It is, however, difficult to speak of a real soul-journey in this connection. Furthermore, as emerges from Le Jeune's description of the séance the medicine-man was singing his chants from his place in the lodge until the spirits arrived, whereupon he consulted them. The situation thus did not seem to conform to the idea of a soul-journey.

The Central Eskimo performance gives us more conclusive evidence of soul-flight. Here the shaman's soul flies away to some cosmic region while his body which is securely bound with cords lies inanimate on the ground. After having woken up from his deep trance the shaman tells the audience of his journey in the other world (Boas 1888: 594). His Yakut colleague makes a similar journey to the supernatural world during the conjuring séance.

Although the data are difficult to interpret, it would seem that

29. The climbing of the shaman seems often to be a part of the annual tribal ceremony (cf. Hultkrantz 1963: 107 f.). The Colville conjuring séance was apparently held in connection with the Winter Dance which is an annual ceremony related to the Plains Indian Sun Dance.

30. Cf. above, footnote 28, and the words directed to the sceptical Le Jeune by his host: "Enter thou thyself into the tent, and thou wilt see that thy body will remain below, and thy soul will mount on high" (Thwaites, ed. 1896–1901, 6: 169).

the idea of the soul-journey does not primarily belong to the Shaking Lodge complex, except in its Arctic extension. The common routine is that the spirits called up by the conjuror depart to gain the information which has been demanded. Sometimes they do this on their own initiative, as we have seen in the Arapaho séance, sometimes they are sent away by a commanding spirit, the control, as among the Montagnais (Burgesse 1944: 52).

6. The curing. Shamans are primarily healers, supernaturally endowed. The juggler in the conjuring ceremony, however, is not necessarily a healer, not, for instance, among the Ojibway where medicine-men are divided into three different categories, healers, conjurers, and seers; the members of the Medicine Lodge then are not included here (Jenness 1935: 60 ff.). If curing occurs in the Spirit Lodge, it is usually of subordinate importance, the greatest weight being laid on the searching for information, for instance, information about the causes and remedy of a certain illness which afflicts somebody in the audience. In the Plains Cree performance the spirits determine the location of a person's illness by hitting his body with a rattle. "Once the exact spot of the sickness has been found, the spirit pounds that particular area quite hard" (Dusenberry 1962: 171).

There are, to my knowledge, only few cases of actual curing in combination with the conjuring act described in our sources. One of them has been demonstrated in the foregoing account of the Arapaho rite; on the whole we receive the impression that the *yuwipi* performance has inherited the curing activities associated with the shamanism of former days (cf. also Feraca 1961: 162; Hurt and Howard 1952: 287. See also Ruby 1955: 44 ff., 62 ff.). Another case emanates from the Ojibway. Jenness tells us that sometimes "the helping spirits cured sickness by exchanging the soul of the patient with that of a man in perfect health; the latter merely felt indisposed for a short time until his new soul regained strength" (Jenness 1935: 67). The Saulteaux jugglers were formerly capable of restoring the soul to the body of a recently deceased person. In other words, they could cure cases of disease through soul loss by dispatching their supernatural helpers to fetch the patient's soul in the land of the dead (Hallowell 1942: 64). (As mentioned above there is otherwise outside the Eskimo area no information of the American conjurer's soul going to the realm of the spirits.) In some places diseases due to witchcraft or the transgression of a taboo can be cured in the Spirit Lodge. If a man has cast a spell over another man the spirits abduct his soul to the conjuring lodge and force him to confess there, whereupon the sick man is said to recover (Jenness 1935: 60 ff.)

It is, however, important to note that information of curing in the conjuring ceremony as such is rare and that the task of the jugglers is primarily to elucidate the nature and treatment of the disease, but not to treat it. The conjurer is a diviner, whether he traces lost objects, discloses past incidents, reveals future events or discovers the cause of diseases.

This summing up of some essential features of the Spirit Lodge complex may now help us to establish its position and relation to shamanism as such, and particularly shamanism in America. The Spirit Lodge is evidently a variety of shamanism characterized by its divining functions. Herein lie its limitations: the shamanistic trance is there, and so are the helping spirits, but the curing activity so typical of shamanism is absent, or principally absent. The act of divining shows a certain affinity with the shamanistic pole-climbing performances and may originally have been related to these. The shaman does not himself make soul-journeys to distant regions during the conjuring performance, except among the Arctic peoples where such journeys belong to the regular shamanistic pattern; instead, spirits are summoned and asked to make the necessary expeditions. These spirits represent different categories, but their leader, the control, is a ghost in several quarters. Specific features express the presence of the spirits: the shaking tent, the Houdini trick, the confusion of voices, etc. The spirits visit the shaman whilst the latter is in a trance; where soul-journeys and, possibly, possession occur the ecstasy may be very deep, but this is not typical.

It seems realistic to claim that the Spirit Lodge is a particular form of a divinatory practice which has developed within general shamanism, the latter concept used in the sense in which it was defined at the beginning of this article. In the north, its basic structure has been overlayed by Arctic shamanism (cf. the soul-journeys and the secondary motivation of the Houdini trick), whereas in the south, that is among Woodland Algonkian groups and Plains-Plateau tribes, it has retained its original character which has become fixed into a rigid ritual pattern. In this way it has become the most spectacular and interesting manifestation of shamanism in North America south of the Arctic zone.

6

The Cult of the Dead
among North American Indians

THE FOLLOWING INVESTIGATION takes up a theme which at first sight may appear outmoded and little rewarding. Outmoded, because this theme belonged with the evolutionistic approaches of fifty years ago, and practically no more modern works treat it; little rewarding, because North American Indians in general have had little inclination toward a pronounced cult of the dead. However, the latter circumstance presents us with some clues to an understanding of why and where such a cult may occur. In a wider perspective, from phenomenological points of view, the cult of the dead, or ancestor worship, may be referred to as an important aspect of the study of death.[1] In certain cases it also represents a dimension of the study of theism. It seems less apparent, however, that it constitutes a stepping-stone to the belief in gods, as Spencer and Karsten thought (Spencer 1876: 502 f.; Karsten 1935: 293).

1. In a recent article the Lancaster scholar Daniel Miranda suggested a subdisciplinary status for the study of death within the comprehensive field of phenomenology of religion. His is an attempt "to taxonomically arrange the subject of death in an orderly pattern for more thematic treatment" (Miranda 1977: 86, 90).

The State of Our Knowledge

Very little has been written on the cult of the dead in North America, presumably because of its restricted importance. There are some generalizations in Schoolcraft's famous work on North American Indians, but they concern death customs rather than the cult of the dead (Schoolcraft, ed. 1851, 1: 41). Daniel Brinton adequately remarked that "ancestral worship ... is a branch of the religion of sex, for only when the ties of relationship are somewhat strongly felt, can it arise. In America it existed, but was not prominent" (Brinton 1868: 274 f.). The observation of the role played by social structure is quite correct and has in later days been emphatically stressed by A. R. Radcliffe-Brown (cf. Radcliffe-Brown 1952: 163 f.). At the turn of the century Miss Laetitia Moon Conard discussed the possible existence of a cult of the dead among the Algonkian-speaking peoples of eastern North America. She found that, generally speaking, there was no such cult. The deceased appear to us as feeble beings, just shadows of men, she says; they need the assistance of the living in order to procure nourishment and clothes, tools and weapons, even fire. "Ils ne sont pas des puissances supérieures, mais de pauvres êtres sans force qui sont placés dans la dépendance des vivants" (Conard 1900: 242). This is indeed the reverse of a cult of the dead.

The first more general appreciation of the cult of the dead in America appeared in the *Encyclopaedia of Religion and Ethics* in 1908. In a general article on the subject W. Crooke said that ancestor worship existed in various forms throughout America—but then, he included reincarnation ideas and carved grave posts to such worship (Crooke 1908: 426, 429 f., 432). Stansbury Hagar conceded that the dead as a rule could return to earth to warn, protect and instruct the living. However, "strictly speaking, instances of true worship of ancestors or of the dead in America are rare. The dead are seldom confused or identified with the various deities, whose attributes, with few exceptions, clearly reveal their origin in the personification of natural phenomena" (Hagar 1908: 433, 435 f.). Hagar added that information was all that was asked of the dead, seldom anything else. The evidence is moreover slight that the dead were regarded as superior beings (Hagar 1908: 436). We must, of course, realize that Hagar's account was written before there was any thorough knowledge of American archeology and ethnology.

Later pronouncements are short statements, nothing more. Hartley Burr Alexander simply declared, in his survey of North

American mythology, that Indians performed rites to secure the assistance of the dead—a sweeping statement (Alexander 1916: xvii). Ruth Benedict remarked that the idea that one may seek guardian spirits among the dead is nearly absent in North America (Benedict 1923b: 47). She pointed out that the association of masked gods with impersonal dead in the Pueblo area is unusual in America, "and even that is slightly developed" (Benedict 1938: 662). K. Th. Preuss found a main distinction between North and South American religions in the fact that in the latter continent guardian spirits are usually identical with dead persons, in particular shamans, and thus we have a cult of the dead here (Preuss 1929: 209 f.). Wilhelm Schmidt, again, considered real ancestor worship to be rare in all of America with the exception of Peru during Inca time (Schmidt 1930: 68). His view that such worship belongs with agricultural societies and other societies influenced by them was shared by Walter Krickeberg (Krickeberg 1935: 332–35). In his comprehensive work on the fear of the dead Sir James Frazer arrived at the conclusion that American aborigines had some worship of the dead, although it was far less important and extended than the same sort of worship in Africa—a rather trivial conclusion (Frazer 1933: 69). About the same time Robert Lowie succinctly wrote that ancestor cults "are rarely typical of American Indians, hence they are not an inevitable stage in religious evolution" (Lowie 1940: 308).

Here, then, Spencer's evolutionism is refuted with the aid of the American evidence. Paul Radin for his part assigned a rather late date to the rise of ancestor worship. He strongly insisted (like Father Schmidt earlier) that there were no well-authenticated traces of this worship among food-gathering, fishing, and hunting peoples (Radin 1937: 74).

There has been little written on our subject during the last forty years. One notable exception is however Ruth Underhill's short characteristic in a paper on American religions. She states that the spirits of the dead did not play the important part sometimes found in the Old World. Certainly, they could cause illness, act as guardian spirits, or become reincarnated. However, only a few might be elevated to powerful spirits and gods (Underhill 1957: 129). The present author has discussed the poor development of North American Indian ancestor worship in some papers, but only briefly (Hultkrantz 1959: 702; Hultkrantz 1963: 134 f.; Hultkrantz 1977: 436).

This negative appreciation of the role of ancestor worship in North America is well founded in the materials at hand. With the exception of particularly the Pueblo area, a real cult of the dead is scarcely mentioned in our sources.[2] There are even direct denials. John Chapman, contrasting ideas and customs among the Ingalik of Alaska with the Batak of Sumatra, says that ancestor worship is found among the former "only in a rudimentary form, if it is to be found at all " (Chapman 1921: 301). We have seen Moon Conard's conclusion, built upon the perusal of a vast material, that Algonkian Indians lacked a cult of the dead. David Mandelbaum tells us that the Algonkian Plains Cree did not believe that the dead souls bestow power on man, but it was possible to beseech them to petition the higher powers to render aid to mortals (cf. below) (Mandelbaum 1940: 251). A bit confusingly, Lowie gives the information that among the Crow ghosts occasionally occurred as spiritual patrons, although ancestor worship in any form was totally lacking (Lowie 1925: 23). Similarly, James Owen Dorsey disclaims for the southern Sioux Indians—Omaha, Ponca, Kansa, and Osage—all worship of the ancestors (Dorsey 1894: 371). The Yana Indians of northern California were apparently also devoid of such worship (Gifford and Klimek 1936: 84).

A particular reaction against anything associated with death, the dead person, his belongings, the lodge in which he died, characterizes Athapascan and, to a certain degree, Shoshoni-Paiute, Yuman, and Piman peoples in western North America (see the maps in Driver 1961: map 30; and Driver and Massey 1957: 385, map 149.).[3] The Southern Athapascans in Arizona, New Mexico, and Texas, have a fright of death which ascends to morbid proportions. Writing about the Lipan Apache "death complex," Morris Opler states that its extensions "involve almost every aspect of Lipan thought and life" (Opler 1945: 140 f. Cf. however below, footnote 22). The fear of ghosts penetrates Apache and Navajo existence. No wonder, therefore, that the latter could not be induced to adopt the Ghost Dance or the Christian religion with their resurrection themes (Hill 1944: 523–27; Reichard 1949: 67). In such a milieu there is, of course, no qualification for the existence of a cult of the dead. Considering the many loans the Navajo have made from the Pueblo peoples, not least in the area of ceremonialism, the distance between their fear of the dead and the ancestor worship of the Pueblo groups is striking.

2. In tribal South America the cult of the dead is a bit more conspicuous, particularly among the woodland Indians (see Zerries 1961: 348 ff.).

3. Cf., however, the too rash conclusions in the latter work (Driver and Massey 1957: 392).

Specification of the Subject

Before turning to a closer investigation of the evidence certain clarifications must be made. My investigation is a case of regional phenomenology (typology) (Hultkrantz 1970b: 85 ff.), which means that it is comparative within certain geographical limits. The area of investigation, North America, is indeed most extensive, and this circumstance calls for certain restrictions of the theme. Firstly, I have deliberately concentrated the account on the cognitive aspects of the cult of the dead which, in a comparative perspective, are of paramount theoretical interest. Of course, a closer study and systematization of such behavioristic facets as offerings, cult groups, prayers, and dances would have increased the value of this investigation, but considerations of space have prevented this operation. Secondly, the margins of the cult have been restricted to cases in which attitudes of veneration and accomplishment are unequivocal.

By *cult of the dead* or *ancestor worship* I mean ideological premises and acts of worship concerned with deceased persons, or groups of (presumably) deceased persons, who may bestow some benefit upon their devotees. The difference between cult of the dead and ancestor worship *stricto sensu* is that the former concept is more inclusive, also taking in other dead persons than the subject's own ancestors, whereas ancestor worship only refers to the latter.

Now, some students define ancestor worship in the same way as I have but reserve the term "cult of the dead" for ideas and actions connected with the disposal of the dead, and include observances directed against malevolent ghosts in "ancestor worship."[4] This seems less advisable. A cult is a set of notions and rites aiming at the veneration of a supernatural being (cf. Latin *cultus*). Neither funeral concerns nor apotropaic rites against dangerous ghosts seem to fall within this definition. And since worship is a direct translation of "cult" the same rule holds in that case.

In order to make the record straight I shall discuss these points a little closer.

1. Burial gifts are no real offerings to the dead. It is a well-known fact that gifts for the dead are placed at (or in) the grave, or burned at the grave in order to release their spiritual essence.[5] Such

---

4. Cf., for example, the article on ancestor worship in *Funk & Wagnalls Standard Dictionary of Folklore, Mythology, and Legend* 1949, 1: 54).

5. There are no modern surveys of these customs in America, but see the following works: Yarrow 1880; Bahnson 1882: 182 ff.; Bushnell 1920; Bushnell 1927.

gifts may be made even long after death had occurred. Thus according to the Nootka of Vancouver Island, it may happen that the dead visit the living with good intentions. It is then practice of many families before going to bed to place a meal of dried fish and potatoes beside the fire for the refreshment of the dead visitors (Sproat 1868: 174). Now, some authors have called such customs instances of a death cult. For example, Schoolcraft notes that North American Indians "worship the spirits of their ancestors. They both place cakes on their graves and sepulchres, and pour out libations" (Schoolcraft, ed. 1853, 1: 61). Moon Conard makes use of the (French) word "offrande" in order to characterize a gift to the dead (Conard 1900: 244). Although the boundary line between worship of, and gifts to, the ancestors is not clear-cut, as will be shown in sequence, in the vast majority of cases we are facing two different classes of phenomena. Already seventy years ago Hagar pointed out, with reference to American Indians, that the customs of burying clothing and tools with the body and leaving food and drink upon the grave expressed the service of love seeking to provide for the material wants of the dead. "It was not worship" (Hagar 1908: 435). Although not only love, but also fear of contamination with the dead or the death substance may lie behind these customs, the conclusion seems to be correct. The same differentiation between cult of the dead and grave gifts has been drawn by theoreticians like Reidar Christiansen and Marcel Mauss (Christiansen 1946: 14; Mauss 1947: 187).[6]

2. Preventive rites directed against dangerous ghosts are not to be included in the cult of the dead. Out of the enormous material on such apotropaic and propitiatory rites I select the following for illustration. Like most North American Indians the Blackfoot believe that ghosts may appear as owls. In order to ward off the evil the owls may bring, the Blackfoot use black paint on their faces (McClintock 1923: 114 f.). Schoolcraft's informant on the Dakota of Minnesota, Philander Prescott, reported that these Indians ascribed bad luck in hunting to some misconduct such as neglect of honoring the spirits of the dead (Schoolcraft, ed. 1852, 2: 195). The Northern Paiute living close to Pyramid Lake, Nevada, "offered" to the dead food, beads, and other objects while an old man said, "Don't come back, stay away, we don't want you" (Stewart 1941: 414, 444).

These precautionary measures cannot always be grouped together with apotropaic rites associated with death (such rites aim at

6. Strangely enough, the British handbook of anthropological field work confuses the issue (see Seligman 1951: 178).

getting rid of the dead person's soul, or ghost). Nevertheless, their general negative import precludes me from counting them to the cult of the dead. I am aware that other authors would accept them as part of ancestor worship. However, there is no veneration of the ancestors involved, no information that they might be resorted to, no hint of their permanence in belief or ritual. If we talk of a cult of the dead we certainly mean a cult with some permanence, and with not only negative but also positive aspects.

3. Ancestor worship in a proper sense is as we saw part of the cult of the dead. However, "ancestor worship" may be used as a term for the cult of the dead as well. If the dead whom the Indian turns to in prayer are looked upon as a collective, it is not reasonable to expect that they are his own ancestors unless they are explicitly identified as belonging to his lineage, and that is not commonly the case (cf. below). From a tribal point of view all dead in the past are common ancestors, and the distinction is therefore mostly of purely academic interest. (The case is, of course, different in the homeland of ancestor worship, Africa.)

Some of the ancestors are portrayed as clan-founders and have as such an enhanced prestige. (It is another matter whether they really once existed as humans or are mythic figures.) There is also the figure of the Ancestor, or First Man, who is sometimes identified as the culture hero, or some other cosmic divinity (cf. the survey of American concepts in Tylor 1891, 2: 311 f.). However, although Father Schmidt has played on the importance of First Man in American Indian mythology this figure is too little investigated to be discussed in this article.[7] He definitely belongs primarily to mythology, not to the cult and practical religion, and therefore should not be mixed with other ancestors.

As we observed earlier, Lowie and Underhill made a clear distinction between ghosts as spiritual patrons and ancestor worship. If we talk of a cult of the dead instead of ancestor worship, this distinction should fall away. One could object that the cult or worship feature is less apparent in man's attitude to guardian spirits, but then, as Underhill extravagantly formulates it, "worship is not an Indian custom" (Underhill 1965: 78). In other words, the gap is smaller than we think. It is therefore natural to include guardian-spirit beliefs in this investigation.

Some words should be said about the place of scalping cus-

---

7. Conard's suggestion that the Ojibway culture hero is a divinized ancestor is rather worthless (Conard 1900: 243 f.).

toms in North American cults of the dead. Whatever the origins of scalping—and it is doubtful that they should be looked for on the American continent—the custom was primarily a means of procuring war trophies (cf. Clark 1885: 325 f.; Friederici 1906: 118 ff.; Mooney 1910: 482; Krickeberg 1935: 317 ff.). At the same time the scalp preserved an identity with the scalped man that made it the object of religious beliefs (Friederici 1906: 103, 112, 114; Krickeberg 1935: 318 f.; cf. also Lévy-Bruhl 1927: 307).[8] In several cases the scalp achieved the same status as the deceased in the cult of the dead. It is therefore necessary that also these cases will be observed in the following survey.

Finally, the Ghost Dance and other modern movements will not be discussed here. There is certainly no "cult of the dead" present in the Ghost Dance,[9] although the deceased relatives are called in for aid: their return is thought as restoration to life, not as a visit of spiritual apparitions.

General Presentation of Facts outside of the Pueblo Area

We shall now study the occurrence of a cult of the dead in the different North American Indian culture areas, in the tense of the "ethnographic present."

Alaska and western Canada is the home of Athapascan-speaking tribes and, as we have found earlier, they shun death and pollution from the dead. Nevertheless, some notices indicate that they are not indifferent to the power of the dead. Each autumn the Ingalik in western Alaska offer salmon and biscuits at the grave boxes of the dead. The dead are supposed to eat the food and bless the givers (Parsons 1921–22: 69). It is also known that power may be had from a tree that springs up from a powerful shaman's disintegrated coffin (Osgood 1959: 131). Among the Coyukon dead shamans are prayed to and their help is besought in difficult situations by the people among whom they once lived. A woman whose husband was moribund offered presents such as moccasins to deceased shamans

8. In an unpublished manuscript by Leslie Spier, discussed in La Barre 1938: 24 n. 8, Spier presents evidence bearing on the religio-magical significance of the scalp complex in the Southwest.

9. It is thus not correct when Benz refers to this cult as an "Ahnen-Kult" and assures us that the Ghost Dance shirts were imbued with power from the "Ahnengeister" (Benz 1971: 70).

and prayed at the fire, "Here I am giving you presents; I give you
the things with which we make you thrifty, that you may come
to my assistance." When the husband died her offerings ceased (Jetté
1911: 719 f.).

Another northern Athapascan people, the Hare at the Mackenzie River delta, offer food into the fire for the dead so that they
will not disturb the people's hunting luck (Hultkrantz 1973a: 127). We
hear that the dead belong to the following of the thunderbird which
returns each spring to the north after its winter séjour down in the
south (Petitot 1886: 283 f.).[10] The Beaver in northern Alberta offer food
for the dead into the fire, asking them "to give us more of what we
have put in the fire" (Goddard 1916: 230).

The North Pacific Coast tribes have long been considered
having traces of ancestor worship (cf., e.g., Friederici 1929: 467).[11]
Duncan Strong found thirty years ago archeological evidence of a
"ghost cult" on the Columbia River (Strong 1945: 244–61). Joyce Wike
locates to the Northwest Coast "widespread, important, and systematized beliefs concerning the relationship of the living to the
dead" (Wike 1952: 98). To her, this is most natural in view of the
extremes of status differentiation and hierarchical ranking found in
this area.

The Tlingit of the southern Alaskan coast invest the drowned
and departed shamans with power. According to a tradition, the spirit
of a drowned man dwells in an underwater hole at Hazy Island.
People go to the island to put food in the water and ask the spirit for
good weather and a safe journey. The spirit helps those who show
respect for wild life but persecutes those who disregard the laws of
food conservation (Garfield and Forrest 1948: 139). H. J. Holmberg
mentions that the shaman candidate seeks up the grave of a shaman
and cuts out one of the latter's teeth, or he cuts off one of his little
fingers. In this way he attracts the guardian spirits he needs—
presumably those of the deceased shaman (Holmberg 1855: 70. This
account was later rendered in Krause 1885: 285 f.). We are also informed by Holmberg that each time a Tlingit in his canoe passes a
shaman's grave he throws some tobacco into the water in order to
receive the benignity and favor of the shaman (Holmberg 1855: 72;
Niblack 1890: 356; Swanton 1908: 467). Occasionally ordinary dead

10. The same association between the thunderbird and the dead coming from
the south may be observed in Saulteaux (Ojibway) beliefs (see Hallowell 1940: 40).
11. The totem poles so characteristic for this area are here interpreted as
ancestor trees ("Ahnenbäume").

can also grant powers, at least indirectly, through the influence of the sun. If we may believe John Swanton a dead person who is very much thought of is, at sunset on the day of the funeral, attended by his clansmen in festive blankets and with canes in their hands. As the sun sinks closer to the horizon they stretch out their canes toward it and utter some prayers like these: "Let me be rich," "Let me come across sea otter sleeping," "Let me kill seal," "Let me kill land otter" (Swanton 1908: 429 f.).

If Haida Indians on Queen Charlotte Islands are poverty-stricken, their dead kinsmen are supposed to send them property (Swanton 1909: 35). On the other hand, we are told that the Bella Coola on the British Columbia mainland make offerings to their dead without the hope of receiving favors from them (McIlwraith 1948: 110). It is not quite clear if the Kwakiutl immediately south of them understand the dead as helping, benevolent beings. It is certain that their dead can be malevolent (Boas 1966: 168). The southern neighbors of the Kwakiutl, the Nootka, think that the spring salmon are sent up from the underworld by the spirits of the departed (Sapir 1922: 594). An early Spanish source imparts the information that among the Nootka the dead are most important in controlling the food supply (see Wike 1952: 99 f., quoting Espinoza y Tello, 1792). The amount of mummies and skulls from dead people in Nootkan ceremonial houses has been described in several works. After a successful whale hunt the chief goes to the ceremonial house where he offers part of his catch to his ancestors (Wike 1952: 100).[12]

The idea that the salmon come from the land of the dead reappears among the Quinault south of Mount Olympus. Here, however, the dead may prevent their coming; they do not, it seems, facilitate it (Olson 1936: 142). On the other hand, it is said that before the season of whaling a whaler had to rub himself with the bones of one of his male ancestors, "probably the one who had the whaler's guardian spirit" (Olson 1936: 46). Furthermore, we are informed that most personal guardian spirits are spirits of the dead (Olson 1936: 141 f.).

The interference of the dead with the living on the Northwest Coast is clearly expressed in the idea that the dead are present at the give-away feasts, or potlatches.[13] We learn that only one motive underlies the custom of arranging potlatches among the Tlingit, regard for and respect for the dead (Swanton 1908: 434. Cf. Tybjerg 1977: 35 ff., 39 ff.). And among the Bella Coola the most important

12. Several older authors are quoted.
13. For the meaning of potlatch, see McFeat 1967: 72–133.

feature is the return of a dead ancestor or ancestors (McIlwraith 1948: 186, 242 f.). Similar examples could be had from other tribes within the area (Wike 1952: 100 f.). Indeed, Kaj Birket-Smith emphasizes that the one reason for giving a potlatch found everywhere is the memorial feast for the dead. He concludes that originally the potlatch institution was therefore probably connected with the death feasts (Birket-Smith 1967: 36).

There is also some evidence that the Plateau tribes, adjoining the Indians of the North Pacific Coast, believe in the protection of the dead. "Some powerful shamans of the Lower Lillooet had the dead as their guardian spirits, and obtained from them their knowledge. To this end they trained by sleeping in burial-grounds at intervals extending over several years" (Teit 1906: 287). The Shuswap pray to powers like the earth, the sun, the guardian spirits, etc., but also to the chief of the dead and the dead themselves (Teit 1909: 603, cf. 605). James Teit who has given this information maintains that the custom of killing an enemy whenever a close relative had been slain was motivated by the wish to send an offering to the dead relative (Teit 1909: 594; Teit 1906: 245). The argument is scarcely convincing. The shaman of the Thompson Indians places the skull of a dead person in his sweat-house and sings and prays to him all night, asking him to impart his knowledge. In this way the dead person becomes the shaman's guardian spirit (Teit 1900: 354). The Nez Percé in Idaho assured Herbert Spinden that ghosts, which to some extent are held in fear, are never called upon for help of any kind (Spinden 1908: 260). There is certainly talk about a "day ghost" as a special tutelary spirit good for laying a ghost, but the character of this spirit is not described (Walker 1968: 28). The Flathead of the Bitterroot Valley imagine that ghosts warn the living (Fahey 1974: 14).

We now turn to the Algonkian Indians of eastern North America. In some older documents from the last century there is mention of prayers directed to the dead at their funerals. Thus at an Ojibway funeral an old man praises the virtues of the deceased person, prays for his blessing, and asks him to interfere, in favor of his living relatives, by sending game in abundance (Jones 1861: 99). Similarly, among the Ottawa (neighbors of the Ojibway close to Sault Sainte Marie) the headman of the family speaks at a funeral, calls on the deceased of the family group, and implores them to accept food prepared for them and "to assist him in the chase" (Henry 1809: 130 f.). Moon Conard who quotes these two instances finds it improbable that such prayers are directed to the dead on the occasions of funerals (Conard 1900: 242 f., 243). Her reservation is understandable.

However, two similar accounts could scarcely be wrong. It seems reasonable to postulate that occasionally such events have taken place. There is other evidence that the deceased took care of the food supply. The Jesuit Father Allouez clearly states that the Ottawa thought the departed governed the fishes (Kenton, ed. 1954: 322).[14]

The best analysis of the Ojibway idea of ghosts as spiritual helpers emanates from Hallowell. The Ojibway group investigated by him are the Berens River Saulteaux, east of Lake Winnipeg. He notes their general custom of throwing food and tobacco for the dead in the fire.[15] The dead will then report this to the master of the dead (an instance of the "boss" concept so typical for the Ojibway[16]), and the living will then receive some kind of blessing, such as long life (Hallowell 1940: 37).[17] Hallowell also found that the Saulteaux, in performing the Dream Dance—which had been given them by the ancestors long ago—expected blessings from the dead (Hallowell 1940: 41). In the so-called ghost dance (not to be confused with the famous Ghost Dance of 1890) the drum is a medium of communication between the living and the dead (Hallowell 1940: 45–48). The dead also occur in the role of personal guardian spirits investing their clients with their power or skill (Hallowell 1940: 38 f.). It seems that in the latter capacity they only appear in spontaneous dreams, not in deliberately sought visions. Furthermore, according to Hallowell, it is the master of the dead that functions as a guardian spirit, not anyone from the mass of the dead.[18] The author insists that the spirits of the dead are not central in Saulteaux religious ideology but are peripheral to other spiritual beings with whom they tend to coalesce, such as the guardian spirits (Hallowell 1940: 50).

It is interesting to study the relations to the dead among the Plains Cree, close neighbors and relatives of the Ojibway. Their dead do not appear in visions, nor are they able to bestow power on human beings. No offerings are made to them. They are, however, asked to petition the higher powers to render aid to living men (Mandelbaum

14. Smith 1933: 26 f. thinks Allouez refers to the Potawatomi.

15. Jenness reports that the Ojibway on Parry Island never drink whisky without pouring a few drops on the ground as an offering both to the Great Spirit and the shadows of the dead (Jenness 1935: 107).

16. On the application of the animal-boss concept to the master of the dead, see Hallowell 1940: 39. Cf. below.

17. Hoffman mentions a tradition according to which a young boy in a trance visited the land of the spirits and received a ginseng root from its master for the people on earth (Hoffman 1891: 241 f.).

18. The usual guardian spirit is a supernatural animal representing the entire species (see Jenness 1935: 54).

1940: 251). Also the Plains Ojibway assert that the dead are never seen in visions and can impart no power (Howard 1965a: 98). However, as we shall presently see these statements do not exhaust the possibilities.

One trait characteristic for both the Ojibway and the Plains Cree is the custom of addressing the dead as intermediaries for prayers to the high supernatural beings. The same custom prevails among the Fox, southwest of the Ojibway. The ruler of the land of souls receives a newly dead person as visitor. The dead person tells him the names of the persons who have made tobacco offerings at his demise. The ruler of the dead is pleased, listens to their prayers, and brings to pass the things they ask (Jones 1911: 225; Michelson 1925: 370 f., 395, 401, 433, 469). If a person has become adopted into a family as a substitute for a recently dead person, he enacts the transmission of the gifts and prayers in a particular ceremony (Michelson 1925: 359. On adoption rites in North America see Wachtmeister 1957: 86–92).

Whilst we hear of offerings to the dead among other Algonkian groups, without knowing however if such procedures invoke their positive interference in human life (Skinner 1920: 102; Speck 1935: 52; Skinner 1909: 52), the idea of the dead as intermediaries seems to have its center among the Algonkian tribes around the Great Lakes. Its southernmost occurrence may be found among the Shawnee where the living send maize and meat to the Creator through an old dying woman, thus causing the Creator to give them help (Voegelin 1936: 15). Among the Lenape or Delaware, again, the dead person can become a guardian spirit in the vision-quest (Harrington 1921: 54 f., 71 f.).

Also the Siouan Winnebago, neighbors of the Fox, partake in the "middleman complex." At the burial one of the mourners throws some tobacco behind himself and exhorts the dead person to act as a mediator. Arrived at his destination, the deceased person asks Earthmaker (or a supernatural old woman) to send war honors, food, and long life (Radin 1923: 141–52, 281). As a Winnebago Indian testifies, "Always, in the past, has the request of a ghost been successful" (Radin 1945: 89).

The idea of the dead man as a mediator between man and the spirits may reflect influences from the Spirit Lodge séances (cf. below).

Archeologists have shown that the Southeast was a center of developed mortuary customs in pre-Columbian days. We know now that the advanced Hopewell culture, with roots in southern Illinois some centuries B.C., was characterized by complex burial ceremonies at huge burial mounds (cf. Willey 1966: 273–80). The Hopewell culture was succeeded by the Mexican-inspired Mississippian culture about 700–800 A.D. Although primarily noted for its rectangular temple mounds, this culture retained the rites around prominent dead (Willey 1966: 292–310). This was demonstrated by the Natchez on the Lower Mississippi: they still represented the temple mound tradition in the eighteenth century, and their elaborate death rituals with executions of human beings at the death of the ruling prince were noted by the French (Swanton 1911: 138–57; Hudson 1976: 327–34).[19] There are hints that the sacred chiefs of the Tekesta and Biloxi Indians received offerings and adoration after their death (Swanton 1946: 722, 727). There is no such evidence concerning the Natchez king, however, and we are on the whole little informed of what the dead chiefs could do for their people.

The Prairie and Plains Indians are usually known for their great fear of ghosts. The picture varies, however: the Dakota evince features that remind one observer of Chinese ancestor cult, whilst the Lipan and Kiowa Apache fear everything having to do with death (Gauvreau 1907: 313. On the Lipan, see above. Kiowa Apache, see Opler and Bittle 1961: 383–94.).These differences mirror the mixed ethnic composition of the central grassland area. We have seen how the dead relatives of the Plains Cree are thought of as being able to help, indirectly, their living kinsmen. Another Algonkian group, the Blackfoot, have the belief that a dead husband may impart power to his widow if she wears a lock of his hair (McClintock 1910: 144 f.). The Gros Ventre, also Algonkian, say that occasionally a dead person becomes the guardian spirit of a surviving relative. Father Cooper, who is our authority here, points out however that "no cult of ghosts existed, and no prayers or food offerings were made to them" (Cooper 1956: 23 f.). As said before, the guardian-spirit relationship is *de facto* cultic in character.

Passing over to the Siouan Prairie and Plains Indians, we notice that the Mandan of the northern Missouri bring back the skulls of those who have died away from their village. Such a skull "was considered sacred and was prayed to. Young men who addressed it as father would request permission to fast near it" (Bowers 1950: 101). A similar custom has prevailed among the Hidatsa (Bowers 1965: 170 f.). Although Lowie did not attribute ancestor worship to the Crow he

19. There are reasons to believe that the Natchez also partook in the circum-caribbean high culture (see Sears 1954).

found one exception: the medicine-man Big Iron told the Crow to lay down beads at his tree-burial, then he would fulfill their prayers; and they did so (Lowie 1935: 255). One Crow family owned a bundle containing the skull of Braided Tail. It was an oracle in matters of warfare, hunting, and disease, and it located lost property (Nabakov 1967: 135, 209).

The westernmost Assiniboin (Stoney) in Alberta can meet ghosts who promise them success in hunting and keep their word (Lowie 1909a: 50). The Assiniboin chief, Tchatka, was buried in a big tree to which, when passing, the Indians made offerings. They believed he could provide them with buffalo and other animals, or drive the animals from the country (Chittenden and Richardson, eds. 1905, 3: 1140 f.).[20] Edwin Denig has recorded an Assiniboin prayer to the spirits of a person's dead relatives in which the petitioners ask for successful buffalo hunts, long life, aid in wars, and revenge on the enemy. The prayer is associated with a feast for the dead (Denig 1930: 484).

The Dakota Indians pray to their dead and give them offerings, and the dead listen to them (Eastman 1911: 156; Riggs 1883: 149; Pond 1889: 243 f.; Pond 1908: 404). More specifically, Philander Prescott assures us the Dakota pray to their dead to show them where to find a deer or bear or other game (Prescott 1853: 226. Cf. Prescott 1852: 195). Also other things, for instance, good weather are asked for (Prescott 1853: 237; Pond 1908: 405; Wallis 1947: 35).[21] The famous Dakota interpreter George Bushotter gives the information that at the so-called ghost feast offerings are given to the dead, whereupon a woman asks for many horses and a long life (Dorsey 1889: 148. Cf. Fletcher 1884: 300).

Although James Dorsey insists the Omaha on the middle Missouri do not venerate their dead, he mentions that they pour out some of their sacred meals as offerings to the ghosts (Dorsey 1894: 421). Alice Fletcher and Francis La Flesche interpret the Omaha attitude as reverence, not worship (Fletcher and La Flesche 1911: 601). The Ponca apparently embrace the idea that the dead promote the welfare of the living. Consequently, the manes receive offerings of food (Fletcher and La Flesche 1911: 310; Howard 1965b: 154).

If we turn to the Shoshonean groups on the western Plains they, too, despite their fear of ghosts, have favorable dealings with

---

20. The dead person is here portrayed as a master of the game.

21. On the North American beliefs that dead may influence the weather, cf. further Spier 1930: 274 f.

them. The Wind River Shoshoni in Wyoming have sometimes ghosts as their guardian spirits. Thus a man who buried the scattered bones of a dead person once received ghost power (Hultkrantz n.d.). Also the Comanche on the southern Plains have medicine-men with such power (Wallace and Hoebel 1952: 174).

Our impression that the worship of the dead has been more diffused in the Plains area than imagined before is strengthened by the wide occurrence of ghost controls in the Spirit Lodge ceremony. This ceremony, model for the so-called spiritualistic séances in the modern western world, is really a shamanistic performance in which the acting conjurer divines the unknown with the help of a main spirit and other lesser spirits. On the Plains the main spirit is most often a ghost or an owl, the latter embodying a ghost (Cooper 1944: 3–4, 61 ff., 81; Hultkrantz 1967b: 62 f.). The ghost imparts information but does not bestow power on the medicine-man. Since the ghost is the central spirit also in the Siberian Spirit Lodge, and the two areas of distribution are evidently linked with each other (Hultkrantz 1967b: 54, 63), it seems probable that we are facing an original dependence here on the craft of ghosts (Hultkrantz 1967b: 63). For further details concerning the role and diffusion of ghosts in the North American Spirit Lodge, I refer to Cooper 1944 and Hultkrantz 1967b and to an article by Donald Collier (Collier 1944: 49).

In the Basin area west of the Rocky Mountains, offerings of food, tobacco, etc., to the dead occur but mostly only with a preventive aim (Hultkrantz 1976b: 146). However, the Paviotso include ghosts among the spirit-patrons of the vision-quest (Park 1938: 15, 18).

In spite of all mourning anniversaries, ghost personifications, and ghost dances, the California Indians do not give us much positive evidence of a cult of the dead. There are exceptions, however. The Patwin, northeast of the San Francisco Bay, celebrate a so-called *hesi* ceremony with impersonifications of ghosts. The latter appear "for the purpose of bettering the crops" (Loeb 1933: 212), "they named the various kinds of acorns in order to promote their growth" (Loeb 1933: 217). The *kuksu* cult in North Central California revolves around a mythical ancestor, but the latter is more a divinity than a dead person.

Of the nomads in the Southwest, the Apache are known as particularly ghost-fearing (see above). And yet, at the turn of the century a Western Apache medicine-man declared that the ghosts who dance around Chromo Butte "to whom we always pray," and the gods of the dead would one day come and help the Indians against the whites (Reagan 1930: 288). Since this pronouncement is so atypical for the Apache we may surmise here an influence from the Ghost

Dance doctrine, in spite of everything that can be said against it.[22]

We proceed to the southwestern village tribes. The Papago medicine-man may enter into contact with dead relatives appearing as owls. By offering tobacco to the ghost, the medicine-man receives from him news about enemy strategy, etc. (Underhill 1938: 75 f., 82 f.). The Pima are said to have offered prayer-feathers and prayer-sticks to the dead at ruins in old times, this being a Pueblo custom (Parsons 1939, 2: 995 n.). Offerings of food and water on Pima and Papago graves are, however, recent (Drucker 1941: 209). Expressions of veneration for deceased "matrons" are, in vague terms, reported from the Seri of northwestern Mexico (McGee 1900: 12, 292). The Cáhita, southern neighbors of the Seri, know some people who pray to the dead for assistance and are known to talk to the dead (Beals 1943: 55). In the acculturated Mayo society of the same region, the dead ancestors, or santos (saints), look after the interests of the villagers. In October or November, when the dead visit the places of the living, they bring the first cold rains of the season, which are followed by colds and diseases (Crumrine 1977: 68, 72, 87).

Far to the south in western Mexico, the Cora and Huichol make prayer-sticks for the dead, like the Pueblo Indians. These sticks are among the Cora used for the supplication of slain enemies in times of drought, for the dead enemy is a rain-maker (Parsons 1939, 2: 1012). The association between rain and the cult of the dead shows both affinities to Pueblo rain ideology and Meso-american ancestor worship. The Huichol furthermore believe that departed relatives may give luck in hunting (Lumholtz 1900: 63 f.).

Evidence from the Pueblo Area

The main area of ancestor worship in North America is, as has been indicated, the Pueblo area in New Mexico and Arizona. Says Ruth Bunzel, "The worship of the dead is the foundation of all Zuñi ritual. The dead form part of the great spiritual essence of the universe, but they are the part which is nearest and most intimate" (Bunzel 1932a: 483, cf. 509). Similarly, Mischa Titiev means that the cult of the dead is "one of the most essential elements in the religious mosaics of the Hopi" (Titiev 1944: 173). These pronouncements from two of the

---

22. There are indeed signs that the Western Apache had a more moderate fear of the dead (see Kaut 1959: 100 f.).

foremost students of Pueblo Indian religion are, however, in conflict with some other statements. Thus Alexander hestitates to talk about an ancestor worship since the spirits of the dead have been identified with divine rain-makers (Alexander 1916: 310). Also Paul Radin sees here an "illegitimate extension of the concept ancestor-worship" (Radin 1915: 282).[23] According to Elsie Clews Parsons, there is little recognition of the deceased relatives in Hopi ritual, for they are rarely or never prayed to (Parsons 1939, 2: 1100 f.). Perhaps it would be safest to say that the majority of Pueblo Indians had a cult of the dead which, however, had a weak anchoring in Hopi culture—not because the latter had been influenced by the Navajo, as Parsons thought, but because its historical roots are in the death-fearing desert culture.

In the Pueblo area the cult of the dead has become mixed with the kachina ideology, and this to such a degree that the connections are difficult to analyze (Parsons 1939, 2: 965. Cf. Hultkrantz 1953: 185 ff.).[24] The kachina are in general identified as rain spirits, or as representatives of rain spirits; they are said not to bring rain themselves, but to interfere with the rain gods on behalf of the humans (Dockstader 1954: 10; Stevenson 1898: 40; cf. Fewkes 1897: 312). Some examples will illustrate the complicated patterns. The importance of the rain for the crops is most obvious in the arid western part of the area, whereas in the eastern part the Rio Grande holds vast resources of water. In one respect the kachina cult differs from all other cults of the dead in North America: it is a collective cult organized by a society. The collectivism of the agrarian Pueblo culture is also expressed in the fact that the dead are addressed without distinctions, although single kachinas may carry individual (mythical) names.

If we start with the Zuni who—together with the Keres Pueblos—by some are identified as the main originators of the kachina cult (Underhill 1954: 650), we notice that Bunzel observes three classes of dead people who receive the cult: (1) the newly dead, who may produce rain after their decease (Bunzel 1932a: 483); (2) the ancestors, identified with the clouds and the rains, and to whom the Zuni pray for life, old age, health, power, rain, and fecundity (Bunzel 1932a: 510); (3) the kachinas (here called *koko*), originally, in the mythological age, children who had died following a taboo contamination, and later on, a concept taking in the dead at large. Bunzel

---

23. Lowie speaks of "the suggestion of an ancestral cult" in the Pueblo area (see Lowie 1925: 175).

24. The word *kachina* is Hopi (originally Keresan) but is used as a technical term for the same class of spirits in other Pueblos.

emphasizes that the identification of the dead with the kachinas is not complete: prayer-sticks are offered to the old people and the kachinas, and their sticks are different (Bunzel 1932a: 516 f.). The kachinas are especially associated with clouds and rain but may also stand for other activities (Bunzel 1932b: 844). The kachina worship is expressed through dances in which male Zuni don their masks and costumes.

Turning to the westernmost Pueblo people, the Hopi, we learn that according to J. W. Fewkes "ancestral worship plays a not inconspicuous part in the Hopi conception of a Katcina" (Fewkes 1897: 251). The person who dies becomes a kachina and is asked to bring the rain and intercede with the gods to fertilize the fields. The dead person is addressed "by the same name as that given to the ancestral personations," the kachinas (Fewkes 1901: 82; Fewkes 1920: 526). Furthermore, the kachinas are better described as general rather than as specific ancestors (Fewkes 1923: 498; Titiev 1944: 172. Cf. also Kroeber 1916: 277). There is the complication, however, that not all kachinas are spirits of the deceased. Animal deities, stars, and other powers appear among the kachinas (Titiev 1944: 108 n. 43; Hartmann 1978: 54 f., 66. Cf., however, Tyler 1964: 286). Even sun worship is part of the Hopi kachina cult (Fewkes 1920: 513). The latter is, in fact, more developed and refined than the Zuni kachina cult. Of course, the dancing of the masked kachina impersonators is also in the Hopi Pueblo the major trait, and acts promoting fertility and curing diseases are included (Dockstader 1954: 15 ff.).

As Edward Dozier has pointed out, the Western Pueblo rituals revolve around the kachina cult, whereas among the Eastern Pueblo Indians, where water is easily accessible (Rio Grande), this cult is less important (Dozier 1971: 238. Cf. also Dozier 1961: 117). In the Keresan-speaking pueblo Cochiti, the kachinas are called *shiwanna* and consist of dead persons. They make rain and thunder, and give health and life. By putting on the sacred mask the men take on the personality of the *shiwanna* (Dumarest 1919: 172–75. See also Goldfrank 1927: 34, 57). The Tanoan-speaking inhabitants of Taos, the northernmost of the Rio Grande pueblos, travel each summer to their sacred Blue Lake to worship the kachinas, "the ones that send all what they get" (Parsons 1936: 100). They are the "cloud boys," who come with rain and thunder but are not identical with ordinary dead; only good chiefs, their wives, and men dying in the mountains become kachinas after their death (Parsons 1936: 109). The restricted occurrence of kachina dancing and the maskless dancing point to the recency of the kachina complex in Taos (Parsons 1936: 114 f., 116).

The emergency of the kachina cult has been vividly discussed in the past. The theory that the kachina are basically clan totem beings has been vindicated from Fewkes to Titiev (Fewkes 1901: 82 f., 85; Titiev 1944: 129).[25] Parsons found it probable that the kachina cult had partly developed out of the Catholic cult of the Saints, and pointed to the several parallels between them. This would in her opinion explain the differences between "ancestors" (the dead in general) and "kachinas" (the Saints). The other component of the kachina complex would have been indigenous rain spirits (Parsons 1930: 582, 590 ff., 596 f.). In her last great publication on Pueblo Indian religion, Parsons assumes, more cautiously, a stimulation from the Spanish worship of the Saints (Parsons 1939, 2: 1069 f., 1077 f., 1121). Increasingly archeological evidence has shown that the kachina cult is pre-Columbian (Mogollon) in origin (Hawley 1950: 296 ff.; Dockstader 1954: 31 ff.; Anderson 1955: 404 ff., 410, 416 ff.; Kelley 1966: 95–110. Cf. also Riley 1974: 33). A suggestive background is given in Parsons' observation that the cultic performances of the kachina dancers had their close counterparts in Aztec religion (Parsons 1933: 75 f.; Parsons 1939, 2: 1020; cf. Anderson 1955: 409 on parallels to the Tlaloc cult; and Riley 1974: 33). The general pattern against which the kachina worship should be seen is furnished by the fertility idea: like in other agricultural preindustrial areas the powers of fertility and the spirits of the dead are located in the same region, the underworld. Thus it is not surprising, writes H. K. Haeberlin, "that in a culture like that of the Pueblo, where almost every cultural phenomenon seems to be focused on the idea of fertilization, the deceased and especially the ancients should likewise have become associated with this idea" (Haeberlin 1916: 28).

The cult of the dead in the Southwest also affected the scalping complex in the old days. The scalps, as representatives of the dead, are thought to execute the powers of the latter. Among the Zuni the scalp passes through a cleansing ceremony and is thereafter prayed to as a rain-maker (Bunzel 1932d: 679 ff.; Parsons 1939, 2: 621. Cf. Stevenson 1904: 207). Parsons writes that presumably in all the pueblos scalps have been rain-senders (Parsons 1929b: 138 n. 269). They also have curative powers, as in Isleta, or promote population growth, as in Taos (Parsons 1928: 461; Parsons 1936: 23). Similar conceptions prevail outside the Pueblo area. Pima and Papago scalps are supposed to bring rain and cure diseases, and are nourished with tobacco smoke (Parsons 1928: 461; Parsons 1939, 2: 997; Underhill

25. This theory concerns primarily the Hopi kachinas.

1946a: 192 f., 199, 210; Spier 1936: 10). Beals's hypothesis that the Acaxee of Mexico took the skulls of enemies for rain-making is without foundation (Beals 1933: 31 n. 77).

The southwestern cult of the scalps may have been an intensification of a cult pattern of a somewhat wider occurrence. The Kiowa (who are, certainly, linguistic relatives of the Taos Indians), a southern Plains people, pray to a certain shield to which scalps are attached. Those who give offerings to it may achieve safety in war or cure for sickness (Parsons 1929a: 110). The Caddo in approximately the same area offer tobacco to scalps (Swanton 1928: 705). The reason is not known.

Conclusions

It is obvious that in one form or another a cult of the dead has existed over most of North America. The Great Basin and California (at least the desert part) seem to be the great exceptions on our map. The sources on the Southeast are not sufficient for a clear judgment, and the same could be said about our source material on the Coast Algonkian groups. The general impression is that there are faint traces of, and a vague tendency to, a cult of the dead in all areas except those where the fear of the ghosts has been too strong (Southern Athapascans, Desert Numic).[26] All over North America the ghosts are feared, and yet, their power and protection is sought.

This general, vaguely supplicating attitude, often expressed in simple prayers by single individuals and accompanied by small offerings of tobacco or meat in the fire, stands halfway between respect and reverence for the dead person at burial and an institutional cult of the dead. At times it is formalized in more fixed patterns, some recurrent, others localized.

Recurrent patterns are:

1. The dead are conceived as personal guardian spirits. This idea is noticeable here and there, on the Plateau, among the Algonkian Indians (Ojibway, Lenape), on the Plains (Gros Ventre, Shoshoni, Comanche, etc.). These are also the areas where the guardian-spirit ideology has its strongest anchoring. In other words, the nondescript cult of the dead has been reinterpreted within this domineering belief

26. Numic is the generic term for the Northern Paiute, Shoshoneans, and Southern Paiute.

complex. Contrary to Radin's assumption, the cult of the dead seems to have given in to the guardian-spirit ideology, not the other way round (Radin 1915: 281 f.). The fear of ghosts has probably precluded a wider distribution of the ghost-tutelary idea. In places, as among the Ojibway, there is a tendency for the ghost helper to coalesce with spirits of nature (cf. above).

2. The dead are conceived as masters of the game. Such notions are found on the north Pacific Coast where they are mostly coupled to the salmon run (Nootka, Quinault?), among the Algonkian Indians (Ojibway, Ottawa), and on the Plains (Assiniboin, Dakota). That is, the dead are not specialized masters of the game, as the true animal bosses are, but they meet such desires as are usually directed to the masters of the game. In my opinion this function of the dead has become possible because the idea of a master of the game has become eclipsed by the guardian-spirit complex (cf. Hultkrantz 1961b: 62). This interpretation might be contested, but I offer it as a hypothesis.

3. Occasionally, the cult of the dead appears as tied up with a symbol of the dead person, his skull (cf. Nootka on the Northwest Coast, Crow, Mandan, and Hidatsa on the Plains and Prairies), his hair (Blackfoot, Siouan tribes), his scalp (different groups in the Southwest). This feature has not been exhaustively treated here. It deserves an investigation of its own.

Localized patterns are:

4. The "ghost cult" of the North Pacific Coast is difficult to assess, but there is no doubt that an emphasis on the presence of the dead in potlatch ceremonies is current in this area. The prevalent x-ray art, possibly connected with the death and life rites of shaman candidates and members of secret societies, should also stress the importance of the death motif. The dead live mixed with the spirits of nature (cf. Swanton 1905: 15, 34 ff.); indeed, the Quinault may have thought there were more ghosts than natural spirits in the supernatural realm (Olson 1936: 141). Consequently, ghosts are sometimes responsible for natural phenomena, as among the Kwakiutl.[27] In this general atmosphere the dead person is a natural resource of help and power.

5. The dead function as intermediaries between man and the powers above in the Central Algonkian area, including the Siouan Winnebago. The powers which help man are different but usually either the Supreme Being and the guardian spirits or the master of the dead. The dead are often the recently dead, and the petitions are

27. Earthquakes, for instance (see Boas 1932: 232).

delivered at their funeral ceremonies. The rich ritualism around the latter among, for instance, the Fox may have paved the way for the development of the complex. However, I also find it possible that the elaboration of the role of the ghost helper in the conjuring or Spirit Lodge could have stimulated the central idea, the dead as intermediary beings.

6. Ghosts of their transformations (owls) act as informants and spirit controls in the Spirit Lodge complex on the Plains. Here we evidently face an idea and a rite complex that has historical connections with Siberian practices. The fact that ghosts are informing spirits on the Plains, but not so much in surrounding areas where this ritual complex occurs may be ascribed to conservatism, but also to the intense interests in ghosts on the Plains. As has emerged, the idea of the dead as helpers is more distributed in this area than in any other area, excepting the Northwest Coast and the Pueblo Southwest.

7. A real cult of the dead is present among the Pueblo Indians where the dead are more or less interpreted as cloud and rain spirits. This cult, with a pronounced collectivistic character and direct association with the demands of the agriculturist, probably originated with the Keres Indians in the Mogollon culture (about A.D. 500) in the southwestern corner of New Mexico. Here, large ceremonial structures (kivas) formed the scenes of the kachina dances. Whether this cult of the dead is entirely a product of the requirements in an agricultural environment, or has also been stimulated from other sources— Central Mexico in the first place—will not be discussed here. I lean toward the last interpretation.

The North American materials give rise to several observations. One is that the cult of the dead is only rarely, and then primarily in the Central Algonkian and Plains areas, combined with rituals at graves. The Algonkians honor the dead at mortuary services, the Plains people give homage to particularly great persons at their graves. Another observation is that the dead are almost always conceived as anonymous collective spirits, except where rites are tied up with their burials and graves or great leaders are venerated. Certainly, we hear about individual cases here and there where personal ancestors have been prayed to; but they are less representative.[28] It is therefore impossible to say if there is generally any difference in attitude between the cult of the ancestors and the cult of the vast host

---

28. Particularly the Pueblo Indians disavow the personal attachments. A Zuni Indian "prays to *the* ancestors, not to his own ancestors" (Bunzel 1932a: 510; cf. also Benedict 1938: 651 f.; Underhill 1946: 156).

of the dead (cf. Jensen 1963: 287). A third observation is that large rituals of petition including dancing primarily occur among the Algonkians of the woods and the Pueblo Indians. The most important rituals take place among the latter.

The North American data demonstrate in an interesting way the rise of a cult of the dead from inchoate beginnings. I am thinking here of evolutionary levels as these may be defined in conjunction with social structures, not of historical developments in a strict sense. Terrence Tatje and Francis Hsu have suggested that there is a connection between certain kinship contents and ancestor cults (cf. Tatje and Hsu 1969: 153–72. Cf. also Swanson 1960: 97–108). We have reasons to suspect that the cult of the dead tends to belong with unilinear societies (Radcliffe-Brown 1952: 163 f.; Swanson 1960: 108). A quick glance at the North American ethnographic map will show that the main zones of the cult of the dead, the northern Northwest Coast, the Central Algonkian area, and the western Pueblo area, are all characterized by lineage systems (Driver and Massey 1957: 410, map 156). The trouble is, however, that in the important Pueblo area the Eastern Pueblos are primarily bilateral in social structure, and unilinear only with regard to moiety membership (Eggan 1966: 114, 133). Fred Eggan interprets this so that there had once been a unilinear social structure which in the east changed to bilateral due to migrations (Eggan 1966: 136 f.) In view of this hypothesis we might say that the complex, unilinear societies of the Pueblo Indians should have provided the right soil for the growth of a worship of the dead, whereas the more loosely, bilaterally organized societies of many hunting tribes rather precluded such a development.[29]

The path of evolution seems clear. There is everywhere, also among the Pueblo Indians, a fear of the dead tempered by their affection for them. The conviction is spread that the dead help, destroy, or master one's existence in some mysterious way. People remember their achievements during life, their care, their wrath. As dead they continue to exert the same influence, but now in a supernatural nimbus. Unpremeditatedly, the living turn to them, talk to them, pray to them. By and by this attitude is strengthened and patterned. Institutional forms develop, particularly in unilinear societies. In North America where classical nomadism fails, it is primarily in the tightly settled agricultural areas that such changes have taken place.

---

29. Note also that the kachina cult is much weaker in the bilaterally organized Rio Grande pueblos than in the western pueblos (Eggan 1966: 133).

ECOLOGY AND RELIGION

7

Feelings for Nature
among North American Indians

I T IS A TRIVIAL TRUTH nowadays that experiences of nature have not been responsible for the birth of religion, as was formerly thought. Modern research sees the growth of religion against the background of tradition, social structure, unconscious psychological processes, ecological integration, and similar factors, without, however, assigning it to any particular cause. In that connection the feeling for nature is considered to play an enriching but not really creative role.[1] At most scholars speak about its forming influence, its property of a component of the structure of experiences that forms the religious world in a

1. This was pointed out already by Émile Durkheim in 1912 (Durkheim 1954: 84 ff.) and has also been stressed by E. E. Evans-Pritchard (Evans-Pritchard 1965: 54). Any careful student of North American Indians will notice that impressive spectacles such as a thunderstorm over the Plains or a great earthquake in California have not given rise to major religious ideas. Certainly, the world renewal ceremonies of the northwestern Californians may have been influenced by the experiences of earthquakes in the region, but there is no evidence that such experiences gave rise to them (cf. Kroeber and Gifford 1949).

This is a revised and much expanded version of a lecture that the author held at several universities in the United States and Canada in the fall of 1977.

"primitive" society. Robert Thouless, the psychologist of religion, identified three basic religiously inspiring aspects in the experience of nature, the experiences of benevolence, harmony, and beauty (Thouless 1923: Ch. 3). He might also have adduced the experiences of uncanny agencies and of fright, of the destructive powers of nature.[2] All these experiences basically constitute a unity although stress is now laid on this, now on that emotion as places and situations change.

Most of us share, I think, the impression that in Indian North America religions are frequently deeply imprinted by man's identification with nature. Moreover, it seems that feelings of harmony and beauty preponderate over other emotions. Man meets the divine in quiet meditation in solitary places, and he experiences his connections with the animals, the plants, the ground, the mountains, and the lakes in light visions as well as in ecstatic dances. He perceives, we might say, his identity with or relation to the cosmic totality, symbolized by such figures as the cross, the circle, and the world-tree, in mysterious holistic experiences (cf. Coe 1976: 18 ff.; Vastokas 1977). The thought is close at hand that North America, "the most beautiful of the continents" in the words of Werner Müller (Müller 1972: 57),[3] by force of its wonderful nature has inspired a feeling for nature that has left lasting traces: first of all in the sphere of religion, secondly in the much talked-of Indian conservationism, the saving of plants and animals for the benefit of future generations, and the ecological balance. The latter argument has lately been often produced in current ecological debate, for instance in Europe.

These are indeed enticing lines of thought, but are they correct? Should we regard, in an historical perspective, the American Indian as a nature-lover and conservationist, whose inspiration of nature created new religious forms? As we shall find, this view of the Indian attitude to nature needs certain important qualifications. Moreover, there is a twist to the issue of the relationship between feeling for nature and religion.

There is, in fact, much to say against any generalization of Indian relations with nature in North America. The continent is large

2. The Utrecht anthropologist J. van Baal assures us that primitive man's view of nature is that it is "untransparent and hostile" (van Baal 1979: 492). This is a wrong generalization. Possibly some of van Baal's experiences of man's interaction with nature in tropical areas have suggested his surprising dictum.

3. Müller has discussed the relationship of the Indians to their surrounding nature in several works that have passed unnoticed by American scholars. Beside the reference just given, see also Müller 1976.

and complex, geographically as well as ethnographically. From the cultural point of view there is no universal American Indian. In the same way there does not exist, and has not existed, a common Indian attitude to nature.

By this statement I do not mean to say that there has not been, as Christopher Vecsey aptly puts it, an integration between environmental relations and religion among the Indians (Vecsey 1980: 2). On the contrary, everywhere the outlook on religion as well as the structure of religion were dependent on the interaction between the natural environment and culture. In a series of articles I have tried to demonstrate that natural environment intervenes in cultural and religious developments in an active, reorganizing way among those peoples who are considerably dependent on this natural environment (cf. German *naturvölker*, "peoples of nature"). The more primitive the technological requisites, the more exposed to natural forces a culture is, the more does a people's imagination revolve around the determining factors released by the culture-nature juxtaposition. On the basis of Julian Steward's culture-ecological principles (cf. Steward 1955: 30 ff.),[4] I have constructed a religio-ecological methodology that briefly implies that nature's integration with culture releases a mechanism that directly or indirectly transforms the structure and pattern of religion (for a presentation of the method, see Hultkrantz 1965b, 1979a). We could add here that it also transforms the perspective on the natural environment. The forms of religion (and the perception of nature) are influenced by the ecological integration in two major ways, through a filter of technological possibilities, value patterns, and belief traditions, and through the bond that obtains between religion and world-view on one side and the ecologically affected cultural structure on the other side. This model does not presuppose that religion is to be derived from material conditions, but it demonstrates that certain religious aspects, primarily those that attach to technology and economy, are formed according to the pattern of integration. Secondarily, the ecological integration affects religion through its impact on religious structure that forms much of religious thinking and religious organization.

Proceeding from this model we may extrapolate the attitudes to nature in different Indian cultures. If we know the environmental conditions, the cultural structure, and the value pattern that it implies, we have the keys to the intepretations of nature current in a

4. There are newer models, like Marvin Harris' ecological materialism, but I find them less useful or convincing.

certain culture. In other words, ideology constitutes the postulate of environmental evaluation and not any spontaneous experience of nature. Therefore, every experience of nature varies according to the "cultural type." Some examples will illustrate this.

If first of all we take a look on the hunting cultures as they are represented among Algonkian hunters in eastern Canada and northeastern United States, we find a very close relationship between man and game animals (for a survey of Algonkian hunting religions, see Flannery 1946). This relationship is manifested in the religio-ritual complex of "animal ceremonialism," that is, the hunter's religious belief in and ritual attitude to the game animals and their supernatural masters or "owners" (see, e.g., Hultkrantz 1979d: 140 ff.; Hallowell 1926; Lantis 1938; Gunther 1928; Casagrande 1952; Paulson 1959, 1965; Driver and Massey 1957: 253 ff.; La Barre 1970: 141 ff., 158; cf. the interpretations in Smith 1980). Such characteristic features as the supplication to the animals or their elders for forgiveness of having killed the animal, or for sending their likenesses to new successful killing, the burial of the animal bones in anatomical order so they can be resuscitated, and the elevation of the animal skulls on poles, belong here.[5] Similarly, the vision-quest complex, so widespread in North America, points to the same intimate association between man and animals: the spirits take the appearance of animals and give hunting luck, among other things (Benedict 1923b).[6] Totemism is also anchored in hunting life (among societies with lineages), and in many rites and dances animal gods are venerated (like the eagle or the thunderbird) or represented (like the buffalo).

It is, of course, natural that the animal stands in the foreground of the hunter's attention: his whole existence revolves around the availability of animals.[7] The forms of interpretation focused on the game animal may be extended to plants, trees, mountains, and lakes as well, but the pattern is always adapted to the animal world.[8] Calvin

5. It is interesting to note that the ritual burial of the buffalo was supposed to bring about the resuscitation of the buffaloes in the Ghost Dance (Mooney 1896: 821)—but at that date there were no more wild buffalo on the Plains!

6. Writing about the Beaver Indians, the Ridingtons tell us that through their vision-quests children become "practicing ethologists, able to understand the behaviour and communications of animals," see Ridington and Ridington 1970: 57.

7. The hunter's dependency on the game for food, clothing, housing, and utensils is well illustrated in, for example, Francis Parkman's description of an Oglala Sioux camp (Parkman 1950: 116).

8. Thus the beliefs and practices concerning the regeneration of the corn in agricultural Eastern Woodlands can be retraced to the hunting ideology, cf. Witthoft 1949.

Martin has rightly observed that the sympathy between human and animal persons is basic to the Subarctic hunter's relationship with wildlife (Martin 1980: 39).[9] More than any other scholar, Martin has stressed that the Indian temperance vis-à-vis the game was due to the conviction that the supernatural masters of the animals punished all overkilling of their subjects. At least this was the belief of the Algonkian tribes (Martin 1978: 71 ff.; see also Hultkrantz 1961b; cf. Underhill 1965: 42 ff.). Here, then, a religious concept provided the social control for the protection of the most precious part of the natural environment.

In other parts of North America where gathering pursuits mingled with hunting, the attention of the Indians was more often directed on the well-being of seeds, roots, and trees. An elderly Wintu woman from north-central California, Kate Luckie, declared about 1925 that "the white people never cared for land or deer or bear. When we Indians kill meat, we eat it all up. When we dig roots, we make little holes. When we build houses, we make little holes. When we burn grass for grasshoppers, we don't ruin things. We shake down acorns and pine nuts. We don't chop down the trees. We only use dead wood [for fuel]. But the white people plow up the ground, pull up the trees, kill everything. The tree says, 'Don't. I am sore. Don't hurt me.' But they chop it down and cut it up. The spirit of the land hates them" (Du Bois 1935: 75 f.). What Luckie here calls "the spirit of the land" is the being that protects and guarantees the resources of nature. The careful watching of animals and plants was necessary for the existence of the Wintu. In an informative article Ann Gayton has described the intimate connection between environment, ecology, and religion in central Californian cultures (Gayton 1946).

The same attitude to the vegetation prevails in tribes that combine hunting and agriculture, for instance the Fox of Wisconsin and Iowa. The trees, says the Fox Indian, speak to each other and make love to each other: "Early in the spring the trees begin to woo. By and by wind comes along and helps them meet. Then we see the trees bend their heads over toward each other until they almost touch, and presently they hold their heads up straight again. Often the whole forest is making love. It is then when we hear from a distance the trees murmuring in low voices. ... When the trees are happy, we can hear their pleasant voices laughing. Often the trees are

9. For a testimony on the Indian hunter's affinity with the animals in the western part of North America, see Chapter 9, "Attitudes to Animals in Shoshoni Indian Religion," in this book.

sad, and that makes our hearts sad" (Fox 1939: 20). The anthro-
pomorphization of the trees, which reminds us of the anthropo-
morphization of the animals, calls forth a treatment of them that has
its close parallels in the animal ceremonialism. "We do not like to
harm the trees. Whenever we can, we always make an offering of
tobacco to the trees before we cut them down. If we did not think of
their feelings, and did not offer them tobacco before cutting them
down, all the other trees in the forest would weep, and that would
make our hearts sad, too" (Fox 1939: 21).

In the same way another hunter-and-farmer people, the
Hidatsa of the Missouri, refrained from cutting down the cottonwood
trees in the old days. When in springtime the river swept some tall
tree into its current, it was said that "the spirit of the tree cries while
the roots yet cling to the land and until the tree falls into the water."
In the 1870s old Indians complained that the misfortunes of the tribe
were due to the modern disregard for the cottonwood (Matthews
1877: 48 f.).

In the intensely agricultural areas, such as the Pueblo Southwest, the attention to the animals and trees has been supplanted by a
belief and ritual complex centered around the grains and other
agricultural products. Myths, beliefs, and ceremonies surround the
most sacred plant among the Hopi of Arizona, the corn, "divinely
created for man in the First World" (Waters 1963: 165), that is, the
deepest underground world from which the people originated. Man
rose to the present airy world just like the corn does every year. A
perfect ear of corn is saved for rituals and represented as the Corn
Mother. At harvest time a man selects some small ears of corn from
his cornfield, saying, "Now you are going home." Then he carries
them home, singing all the time. His wife carries them to the storage
room, where she stacks them on the floor (Waters 1963: 166). This
ceremony is a counterpart to the rites around the last sheaf in European folklore.

While the Hopi pay particular attention to the maize, they are
not indifferent to other parts of nature. A Hopi Indian told me that his
people show respect for and friendship to all animals, both domesticated and wild animals. He informed me that "horses are not to be
treated as possessions which can be tamed, but as personalities in
their own right." This attitude is probably a heritage from the ancient
days when the Hopi were (Shoshonean) hunters. The Hopi are a
most conservative people.

My point is, however, that the Indian veneration of nature is
specific, not general. Vecsey and Venables have correctly emphasized

that there was, among Indians, no general love of all nature (Vecsey and Venables 1980: xxiii; cf. Vecsey 1980: 25). I should like to add that as a rule the Indian is not contemplating the beauty of nature, as some romantic writers try to make us believe.[10] His attention is directed to some particular objects in nature that mean something to him at a certain moment: the hunter concentrates his thought on the animal, the agriculturalist on the plant, and so on. Only in retrospect, and as an effect of an entirely different line of reflection, may a more inclusive feeling for nature emerge (cf. below). We shall soon see examples of this.

There are, however, many complications in the Indian attitude to nature, some of which are not so easily solved by the application of an ecological model. One such complication has been observed by Vecsey, namely, the tension between exploiting and loving the environment: "they were not in perfect harmony with nature; there was a tension in their relationship" (Vecsey 1980: 31, cf. 12 f., 22 ff.). We could add, the more exploitation, the greater the unbalance in the Indian way of viewing nature (cf. below). The same author emphasizes the two sides of nature that were as evident to the Indians as they are to us, the nurturing and attractive, and the destructive and dangerous (Vecsey 1980: 36). My discussion of the Indian fear of the glaciers of Yellowstone brings out this more gloomy side of Indian relationship with nature (see Chapter 10 in this book, "The Indians and the Wonders of Yellowstone"; and Hultkrantz 1979b).

Still another point to be observed is that some natural features in the unfertile terrain attract greater attention than others, and not just because from our point of view they inspire more awe or harmony. During my stay among the Shoshoni in Wyoming, I observed that the spirits are supposed to frequent mountain crevasses and lower mountains, for instance the Big Horn Mountains, whereas more rarely they had their place of abode on more majestic mountain formations like the Teton Range. Presumably the spirits had from the start been tied to mountain passes, favorite vision localities and other places that were vital for the Indian life-way.

Sometimes two tribes that basically share the same type of economy and live as neighbors may, for cultural and ecological reasons, expose different reactions to their surrounding environment. Thus we are told that in Alaska the Eskimo learn everything about

10. It is another matter that the Indian is more or less one with his natural environment and feels at home there. See, for instance, the scenes immortalized by Edward S. Curtis' camera (Brown 1972).

the animals and their habits, whereas—surprisingly—their inland neighbors, the Kutchin, learn everything about the landscape. Richard Nelson who has made this observation explains the Kutchin attitude with the statement that "in the boreal forest the key to success in hunting and trapping is knowledge of the landscape" (Nelson 1973: 275 f., 301 ff.). This may be true, but Nelson's own data suggest that much knowledge of animals is needed as well.

Most disturbing is that some observers may even receive the impression that Indians do not show any consideration for nature at all. On many Indian reservations in North America (and at many Eskimo settlements in Greenland) the casual visitor may find the space outside the houses encumbered with plastic trash, fractured glass bottles, old tires, and wrecked cars. It seems that the residents are indifferent to this pollution of nature. However, it would be wrong to interpret their attitude in these terms. The reason for their behavior is quite simple: once all used material could be thrown out from the tent, lodge, or house to decay in nature; today this custom still prevails, but unfortunately the modern material is more permanent and consequently remains on the spot.

It is more disturbing that Indians treat their dogs badly, and as far as we know they always have done: numerous travellers' reports testify to this. Many of us have observed that reservation Indians sometimes kick their dogs so they sneak away howling and limping to hide themselves. I have even seen sober Indians drive their cars over their dogs without hesitation. Certainly, such incidents make you contemplate the use of the word "dog" in some tribes as an invective. The denigration of dogs is, however, no sign of a general indifference to the animals. It is most probably due to the basic experience that the (half-wild) dogs do not earn their living but live on the food scraps and refuse that their human masters throw to them.[11] Another domesticated animal, the horse, received different treatment: among the Blackfoot, for instance, it was held to possess supernatural powers (Ewers 1955b: 290 f.).

Our findings so far may be summarized as follows: the Indians have had a very diversified attitude to nature. I concur with Christopher Vecsey who maintains that they loved "particular locations, particular aspects of their environment" (Vecsey 1980: 25). They did so partly because they were dependent on nature (Vecsey 1980: 13), and took advantage from the nourishing and protective resources

---

11. The Lenape contrast their domestic animals with wild animals which are considered "pure": Speck 1931: 50 f. Cf. also Vecsey 1980: 29f.

that nature could supply. In the same way they tried to avoid all the dangers in nature, or what they supposed to be dangerous. Wilbur Jacobs is certainly right when he claims that the Indians were America's first ecologists (Jacobs 1980: 49), but I should like to qualify his statement: they were so because a depletion of the wild or a destruction of the soil meant hunger and starvation in the Indian camp (cf. also Vecsey 1980: 8). In particular, their careful hunting methods deserve our praise. It is less easy to appreciate the slash-and-burn ("swiddening") procedures of the agriculturists which, at a high population figure, could have devastating consequences (Harris 1978: 102 ff.).

Selected portions of natuɾe were thus in the focus of Indian interest and care. What about the rest of nature?

We seek in vain for a pure aesthetic beholding of nature. An educated Seneca Indian well initiated into the traditions and values of his people once told me of the widely divergent reactions of Indians and whites when they move to new regions. The white man, he said, is impressed by the appearance of the landscape and meditates over its beauty, whereas the Indian first of all asks, where are my medicines? (the medicine bags, the cultic paraphernalia). An Indian, he explained to me, feels lost if he is without his medicines in a new, foreign country. I also noticed that the same Seneca Indian, whose acquaintance I made in Scandinavia, was entirely indifferent to those feelings of euphoria, longing, and wistfulness that overtake the Scandinavian when spring sets in. He confirmed himself the truth of my observation.

In this connection it should also be said that in myths, legends, and belief statements the appearance of the supernatural is not described as surrounded by a *mystère* of nature as is the case in some European and Euro-American romantic essays. Modern American Indian poems have some tint of it, but this is evidently a new development.

The obvious conclusion we can draw is that the aesthetic enjoyment of nature is a peculiar development of the white man's civilization, first heralded by Rousseau and—in the New World—by Thoreau. The American Indians were practical people, nature was to them the means of subsistence, housing, dress, transportation, and so on. Just as little as they performed art for art's sake—it was always part of their technological, social, and symbolic activities—did they pursue a contemplation of nature to satisfy their aesthetic "needs." Their cultures simply did not provide for such needs.

However, aesthetic evaluations could spring forth from

dimensions of thought that were meaningfully integrated with Indian cultural systems. This brings us to our next subject, the relations between nature and religion in Indian metaphysical thought.

We have seen that the American Indian has a selective approach to nature. In his practical, everyday pursuits he does not experience nature as a scenery of beauty. There are traces of an appreciative view of nature's gifts in myths, tales, and speeches, but they stand for other values than the purely aesthetic ones. For, if there was no aesthetic indulgence in the beauty and drama of nature there was, on the other hand, an experience of nature as a realm of mystery. Nature revealed a reality of a higher order, "the great supernatural" (*wakan tanka*) as the Dakota call it, God, or the upper spiritual world.[12] The insight of this otherness was, of course, part of the religious tradition, but it was also nourished by solitary meditation and ecstatic visions. The outcome of it all was a consciousness of harmony and beauty in the landscape as long as it reflected the divine or mysterious presence.[13]

Our best examples of this close experience of the connection between religion and nature come from the Plains Indians. Here we meet the idea that there is an essential relation between man and nature because the Supreme Being dwells in all living beings. The Plains Cree Indian Stan Cuthand told me and some other whites that "the Supreme Being is in everything, he is in all of nature, in man and all the animals. He is a mystery—you can never grasp him." In the same way the well-known holy man of the Oglala, Black Elk, explained to Joseph Brown that "all things are the works of the Great Spirit. We should know that He is within all things: the trees, the grasses, the rivers, the mountains, and all the four-legged animals, and the winged peoples [the birds]; and even more important, we should understand that He is also above all these things and peoples" (Brown 1953: xx; cf. also Brown 1964: 16 ff.).

Thus the divinity manifests its being through nature. Allan Wolf Leg, deputy for the Northern Blackfoot, recently made the following statement: "In the Indian religion there is God, the Indian people, and Nature in between. We do not have Jesus Christ, yet on

12. When Richard Slotkin says that "to the Indian the wilderness was a god" this is of course a simplification of facts (Slotkin 1973: 51).
13. Cf., for instance, Curtis' famous pictures which often show the Indian in meditation in nature. A portfolio of such pictures is presented in Brown 1972.

the other hand he existed among those people who made up Christianity. The same God, the same human beings, though of a different race, but this has Christ, that has Nature" (Waugh and Prithipaul 1979: 4).[14]

Inasmuch as nature reveals God it is man's duty to care for the well-being of nature. This thought is clearly expresed in the Assiniboin Chief John Snow's book of his tribe and their world:

> We believe that the Creator made everything beautiful in his time. We believe that we must be good stewards of the Creator and not destroy nor mar His works of creation. We look upon stewardship not only in terms of money and the profit of a hundredfold, but in those of respect for the beauty of the land and of life in harmony with the succession of the seasons, so that the voices of all living things can be heard and continue to live and dwell among us. If an area is destroyed, marred, or polluted, my people say, the spirits will leave the area. If pollution continues not only animals, birds, and plant life will disappear, but the spirits will also leave. This is one of the greatest concerns of Indian people (Snow 1977: 145).

Here, the ideological motivation behind the feeling and care for nature is quite evident.

The Plains Indians have been chosen as main references here because more obviously than other Indians they evince the ideological basis of nature conservationism and nature veneration. Most certainly their ecological situation has motivated this close connection. As specialized hunters, they have felt their affinity to all living beings and their intimacy with the wide, open environment that was theirs for hunting. The Plains Indian identification of nature with God or the supernatural world has been called "cosmotheism" by Horst Hartmann (Hartmann 1973: 186 ff.), and Werner Müller compares it with the Chinese "universism" (Müller 1976: 40).

However, in less lyric, outspoken forms the same attitude occurs sporadically also in other parts of North America where hunting plays a major role. Certainly it is implied in the Choctaw Indian's reference to the Great Spirit as manifesting himself in thunder, the voice of the winds, and the sounds of the waves (McKenney 1846, 2: 90), or in the Menomini Indian's conviction that rocks, stones, and the

---

14. This dichotomy between the white man's inspiration through Christ and the red man's inspiration through the spirits of nature is widely acknowledged among Plains Indians. Cf. also Hultkrantz 1969.

smallest animals are all *manitou* (Skinner 1913: 84). Even modern Indians whose religious traditions are broken easily ascribe to such a view. Recently, a Chumash Indian declared, "I use sacred land every day to exist on. When you have respect for your religion and your tradition, everything around you is sacred" (Craig and King 1978: 52).

The perspective represented here—that nature is sacred because it reveals, or symbolizes, the Great Mystery—is not absolutely new in American Indian research. It is more or less implied in W. C. MacLeod's view of Algonkian conservation philosophy (MacLeod 1936), and it is clearly expressed in Stewart Udall's analysis of Indian ideas of their relationship with the natural environment (Udall 1972: 4). A few years ago Clara Sue Kidwell claimed that "the concept of nature as a metaphysical basis for Indian culture has not been fully explored" (Kidwell 1973: 45). More recently, Vecsey has emphasized that the American Indian recognition of their dependence on nature was a conceptual aspect of their religion (Vecsey 1980: 13). My particular point is that religious belief, and nothing else, elevated nature to a beautiful and harmonious structure in the Indian mind.

This is, of course, evident to American Indian thinkers today. One of their spokesmen, Vine Deloria, writes, "In seeking the religious reality behind the American Indian tribal existence, Americans are in fact attempting to come to grips with the land that produced the Indian tribal cultures and their vision of community" (Deloria 1973: 88). So it is. We now understand what Joseph Brown means when he says that he discovered how Black Elk, in speaking about animals and natural phenomena, really was explaining his religion (Brown 1964: 16, 1972: 9).

The cosmotheistic interpretation of nature underlies most North American Indian cultures, but it has been weakened among some agriculturists. There are two major reasons for this change, it seems: first of all the digging into the earth that could have destroyed the concept of a sacred ground, Mother Earth,[15] and secondly the separation of cultivated lands from wild nature.

Mother Earth is a common idea among Indians over large parts of North America, it occurs among hunters as well as among

---

15. It is interesting to note that whereas incision into the ground was condemned as an act of sacrilege, killing of animals was quite legitimate if performed properly. Cf. Vecsey 1980: 181 n. 83.

agriculturists. Whereas in myth she may be portrayed as an individual, anthropomorphic goddess, she appears to be identical with earth in ritual and everyday beliefs (cf. Hultkrantz 1972b: 166). When the whites tried to induce the Shahaptin Indians of Washington to cultivate the ground, their spokesman Smohalla reacted violently, and retorted to the white agent:

> You ask me to plow the ground! Shall I take a knife and tear my mother's bosom? Then when I die she will not take me to her bosom to rest.
>   You ask me to dig for stone! Shall I dig under her skin for her bones? Then when I die I can not enter her body to be born again.
>   You ask me to cut grass and make hay and sell it, and be rich like white men! But how dare I cut off my mother's hair? (Mooney 1896: 721).

We can imagine how the slow transition from plant collecting to horticulture involved a change in world-view, not so rash perhaps, but over the centuries. The hoe of the agriculturist made more damage to the soil than the simple digging stick of the root collector, and the burning of the woods—in order to achieve clearance for farming lands and fertilization—killed off the trees, drove off the animals, and changed the landscape.

Certainly, the immaculate ground became no dominant religious concept among the real agriculturists. She could still play an important creative role in myth, as she does among the Zuni. However, she was usually replaced in both myth and cult by the Corn Mother (or Corn sisters among the Iroquois, Corn maidens among the Pueblo Indians). The death and birth of the corn, features in both vegetational life and cultic events, are themes widely dealt with in myths.

The separation of wilderness and cultivated ground in the collectivistic village society of the agricultural tribes tended to degrade natural environment. The former affinity with the pristine woods and mountain meadows associated with hunting life[16] was sometimes changed into an indifference, and even hostility toward once favored places. The process is easiest to follow in northern Asia (Paulson 1962:

---

16. Cf. Standing Bear 1933: xix: Indians know no wilderness. This statement from a representative of a hunting tribe does not contradict our earlier observation that nature may be dangerous and destructive.

79 f.), but it may also be tracked in North America, although less evident here. This is probably due to the fact that, as we have seen, North American agrarian peoples retained the hunting and collecting as secondary economic activities. The chasm so characteristic in Europe and Asia never developed to the same depth in North America. However, we can observe a slackening of connections with natural environment in some specific spheres, as evidently was the case among, for instance, the Iroquois.

The Iroquois Indians were planters, although they supplemented their cultivation of maize, squash, and beans ("the three sisters" in religious thought) with hunting of deer and bear and with fishing. My Iroquois informant, mentioned in the foregoing, pointed out that among the agricultural Iroquois the bonds with nature still persisted. The Iroquois consider, he said, that there is a reciprocal relationship between nature and man: if you take something from nature, you have to give something else back. If you take an animal, you must in return give an offering of tobacco.

However, to some extent the Iroquois were kept out from their natural environment. They lived in settlements consisting of perhaps a hundred longhouses, situated on heights of land and surrounded by palisades. The wilderness outside held attractive game animals but also unpleasant shrubs like the poison ivy and unpleasant animals like the skunk and the rattlesnake. In contrast to surrounding Algonkian tribes, the Iroquois youth did not go out into the wilderness to seek a guardian spirit (cf. Benedict 1923b: 32 f.). It seems characteristic that in Iroquois religious beliefs we find the idea of the woods housing a species of ugly, bodyless spirits with distorted faces, called "false faces" (since they were impersonated by masks in a secret curing society). Their looks are so frightening that those who meet them in the woods are afflicted by paralysis. These spirits send pestilence and other diseases, and may eat human beings who stumble upon them (Morgan 1901, 1: 157 f.; McElwain 1980, with literature references).

These dark aspects of nature may have contributed to its partial desacralization. Speaking about the Iroquois as conservationists in theory, William Fenton emphasizes that "in practice they often contributed to the decline of species" (Fenton 1978: 298). Similarly, my Iroquois informant admitted that his people did not always show the same consideration for parts of their environment that they afforded the game animals. Thus when they harvested wild cherries they broke off the whole tops of the trees. Nor did they save the feathered game. The Iroquois were largely responsible for the extermination of the passenger pigeon (*Ectopistes migratorius*). My informant told me how the Iroquois watched these birds flying in enormous flocks, and later on broke their eggs and removed the chickens.[17]

It seems that in this case the original respect for nature as a manifestation of the supernatural was gradually lost in a partly agricultural setting. However, there is also another possible explanation to which we now turn.

The sacred unity between the supernatural powers, man, and environment so characteristic for North American Indian hunting societies could also be dissolved through the influence of the white man's value patterns. It is perhaps in acculturative situations that we perceive the most devastating changes in the Indian's feelings for nature. Under white impact the old ethics were broken up, and the traditional life values were lost or nearly so.

In some penetrating studies Calvin Martin has shown how the use of the country and the relationship to animals and trees among Indian hunters originally were determined and controlled by tribal religious values. He observes that among the Micmac on the eastern coast of Canada "the entire Indian-land relationship was suffused with religious considerations which profoundly influenced the economic (subsistence) activities and beliefs of these people" (Martin 1974: 4). The Micmac, therefore, killed only the animals they needed (Martin 1974: 11, 1978: 32 f.). The mechanisms of control functioning here were among others the beliefs in masters of the game and the animal ceremonialism (Martin 1978: 35). When the Micmac converted to Christianity these mechanisms fell away, the animals were slaughtered wastefully, and starvation as well as social disintegration followed.

This far I am prepared to agree with Martin. However, it is more difficult to follow suit when he introduces a complicated cause-and-effect argument where European disease, Christianity, and the fur trade are blamed for the corruption of the Indian-land relationship among the Micmac, the Ojibway, and other Algonkian Indians (Martin 1978: 61, 154 f., 1974: 25). Martin thinks that the spread of

17. Ironically, Wilcomb Washburn attributes the indiscriminate killing of the pigeons to the whites (referring to James Fenimore Cooper's *The Pioneers!*), contrasting the white American attitude to nature with the respectful attitudes of the Eskimos and Indians (Washburn 1961: 35).

European diseases was brought on by the animals, in particular the beaver, according to Indian beliefs. There was, he says, in Indian understanding a conspiracy between the animals directed against man, with the effect that man turned to hostility to the game animals (Martin 1978: 144 ff.). However, such a causal chain cannot be proved to have taken place. The whole theory is based on a conversation between two aged Cree and the trapper David Thompson and refers to an ancient tale of the mythical beavers (Martin 1978: 106 ff.).[18]

Martin also argues that the commodities of the fur trade, not least the big gains and the technological equipment, lured Indians to abandon their old cautious hunting techniques, thus nullifying supernatural sanctions against overkilling game (Martin 1978: 153 f.). This sounds more likely. However, we should keep in mind that Indians normally reacted against white mass slaughterings (cf. Kohl 1859b: 497; Rich 1960; O'Neil 1977: 83), and did not join in until their world-view had been partly disenchanted by Christianity, their old life-ways demolished, and their very survival was at stake (see Vecsey 1980: 28 ff.). Certainly, the despiritualization of nature was the factor that paved the way for the overhunting.

A similar course of events took place among the Plains Indians when the buffalo became scarce in the 1870s. However, the Indian part in the drama of extermination has been misrepresented in contemporary descriptions. In a report to the American Congress in the late 1880s, William T. Hornaday accuses the Indians of having slaughtered the last buffalo, the so-called northern herd. (The Union Pacific had divided the buffalo in two main herds in the late 1860s.) Still in 1874 a reliable observer, Lieutenant G. C. Doane, estimated there were as many as four million buffalo in the northern herd east of the Big Horn Mountains (Burlingame 1942: 71). The great Indian assault set in the following years, according to Hornaday: "Up to the year 1880 the Indians of the tribes previously mentioned [the Sioux, Cheyenne, Crow, Blackfoot, Assiniboin, Gros Ventre, Shoshoni] killed probably three times as many buffaloes as did the white hunters, and had there not been a white hunter in the whole Northwest the buffalo would have been exterminated there just as surely, though not so quickly by perhaps ten years, as actually occurred. ... From all accounts the quantity of game killed by an Indian has always been limited by two conditions only—lack of energy to kill

18. It is most unlikely that Indians would suppose the animals should have reacted *in corpore* against man. As one Indian once said to Frances Densmore, how could nature ever be angry with Indians when everything they have was given them by nature (Densmore 1948: 95).

more, or lack of more game to be killed" (Hornaday 1889: 505 f.). So speaks an inveterate Indian hater, a person who is out to free his white compatriots from the charges of having extinguished the precious American buffalo.

As we now know, the real destroyers were the whites. The hunters employed by the railroad companies furnished the railroad workers with buffalo meat in enormous quantities. Dude ranchers and European high class society amused themselves in buffalo shooting. Masses of buffalo were killed just for their hides that were brought to the big merchant houses for sale, while the carcasses rotted on the Plains. White military leaders advised the government to shoot off the buffalo so the Plains Indians became starved and ruined—the best way to bring down their resistance. Certainly, the mass slaughter was organized and executed by the whites.

Nevertheless, in the last hours of the old Plains culture the Indians contributed to the annihilation. However, in all fairness it should be said that they were drawn into the process. As Frank Gilbert Roe has pointed out, the whites equipped the Indians with guns with which they could hunt the big game (Roe 1951: 450 f.). This certainly enabled them to kill more buffalo than before. Another important factor was the accelerating scarceness of buffalo herds. The contraction of the northern herds to parts of Wyoming and Montana forced those Indians whose whole existence, biological and cultural, depended on the buffalo, to move within short distances from each other. A competition took place which resulted in an onslaught on the remaining herds. Apparently the very smallness of the herds made the Indians desperate. The end came very abruptly. The last herd of about 10,000 animals was wiped out in the fall of 1883 at the Cannon Ball River in North Dakota. The hunters were Sitting Bull and his men, but also a crowd of whites (Garretson 1938: 153). Reverend John Roberts, Episcopalian missionary to the Shoshoni and Arapaho Indians on the Wind River reservation, remembered that in 1883 "3,000 buffalo robes were brought by the Indians to the local trader's store, and elk, deer, antelope by the thousands" (Mokler 1927: 102). Next year the buffalo were gone.

According to the Indians, the buffalo dwelt beyond the horizon, or under the ground (Mooney 1896: 906). As we know, the bringing back of the buffalo was a main point in the Ghost Dance doctrine.[19]

19. Cf. above, footnote 5. The idea of the return of the buffalo seems to reiterate the mythical events in Cheyenne sacred history when the buffalo emerged and followed the culture hero Erect Horns from the holy mountain (Dorsey 1905a: 48; Powell 1969, 2: 470).

As far as we can discern, the Plains Indians in those days suffered from feelings of deprivation and desperation: their whole world was threatened in its existence, shortage of food, and military defeat, made it impossible for them to continue their ancient pattern of life, and traditional tribal religions seemed out of place. No wonder that in this confused situation the bars of indiscriminate killing of the game gave in.

This process of secularization which started in the wake of white colonization has continued until this day. Where the old beliefs are gone, red man's particular relationship to nature is there no more. A Slavey Indian from northwestern Canada told me some years ago that, in accordance with the traditions of his tribe, he does not kill more animals than he needs; but, he added, his tribesmen have no such hindrances, they waste the game.

No wonder that many thoughtful Indians long for the days when nature was virgin and unspoiled, when the Great Spirit offered his children a rich flora and fauna, and revealed his own essence in the beauty and dramatic force of the landscape. These nostalgic feelings have perhaps found their most moving expression in the following reflections on the past by an old Omaha Indian:

> When I was a youth, the country was very beautiful. Along the rivers were belts of timberland, where grew cottonwood, maple, elm, ash, hickory, and walnut trees, and many other shrubs. And under these grew many good herbs and beautiful flowering plants. In both the woodland and the prairies I could see the trails of many kinds of animals and could hear the cheerful songs of many kinds of birds. When I walked abroad I could see many forms of life, beautiful living creatures which *Wakanda* [the Supreme Being] had placed here; and these were, after their manner, walking, flying, leaping, running, playing all about. But now the face of all the land is changed and sad. The living creatures are gone. I see the land desolate and I suffer an unspeakable sadness. Sometimes I wake in the night and I feel as though I should suffocate from the pressure of this awful feeling of loneliness (Gilmore 1929: 36).

Much of the old environment is irreparably lost, but much remains to be taken care of. Fortunately the new Indian spirit is very ecology minded, and there is a fair chance that coming generations of American Indians will restore the old sound perspective on nature that was so well represented by their ancestors.

8

The Owner of the Animals in the Religion of the North American Indians

BEFORE THE ARRIVAL OF THE WHITE MAN IN THE NEW WORLD, the American scene was in extensive areas dominated by hunting, fishing, and the collecting of food as compared with other and more advanced means of livelihood (see the maps in Wissler 1950: 2, 20; and in Driver and Massey 1957: 177). In North America cattle-rearing was entirely absent; agriculture was practiced among the tribes in eastern U.S., above all in the southern states (except the coastal tracts), and among various groups in New Mexico and Arizona, especially the Pueblo peoples. In the Great Basin and in the Plateau area, wild plants and berries were collected, but small game was hunted on the side. The Indians of the Northwest Coast were fishermen. Everywhere else, hunting occupied the foreground of the men's occupations: they hunted caribou and moose in the Canadian wilderness, buffalo and other big game on the Plains and in the forests of the Rocky Mountains. Even in those tracts in which agriculture had gained a footing, the men were often also hunters, indeed, more hunters than farmers (Driver and Massey 1957: 227, map 39).

These economic conditions are, moreover, reflected, right

135

into our own times, in the religious conceptions and usages of the Indians: it is the hunter's religious ideology that gives to the spiritual life its form and meaning. How often do we not hear talk of the way in which the medicine-man tries to invoke the game, or how the guardian spirit blesses the hunting luck and how after death the Indian is awaited by the happy hunting grounds. Notions of this or a similar kind confront us everywhere in the nonagrarian areas, indeed, even in the agrarian regions, at least in eastern North America. As Witthoft has shown, even the agrarian religious conceptions and rites in the last-mentioned area have their roots in old hunting culture (Witthoft 1949: 84). Only in southwestern North America, chiefly among the Pueblo Indians, is the agrarian ideology firmly established. The sharp difference between hunting and agrarian religion in this part of North America has inspired Underhill to a basic study of the problems pertaining hereto (Underhill 1948).

Little has otherwise been done in accounts of the religion of the North American Indians to stress the close connection between and the dependence upon hunting. Discussions have been connected with many essential aspects of the religious life, such as the Great Spirit, the guardian spirit complex, the initiation rites, etc., but only the most casual attention has been devoted to some of the religious conceptions and rites which from the hunter's point of view have the greatest significance. The work which has shed most light upon old Indian hunting rites and religious notions pertaining hereto is Hallowell's almost classical study of the bear cult (Hallowell 1926). Juel has in a longish essay discussed the so-called animal ceremonialism centering round the bones of marine animals (Juel 1945), and Frazer and Paulson have given brief surveys of the ceremonial treatment of above all the bones of land animals (Frazer 1955: 204 ff.; Paulson 1959: 182 ff.). The salmon ceremonies on the Northwest Coast have been described by Erna Gunther (Gunther 1926; Gunther 1928). Regional studies of animal ceremonialism have been written by, e.g., Birket-Smith, Lantis, and Speck (Birket-Smith and de Laguna 1938; Lantis 1947; Speck 1935). But no exhaustive investigation has yet seen the light.

The same applies to the conceptions of the animal guardian or owner, so important for the whole hunting ideology and according to H. B. Alexander "one of the most distinctive of American mythic ideas" (Alexander 1916: 292). The animal guardian may be defined as a supernatural ruler whose function is to exercise stewardship over the wild animals, especially the animals which are hunted by man. He protects these animals, sees to it that if they have been slain by man, they get a correct ritual burial, and sanctions or prevents the hunter's slaying of them. These functions may also be exercised by rulers of other origin (the Supreme Being, the master of the woods, etc.), but they are typical of the animal guardian and motivate his existence.

It is only during the past decade that closer attention has been paid to these conceptions. The author has given a survey of the owner or guardian notion in its connection with the soul belief (Hultkrantz 1953: 497 ff.). Pettazzoni has sought another point of contact for the owner concept, viz., the conceptions of a Supreme Being (Pettazzoni 1956: 354 ff.). Haekel, finally, has given a list of the meso-American conceptions of the animal guardian (Haekel 1959: 60 ff.). Only the last-mentioned article concentrates upon the owner concept in its various aspects. No similar investigation has been undertaken for North America proper. What is perhaps the religious concept most typical of the hunting peoples has thus not been properly investigated here.

In such circumstances it is scarcely surprising that even very eminent researchers have passed over the owner concept among the Indians or else given it the wrong dimensions. In a recently published survey of the Indian religions, Ruth Underhill considers it possible to observe that "the Algonquians believed in an Owner for each sort of animal" (Underhill 1957: 130). Even if other tribal groups are not excluded, the reader is given the impression that the owner was properly domiciled among the Algonkian Indians, whereas he has, on the contrary, occurred rather generally in the hunting cultures of North America—and also in the agrarian cultures. The same view of the owner's narrowly regional occurrence is presumably at the bottom of Birket-Smith's and de Laguna's assertion of the late "intrusion upon American soil" of this concept (Birket-Smith and de Laguna 1938: 505).

A direct consequence of the insufficient attention devoted to this object of research is that it has not been possible to throw clear light upon other religious conceptions closely allied to the concept of the owner. Such dominant complexes of ideas as the belief in the guardian spirit, totemism, and the culture hero can only be understood against the background of the concept of the owner of nature, as will presently appear. A number of the rites connected with the bones of slain animals become comprehensible only if they are set in relation to the belief in the animal guardian. And the picture hitherto drawn of the North American hunter's religion has been so incomplete, so badly proportioned, and so little integrated because attention has not been paid to what I should like to designate as its key figure—the owner.

It is not difficult to indicate the cause of this neglect. To a certain extent research in the field has disregarded the owner concept, and to a certain extent, too, the fieldworkers have misunderstood the figure—the line of demarcation between the Supreme Being and the owner, for example, has not always been kept clear. But behind the uninterested attitude of researchers in the field, one glimpses two deeper causes which may be most simply expressed as follows: an indifferent attitude to the influence of nature upon religion and to the value of ecological methods in the research on culture and religion. During the period in which the great majority of American tribal monographs were written—the first decades of the twentieth century—scientific discussion of culture in the U.S. and Canada was dominated by the conviction of the determining influence of tradition upon culture and religion. It is only since the second World War that interest in the culture-determining role of nature has been extended; and in connection with this ecological methods and viewpoints have been accorded consideration in culture research (Meggers 1954; Steward 1955). An ecological view necessarily implies, as far as religion is concerned, a recognition of the decisive importance of the determinants in the natural environment for the structure and pattern of a given religion, in which connection the natural influence must be graded according to the basic economic and technical level of the culture forming the matrix of the religion. The type of religion thus occurring in a hunting culture should in the highest degree have been formed and attained its significance through interaction with nature's own field of force. Otherwise expressed, the religion should be at one and the same time deeply marked by the experience of nature and the daily intercourse with nature, and dominated by the hopes and the fear connected with the killing of game. By the side of the animal ceremonialism, the concept of the animal guardian constitutes the adequate release for these two tendencies when they occur simultaneously.

This is more than a logical calculation; it is a fact, if one devotes a closer study to the religions of the North American hunters. The distribution of the animal-guardian concept among these Indians cannot here be discussed in detail; I refer the reader to the by no means exhaustive, but compendious list I have drawn up in an earlier work (Hultkrantz 1953: 497 ff.). So much, however, should be said here concerning the occurrence of the North American animal-guardian concept that it has—not unexpectedly—had its chief anchorage among me for this work, and for source data the reader is referred to this

forthcoming publication. So much, however, should be said here concerning the occurrence of the North American animal-guardian concept, that it has—not unexpectedly—had its chief anchorage among
the hunting peoples in the north, especially the Algonkians, whose
primitive culture structure has long been well known. But even in the
more southerly parts of North America, and especially among the
(agrarian) southeastern Indians, whose close kinship with the Algonkians has recently been shown (Haas 1958), the animal guardian is
common. Nor is he missing in western North America, and he is
found far down in Mexico and Central America (Haekel 1959; Zerries
1959: 144 ff.).

There are, on the other hand, remarkable lacunae in this distribution. Thus the Great Basin is badly represented, which may naturally be due to the nature of the source material, though in the main
it has deeper causes than this. Among collectors of wild plants and
hunters of small game like the Indians in this half desert region, one
cannot expect to find conceptions of the animal guardian as pronounced as those of the big game hunters. The hunt is here—from the
point of view of the males—of still more subordinate interest than
among the tillers of the soil in the East. The scarcity of game in the
Great Basin has been not the least of the factors contributing to the
lack of prominence accorded to the concept of the animal guardian.

There are, naturally, also other "guardians" or "owners" in
North America than the animal guardian. The plants have their
guardians, as have also places—and so has man, for the Supreme
Being is, of course, in principle a guardian or owner of men, when he
is not still more closely associated with, e.g., the sky or the world
pillar. In shape and functions the animal guardian may coincide with
the guardians of both plants and localities, as is the case with, e.g.,
Scandinavia's mistress of the woods (these views already advanced in
Holmberg 1917: 46, 52). As we shall see, the same thing applies in
North America. But it is incontestable that the animal guardian as
such is especially well represented here and has a far more dominant
position than other types of owner, at all events in the hunting
religions. Among the agrarian peoples the plant guardian, as a rule
the corn goddess, naturally occupies a prominent place. In this connection a comparison with the hunting peoples in South America and
northern Eurasia is interesting. In South America the animal guardian
seems to be very common, but also the "bush spirit," in many cases
scarcely to be distinguished from the animal guardian, is often met
with here—quite naturally, since hunting and agriculture occur side
by side in this continent (Zerries 1954). In large parts of northern
Eurasia we find another situation. Here, as e.g., Holmberg (Harva)

has shown, the dominant figure is the guardian of place, i.e., as a rule the master or mistress of the woods, sometimes also the water sprite; this naturally does not mean that among many tribes, as among the Yakuts, forest and animal guardians do not occur side by side (Harva 1938: 389, 394). According to what Dr. Ivar Paulson has informed me, one can, roughly, proceed on the assumption that the place guardian has the ascendancy in the western and the animal guardian in the eastern parts of northern Eurasia. Here, as in so many other cases, we thus find an unbroken transition between the Siberian and North American religious conceptions.

Against the background of this wide intercontinental distribution, it appears most correct to presuppose that the notion of the animal guardian constitutes a very ancient religious concept, perhaps more primitive than other owner concepts. It seems, better than any other owner concept, to incorporate the religious tendencies of the hunting culture. Cooper has in a way given expression to the same thought in describing the complex of beliefs connected with the animal guardian (and the ritualism pertaining thereto) as "more archaic than the taiga economy" and as "a very basic feature of religious culture, not only in southern South America, northern North America and northern Eurasia, but also among some African and Oceanic Negritos" (Cooper 1946: 300). There can be no doubt but that the animal guardian belongs to the ancient religious heritage in what is historically and structurally man's oldest culture formation, the hunting culture. This figure is therefore of the very greatest importance for research on the lines of development followed by religion.[1]

The rich, at once various and uniform North American material concerning the concept of the animal guardian would seem able to give us certain clues as to how it has developed. It is, of course, always difficult to reconstruct the prehistory of a religious idea from ethnographic material in the present. But the distribution of the idea and its adaptation to a certain cultural "ecotype" gives certain clues to the forms it may have taken in the past. On the basis of the North American material one may make the following general observations:

1. The concept reflects the social and economic structure of the ancient hunting community. In principle, the owner may be said to correspond to the role played in the little hunting community by the head hunter, the "head-man." Just as this community consists of

1. All the more remarkable is if that modern religio-phenomenological surveys, e.g., van der Leeuw's and Eliade's, entirely neglect the animal guardian, and also the owner as a type conception. Cf. herewith Tylor's excellent account in Tylor 1873, 2: 329 ff.

persons who are more or less related to each other and to the leader—the really primitive bands are, as we know, constituted by uncomplicated family groups, sometimes simply by single families (cf. Steward 1936)—there is an elementary kinship between the owner and the individuals over whom he rules. In more complicated cultures this relation may then vary according to the model supplied by the relations in the human society. Here, as elsewhere in the history of religions, we find that the social structure has served as a model for the pattern of religious concepts.

2. As the game occupies the focus of hunting interest, its habits are made the subject of intensive study on the part of the hunter. Especially does he note the fact that in certain animal species single individuals act as leaders and guardians of the entire herd. At the same time it is natural for him to identify himself with the game.

3. The owner of the animals is the guardian soul of an animal collective, and as such built upon the soul conceptions (Hultkrantz 1953: 497 ff.). The transition between the soul of the individual animal and its collective guardian soul or owner can be instanced both in North America and in Siberia. Judging from North American data the concept of the animal guardian appears to be best developed in those places in which soul dualism prevails and in which, accordingly, the free-soul is conceived to possess the attributes which convert it into a guardian soul (Hultkrantz 1953: 374 ff.). It is, however, not certain whether other factors, above all the frequency of big game, have not meant more for the pregnancy of the owner concept.

4. The animal guardian owns and rules over the animals in the same way as the Supreme Being rules over human beings, animals, and the entire universe—the perception of dependence characterizing the religious feeling has here been transferred from the world of man to that of the animals. The feeling of solidarity between man and the animals has facilitated the transference.

If, as I presume, the concept of the animal guardian has these prerequisites—all of them interacting on or reinforcing each other—there is no need to have recourse to any artificial theory as to his splitting off from the high god.[2] I have here taken up a stand against

2. It should in this connection be pointed out that Geo Widengren, who particularly stresses the significance of the splitting-off process, is doubtful of its extent as concerns "all the natural objects regarded as deities which are subjects of a cult, such as Mother Earth, mountains, rivers, trees, springs etc."; one may probably also account nature's rulers as belonging to this category. "How the worship of these entities arose still constitutes a problem difficult of solution. One may regard them as split off from the pantheistically conceived high god, but the whole question calls for a number of special investigations" (Widengren 1945: 131).

those scholars who seek the origin of the animal guardian in a higher, gradually degenerated conception of God (Schmidt, Haekel, and Jensen), and for those who assert his primary nature (Friedrich, Zelenin, and Zerries). The given conditions seem to be so predominantly in favor of the last-mentioned alternative that in the absence of reliable datings in this field it must be regarded as the probably correct solution.

The North American animal guardian was presented as early as in the Jesuit relations of the seventeenth century, and from these he found his way to the first really scientific comparative religious works published, those of Lafitau and de Brosses.[3] Although he had been duly mentioned by both Tylor and Alexander, as shown above, he has in the course of time come to be obscured by another concept, which has given rise to a good deal of discussion, viz., the visioned or guardian spirit (Benedict 1923b). In modern accounts of North American religion he does not occur at all or is only briefly glimpsed. It may, therefore, be of interest to make cursory mention of this spirit's forms and functions.

In North America we can distinguish the following typology for the animal guardian:

1. The particular animal species has its own supernatural owner. This is a very common belief in North America. But it should be noted that not every species necessarily has its guardian. In general it is chiefly the economically valuable animals that are conceived as having guardians: they claim the hunter's attention, it is them that with every spiritual and material resource he tries to slay. But this is no rule without an exception. The mighty bear is also the object of the hunter's keen interest; the slaying and eating of the animal and the treatment of the corpse are hedged about with rites which stress its supernatural character, but the cult commonly addresses itself to the soul of the individual animal, less frequently to the bear guardian. We find the same thing in northern Eurasia. It cannot *in et per se* be the bear's dangerousness and strength that have given it this individual position—the moose is generally considered by the Indians to be more dangerous than even the grizzly bear, but it is not the object of the same ritual attention as the latter. The cause of the special position

---

3. The Indians, says Lafitau, "croyent que chaque espece a dans le Ciel, ou dans le pais des Ames, le Type & le modele de toutes les autres, qui sont contenuës dans cette espece: ce qui revient aux idées de Platon" (Lafitau 1724: 360 f. See also de Brosses 1760: 57 ff.).

of the bear cult is rather to be sought in deep-lying historical conditions (see Hallowell 1926).[4]

2. The guardians are sometimes ranged in hierarchical order. The chief reasons for this are the animals' varying importance or food value for the hunter, their differentiated physical potential or supposed mystical capacity and, not least, the social pattern in the human world.

3. In some tribes the animal world has been divided up between two guardians or owners, one for the birds and the animals living on the ground, another for the creatures of the rivers, lakes, and the sea. This dichotomy is reminiscent of the cosmic dualism finding expression in, *inter alia*, mythology and the tribal division into sacral moieties. The great guardian is generally identical with the most powerful guardian of the land animals and sea animals, respectively.

4. This powerful guardian is also conceived by many peoples as a general animal guardian, a ruler over all animals. He may be exemplified by the bear sprite in the Eastern Woodland, the buffalo sprite on the Plains and the sea goddess Sedna of the Eskimo. In southwestern North America this high guardian is identified with the star-beings, precisely as is the case in South America.

It is only natural that with its wide range the concept of the animal guardian should easily merge into or be transformed into concepts in line with its dynamic tendencies. A genuine religious idea is, of course, never static, it is subjected to constant change, just as are other culture manifestations. Under the influence of the strict historicistic tendency in ethnology and comparative religion this continuous process—or evolution, as it was called in older research, and as it may still be called—has doubtless been somewhat obscured, since changes in the spheres of religious life are so difficult to trace in the absence of direct testimony. But the dynamism of religion is a part of the life of a religion and must not be neglected if one wants an all-round picture of the religious reality. From the detailed analysis of the contact between the conception of the animal guardian and other religious conceptions, however, we should be able to get some insight into the course of its development, an insight applying less to the individual cases than the general trend of the changes.

In the following only a few points of the many I should like to make will be mentioned concerning the evolutionary forms of the

4. Ritually buried bear skeletons are among the oldest traces of religious cult in the European palaeolithic age (see, e.g., Maringer 1956: 86 ff., 142 ff.).

animal guardian and its connection with other religious concepts in North America.[5] Readers seeking source documentation and a more detailed discussion of the mutatory process are referred, now as previously, to my work on the conception of the animal guardian in North America.

1. The animal guardian has a tendency to merge into other, closely allied guardian or owner concepts such as the water sprite: he is less frequently assimilated with the master of the woods, who is, for the rest, a figure seldom mentioned in North America. So much is clear, that the animal guardian cannot have been differentiated from the master of the woods as a special form of the latter, as some researchers seem to think.

2. The animal guardian is sometimes identical with man's guardian spirit beheld in vision, but this identity is by no means self-evident, as one is tempted to think from Ruth Benedict's statements on the subject. In the majority of cases we are left without information as to the relation obtaining between the two types of spirit. There frequently appears to exist a psychologico-functional distinction between them, but this may naturally be secondary, and a common origin is far from improbable.

An interesting question in this connection is whether the guardian spirit has ousted and replaced the owner of the animals as the genius of the hunt. The owner of the animals not only rules over the animals, he is also, as we know, in virtue of his dominion over them, the one who permits the hunter to succeed in his intention or the one who thwarts him in this. But also the guardian spirit gives luck in the hunt, above all as regards the animals whose shape it has assumed; good health, virility, fortune in the hunt and in war were what the Indian most of all expected from his guardian spirit. The problem here adduced does not, of course, exist where the owner and the guardian spirit are conceived as one and the same person. But what is the solution in other cases? Unfortunately, our material is so inadequate that it does not permit of any definite conclusion. On one case, among the Naskapi on Labrador, it is obvious that both "the Great Man," man's guardian soul, and the animal guardian can give hunting luck; but guardian soul and guardian spirit are cer-

---

5. A strict account of the phenomenology of the animal guardian does not here come into the question. Such important problems as its sex, outer form (invisible, anthropomorphic, theriomorphic, etc.), the degree of biological reality (some sprites are obviously animals of sensational size or color), and the degree of distinct personality cannot in this brief account be made the objects of investigation.

tainly not the same thing (see Hultkrantz 1953: 374 ff. See also Paulson 1958: 310 ff.).

But these views take us further. Among the Naskapi the spirits beheld in vision—those of the shaman possibly excepted—seem only to have brought hunting luck, this because they were always identical with the animal guardian. Sometimes the latter revealed itself only incidentally in dreams giving a good omen for the hunt. Examples like these seem to indicate that the belief in the guardian spirit may possibly have evolved from the belief in the owner, even if this is a very bold assumption. It must in this connection be borne in mind that the belief in the guardian spirit flourishing in North America is a "democratized shamanism," as Lowie has so aptly pointed out, and that the problem is therefore a complicated one: ought the shaman's guardian spirits also to be conceived as animal guardians (Dittmer 1954: 92)? At least one researcher has (on weak grounds, it is true) contested this, but his objection refers to the historically uniquely developed Siberian shamanism (Findeisen 1956: 48).[6]

3. If there is a genetic connection between the animal guardian and man's guardian spirit, new light is herewith thrown upon the essence of the so-called individual totemism: there is a mystical connection between the Indian and the animal species in whose shape his guardian spirit appears. This essential connection may naturally arise in any case, through a natural attraction; but it becomes more comprehensible against the above-adduced background.

4. In North American mythology there is frequent reference to the primeval prototypes for the different animal species: the hare, the beaver, the wolf, and so on. One thus finds in the mythology the same corporative view as lies behind the idea of the animal guardian, and the points of resemblance frequently extend to the outer contours of the conceptions: both may be represented as the origin of the animal species or as their chiefs. Now it is undoubtedly difficult in many cases to trace a real connection between the theriomorphous spirit-beings of the religion and those of the mythology, since religion and mythology may actually represent two fundamentally different worlds (see Hultkrantz 1956a). But this distance is probably due to the more dynamic nature of religion and the more static nature of mythology and not to any original gulf between the two. Thus one should not rule out the possibility that the animal prototypes of the myths really reflect the conception of the guardian.

6. Siberian shamanism has, as Dr. Ivar Paulson has informed the author, attained an obvious historico-regional fixation; one can distinguish 3–4 characteristic shamanistic regions.

5. The culture hero, one of North America's best-known and most-debated mythological figures, is often described as a prototype of the animals. His person and functions show, moreover, such great affinity with the conception of the animal guardian that an original and not merely secondary connection between them appears probable. Pettazzoni and Kock have traced the notion of the culture hero direct to the concept of the animal guardian (Pettazzoni 1956: particularly the epilogue and 376; Kock 1956: 125 ff.). The problems here unfolded are, however, so widely ramifying that they cannot be discussed in this short chapter.

The points concerning the North American animal guardian advanced here are not without interest in a wider context. The conceptions and their tendencies have, certainly, their counterparts all over the world, especially in the hunting cultures (with the possible exception of that of Australia). In this connection the North American material is particularly well qualified to serve as a model: it is rich and varied, the milieu in which it occurs is fairly untouched by the cross-currents of ideas deriving from the high cultures, and its connection with the existing conditions of culture and nature is very distinct.

9

Attitudes to Animals
in Shoshoni Indian Religion

ELIGION, ALTHOUGH INHERENT IN MAN, borrows its expressions from the setting or milieu in which man appears. The forms through which man expresses the supernatural are all drawn from the cultural heritage and the environment known to him, and are structured according to his dominant patterns of experience (Hultkrantz 1966a). In a hunting culture this means that the main target of observation, the animal, is the ferment of suggestive influence on representations of the supernatural. This must not be interpreted as meaning that all ideas of the supernatural necessarily take animal form. First of all, spirits do appear also as human beings, although generally less frequently; the high god, for instance, if he exists, is often thought of as a being of human appearance. Second, although spirits may manifest themselves as animals, they may evince a human character and often also human modes of action.

All this is apparent in Shoshoni Indian traditional religion as it lives on today. Since prehistoric times Indians of the Shoshonean linguistic stock have roamed about in the wide region between the high plains of western Wyoming and the Pacific Ocean at the coast of

California. The desert or semidesert area between the Rocky Mountains and California, Great Basin, has been the center of distribution
of the Shoshonean groups. However, the easternmost Shoshoni
extended out on the Plains east of the Rockies. The present article
deals with these Shoshoni, nowadays called (after their reservation)
the Wind River Shoshoni. In contradistinction to the Basin Shoshoni
who subsisted mostly on seeds and nuts which they gathered, the
Eastern Shoshoni mostly hunted animals, in particular the buffalo,
and they achieved in the eighteenth century a veneer of Plains culture
(characterized by mounted warriors, war-honors and a war society, teepees, Sun Dance ritual, etc.) (Hultkrantz 1968b. See also
Hultkrantz 1961c.). The old political, social and economic patterns
ceased to exist during the first decade of reservation life in the 1870s.
Still, much of the religious life survived this change, for instance, the
vision-quest, the power of the medicine-man, and the Sun Dance.
Also the characteristic mythology continued to flourish. Today, much
of the traditional religion is gone, and in particular the younger generations turn away from old tribal beliefs. The visitor to the Wind
River Shoshoni will find, however, that there are still medicine-men
around and still celebrations performed of the yearly grand ceremony,
the Sun Dance. And a careful observer will learn that the oldtimers
even today preserve religious beliefs of the past. Many of these beliefs
concern the animals and the zoomorphic representations of spirits, as
may be expected in a former hunting culture.[1]

The Shoshoni are keen observers of animals. In particular
they know the animals good for food, like the buffaloes. They have
many names for the buffaloes according to their age and sex, and for
different parts of the bodies of these animals. Also a useful domestic
animal, the horse, is known under many names. On the other hand,
animals and birds which do not play any cultural role are often
classified under group names; for instance, *ka:kh* means both raven
and crow. Our conclusion must be that the idea of the animal is
structured culturally, that is, the animal is seen not exactly as a biological being, but as a being colored by cultural values, and judged from
cultural premises. It plays the role ascribed to it by cultural tradition.

A closer view reveals that this structuring or patterning
appears in two different connections. Firstly, as emerges from what

1. The following account describes the beliefs of the former Plains Shoshoni
who constitute the greater majority of the present Wind River Shoshoni. No particular
attention will be given to the remnants of the earlier Sheepeater population once
sparsely distributed in the mountain areas of Wyoming (see Hultkrantz 1966–67a).

has just been said, the animals occurring in the Shoshoni hunting area function according to selective criteria. Secondly, zoomorphic beings are conceived on different planes of cognition. Also in this case they represent, of course, a selective approach to nature.

Like most other peoples the Shoshoni distinguish between a natural and a supernatural reality. The former is the common, every-day world where one event follows the other in an ordinary, expected way. The supernatural world, on the other hand, often breaks through into the natural world but may also run parallel to the latter and manifest itself in the ordinary pattern of events. It is not founded in an exterior chain of causalities but in religious belief. Now, natu-ralism and supernaturalism are the two main levels of cognition referred to above. The animal which the hunter approaches may be a real (natural) animal, or it is the abode or rather the manifestation of a spirit. Sometimes the two conceptions blend, so that what appears from the outset to be an animal reveals itself as a spirit. In principle, however, the difference is sharp and uncompromising.

The changing attitude to animals depending on whether they are just animals or manifestations of spirits is well illustrated in the Shoshoni Indian's relationship to bears. The Wind River Shoshoni have quite a lore on bears, an animal species which apparently has fascinated them more than other animals. Why this has been so is open for speculation. Hallowell has shown that the so-called bear ceremonialism, centering on the ritual funeral of the slain bear, and in particular the orderly deposition of its skull and bones, has been spread over a wide area from the old Laplanders in Scandinavia to the Lenni Lenape of Delaware and adjacent regions (Hallowell 1926). This ceremonialism has been associated with an attitude of reverence and devotion on the part of the participants. There are no indications that similar rites ever occurred among the Shoshoni, but some of the awe and respect they felt for the bear may reflect the extraordinary posi-tion assigned to this animal in other tribes.

One of my Shoshoni informants, a reputed medicine-man, saw in the company of a white man (the identity of this man is unknown to me) some bears perform the Sun Dance at a place called Sweetwater Gap. This happened at sunrise on a day in spring. My informant watched the bears at a distance of about fifty yards. He was cautious, for bears are "wicked animals when dancing." If they had discovered him they would have hunted him mile after mile, he said. The bears were dancing in front of a pine tree painted yellow, red, and green. They made four steps forward and four steps backward, and all the time they were looking at the pole. They also sang, and their singing was a growling. They had built a fire there. My informant thought that this "midnight-fire" had been made by one of the bears who, he surmised, was a *puhagant,* a medicine-man. He added that when dancing the bears pray for their youngsters. "They act just like a person. They are smart."

It is evident that the pattern of this curious event has been borrowed from the Sun Dance ritual; the informant in question is himself a firm believer in and a noted leader of this ceremony. Many details, in particular the four steps forward and backward, remind us, however, of the Bear Dance of the Ute Indians (Opler 1941). And, indeed, the informant knew about this dance and pointed out, quite correctly, that in some way it had to do with the reinvigorated activities of the bears after their coming forth in the spring. The scene supposedly witnessed by this informant is nevertheless difficult to account for psychologically. Perhaps he had, at some sun-up, watched some bears perform the characteristic, swinging movements which can be observed by anyone at a zoological garden. Perhaps he had also seen the first rays of the sun color the trees and create illusions of burning fire. And all these visual impressions had then been systematized into a pattern suggested by the observer's experiences from the Sun Dance and the (Ute) Bear Dance.

Whatever the background of this mysterious experience, to my informant it was a proof that in spite of their marvelous qualities these bears were animals, not spirits. He assured me that although bears act like human beings they cannot talk to me, and I cannot talk to them. "Spirit-bears can speak to you, but these bears are regular animals." Their almost human qualities simply show that bears have a psychic equipment which matches man's. Every human being has two main souls, the soul of the body or vital principle, *mugwa,* and the dream or free-soul, *navužieip,* which may leave him when he sleeps and often acts as an adviser and guardian of its owner (Hultkrantz 1951). The soul system of most animals is in comparison much simpler. Each animal has a body-soul, *mugwa*—"if it didn't, it would be lying on the ground, dead," explained my informant. The animals lack, however, the dream-soul, the *navužieip,* with one exception: the bears seem to own it. Speaking about bears in general and the sun-dancing bears in particular my informant attributed both sets of souls to them: "The bears have got *mugwa,* for they can move. But they must also have *navužieip,* for otherwise they shouldn't have had power to throw that paint on the tree." He added that after death the bear's *mugwa* goes to the realm of the dead, like the *mugwa* of all other animals.

True bears are never spirits—indeed, no spirits have souls—but spirits may appear in bear form. That is, they do not take a bear's disguise as they please, but they show themselves as bears because their nature comes close to that of the bear. As my Shoshoni informant said, "all spirits are different," never identical, differing in qualities and capacities. He went on: "The Bear spirit looks like a bear, but is different from the bear in that he suddenly appears and suddenly disappears. He is like a *hïgien* (shadow). He has a bear's form, but is a spirit. He figures as a bear because *tam apō* [our father=the Great Spirit] made him that way. But he has nothing to do with the animal bear and other bears."

The Bear spirit is one of a host of spirits, all called *puha*, meaning supernatural power, whose main function it is to manifest themselves in visions to human clients who seek their help, and to bestow their power upon them. In other words, the *puha* are the guardian spirits of the Shoshoni visionaries. As is well known, the vision-quest is a ritual that occurs, or has occurred, among the Indians all over the North American continent, with the exception of the Indians of the Southwest (Benedict 1923b). It has been summarized by the American anthropologist Clark Wissler as follows: "The procedure usually takes this form: if a youth does not have a dream or vision which his superiors regard as supernatural, he is instructed and prepared for the inducing of such an experience and left in a lonely place to fast and pray, day and night. If a spirit appears, it is usually in animal form and that animal becomes in a sense the individual guardian of the supplicant. This guardian is, however, conceived of as a spirit and not merely as a bear, eagle, wolf, etc., which are, after all, but the objective links between the individual and the source of spiritual power (Wissler 1950: 199). Wissler then goes on to demonstrate that the so-called medicine bags (he calls them "medicine objects, or charms") are the material bonds between the Indians and their personal guardians. Very often these bags consist of skins of animals, and their contents may be claws, ears of an animal, feathers, etc. The figure of the spirit is not infrequently painted on different utensils, such as the teepee cloth, the shield, or the shirt.

The Shoshoni vision-quest follows the pattern outlined above. It should be added, however, that among the Shoshoni as among all the western Plains Indians not only youths but also adults formerly took part in such quests and achieved guardian spirits, often one after another at successive occasions. Today, only single medicine-men keep up the old custom. They direct their steps to solitary hills or to the rock-drawings in the foothills of the Rocky Mountains, pass away the night there by smoking and singing and, finally, dreaming, and then meet their future guardian spirits if they are lucky. In most cases the spirit shows itself as an animal, but anthropomorphic spirits are not rare. For instance, one medicine-man told me that he had seen in waking visions "those powers which are around us in the country" dressed up as Indian old-timers. Even the sun, the moon, and the evening star appear as *puha.* The rule is, however, that the spirits take animal form. According to my informants, otters, eagles, and buffaloes have been common spirit disguises, but also other animals and birds, such as jackrabbits, hawks, and magpies have figured in this connection. It seems that *puha* can appear in most animal forms. Certainly, one of my informants, himself a medicine-man, was quite convinced that *puha* could never appear as deer, but this was contradicted by other informants. I never heard, however, of anybody having smaller mammals like chipmunks and moles for guardian spirits. They are not impressive enough.

This observation brings us over to the fact that although the spirits are independent of the animals whose form they have taken, they do represent in their powers the specific qualities of these animals. One knowledgeable informant said this: "The buffalo can appear as *puha* because he is big and strong. It is not so that all buffaloes are *puha,* but the spirit may take on the shape of the buffalo." The same informant stressed emphatically that each spirit animal endows his client with the capacity characteristic of the animal in question, and nothing else. For instance, the turtle equips you with the ability to cure the sick, for the following reason: the doctor has to see through the patient in order to diagnose the disease, just like the turtle who is able to see through water. It is easily understandable that a person with beaver-power is a good swimmer, a person with deer-power a swift runner, etc.

Similarly, the bears—to whom we now return—express strength and fortitude, and other qualities as well. Here is a vision account narrated to me by the most respected medicine-man of the Wind River Shoshoni in the 1940s: "When the sun went up in the east I dreamed about three bears sitting under a pine-tree. I shot at them. One of them came forth to me and said, Look now, you see all these bullets twisting the fur here?—Yes, I see them.—This is the way I am: the bullets cannot kill me.—It really looked as if the bear had mud twisted in his coat. The bear said, I want you to cut one of my ears. You should fasten it in a rope hanging down from your side. In this way you will dance the Sun Dance.—The dream ended. Later on I stumbled upon a dead bear, took his one ear and carry it now in the Sun Dance. No bullet can kill me. This is true. I never tell lies. That's the way I like to be." The same medicine-man also told me, referring to this vision, "The bears often come to me in my dreams, they rustle and scratch, but don't hurt me." He did not tell me, however, whether he could mingle with real bears without being hurt by them. In principle, these bears ought not to be affected by his owning bear *puha*. But in practice the case is the reverse. That is, a person enters into a certain relationship with the animals whose shape his guardian spirit has taken. The Indian cannot keep the spirit and the animal apart. Whether we accept Lévy-Bruhl's concept of the *participation mystique* or not, here we have the germs of such phenomena as nagualism and totemism (Hultkrantz 1963: 68 ff.).[2]

The close connection between the bears and a person who has the bear as his *puha* was repeatedly pointed out by my informants. One of them had the following to say on the subject. "A Shoshoni who has the bear as his guardian spirit may treat the bears in whatever way he pleases. Any other person will however be torn to pieces by a bear if he tries to deal with it. A man who has the bear as his *puha* may kill the bear, but not eat it.[3] He may, however, leave the meat for his family [to eat]. The same rule holds for any animal a person has as his *puha*."

Another Shoshoni, a medicine-man, volunteered the following information: "The bear is an animal that gets mad, therefore no good *puha* for a family-man: he will get mad over nothing. One man with bear *puha* was Pinji:z ["cross-legged"], a good, strong

2. The Shoshoni never developed totemism and have no clan-animals since the unilinear descent system which is the basis of clans was lacking among them.

3. Opinion is divided on this point, however. Another informant said, "A fellow who has beaver *puha* cannot kill the beaver animals. But other fellows who try to trap them, often at the same place as where the beaver *puhagant* [medicine-man] tried in vain, they will get them. I have noticed that myself. It is the same thing with other *puha* and animals. I don't know how to explain it; nobody now living knows. Furthermore, *puha* says in the dream, 'Don't try to kill me, for if you do your medicine will be destroyed.' Therefore, when I am hunting elk I don't kill it, but ask my grandson to do the killing, for I have elk medicine."

medicine-man. When he got mad he growled like a bear, and the hair on his head stood up like the hair of a bear."[4] Pronouncements like these show that since man takes part in the spirit's power, and the latter is somehow identical with the qualities of a certain animal, man is related to this animal.[5] It is too strong to speak here about a possession (in the psychological sense) by the animal, but the connection between man and animal is close to identity.[6] In contradistinction to the Mexican *nagual*, the Shoshoni guardian animal is not born with the individual, but associated with him in a later phase of his life. You never know with whom you will be united. Said one of my informants who had the eagle for guardian spirit: "The eagle said in my dream, 'You should never want to eat beaver-meat. Some day you might get some *puha* from the beaver, if you stay with what I tell you.' It came true to me."

Paul Radin has suggested that the North American guardian spirits have been recruited among the *genii loci*, a possibility that Benedict has found to exist only among the Central Algonkian Indians in the Eastern Woodlands (Radin 1915: 294; cf. 286 ff; Benedict 1923b: 46). As to the Wind River Shoshoni, the *puha* are said to exist in multiplicity within certain definite areas, known by the old men—on the north side of a well-known butte, among the hills north of Big Wind River, etc.—but even so they are not in any way the "owners" of this country. In fact, when we meet animal spirits as *genii loci* they are never to be confused with the guardian spirits.

The *genii loci* are in some cases conceived in animal form and then consequently represent another level of the supernaturalistic cognition of zoomorphic beings.[7] The most well known of these *genii*

---

4. The same informant also recalled a medicine-man of the old days who called on his bear *puha* by taking on a bear's hide and growling like a bear. (He did not, however, cure the sick in this way, as did the Blackfoot medicine-man White Buffalo portrayed by Catlin.) My informant did not appreciate bear *puha* too much—and he ought to know, for he was loaded down with all sorts of *puha*. "The bear is tricky. There is only one thing I like about him, and that is to get some paint from him. If you have been hurt or you have rheumatism, you put the paint on the sick place. That is the best thing you can get from a bear."

5. The close connection between man and his *puha* is, i.e., stressed by the fact that loss of *puha* may mean sudden or gradual death.

6. The psychological background of this phenomenon has been rightly appreciated by Frances Densmore: "The bird or animal that appeared to the Indian in his dream was an embodiment, to some extent, of the power that he desired and, by his individual temperament, was best fitted to use" (Densmore 1953: 220).

7. Like most tribes on the Plains the Shoshoni have few localized spirits. Those who exist seem mostly to stem from the reservation era.

loci are the water sprites. One of the Shoshoni mythic tales tells us that there are spirits in the form of muskrats in the waters. More common, and functioning more in actual beliefs, are the stories of the water-buffaloes, *pa:gwic,* who haunt Bull Lake and Dinwoody Lake and also certain spots in the Big Wind River. The Shoshoni refer to a tale about two Ute scouts who transgressed the rules of scouting by eating a rabbit and a water-buffalo raw; one turned into a rabbit, the other into a water-buffalo who immediately descended into a lake close by and disappeared there. In another story it is told how once some Shoshoni hunted buffaloes near Bull Lake. When the buffaloes dived down into the lake and did not reappear, the hunters understood that they were no real buffaloes but the spirits of the lake. I was informed that these mysterious beings are still there. It brings bad luck to see them, and nobody has seen them for a long time. However, you can hear them in the early spring when the ice is still covering the surface of the water. One Indian told me one can hear their noise when the ice cracks. Is this perhaps the empirical foundation of these beliefs?[8]

Perusal of comparative literature on Shoshonean peoples has convinced me that the water-buffalo is a concept peculiar to the Wind River Shoshoni. The buffalo of the dry plains has here become identified with the mysterious owners of the lakes in the Rocky Mountain chain. The concept mirrors the belief in miraculous powers in the buffalo and the awe for waters natural to a population on the plains.

There are vestiges of a third level of zoomorphic representation in Shoshoni religion, the lord or master of animals. Hunting peoples in Africa, Europe, Asia, and America have developed the idea of a supernatural owner of the animal species, or of all animals, who protects them, commands them, and at request from hunters delivers them to be slayed and eaten. The concept is not infrequent in North America (cf. Hultkrantz 1961b). The master of animals is a spirit, generally figured as an animal. The Shoshoni have possibly in very remote times known the coyote, or rather the mythical Coyote, as a master of animals. With the impact of Plains Indian culture, the buffalo and the eagle have halfway achieved the position as master of animals and master of birds, respectively (Hultkrantz 1961a). In all fairness it should be pointed out, however, that this type of concept is very little noticeable among the Shoshoni.

The fourth and last level of zoomorphic religious representa-

8. Another informant maintains that he saw a true water-buffalo in the City Park of Denver. It dived under the surface of the water when looked upon.

tion belongs to mythology which, among the Wind River Shoshoni, is a cognitive segment different from religion (Hultkrantz 1956a). Thus the Supreme Being is anthropomorphic in cult and daily beliefs, but to a certain degree theriomorphic (wolf) in the myths. Actually, in mythology all acting personages are animals, or rather the prototypes of the present animals, whose deeds set the pattern for their present-day descendants. The chief actors are Wolf, the camp chief, and Coyote, his announcer. The latter is, phenomenologically seen, the trickster and, to a slight extent, the culture hero. It is said that in mythological times, that is, the formative times in the beginning of the world, all animals were human beings which only later changed into their present animal form.

Shoshoni mythology, and the roles played by animals in it, offers a particular and involved problem that will not be discussed here. The important thing is, in this connection, that animal beings dominate mythology as they dominate religion. In this hunting milieu the animal offers the closest tie between the world of realities and the world of spirit.

10

The Indians and the Wonders of Yellowstone

A Study of the Interrelations of Religion, Nature, and Culture

Introduction

IT IS GENERALLY RECOGNIZED THAT geographical enviroment—topography, climate, nature and distribution of fauna and flora, access to water—appreciably influences the development of every culture. The degree of this influence is usually directly proportional to the primitiveness of the community; for, as J. H. Steward puts it, structurally simple communities "show minimal borrowing and conspicuous environmental conditioning" (Steward 1938: 1). The influence of nature asserts itself in two different ways: it provides the physical and spiritual material on which culture can build; it also checks, transforms, and canalizes already existing culture forms. The older ethnologists, like many geographers of today, exaggerated the culture-creating power of the physical environment ("environmental determinism") (cf. Bates 1953: 704). Modern students of culture realize that the natural environment is not in itself productive of, but tends to promote, restrict or eliminate culture (see, e.g., Forde 1949: 460 ff.; Goldenweiser 1946: 443 ff.; Herskovits 1949: 153 ff.; Kroeber 1939: 205 ff.; Lowie 1940: 356 ff.; Wissler 1912: 217 ff.; Wissler 1926: 211 ff. Cf. Ginsburg 1934: 92 ff.; Odum 1947: 86 ff.).

The influence exerted on a culture by the natural environment is either direct or indirect. Direct influence acts independently of every expression of cultural activity; it is a strictly mechanical process. As an example one might mention the influence of the natural environment on the economic system of the Californian aborigines. As is well known, these Indians never tilled the soil. In this connection Sauer adduces the following: "Lack of contact with agricultural peoples can hardly account for the absence of agriculture on the Pacific coast of the United States. The Indians of southern California were in communication with agricultural peoples along the Colorado. It is not likely that California Indians refrained from experimenting with the crops grown on the Colorado river. The resistance to the westward diffusion of agriculture was probably environmental rather than cultural. The crops which were available had little prospect of success in winter-rain lands. Maize and squash especially were ruled out by the rain regime, but the conditions also are predominantly unfavorable for beans" (Sauer 1936: 294 ff.). Here nature itself placed obstacles in the way of cultural expansion.

Actually, the indirect influence of nature is culturally conditioned. There are two different types of such influence. In the first place we not infrequently find—especially in the modern community of our days—that culture produces the external physical conditions for nature's effect upon it. Indeed, the circumstance that nature is nowadays in many places curbed within the cultural field of power, a passive instrument in the culture builder's hand, by no means eliminates the fact that it at the same time, in one form or another, modifies and contributes to the building up of our modern culture.

The second type of culturally conditioned natural influence appears when culture supplies concepts, mental patterns, evaluations, by which nature is given a chance to affect the cultural development. Nature and its phenomena are judged according to the system of values established within the social group on the basis of inherited tradition, internal development, loan from other groups, and adaptation to the natural environment. It is when the ingrained scale of values, the traditional conceptual material, no longer suffices that the influence of nature gets freer play.

As a rule, nature does not disturb the cultural balance, not even new impressions have a disturbing effect: they are merely associated to already known conditions. It is said of Sacajawea, the legendary Shoshoni woman acting as guide for Lewis and Clark 1805–1806, that upon reaching the Pacific she espied seals basking on the rocks offshore. She told her tribesmen that these beings were humans dwelling in submarine caves, and that they dived below the surface as soon as she approached to chat with them. The Shoshoni were completely taken in by her tale. On the other hand, they disbelieved her when she told them of fishes as big as a room—evidently whales—that she had encountered on the coast (David 1937: 310 ff.).[1] The seals were easily associated with existing notions of water babies and water women, but for whales prototypes were lacking.

The more radically natural phenomena contrast with the expectations within the cultural pattern, the more intense is their effect on the culture. If owing to their violence or their alien character they break through the frame of current concepts of nature, they are liable to glide over into the religio-mystical sphere. And even if within this they find links with the existing religious conceptual pattern it is not always so certain that safeguards against them will be available in the form of practical ritual observances.

In the following paragraphs we shall examine a specific case where the tension between nature and culture has become acute and where consequently the former reacts detrimentally on the cultural situation. At the same time we shall find what a significant factor religion may be for settlement and geo-cultural diffusion. The scene is Yellowstone National Park, and the actors are the Indian tribes of the Yellowstone region, among them the Shoshoni just mentioned (see Hultkrantz 1954a).

Indian Reticence Concerning Yellowstone and Its Causes

There are probably few areas on the North American continent that would seem more apt to spur Indian fantasy and to give rise to legend than Yellowstone National Park. There is so much there that enchants and spellbinds even the casual visitor, that makes him rejoice at nature's beauty or sense his littleness in the face of this world of wonders: the brilliantly colored cliff walls and the majestic waterfalls of Yellowstone Grand Canyon, the petrified tree trunks of the forests, the darkly forbidding glass mountain Obsidian Cliff,[2] the thermal springs, the spouting geysers, gases and subterranean rumbles, the peculiar whining sound in the mornings over the big lakes, where it has also happened that lightning has flashed and thunder boomed

---

1. An old squaw, Pandora Bogue, stated: "She also said that she had seen people sitting on rocks out in the water. They talked among themselves but she could not understand them" (*Wyoming State Journal*, October 2, 1941).

2. These "glass mountains" are obsidian formed by the sudden cooling down of lava.

from a cloudless sky.[3] This is a world of grandeur and mystery. It stands to reason that the first whites to view the Park—among them the scout, trapper, and champion braggart Jim Bridger—painted its wonders in grossly exaggerated colors (Chittenden 1918: 44 ff.).

Yet, strangely enough, this attitude of boundless enthusiasm is in sharp contrast to the reserve and reticence of the neighboring Indians. Chittenden, the national park's foremost chronicler, finds it remarkable that so little knowledge of the area has been obtainable from the Indians. Lewis and Clark were duly informed by them of all the outstanding geographical features lying ahead on their trip but never of the fairyland around the Yellowstone's springs. "There is not a single instance on record, so far as we can discover," Chittenden states, "except in the meager facts noted in an earlier chapter, where rumors of this strange country appear to have fallen from the lips of Indians. And yet it was not a region unknown to them, for they had certainly passed back and forth across it for a long period in the past. Their deep silence concerning it is therefore no less mysterious than remarkable" (Chittenden 1918: 81). Chittenden inclines, however, to the view that Yellowstone Park in reality had been a *terra incognita* for most Indians in the vicinity (Chittenden 1918: 9, 14). In his opinion the reason can scarcely have been that "superstitious fear" deterred them from visits: in that case there ought to exist traditions of a more striking kind connected with the park, yet such traditions are lacking. No, the real reason is presumably practical, says Chittenden, and has to do with the local topography and climate. An impenetrable woodland covered with snow for three-quarters of the year, which in former days could not compare with the surrounding valleys as a hunting ground, could obviously not exert any great attraction on the Indians, opines Chittenden (Chittenden 1918: 11 ff., 82).

Chittenden must be right at least in part. The natural obstacles to an Indian penetration of the park were formidable. Lofty mountain rims barred the way for the surrounding Plains peoples; the high Absaroka Range to the east was negotiable only via Sylvan Pass at the North Fork of the Shoshone River (Shimkin 1947b: 256. Cf. Linford 1947: 16, 17). To the south and southeast access was facilitated by the Ishawooa, Two Ocean, and Togwotee Passes; to the west the gateway consisted of the Targhee Pass. Otherwise, the Yellowstone Valley north of Mammoth offered the best route (Bauer 1948: 81).

---

3. The event dates from 1885 (Haynes 1947: 104).

Spouting hot spring in the Norris Geyser Basin, Yellowstone National Park.

However, once in the park the visitor was stopped by a wild, savagely broken-up country full of undergrowth and tall mountain ridges, and snow-covered for the better part of the year. Neither were the park's allurements so very great; from the Indian viewpoint obsidian and horn (from mountain sheep) were its chief assets. In addition, the habitats proper of the Plains Indians were located at a relatively great distance from the park.

Hence it is not so strange if for climatic and geographical

reasons the park was rarely entered by neighboring Indian tribes. Much evidence points to the fact that these latter were rather sparing with their visits. Trails were comparatively few and almost untrodden. Old trappers said that the large majority of Indians in the vicinity never saw the country. And even outstanding Indian guides thoroughly at home in the outer wilderness were completely lost as soon as they got into the park area (Chittenden 1918: 9). Unfamiliarity with the natural conditions within the park seems to have been the chief reason why about 1872—just as the fame of its wonders had reached all over the United States—hordes of Indians trekked to this area out of pure curiosity (Cramton 1932: 36).

Thus it might be said that Indian reticence regarding the park must at least in part have been due to the fact that they actually lacked knowledge of it, and that this ignorance was connected with their difficulty in gaining access to the park: only a relatively small number of individuals from any neighboring Plains tribe may actually have entered the park area. Nevertheless, even the most casual lone visitor to the park could scarcely have avoided noticing its peculiarities and then mentioning them to his fellow tribesmen. True, a certain lore connected with the park's curiosities did actually exist among the surrounding Plains Indians, although for some reason this subject was never willingly brought up by them. It is the Indian tendency to close up in this connection that seems so strange to us (see further below). Moreover, as we shall find, the park region proper was inhabited by a primitive Shoshoni group, the Dukurika or Sheepeaters, who apparently had their settlements not far from the geyser areas—yet without knowing much about them.

All these circumstances conduce to putting the Indian attitude in a different light. Indian reticence must have had other and more significant causes than those adduced by Chittenden. In other words, it seems indeed probable that the very motive rejected by Chittenden—"superstitious fear"—played a most significant role in this connection. One of the first superintendents of the national park, Col. P. W. Norris, was fully convinced of this. He records that the park's "few yawning, ever difficult, often impassable, cañon-approaches along foaming torrents; the superstitious awe inspired by the hissing springs, sulphur basins, and spouting geysers; and the infrequent visits of the surrounding pagan Indians have combined to singularly delay the exploration of this truly mystic land" (Norris 1881: 27).

The question is whether the religio-magical factor here was not decisive.

Yellowstone Park in the Indian Conceptual World

Indian acquaintance with and reaction to the park are attested on the one hand by the Indian place names (of which some have been preserved on the map), and on the other by Indian popular tradition.

The Indian place names have mostly a neutral, matter-of-fact meaning and do not appreciably reflect the impressions the park must have evoked. The park as a whole seems to have passed among some Indians—which of them is uncertain—under the designation "Summit of the World," a name marking both its altitude and its role of continental divide (Chittenden 1918: 156). Yellowstone, or "Rock Yellow River," was originally the Hidatsa Indians' name for the river itself (and probably also that of other Indian tribes); very likely the name was derived from the yellow walls of the Grand Canyon. The Crow Indians called the river also "Elk River" (Chittenden 1918: 3 ff.). Formerly, the Shoshoni River east of the park was called "Stinking Water" also by the whites, because it runs past a spring with a very strong odor (Chittenden 1918: 103). The Shoshoni name it "Bad Water River." And in their tongue the geyser areas of the national park are "Water-Keeps-On-Coming-Out."[4]

The above-mentioned place-names are soberly descriptive and, as we have said, tell nothing about the Indian emotional attitude to these natural phenomena. But they prove that the Indians were once familiar with the park's mysteries. If they never described them in detail, this must be attributed to religio-magical causes.

The Indian popular tradition in connection with Yellowstone Park is not rich, but it exists just the same. The greater part of the material comes from the Shoshoni peoples, in the first place the Wind River Shoshoni.[5] The characteristic feature of the material collected is restraint: it is possible to trace a certain hesitancy on the part of the Indians to tell what they know about the park's peculiarities. This restraint applies particularly to the geyser regions.

In a letter from St. Louis dated January 1852, the well-known missionary Father de Smet gives a detailed account of the geyser areas, which he apparently had no chance to see personally. Having

4. By way of comparison one might mention that among the hot springs outside the Park Thermopolis Hot Springs are known by the Shoshoni name "Water-Hot-Stand" and Washakie Hot Springs by the name "Smoking Waters" (see Shimkin 1947c: 252; and Hultkrantz n.d.).

5. The author carried` on field research among these Indians and the Sheepeaters in 1948. Where no source is stated in the following the data are the author's own.

Volcanic activity in the lava beds of the Norris Geyser Basin, Yellowstone National Park.

mentioned the volcanic district, he writes, *inter alia:* "The hunters and the Indians speak of it with a superstitious fear, and consider it the abode of evil spirits, that is to say, a kind of hell. Indians seldom approach it without offering some sacrifice, or, at least, without presenting the calumet of peace to the turbulent spirits, that they may be propitious. They declare that the subterranean noises proceed from the forging of warlike weapons; each eruption of the earth is, in their eyes, the result of combat between the infernal spirits, and becomes the monument of a new victory or calamity" (Chittenden 1918: 41 ff.).

Unfortunately, de Smet does not say which particular Indians it was that held this view. Col. Norris, the esteemed park superintendent quoted above, reports in 1881 that the Crow, the Shoshoni, and the Bannock occasionally, but extremely rarely, crossed the difficult passes to the park. "It is probable that they were deterred less by these natural obstacles than by a superstitious awe concerning the rumbling and hissing sulphur fumes of the spouting geysers and other hot springs, which they imagined to be the wails and groans of departed Indian warriors who were suffering punishment for their earthly sins" (Norris 1881: 35). Although more influenced by Christian ethical precepts than the missionary's account, this report in the main corroborates de Smet.

To my knowledge, no further detailed accounts of Crow and Bannock conceptions relative to the geysers exist.[6] On the other hand, we know a little about how the Wind River Shoshoni viewed the geyser region.

In the year 1880, the Shoshoni Indian Wesaw, an intelligent old redskin who had more than once been a guide through the park, had a conversation with the aforesaid Col. Norris on the shores of Yellowstone Lake. According to Norris, Wesaw stated "that his people, the Bannocks, and the Crows, occasionally visited the Yellowstone Lake and River portions of the Park, but very seldom the geyser regions, which he declared were 'heap, heap, bad,' and never wintered there, as white men sometimes did with horses" (Norris 1882: 38). In the autumn of 1948 one of Wesaw's descendants, George Wesaw, told me the following: "The Indians prayed to the geysers because they believed that there were spirits inside them. Sometimes, when nearing enemies, they let the water from the geysers spray over themselves so that they became invisible." On the other hand, the old squaw and medicine-woman Nadzaip denied that she knew the national park, which she dryly referred to as a "vacation country." It may be added that the historian Dr. Hebard gives a casual account of Shoshoni notions concerning the geysers, but it seems to have been taken from de Smet's letter quoted above (Hebard 1930: 307).

While these Shoshoni, and probably also the Crow and the Bannock, all living in the vicinity of Yellowstone Park, had developed

---

6. Discussing the springs at the upper reaches of the Yellowstone River, Denig writes (1856): "The (Crow) Indians describe others to be of a poisonous nature to animals, 'tho the same water is said not to affect the human species" (Denig 1953: 22). Sober appraisal of the effects of the springs does not necessarily argue against their simultaneous supranaturalistic interpretation of the nature of the moving forces.

definite conceptions and ritual precautionary measures, the Indians living farther off who occasionally visited the park stood appalled before its wonders, terrified, and unable either to form a clear conception about them or to protect themselves against their terrible power.

In the year 1845 the Blackfoot chief Painted Wing and his two hundred and seventy-five braves strayed over into the park area while pursuing Shoshoni who had appropriated their horses. But the whole band got scared and took to flight. Many years later the chief's son visited the park and soon understood why his father had fled: "Blackfeet Indians saw something go boom. Blackfeet run away. Never come back. I come back now. Find long smoke everywhere but no fire" (Linford 1947: 251). A Blackfoot tale says, however, that in times past Blackfoot ventured as far as the hot springs and camped there in order to get yellow pigment out of the ground. They dug a tunnel underground, but in the course of this job the walls collapsed and buried them alive (McClintock 1910: 216).

In 1834 an official of the American Fur Company, W. A. Ferris, visited the Upper Geyser Basin accompanied by two Kalispel Indians. These were impressed in particular by the biggest geyser (Old Faithful?). Ferris writes: "The Indians, who were with me, were quite appalled and could not by any means be induced to approach them [=the geysers]. They seemed astonished at my presumption in advancing up to the large one, and when I safely returned congratulated me upon my 'narrow escape.' They believed them to be supernatural and supposed them to be the production of the Evil Spirit. One of them remarked that hell, of which he had heard from the whites, must be in that vicinity" (Chittenden 1918: 38 ff.). When pagan conceptions did not suffice, Christian ones were resorted to.

Nez Percé Indians who trekked through the park in 1877 seem to have been astonished but evidently not unduly scared. Just as they had made camp near Fountain Geyser it started to play. An Indian then asked a white man captured in the vicinity: "What makes that?"(Chittenden 1918: 132 n.).

It would be interesting to know how the shy and primitive aborigines in Yellowstone Park, the Dukurika or Sheepeaters, reacted to these overwhelming natural phenomena. Did they dread them like the other tribes, or had they got used to them? Unfortunately, as far as I know, they have not left behind any traditions whatever in this respect. Doane's account would suggest that the Sheepeaters, contrary to the other tribes, felt thoroughly at home in these queer surroundings (Cramton 1932: 137). This, however, is probably wrong. As we shall find, the Sheepeaters shunned the geyser areas—and the reason for this can scarcely have been anything but fear.

Old Faithful, the most dramatic of all geysers in Yellowstone National Park.

The material thus far surveyed provides conclusive evidence that it was chiefly the hot springs and geysers that were made objects of religious evaluation. However, it is probable that—even if to a much lesser extent—also other natural phenomena of the park were comprised within the sacral sphere. To be sure, of this we know nothing definite, but collateral evidence to this effect is by no means lacking. Among the Shoshoni the mountains, and above all their snow-covered tops, were counted as abodes of the spirits and of the dead. The Teton Range, the majestic group just south of Yellowstone Park, was particularly dangerous. Whoever tried to scale it died a

Dragon's Mouth, a pulsating pool of hot water close to the Yellowstone River, Yellowstone National Park. "The cavernous crater, with green coloring on the rock and its flashing tongue of boiling water and steam, account for its appropriate name" (Haynes 1947).

sudden death, and he who mentioned its name perished by rain or by snow. Probably other tribes living near the Rocky Mountains also imbued these with a supernatural nimbus (Alexander 1916: 132). Hence there might be more than mere poesy in the appellation "Burning Mountains" applied by the Indians to the ranges around the geyser basins.

More questionable is whether also the strange sounds over the Yellowstone and Shoshoni lakes ever had a religious interpretation. A parallel to Bull Lake farther south on the Wind River reservation is of a certain interest. The Indians assert that they are able to hear mysterious sounds over this lake; "rattles and beating drums and battle sounds may be heard in the night—just in the air I think," I was told by the Shoshoni George Wesaw. Bull Lake, with which a number of Shoshoni legends are associated, was conceived of by the Shoshoni as "a scared lake." The phenomena over the lake are possibly of the same nature as the acoustic peculiarities over the lakes of Yellowstone Park.

However, appraisal of the tradition material as a whole leaves no doubt whatever that it was chiefly the spouting hot springs that released religious responses. The reason is clear enough: the violence with which they totally upset the system of expectations connected with the Indians' conception of the world of everyday reality. The cascades and rumbling eruptions of the springs inspired the belief that they were the abode of evil spirits fighting for power in the nether regions, or dwellings for departed ones giving visible and audible expression to their paroxysmal pains, their sufferings in Hades; in Christian reinterpretation the geysers were conceived as the work of the devil.

This legend-forming around the hot springs and related phenomena is in no way peculiar to Yellowstone Park. The Shoshoni imagined that such far less active hot springs as Thermopolis and Washakie Hot Springs—located respectively just outside and inside the Wind River reservation in Wyoming—were the abodes of dark powers. According to Shoshoni tradition, both springs were at one time much hotter than now. Thus one of my oldest informants told me that Washakie Hot Springs had already cooled down considerably before reservation times. It was, she claimed, in former days an active spring, a continually spouting fountain of boiling water. In those days a great spirit lived in it. But the whites caused the water to subside, and "the spirit gradually left it." Another of my informants stated that right in the center of the spring there was a deep hole, and down in this hole, under the water, there resided a dragon that in the olden days spouted up the water. This dragon, which is gigantic, looks like a snake but has wings and claws.[7] The idea that demons and spirits

7. The dragon conception, according to my informant's expressly formulated explanation, is part of old Indian tradition. Yet the dragon's appearance is undoubtedly evidence of influence from European legends.

control the geysers' activity is not restricted to the Shoshoni and their neighbors on the Plains. It is also found in other quarters, as for instance among the Wappo in California (Powers 1877: 202 ff.).

As we have seen, the spirit geysers of Yellowstone Park were the objects of strong feelings of fear and trepidation. If one had to stay in their vicinity it was necessary to propitiate them: according to Father de Smet, sacrifices were made to the spirits, or at least the calumet was proffered. According to George Wesaw, the spirits were prayed to.[8] But a center of religious power having the indifferent character of natural force does not act only negatively; he who knows its secret may turn its destructive activity into useful constructive force. The Shoshoni knew that the sacred springs could be utilized for positive purposes. As we have seen, the hot jet of the geyser provided invisibility-medicine. The hot springs also cured rheumatism. Presumably their "medicine" was of the same kind as the power residing in other hot springs closer to the Shoshoni country, as for instance Big Horn Hot Springs at Thermopolis. Hither came warriors from remote regions to bathe in the steaming water and thus acquire supreme valor in battle. In this connection it should be noted that also the Bull Lake just referred to might impart supernatural powers: Shoshoni who wished to become medicine-men camped for the night on its shores (Olden 1923: 23).

We are now in a position to venture some conclusions concerning Indian reticence in connection with Yellowstone Park.

All data seemingly confirm that most of the neighboring Indian tribes knew of this wonderland and that some of them occasionally stayed there; a smaller group of Shoshoni-speaking Indians, the Sheepeaters, even lived there permanently. But the natural phenomena evoked the astonishment and fear of the natives; they seem to have reacted especially strongly to the geysers, which were conceived of as violent supernatural manifestations of demoniacal beings. It is thus not unnatural to suspect that these forces of nature tied the redskins' tongues. In other words, the phenomena in question were so overpowering, so dreadful, as to break out of the conventional religious pattern and become taboo, that is, to encourage their avoidance both in word and deed. We shall soon see that this view is justified.

---

8. I found no other definite traces of the performance of cult acts within the park area. Stone cult may possibly have occurred here in the form of stone sacrifices on rock piles once serving as corral posts in connection with buffalo hunts (cf. Mulloy 1952: 133, 137).

The Taboo Concept

It is necessary first to discuss, to some extent, the taboo concept. Elucidation of this is indispensable for the argumentation.

As is well known, the Polynesian word "taboo" means something that is prohibited or should be avoided; in Polynesia it is used in both profane and religious contexts (cf. Lehmann 1930). In sociology, anthropology (ethnology), and comparative religion taboo has become a very widely used general concept, though it has lost in firmness of definition in comparative research as it has been defined in so many different ways—perhaps because the Polynesian taboo shows so many varying types (see, e.g, Mensch 1937: 16; Hauge 1945: 126 ff.). In general, however, taboo is nowadays no doubt understood as a prohibition with religious or social sanction whose infringement unleashes an unfortunate, mystical—practically automatic—effect.

This definition embraces some essential aspects of the complex taboo phenomenon, but it requires elucidation. Margaret Mead claims that taboo is characterized by its lack of external sanction (Mead 1934: 503).[9] "Tabu may be defined as a a negative sanction, a prohibition whose infringement results in an automatic penalty without human or supernatural mediation" (Mead 1934: 502). Dr. Mead overlooks the fact that taboo also has an *institutional* aspect: it is authorized by a chief, a god, or by tradition via public opinion. On the other hand, the taboo infringement usually has an automatic effect, showing that in its functioning the taboo is independent of the intervention of outside authorities or their agents. This circumstance points to a quality in the tabooed categories which Dr. Mead has also touched upon in referring the taboo attitudes to "a deep-seated fear" (Mead 1934: 504). The fact is that taboo has also a markedly emotional aspect.

Although taboo may be governed by external, social, or religious, sanction, it receives its real significance from the fear it inspires. Hence, in my opinion, the best definition of taboo is this: taboo are all actions, circumstances, persons, objects, etc., which owing to their dangerousness fall outside the normal everyday categories of existence. True, taboo fear is often associated with the penalties for taboo infringement that may be inflicted by the sanctioning powers: politicial or religious authorities, the culture hero or other deity, public opinion. Yet the fear is mostly concentrated to the dreaded automatic consequences of the infringement—consequences

9. Freud, on the other hand, stresses that the taboo is a prohibition imposed by external authority (Freud 1950: 34).

in which these sanctioning powers manifest their sway in a more convincing manner.

The essential fact is that taboo fear sometimes has a religious implication. True, Mead states that "there is no justification in the facts for regarding tabu as a religious phenomenon." She herewith rejects Marett's thesis that taboo is a negative mana (Mead 1934: 503. Cf. Marett 1909: 90 ff.; Marett 1922: 181 ff.). With this categoric formulation Marett has undoubtedly shot over the mark; numerous instances of cultic impurity fall within the taboo category without its for this reason being necessary to trace their origin to the presence of supernatural power. This, however, by no means signifies that the taboo reaction is not in a large number of cases a reaction to the representatives of supernatural power, gods, spirits, and dark powers, who reveal themselves and their own nature in the "automatic" penalization. We may also assume that in many cases these beings are not the products of solicitude on the part of the authorities—fictive guardians fashioned according to the prototypes of popular belief—but reveal an authentic and genuinely religious faith. A given spot, for instance, is tabooed because from the beginning it has been found eerie, frightening, mystical, and in consequence associated with known or unknown spirit beings (cf. Benedict 1938: 644, 645). The human reaction to these numina becomes complex, but fear seems to be the dominant element.

The distinction here attempted between a religiously motivated state of taboo and a state of taboo maintained by an external apparatus recalls Webster's taxonomy of the taboo categories: "A state of taboo is either inherent in an object, as the necessary outcome of certain activities, situations, or characteristics; or imposed by the arbitrary action of a superior authority; or acquired by contact with anything or anybody tabooed" (Webster 1942: 29). The British folklorist Miss Burstein, too, distinguishes inherent, imposed, and derivative taboos (Burstein 1950: 732). Still closer to my view is an earlier ethnologist, N. W. Thomas, when he classifies taboos as "natural or direct" and "communicated or indirect" (Thomas 1911: 337).

If we consider the matter from the temporal viewpoint, we find that the state of taboo maintained from without often consists of a later extension of, or substitute for, an originally religiously motivated state of taboo. It is then possible to distinguish, with some measure of justification, between a religio-institutional and a religio-emotional taboo. In the former case—which represents a later phase of development—the deity, the prophet, the religious custom, etc., imposes a negative behavior pattern that we might term ritual obser-

Volcanic ground in the Norris Geyser Basin, Yellowstone National Park.

vance; consequently, it is then a matter of a prohibitive taboo (more or less authoritative) where the personal experience is restricted to the infringement of the prohibition. In the latter case—which represents an earlier phase of development—the negative behavior pattern takes the form of spontaneous avoidance, this being the practical consequence of a religious experience. With van der Leeuw we may sum up the course of evolution thus: "Die Scheu, die sich festsetzt, wird zur Observanz" (van der Leeuw 1933: 30). Or, as Webster formulates it: "Fear is systematized in taboo" (Webster 1942: 14).

It is an historico-psychological process of this kind that we must keep in mind when we now return to Yellowstone Park and the Indians.

The Tabooed Natural Park

A number of circumstances indicate that the geyser basins in Yellowstone Park were once regarded as taboo on account of their supernatural perilousness. On the other hand, the national park as such was never made the subject of taboo restrictions; for that matter, it has had the character of a regional unit for only a relatively brief period (since 1872). That just the geyser basins were tabooed is consistent with our earlier observations according to which these basins with their strange phenomena evoked religious responses on the part of visiting Indians. The taboo, in other words, had a markedly religious background.

The circumstances attesting the fact that the regions of the hot springs were taboo are, on the one hand, the Indians' dread of speaking about them, on the other their endeavor to avoid approaching them.

It is a well-known fact that so-called primitive peoples the world over dare not mention the names of dangerous powers for fear of thereby arousing their wrath; by the utterance of its name the demon is "bound" to a person, who thus becomes the nearest object for its destructive activity. The Shoshoni, for instance, once very much dreaded speaking of the evil spirit *dzoavits*, a being that sneaks into camp grounds, kills and devours people; mention of his name alone is enough to invoke his presence. It would be only natural if for analogous reasons they avoided broaching the question of the wonders in Yellowstone Basin. We have already been able to establish that the Indian place names are cautiously descriptive so-called noa names having no direct reference to the menace of these spots. Even more remarkable, however, is the fact that the Indians, as pointed out earlier, show a striking tendency to withhold what they know of the park's wonders, evidently because they dread mentioning the phenomena as such. Both de Smet and Norris state that the Indians spoke of these phenomena with "superstitious fear" or "superstitious awe," while the Shoshoni Wesaw only could characterize the geysers with a single word, "bad." As might be expected in these circumstances, the creation of myths and legends around these wonders of nature is singularly meager. Presumably, Indian assertions that they did not know the park were often evasions, a maneuver to avoid the necessity of discussing the inflammable topic.

As mention of the geysers was taboo, so also was entry into their region taboo. Thus the secretary of the Washburn expedition (1870), Lieutenant G. C. Doane, writes: "The larger tribes never enter the basin, restrained by superstitious ideas in connection with the thermal springs" (Cramton 1932: 157). Ten years later Norris was able to establish that the reason why the Plains Indians so seldom journeyed to the park was much less the hazardous natural conditions than religious awe of the spouting geysers and other hot springs (Norris 1881: 35). The Shoshoni could never bring themselves to winter there, evidently for the same reason (Norris 1882: 38). And Finn Burnett, who knew the Indians well, stated that they "were all very much afraid of the geysers in the Park, and gave them a wide berth" (Letter from superintendent R. P. Haas to D. G. Yeager, August 12, 1929. Wind River Agency Files, n.d.). We have already mentioned how the Blackfoot Indians fled in fear from the park, and how Kalispel Indians on casual visits dared not approach the geysers.

Chittenden is plainly wrong when he opines that the Indians did not shun the park for superstitious reasons (cf. above). The geyser region was dreaded in an eminent degree; and, if we are to believe de Smet, the Indians never dared to approach it without conciliating the residing powers with sacrifices or some other propitiatory measure. We have learned earlier that the springs were sought for religious purposes, for instance, the acquisition of medicine. It seems likely that only distress and mystical yearning for contact with the supernatural powers could overcome the taboo dread.[10] One is here reminded of the attitude of the Shoshoni vis-à-vis their rock-carvings: in everyday life they shun these sacred spots because the spirits are at work there, especially in winter; but Shoshoni braves wishing to have visions of these spirits go there to fast and to pray in solitude. Supernatural power has not only a negative, frightening aspect; under the right ritual conditions it may also be exploited positively. Supplicants at the Yellowstone geysers were probably few because the journey thither was long, difficult, and perilous. For the Shoshoni, the sacred spots located closer to the tribe's hunting

---

10. The same reaction to the spouting springs by the previously mentioned Nez Percé Indians offers an interesting special case. They may have been unduly influenced by Christian mission; their attention and interest may have been damped by the ceaseless activity and fatigue following arduous military exertions.

grounds actually came to mean more to them. For that matter, to these Indians the previously mentioned Bull Lake was the most dreaded of all sacred spots (Shimkin 1947c: 349).

A more concrete view of how consistently the Indians avoided approach to the geyser regions may be gained by studying the location of Indian trails and the distribution of their settlements in relation to the hot springs and the geysers.

As Chittenden has rightly pointed out, Yellowstone Park was never any sort of transit country. All the major Indian routes except Bannock Trail passed outside the park area (Chittenden 1918: 11 ff.). Presumably, the chief reason for this lay in severe climatic and topographical conditions; as pointed out in another context, the park was a less frequented march in the outer domains of the Indian territories (Hultkrantz 1954a: 114). Yet it had its allurements: there was obsidian to be had, there were medicine springs, and there were beaver, mountain sheep, even buffalo—although viewed as a hunting ground the park was far inferior to the surrounding territories. "Superstitious awe" of the peculiarities of this park country no doubt contributed to the fact that the Indian trails were so few and so seldom used.

Best known of all paths was the great Bannock Trail connecting, via the park's northern portion, the home grounds of the Bannock Indians in middle-eastern Idaho with their buffalo hunting grounds near the Big Horn Range. This route, also known as the Great Indian Trail, has been used by Indians and trappers since ancient times; in 1807 John Colter tramped it as the first white man (Haynes 1947: 97, 133, 137. Cf. Chittenden 1918: 23 ff.). It ran from Henry's Lake in Idaho over the Gallatin Range to the vicinity of Mammoth Hot Springs, where it joined another trail coming up Gardner Valley. The Bannock Trail then continued south of Mt. Everts, across Blacktail Deer Creek and the plateau country, finally also crossing Tower Creek not far from where it flows into the Grand Canyon of the Yellowstone but above the high and narrow Tower Fall. Just after crossing Tower Creek the Bannock Trail met another pathway running from the south along Yellowstone Valley. Thence the trail ran further in a northeasterly direction to Bannock Ford, where it crossed Yellowstone River. From here the trail led to Lamar River and followed this as far as the Soda Butte tributary. Here the trail divided: one could go northeast along Soda Butte to the spring waters of Clark's Fork and then along this river to Big Horn Valley; or one could continue to the southeast along Lamar Valley and then via the North Fork of the Shoshoni River as far as Big Horn Valley (see Chittenden 1918: 8; Cramton 1932: 119, 145; Haynes 1947: 97, 131 ff.).

Yellowstone Grand Canyon, Yellowstone National Park.

Some other less frequented trails, too, should be noted here. We have already mentioned the trail along Gardner Valley (see above). Another trail cut across the park in the north-south direction. It ran from Tower Fall Campground Junction on the right side of Tower Creek and close to the Yellowstone River; this spot was also crossed by the Bannock Trail (see above). From this place the trail running south along Yellowstone Grand Canyon led up toward Yellowstone Lake. At first it followed the western bank of Yellowstone River, but just south of Mud Volcano it crossed this river and then continued on the eastern bank as far as the lake (Haynes 1947: 111,

133). The ford at Mud Volcano had also been the crossing for a trail running westward to Nez Percé Creek and Firehole River and further along Madison River—a trail used by Nez Percé Indians on the warpath in 1877 (see Haynes 1947: 111; Chittenden 1918: 8; also Hultkrantz 1954a: 134). From the north end of Yellowstone Lake ran another trail, also used by these Indians, in a northeasterly direction along Pelican Creek as far as Lamar River (Hultkrantz 1954a: 134). But let us return to the Yellowstone Valley trail. Its continuation southward was carefully noted by Chittenden. "It divided at Yellowstone Lake, the principal branch following the east shore, crossing Two-Ocean-Pass, and intersecting a great trail which connected the Snake and Wind River Valleys. The other branch passed along the west shore of the lake and over the divide to the valley of the Snake River and Jackson Lake. This trail was intersected by an important one in the vicinity of Conant Creek leading up from the Upper Snake Valley to that of Henry Fork" (Chittenden 1918: 8. See also Cramton 1932: 7, Jones 1875: 54 ff., Shimkin 1947b: 248 ff.).[11]

How, then, were these trails related to the basins in which the geysers and hot springs were located? The location of these basins appears clearly from Map 1. Patently, the Bannock Trail ran north of the geyser country proper; only in the vicinity of Mammoth Hot Springs did it enter a critical zone. At Mammoth Terrace poisonous gases pour forth from the bowels of the earth, and a number of hot springs and some spouting geysers are scattered over this area. However, the Bannock Trail very likely passed around this danger area, along Gardner River. The north-south Indian route probably did not pass too close by the Grand Canyon, where we have hot springs: Colter, who travelled this route, does not describe the canyon's wonders. Farther south, however, the route passed just by the river but left the western bank as soon as it entered the geyser region south of Antelope Creek. Of the lesser trails referred to, none ran in the vicinity of the geyser areas except the east-west one along Nez Percé Creek and Firehole River, which just skirted the Lower Basin, and the trail running west of Yellowstone Lake, which somehow must have touched Thumb's Basin. It is important to note that no Indian trail was worn in the western part of the park from Norris Geyser Basin to Shoshone Geyser Basin—this remarkable region, which is today cut through by a modern highway, evidently scared away the Indians. To

11. Jones states also that the path along the North Fork of Shoshoni River—which we have earlier identified with Bannock Trail, with its continuation along Lamar Valley—led westward to the north end of Yellowstone Lake.

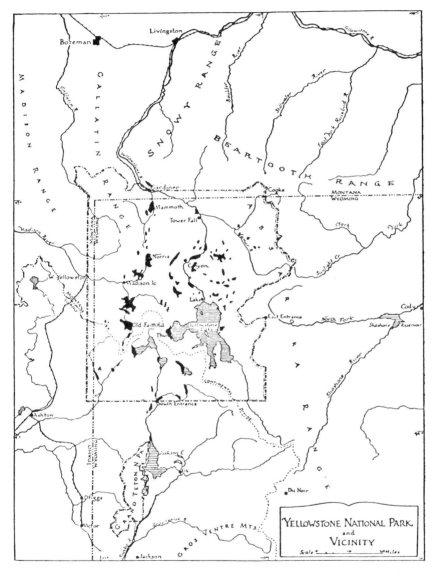

Geyser basins and volcanic areas of the Yellowstone National Park (from
C. M. Bauer, *Yellowstone—Its Underworld,* 1948).

sum up, one may say that the trails within the park were comparatively few and as a rule but little trod, and that they avoided the
geyser basins wherever possible. Inasmuch as the latter were often
located close to the river valleys where of necessity the Indian trails
had to pass, the convergence of a trail with the outer fringe of a geyser
field could not always be avoided.

Settlements, too, were invariably located well away from the
hot springs and fountains. Thus no data are available to show that the
Plains Indians ever made camp in such regions—with one exception:
the aforementioned Blackfoot expedition in search of pigments is
indeed said to have camped by some hot springs (see above). However, the story of this expedition and its sad fate may be regarded as
an *aition* for avoidance of the volcanic areas. That lone Plains Indians
deliberately sought the hot springs for religio-magical or medicinal
purposes has already been stated.

The sole permanent settlers of the park, the Sheepeaters, had
their primitive dwellings—simple huts, caves and skin teepees—
scattered over the whole area (see Hultkrantz 1954a: 124). Such an
expert on the park before the Sheepeaters' removal as Norris points
out that more or less deserted Sheepeater habitations were found
"near the Mammoth Hot Springs, the various fire-hole basins, the
shores of Yellowstone Lake, the newly explored Hoodoo region, and
in nearly all of the sheltered glens and valleys of the Park" (Norris
1881: 35). Thus it is plain that the Sheepeaters were not settled so very
far away from the hot springs and geysers. But neither did they live
too near them (Linford 1947: 251. Later archeological research has
shown that there were settlements around thermal areas. In a subsequent article, "The Fear of Geysers among Indians of the Yellowstone Park Area" [1979], I have discussed this new discovery. I
refer there to Norris' statement that, whereas the geyser areas were
certainly avoided, the Sheepeaters lived close to them [Norris 1881:
35]. Apparently, the local, stationary Sheepeaters adapted themselves
to their strange natural surroundings [Hultkrantz 1979: 37 f.], whilst
other Sheepeaters, like General Sheridan's guides [see below],
avoided them.). They no doubt expressly avoided the vicinity of the
geyser areas; their imperfect knowledge of the park country cannot be
otherwise explained. General Sheridan, who visited Yellowstone in
1882, reports: "We had with us five Sheep-eating Indians as guides,
and strange to say, although these Indians had lived for years and
years about Mounts Sheridan and Hancock, and the high mountains
southeast of the Yellowstone Lake, they knew nothing about the
Firehole Geyser Basin, and they exhibited more atonishment and

wonder than any of us" (Sheridan 1882:11; Chittenden 1981: 11).[12] The distance between the aforesaid mountains and the Firehole Geyser Basin is only twenty to thirty miles.

In this connection it is not without interest to note that the Sheepeaters were held to be a mysterious and enigmatic tribe by their neighbors and linguistic kinsmen, the Plains Shoshoni. The tales circulating among the Wind River Shoshoni of fierce mountain men apparently refer to them. Several Sheepeaters, among them the famous Togwotee, were held to possess supernatural powers which they used for magical purposes. Obviously the Sheepeaters were taken for mystical beings because they showed themselves so rarely and because they lived in such strange localities—the Regions of White Peaks or the Land of Spouting Waters.

Religion, Nature, and Culture

The preceding survey now enables us to approach the problem formulated at the beginning of this chapter, viz., what were the motives for the Indian silence regarding Yellowstone Park and its natural phenomena?

There is no doubt that the inaccessibility of this area and its remoteness from the better hunting grounds must have been partly responsible for the poor knowledge of the country among some of the surrounding Plains tribes. Yet the area is in itself so unique that even the visit there of some lone Indian must have given rise to legends and traditions. Such traditions exist, but not only are they remarkably few, they are also mentioned with great reserve, almost unwillingly. Closer study of the character of these traditions shows that the repressive factors have been of a religious or magical nature. In the writer's opinion the geyser areas in the park have had taboo value, and it is just this taboo (or taboos) that has constituted the chief motive for an Indian reticence otherwise difficult to explain.

A reconstruction of the connection between natural phenomena and their tabooing—and hence the link between religion, nature, and culture—might be stated thus:

12. In recent times the Sheepeaters' imperfect knowledge of the park has been pointed out by superintendent Haas, Wind River reservation (cf. letter from R. P. Haas to D. G. Yeagar, August 12, 1929, in Wind River Agency Files n.d.).

A group of Indians experience the geyser region as a fearsome shock because it conflicts with current expectations within their own culture, and even with traditional religious concepts; only a dim notion of the presence of dangerous supernatural power is entertained, because, among a primitive people, that which terrifies and at the same time appears different is moved up automatically into the religious sphere. However, the sense of insecurity is predominant, and escape from the critical zone is the immediate consequence of the experience. We may characterize the situation by using our previously employed term "religio-emotional taboo." The geyser area was spontaneously conceived of as taboo by those Kalispel Indians, for instance, who from their distant homes happened to stray into its vicinity.

Among the Indians living nearer the perilous districts the emotional relation to the dangerous spots is stablized; the balance within the religious pattern is restored, and thus also man's equilibrium within the frame of his culture—for, as Herskovits has said of religion, "everywhere its effective functioning lies in adjusting man to the universe" (Herskovits 1949: 162). The spouting springs are integrated in the culture pattern when the conceptions around them assume firmer shape—that may be related to existing conceptions—and fixed modes of reaction are developed—that may be related to already existing ritual behavior. The geysers are thought of as the abode of a certainly fairly well defined class of spirits, while at the same time fear remains to prompt careful avoidance of the dangerous places: the taboo has become religio-institutional and is maintained by tradition and public opinion. As we have seen, this means, for instance, that trails are located as far as possible outside the national park, or at any rate away from the vicinity of the geyser regions; it also means that settlement within the park avoids these regions.

Thus the Indian reaction to the wonder world of Yellowstone Park affords evidence of the way in which nature may affect man and his cultural creativeness via religion, which is itself a culture product. Some ethnologists have already suggested a similar line of thought concerning the relation between nature, religion and culture. Thus Forde writes: "Between the physical environment and human activity there is always a middle term, a collection of specific objectives and values, a body of knowledge and belief: in other words, a cultural pattern" (Forde 1949: 463). And Linton says: "Even the natural environment provided by a particular geographic area impinges upon the individual only after it has been filtered through the screen which culture interposes between man and nature" (Linton 1936: 467). Finally Gayton: "the role of external environment in the human environmental [culture] can be of major importance and therefore, through the cultural mechanism, be of deep psychological significance" (Gayton 1946: 267).

Between nature and our reactions to it there lies a cultural filter, a ready-made ideology, an ingrained behavior complex. Confronted with the uncanny, the incomprehensible, the "unfamiliar-different," this filter assumes a religio-magical tint. That is to say, the experience of nature leaves no direct religious traces; it acquires its religious significance from its agreement with or contrast to the religious pattern. Arbman has earlier discussed this matter: "The supernatural occurrence presupposes belief in the supernatural will or force and its mystical way of acting," he writes. "The miracle can thus be understood only from the religious or religio-magical belief in power" (Arbman 1939: 26). At the same time Arbman points out that "certain occurrences—for instance those of an unusual or sensational kind, or happenings whose real causes are unknown, or such as cannot at once and without reflection be referred to a context of experienced reality—are more easily ascribed by faith to supernatural influences than others" (Arbman 1939: 25 n. 4). Radin relates that the Winnebago worshipped stones that had a strikingly queer form and thinks that the stone "deshalb heilig war, weil er ihnen (the Winnebago) nicht in die festgelegte Ordnung zu passen schien" (Radin 1951: 31). But Radin says also: "In der Tat ist jeder auffällig scharfe Stein, jeder steil abfallende Fels ein massgebendes und typisches Kennzeichen des Übernatürlichen, und ein Winnebago würde um diese Dinge wissen, noch ehe er sich ihnen genähert hat" (Radin 1951: 121 n. 9).

Many of the spirits and deities of primitive peoples must have been born out of the intricate interplay of nature, culture, personality, and religion. Hence the process is not so simple as Tylor will have it in his account from West Africa, where a stone is supposed to turn into a fetish just because a Negro happens to hurt himself on it (Tylor 1871, 2: 121 n. 9). Of course, the idea of fetishes and spirits existed in this Negro's brain even before the accident, as a part of the cultural ideology.

The natural phenomena in Yellowstone Park did not give rise directly to definite religious conceptions and behavior patterns among the Indians in the vicinity. The effect they obtained was determined by the value pattern of Indian culture. And the effect was manifold: new religious concepts were brought into being, extensive areas became taboo. And this tabooing rendered impossible *inter alia,*

a more intensive exploitation of the park for transit and for settlement. Thus nature, indirectly via religion, may react upon culture—
upon spiritual as well as material culture.

PERSISTENCE AND CHANGE

11

The Problem of Christian Influence on Northern Algonkian Eschatology

The Issue

THERE IS A DIVISION OF OPINION AMONG SCHOLARS concerning the extent of Christian influence on North American Indians ideas of the hereafter, or "eschatology."[1] Are concepts about a retribution after death, a dual destiny to the next life, a division of the world hereafter into a happy paradise and a realm of terror, a heaven and an underworld, of Christian origin? Has the idea of a ruler in the next world a Christian prototype? Certainly, where there are specific Christian traits like the tormenting of sinners the problem may seem solved. However, this is not always the case, for such features as the transgression of taboos, the punishment of transgressions, and the confession of sins are part of North American Indian religions (on the breach of taboo, see Clements 1932: 203, map 1, 204 ff. On the confession of sins, see Pettazzoni 1931; Spier 1935: 8 n. 7; La Barre 1947: 302 ff. For the whole complex of beliefs involved, cf. Hultkrantz 1979d: 87 f.). Even the dualism between God and a bad spirit (or a less successful competitor

---

1. Eschatology is in this context not the doctrine of the doomsday and the end of time, but the conception of life after death. Here I follow the anthropological use of the term (cf., e.g., Wyman, Hill, and Ósanai 1942).

of God) exists in these religions, at least on a mythological level as is pointed out below.

Some references to earlier authors on the subject may demonstrate how the scholarly position has vacillated. George Catlin, an early observer of the Prairie and Plains Indians in particular, made the following sweeping statement: "I fearlessly assert to the world, (and I defy contradiction,) that the North American Indian is everywhere, in his native state, a highly moral and religious being, endowed by his Maker, with an intuitive knowledge of some great Author of his being, and the Universe; in dread of whose displeasure he constantly lives, with the apprehension before him, of a future state, where he expects to be rewarded or punished according to the merits he has gained or forfeited in this world" (Catlin 1841: 243).

Catlin was guided by his knowledge of Mandan and Choctaw eschatology and generalized accordingly. However, J. G. Müller, our first historian of religions, who had read Catlin's famous work (and severely criticized it), suggested a more rigid, evolutionistic interpretation. In his estimation the northern Indians represented the religious level of fetishism, which corresponded to afterlife conceptions that prolonged the earthly life into an indifferent future state. Only at a later stage of development did a brighter view on the next world develop, but it developed independently of moral evaluations (Müller 1855: 87 ff.).[2] Daniel Brinton, writing thirteen years later, brought up the question of Christianlike ideas in American Indian eschatology. He found very faint traces of any such belief. There was, he pointed out, no doctrine of a punishment in the next world, only a negative castigation of "the liar, the coward, or the niggard." As Brinton said, different fates awaited departed souls, but they were decided by their manner of death or by the punctuality with which burial rites were performed (Brinton 1868: 259 f.).[3] A missionary scholar, John McLean, wrote that little attention was paid to the possibility of hell and a personal devil, "the native intellect being more apt to dwell on the prospect of pleasure than pain" (McLean 1892: 110). At the turn of the century Washington Matthews, who had investigated Hidatsa and Navajo Indians, repeated the same point of view, implying that according to Navajo thinking any supernatural punishments would be enacted in this world (Matthews 1899: 5 f.). Other scholars also like

---

2. Concerning Müller's contributions to the study of North American religions, cf. Hultkrantz 1966–67b: 97.

3. There are, of course, also other criteria, such as age, social position, and divergent burial customs.

Hagar and Henshaw dismissed the retribution idea as an original native concept (Hagar 1908: 437; Henshaw 1905: 109; Henshaw 1910: 284). Finally, Lewis Spence, in his classic book on North American mythology, disclaimed the opinion that Indians should have embraced a belief in punishment after death: "Should a place of torment be discernible in any Indian mythology at the present day, it may unhesitatingly be classed as the product of missionary sophistication" (Spence 1914: 130).

We look in vain for similar general statements on native eschatology during the last sixty years, with the exception of my own writings (see in particular Hultkrantz 1977: 435 ff.; Hultkrantz 1979d: 135 ff.). Certainly, such penetrating scholars on the American Indian as Lowie and Radin give their verdict that the theory of rewards and punishments after death is of little consequence or completely lacking, but these authors then refer to the whole "primitive" field (Lowie 1934a: 307; Radin 1937: 285). The reason for this silence is that the historicistic thinking among anthropologists which broke through during the first two decades of this century skipped all regional generalizations that were not founded on historical and diffusional inferences (Hultkrantz 1967a). Sweeping judgments applying to humanity as a whole were however—most inconsequently—accepted.

There we stand. The time has come to return to the abandoned subject of the Christian impact on Indian ideas of life after death. It is a most important subject. An analysis of Indian conceptions of the hereafter in a temporal perspective should enable us to discover the changes in native thought brought about by Christianity. It should also possibly tell us whether ideas of retribution, dual destiny, and a master of the dead are due to Christian influences or not.[4] It is worth underlining the word "possibly," for any record of native eschatology presupposes, in the old days, the presence of contact with Christianity through the person of the writer. Indeed, Indian middlemen who listened to the Christian message might have diffussed it to their own or other tribes.

The Northern Algonkian Indians will be selected as our test group, for the following reasons: (1) the earliest records on North American Indian eschatology are (with few exceptions) found in the *Jesuit Relations* from the first half of the seventeenth century and concern Iroquoian and Algonkian groups; and (2) there are also late

---

4. Dual destination: dual in the sense used above. Reincarnation beliefs, important in themselves, will not be dealt with here.

documents from the nineteenth and twentieth centuries on Algonkian eschatology, thus offering us a good comparison of changes that have taken place.

General Remarks on the North Algonkians and Their Eschatology

By "Northern Algonkians" is here understood those Indians who belong to the first two tiers of the Central Algonkian languages, as recognized by Carl and Erminie Voegelin (Voegelin and Voegelin 1946: 181 ff. See the survey in Goddard 1978: 583 ff.). More specifically, they are the Cree-speaking Indians, or the Cree proper, the Tete de Boule, Mistassini, Montagnais, and Naskapi in Manitoba, Ontario, and Quebec, and the Ojibway-speaking Indians, including the Chippewa, Southeastern Ojibway, Saulteaux, Ottawa, Mississauga, Nipissing, and Algonkin in northern Minnesota and Wisconsin, Manitoba, Ontario, and the southernmost part of Quebec. Excluded are those Cree- and Ojibway-speaking Indians who live in the Plains area, that is, the Plains Cree in Saskatchewan, Alberta, and Montana, and the Bungi or Plains Ojibway of Manitoba, Saskatchewan, North Dakota, and Montana. The Potawatomi of Michigan were once close to the Southeastern Ojibway but associated themselves with the Fox group —third tier of Central Algonkian languages—in historical times.

The area encompassed is thus, roughly, Canada east of Lake Manitoba and south of the tundra to the St. Lawrence River and Straight of Belle Isle.[5] The Ojibway, Cree, and Naskapi hold most of this area. Ecologically it may be defined as a Subarctic Region covered by the coniferous forest or taiga that stretches from Scandinavia and northern Russia over Siberia into North America (cf. Kroeber 1939: 95 ff.). Because of the harsh climate subsistence in bygone days was by hunting and fishing; only in the south, among the southern Ojibway, has there been some maize cultivation. The northernmost agriculturists were the Ottawa, Nipissing, and Algonkin.

The culture of most Northern Algonkians was therefore one of Subarctic hunters (cf. Spencer and Jennings 1965: 397 ff.; and Graburn and Strong 1973: 6 f.). Characteristic features of their culture were hunting and fishing, the use of snowshoes, toboggans, birchbark canoes, sewn skin-clothing, domelike or conical tents of bark

---

5. The Beothuk have been excluded here since their affiliations to the Algonkians is uncertain.

or skin, wooden or birch-bark vessels, patrilineal or bilateral family group organization and a weak band-chief authority.[6] In the religious sphere we notice several circumpolar features like hunting conceptions (masters of the animals, animal ceremonialism) and hunting magic and divination (scapulimancy, etc.), worship of sacred places (stones, mountains, lakes, etc.), a lofty world-view (heaven as a tent, etc.), shamanism (including the shaking tent rite), and a conception of life after death analogous to that of the surrounding Subarctic world and the village life (Hultkrantz 1965b: 302–313). In addition, each ethnic group developed some peculiarities of its own. For instance, the Cree were frightened of a cannibal being, *windigo* or *witigo*, and the Naskapi held the belief that their free-soul ("Great Man") acted as a guardian spirit (cf. Teicher 1960; Speck 1935: 41 ff.; Hultkrantz 1953: 374 ff.).

The first missionaries despatched to the Northern Algonkians were the Jesuits. In 1611 they had already reached the Abnaki Indians in Maine (Kenton, ed. 1954: xxiii, xxviii f.). A mission was established in 1632 at Quebec for the Montagnais, later followed by missions at Tadoussac, Three Rivers, and other places where Montagnais could be found. Missions at Quebec (Sillery) and Montreal, founded in 1637 and 1641, respectively, served Algonkin and Ottawa Indians (Kenton, ed. 1954: xxx ff.). The Mission at La Pointe, created in 1665, became a center for Father Allouez's activities among Huron and Algonkian groups. From there he founded missions at Green Bay and Sault Ste. Marie among Ojibway and Ottawa Indians. His successor, Father Marquette, established the large mission at Point St. Ignace, across from Mackinaw, where Ojibway and Ottawa received their Christian education (Kenton, ed. 1954: xliv ff.).

The outcome of these missionary enterprises is partly visible in the documents on native eschatological beliefs.

The first scholar to discuss the Christian impact on ideas of the afterlife among the Algonkian tribes was Laetitia Moon Conard who at the turn of the century wrote a paper on this subject (Conard 1900). In her opinion it is in the myths, and not in the rites, that one perceives the changes in beliefs. New ideas reveal their foreign extraction in the imperfect way in which they have been integrated with native beliefs, or they mix in a strange way with aboriginal conceptions. Conard mentions among foreign ideas the distinction between a paradise for the good and a hell for the bad, the Supreme Being as a

---

6. Some of these elements were circumpolar. Cf. Kroeber 1939: 101. For a detailed account of tribal cultures, see Jenness 1934: 270–87.

judge of the souls after their moral fulfillments, and an easy journey for all children to the other world. Conard testifies to the ease with which Indians have embraced Christian notions. Her whole reasoning is otherwise shrouded in an old-fashioned evolutionistic perspective that we may disregard (Conard 1900: 224 ff.).

Conard continues by stating that the realm of the dead was usually situated somewhere on earth, and that the idea of double realms of the dead was not characteristic for Algonkian eschatology, if this idea belonged to it at all before the European influence set in. The author goes on to say that in some reports only one realm of the dead is ascribed to a tribe, while in others two realms are mentioned or we are faced with contradictory statements (Conard 1900: 251).

It thus emerges from Conard's discussion that the doctrine of two realms of the dead among Algonkian tribes was most probably of Christian extraction. The occasional idea of the Supreme Being as a judge (according to a belief among the Cree) conveys the same impression. Conard refers to myths as her main source of information. It is true that many myths (and legends) provide us with rich materials on Indian eschatology as, for instance, the Orpheus tale which was distributed among Algonkian tribes (Alexander 1916: 49 f.; Gayton 1935: 274 f.; Hultkrantz 1957: 31, 41 f., and passim). However, our best sources are the so-called memorates and the reflective or traditional belief statements ("religious sayings") (see Honko 1964; Hultkrantz 1968a). A perusal of Conard's material shows that she has in fact made use of these two latter categories.

The problem of the Christian impact on Algonkian eschatology was reopened by Regina Flannery almost four decades later. Flannery, who evidently did not know Conard's investigations, noticed that there was a "differential treatment in after life according to socio-moral conduct on earth" among Coast Algonkian, Huron, and Iroquois Indians (Flannery 1939a: 162). "It is possible," she wrote, "that the emphasis on differential treatment according to socio-moral conduct, as recorded for the coastal Algonquian and later Huron-Iroquois, may be due to Christian influence, although Swanton ... states that rewards and punishments are sometimes mentioned for Southeastern peoples, but not much stress is placed upon them" (Flannery 1939a: 163). Flannery did not include the Northern Algonkians in her research.

Other scholars who have investigated particular cultures, such as Cooper on the Cree and Kohl and Hallowell on the Ojibway, have been less outspoken on the development of eschatological ideas. Their opinions are discussed in what follows.

The Oldest Descriptions

The first written accounts of the eschatology of the Indians of New France—we are uncertain as to what Indians—are to be found in the first records of the *Jesuit Relations*, 1610–13. Father Joseph Jouvency wrote: "They believe that the appointed place for souls, to which after death they are to retire, is in the direction of the setting sun, and there they are to enjoy feasting, hunting, and dancing; for these pleasures are held in the highest repute among them. When they first heard of the eternal fire and the burning decreed as a punishment for sin, they were marvelously impressed; still, they obstinately withheld their belief because, as they said, there could be no fire where there was no wood; then, what forests could sustain so many fires through such a long space of time? This absurd reasoning had so much influence over the minds of the savages, that they could not be persuaded of the truth of the gospel." It was when a Jesuit priest threw some sulphur—which the Indians thought was earth—on coals, and it started to burn, that the startled red men first "believed in the word of God that there is a lower world" (Thwaites, ed. 1896–1901, 1: 289–91).

Here is, then, a reference to "the happy hunting grounds"—a true aboriginal conception, whatever anthropologists say (La Farge 1956: 51; Stirling 1955: 41; cf. the motivations adduced in Kohl 1859a, 1: 282 ff.)—and a clear testimony of the absence of every idea of post-mortal retribution. A few years later, however, Father Pierre Biard had the following to say: "They have an incoherent and general idea of the immortality of the soul and of future reward and punishment: but farther than this they do not seek nor care for the causes of these things" (Thwaites, ed. 1896–1901, 3: 135). It is, of course, possible to interpret this information as a proof of a native, or recently acquired, idea of retribution. But we have other alternatives as well. We may question the semantics of "reward and punishment": perhaps the Indians referred to social differentiation—according to rank, manner of death, etc.—after death. Or, they may cautiously and courteously have simply nodded to whatever suggestions their white brothers asked for. An early belief, testified to already in 1636, assigns one realm of the dead to the whites, and another to Indians. Said one Algonkin Indian to the missionaries, "You people are sure of going up yonder. Well and good, go there, then; each one loves his own people; for my part, I shall go and find mine" (Thwaites, ed. 1896–1901, 8: 271).

The probable conclusion is that ideas of hell and paradise had, at first, little chance of being accepted by the Indians who preferred to draw a demarcation line between their realm of dead and that of the faithful Christians. However smoothly Indians absorbed Christian ideas, according to Conard's judgment, they were not so willing to accept the idea of a hell where people were punished for all eternity (cf. Hallowell 1940: 35 f.).

Montagnais-Naskapi Eschatology

The first Algonkian eschatology mentioned in detail in the *Jesuit Relations* is that of the Montagnais. The raconteur is the famous Jesuit Father Paul Le Jeune, and the year is 1634.

Le Jeune gives a vivid description of the questions he posed and the answers he received. We are told that the dead go to a large village situated where the sun sets.[7] During their long journey, which they make on foot, they live on bark and old wood that they find in the forests. After arrival there they spend the day as a night and the night as a day. During the daytime they rest, leaning their elbows upon their knees, and holding their heads between their hands, the usual position when people are sick. In the night, which is a day to them, they go hunting: "They hunt for the souls of Beavers, Porcupines, Moose, and other animals, using the soul of the snowshoes to walk upon the soul of the snow, which is in yonder country; in short, they make use of the souls of all things, as we here use the things themselves" (Thwaites, ed. 1896–1901, 6: 177–79).[8]

When the missionary told the Indian about retribution, heaven, and hell, the red man retorted, "In that you lie, you people, in assigning different places for souls,—they go to the same country, at least, ours do; for the souls of two of our countrymen once returned from this great village, and explained to us all that I have told thee; then they returned to their dwelling place" (Thwaites, ed. 1896–1901, 6: 181).

It is perfectly clear from this presentation of the other world that it represented a prolongation of the life on earth, a continued Montagnais existence on the other side of the grave. At the same time, it was upside down, day and night changing places—a conception that we meet quite often in North and South America and in northern Eurasia as well (cf. Alexander 1916: 276; Koch-Grünberg

---

7. The dead are supposed to follow the Milky Way which is therefore called the path of souls (see Thwaites, ed. 1896–1901, 6: 181).

8. A famous and often quoted passage in comparative religion.

1920: 297 f.; Holmberg 1925). This inversion of things stands for the otherness of the next world, its supernatural quality. Moreover, the use of phrases like "souls of beavers" supports this point. The position of the realm of the dead at the very end of the world is a quantitative expression on the same qualitative diversity.

Now, this realm, apparently a fairly happy hunting ground, was the destiny of everybody except, possibly—said the Montagnais informant—the whites. There was positive evidence that no retribution occurred after death, for two dead Indians had returned in a dream and told their living countrymen.[9] The pattern is obvious: a differential eschatology could hold good for the whites but had no validity for the Indians.

The Montagnais comprise the southernmost local groups of the Naskapi, and there is no reason to construct a division into Naskapi and Montagnais.[10] As Frank Speck has noted, since the Jesuit fathers wrote their impressions of the spiritual life among the inhabitants of Labrador, practically nothing was reported until Speck himself issued his study of Naskapi religion (Speck 1935: 15).[11] Speck's information on Naskapi eschatology is somewhat at variance with what the Jesuits were told: "That the abode of souls of the deceased is in the sky, that they manifest themselves there in the form of stars, that they travel over the Milky Way, that they congregate in a dance and illuminate the night sky as the northern lights, are indications of the fundamental eschatology of the peoples of the Northeast" (Speck 1935: 50 f.; cf. Tanner 1944: 690). Flannery, besides pointing out that the northern lights are the dead dancing, says that there was practically no interest in life after death, and that non-Christian natives today are very vague on this point (Flannery 1946: 269).

In actual fact, the difference between Le Jeune and Speck is probably very slight. We noted that even the Jesuit talked about the travels of the new dead over the Milky Way, a concept hardly compatible with the idea of a journey over land to a distant country. Here we may trace two trends of thought on life after death coexisting in the same people, in the same individual: the more prosaic conception of

9. On the whole the North American Indians based their ideas of the supernatural on personal mysterious experiences, dreams, and visions (cf. Benedict 1923b: 23 ff.).

10. I am quite aware of the genetic and physical differences between the Naskapi and the Montagnais, but I see no reason to separate them on this account as Dyke has done (Dyke 1970: 47). Traditions, culture, and language are shared by both ethnic divisions.

11. Cf. the poor information in Turner 1894: 271 f., 342.

travelling over land, nourished by visionary or dream experiences, and the more poetic idea of a skyway, associated with cosmic—or cosmological—meditation.[12] This is not more surprising than the fact that a bereaved Christian mother can imagine her dead child to be sometimes in the grave, and sometimes in heaven. Religious beliefs form different segments, as I have attempted to demonstrate in some earlier works (Hultkrantz 1972a: 349 ff.).

The notion that the dead sing and dance in the realm of the dead is common all over North America.[13] It is, for instance, a frequent feature in the Orpheus theme (cf. Hultkrantz 1957: 106 n. 86). The combination between the dead and the northern lights is, of course, an Arctic-Subarctic invention.[14]

Speck mentions that the dying Naskapi expect to meet, in the next life, the high god or "Great Spirit," *Tce'möntu* (Speck 1935: 78). This sounds Christian, however, and a Christian reworking of an older concept of god seems most probable (Speck 1935: 37). The *Jesuit Relations* do not indicate that the high god was associated with the world of the dead.

Our investigation of Montagnais-Naskapi eschatology over time has demonstrated that it remained virtually the same, until the present, except for the presence of the high-god concept. However, independently of this the missionaries managed to convert the Indians, at least formally, so that they now also embrace the Catholic ideas of heaven and hell (Speck 1935: 32). The theory of religious segmentation, just referred to, could explain why pagan and Christian conceptions of the afterlife survive side by side.

Cree Eschatology

The trouble with the reliable Cree source material is that it is so recent. In the oldest available records from the seventeenth century, the *Jesuit Relations*, there is practically no information concerning Cree views on afterlife. The first more explicit statements emanate, as far as I can judge from the so-called Clerk of California, who spent the

12. Werner Müller considers that cosmic visual patterns are the particular heritage of the Central Algonkians (Müller 1961: 202).

13. I have gone through most published sources on the subject of eschatology in North America and consider myself consequently qualified to make this statement.

14. We do, however, also find the same conception among the Siouan Mandan and Omaha, and possibly, in a Californian Yokuts Orpheus legend (Hudson 1902: 105).

winter of 1746–47 at York Factory (then Fort Nelson). A confusing mixture of native and Christian beliefs is readily observable in his report. At death, he tells us, the fugitive soul reaches a big river. The good pass it to go to a happy land, but the wicked go to a barren land, full of rocks (The Clerk of California 1748–49: 40 ff.).[15] This differentiation of fates after death certainly reflects Christian influence. Jesuit missions existed on James Bay since 1672 and continued to exert an influence on York Factory up to 1696, when the English deported Father Marest. Missionary work was resumed in the 1840s by Wesleyans, the Oblate Fathers, and others (Cooper 1933: 102 f.).

A garbled "Christian" eschatology is also reflected in an obscure account from 1830. According to the latter, the dying person is protected by the Good Spirit on his journey to the world beyond, unless he has been burned alive at the stake in which case he goes to hell (Jones 1830, 1: 268 f.). The mutual attraction of the ideas, burning and tortured prisoners on one hand, burning and being tortured in hell on the other, has here formed a strange eschatology.[16] We notice that a "good spirit" is here in charge of the travel to the land of the blessed. In the Clerk of California's narrative there is no mention of any *manitou*.

Unreliable as these sources are, they bring testimony of a strong Christian impact. However, we may catch some glimpses of more original beliefs. Thus the concept of the northern lights as the dancing dead in the other world was noted down by Umfreville near the end of the eighteenth century (Umfreville 1790: 190). Furthermore, the Plains Cree—who may have separated from the main body of Cree about 1700—depict a country of the dead that is very similar to that of the Montagnais: a world of green grass on the other side of the Milky Way, a country where all departed Cree live a carefree life (Mandelbaum 1940: 251).[17] If we change the prairie grass for the woodland trees, we have what seems to be a realistic picture of the afterworld of the Eastern Cree.

An indirect proof that the precontact Cree lacked the idea

---

15. According to a tradition of a visit of a man to the other world recorded by Hind, the river separates the beautiful country of the south from the trist country of the north (cf. Hind 1860, 2: 129 f.).

16. This is at variance with David Thompson's information that the Cree did not believe in the flames of hell (Thompson 1916: 78).

17. It should be pointed out, however, that in other descriptions of the future life the Plains Cree emphasize the prairie life but also make a distinction between this existence, under the First Ancestor, and a dark, underground existence under the rule of the Evil Spirit—quite obviously a Christian elaboration (cf. Dusenberry 1962: 99 f.).

of retribution, heaven, and hell may be found in the belief, noted by the artist Paul Kane in 1848, that the Christians have a realm of their own to which an Indian might risk coming if he has converted; such an afterlife, of course, a true Cree Indian would resent since it would disrupt his communion with his own people (Kane 1925: 276 f.). As we have observed, such a distinction between a Christian and an Indian afterworld represents a resistance to the Christian doctrine of retribution.

Cree postmortal beliefs as held fifty years ago were investigated by John Cooper, learned anthropologist and theologist. It was primarily the James Bay Cree that caught his attention. Summarizing the evidence he writes, "The concept of the soul and of the future life was very vague. There seems to have been no idea of reward or punishment in the future life. At most some kind of survival was believed in, as evidence, for instance, by the common saying that the northern lights are the dead dancing. The dead did not go to the Supreme Being" (Cooper 1933: 79, cf. 106). The last statement was confirmed by all Cooper's informants (cf. Cooper 1933: 50, 54, 62). Cooper also found that the notion of souls crossing a river to arrive at the land of the dead was unknown (Cooper 1933: 50).

How should this be interpreted? Perhaps as follows. Firstly, present-day Cree have largely forgotten their old eschatology. Cooper certainly claims that the Cree kept their old theism intact (they "drew a sharp line of demarcation between what in their present Christian belief was pre-Christian and what was not") (Cooper 1933: 106). However, the old eschatology must have succumbed in face of the more dramatic Christian eschatology, and only vague traits of the old conceptions of afterlife remain. Secondly, considering the enormous territory held by the Cree, the infusion of Ojibway ideas (the Ojibway took over much of the Cree hunting grounds in Manitoba as a consequence of the fur trade), local Christian influences, migratory mythological motifs, and possible misapprehensions by white traders and missionaries, it is only natural that records of Cree eschatology are varying in content and are even contradictory.

It cannot be proved, but there is every probability that in precontact days the Cree had a picture of the realm of the dead more or less coinciding with that of the early Montagnais.

Ottawa Eschatology

The Ottawa and Ojibway Indians are, as far as we know, the only Northern Algonkian Indians who have known versions of the Orpheus tale. This is perhaps one of the reasons why these Indians have more vivid, exact, and detailed accounts of life after death than their congeners. Another reason may be the fact that the whites came closer to and knew more about these Indians than other Northern Algonkians. After all, we only know the older Northern Algonkian eschatology through the whites.

The Ottawa Orpheus tale—the legend of the White Stone Canoe—was not recorded until Schoolcraft wrote it down in the last century (Schoolcraft, ed. 1851–60, 1: 321–23).[18] The earliest eschatological descriptions of the Ottawa have, however, come down to us through three sixteenth-century authors, Nicholas Perrot, Peter Esprit Radisson, and Antoine de la Mothe Cadillac, the founder of Detroit in 1701.

Perrot's account concerns, it is true, "all the savages who are not converted," but primarily the Ottawa from 1665 to 1699. Perrot tells us that, according to the Ottawa's own testimony, the basis of their beliefs is the tradition that once some of their ancestors had reached the farthest limit of the earth, and passed into the other world, they experienced its pleasures and the friendliness of its inhabitants, but were sent back by the latter since they were not dead yet (Blair, ed. 1911: 92). According to the report of these travellers the land of the dead is beautiful and fertile—the Ottawa were partly agriculturists—has an agreeable climate, and abounds with animals and birds of every kind; as a result, the hunter need never feel any hunger. The dead are happily dancing there, without sorrow, anxiety or the vicissitudes of mortal life (Blair, ed. 1911: 89, 91).

Before attaining this *Schlaraffenland* the dead must, however, pass through certain ordeals. They have to cross a very rapid river, and the only bridge over it is a tree trunk which bends so much that now and then a soul is swept away by the waters and drowned. Young, vigorous people have nothing to fear, but decrepit old people and small infants may perish. Another obstacle is two rising and falling pestles; the person who, in making his passage, is caught between them suffers destruction.[19] Again it is the old and the small children that run this risk (Blair, ed. 1911: 89 ff.).

It is interesting to find that, according to Perrot, the Ottawa also think that the white men have a different country for their dead (Blair, ed. 1911: 92).[20]

18. There are also other versions of this tale in other works by Schoolcraft (see Hallowell 1946: 148; and also McLean 1892: 180 f.).

19. This is the falling and rising horizon, the Symplegades motif (cf. Hultkrantz 1957: 79 f.).

20. There is a story among the Ottawa and Ojibway about a Christian Indian who was neither admitted to the Indian or the Christian realms of the dead (Feest and

Radisson who traded with the Indians between 1652 and 1684 has a similar tale to tell. The deceased person passes through a thick, thorny wood and crosses the big river on a plank that rises and falls all the time. A giant by the river strikes him with a dagger, cutting him in two halves. If the deceased person has been valiant in life the two halves join again on the other side of the bridge. Then there is a new, big forest to traverse for five days. Thereafter, the dead person has to walk through a fire; if he has loved his woman and been a good huntsman, he will pass through it unhurt. Next, he enters a wood where the slain enemies lie on the ground. Finally, dead ancestors come to meet him, and a feast is arranged for the newcomer to the happy land. There follow dancing and sexual delights (Radisson 1885: 236 ff.).[21]

Cadillac's account is brief and clear. The land of the dead, he says, is a fine country, abounding in strawberries and raspberries as large as a man's hand: "They think this region is toward the east, that the air is mild and temperate, that there is no rain, snow, nor wind there, no rocks nor mountains, and all the paths are paved with robes of otter, marten, and beaver; in a word, that it is a land of pleasure, where one never has to bear hunger or thirst, and all are equally happy. They absolutely deny the existence of places where souls are tortured and reject the opinion of the resurrecton of the body" (Kinietz 1940: 296 f., quoting Cadillac, "Relation on the Indians," ms., Edward Ayer Collection, Newberry Library, Chicago).

The characteristic features of these three descriptions of the afterlife are the dramatic journey to the world beyond, in particular the swinging log over the river, and the lyric accounts of the beauty and pleasures of that world—a world for everybody, irrespective of behavior on this earth. We may here make a distinction between the journey and the land of the dead. The former may initially have had its origin in psychic experiences during trance and coma, but its colorful contents are folkloristic motifs that have migrated over wide areas. The swinging or bending log motif, for instance, is a common theme in North America.[22] The concept of the land of the dead, on the other

---

Feest 1978: 783, and there adduced literature; Hallowell 1940: 36). The Feests think the story was spread by missionaries. I think that, on the contrary, anti-Christian and traditional forces lay behind it.

21. A confused and incoherent presentation which I have tried to make more lucid here.

22. I have found it present among practically all the Algonkian tribes of the Eastern Woodlands south of the Canadian border, Ojibway-Saulteaux, Ottawa, Potawatomi, Menomini, Sauk and Fox, Miami, and Shawnee. There is also information

hand, is less influenced by migratory motifs and more formed by existing cultural, social, and natural premises in the tribal unit. The Ottawa land of souls comes close to the Montagnais one. Both seem to belong to what could be called "a primeval Algonkian eschatological pattern."

The Orpheus legend from the nineteenth century (but certainly as such antedating this century) has, in the form it was written down by Schoolcraft, a slightly different eschatology. The long journey is there, although it is to the south, not east. There is a body of water to pass over, and there is, in the middle of it, the island of the blessed with all imaginable joy and beauty. However, the passage over the water is made in canoes, and storms and waves crash the canoes of people whose thoughts and acts have been bad; their bones cover the bottom of the water. It is the Master of Life who allows good people, and all little children, to pass into the blessed land. It is also the Master of Life who, although invisible, orders the living person— "Orpheus"—to return to the living.[23]

Thus after the first accounts of life after death had been written by three authors in the seventeenth century, a reformation of eschatology took place. The new elements were—besides the already extant motif of crossing the water in a canoe, a motif that exists as a parallel phenomenon to the crossing on a plank among many of the tribes, and perhaps is archaic—a kind of retribution idea and the presence of the Supreme Being in the land of the dead. The particular care for small children should also be noted. It is interesting that the passage over the water, the boundary between this world and the other one, has become the test by which the separation of the virtuous from the nonvirtuous takes place. In several other tribes where the plank-over-river motif occurs, the bad people are said to fall off

---

on the same motif among part of the Cree (Franklin 1823: 70). Of the Coast Algonkians only the Lenape (Delaware) seem to have known it. The Huron and Iroquois were familiar with the motif. It also appears in other cultural areas, the Southeast (Cherokee, Choctaw, Seminole), Prairies and Plains (Iowa, Dakota, Hidatsa, Pawnee, Caddo), the Plateau (Carrier, Thompson, Lillooet), the Northwest Coast (Tsimshian, Coast Salish, Quinault), and California (Pomo, Nisenan, Miwok, Yokuts, Mono). Of these tribes the Carrier say the bridge is a snake, and the Ojibway and Menomini trunk bridge is often transformed into a snake. Bridges over chasms are mentioned among the Chickasaw and Natchez of the Southeast and the Bear River Indians and Yurok in California. The Winnebago west of the Great Lakes believe there is a bridge over a huge fire. See also footnote 26 below.

    23. There is a similar tale, but without the Orpheus motif, among the Athapascan Chipewyan north of the Cree (Schoolcraft 1851–60, 5: 173 f.).

the bridge.[24] No doubt we are here facing a change of the story inspired by Christian values. Most probably an older thought has been replaced, the thought that wrong measures like irregular burial, or no burial at all, caused the fall from the bridge.[25] In the same way, the drowning of bad people in the Ottawa legend most probably reflects Christian ideas. So also does the concept of the presence of the Supreme Being in the realm of the dead, and of his aid to small children.

Ojibway-Saulteaux Eschatology

There are plenty of descriptions in the literature of the Ojibway land of the dead, but unfortunately they mostly date from fairly recent times. This means that they are all more or less portraying an afterworld that has been colored by Christian ideas. Because of the southern position of many Ojibway they also evince the integration of Ojibway eschatology with the myth of the divine twins characteristically elaborated in the Medicine Society of the southern Central Algonkians.

It is possible, however, to use the seventeenth-century sources for the Ottawa as testimony of Ojibway eschatology, for two reasons: (1) these sources are without tribal designation, although most experts consider them to be primarily dealing with the Ottawa; (2) the name Ojibway is very inclusive, and the Ottawa may be regarded as a subgroup of the Ojibway. It is even possible to mobilize a third argument, namely, that there is no basic difference between the old Ottawa descriptions of the afterworld and those of the Ojibway in later time, if retribution ideas and the concept of the lord of the dead are disregarded.

An English trader who in 1764 witnessed the burial of an Ojibway child on the northern shore of Lake Superior stated that their ideas of future life "were somewhat different in different individuals." To some, he said, the soul remains in this world, invisible; to others it leaves for a distant country where "it receives reward or

24. This is the case among some Saulteaux (see below), the Menomini, Sauk and Fox, Hidatsa, Cherokee, Choctaw, Seminole, Pomo, Yokuts, and Mono.
25. Irregular death rituals have determined such a fate among the Miami (Kinietz 1940: 209) and Winnebago (Radin 1920: 453, and n. 232).

punishment, according to the life which it has led in its prior state." The virtuous people go to a lovely land abounding with deer and other animals and the sweetest fruits. The bad ones, on the other hand, are removed to a barren country filled up with rocks, morasses, and stinging, gigantic gnats (Henry 1809: 151 f.).

Christian ideas of retribution had thus been accepted at this time. They recur again and again in eschatological descriptions from later times but, curiously enough, they do not stand alone.

In Peter Grant's memories of the Saulteaux in 1804 we are told that good people go southward to a delightful place stocked with fine game. Here, on the banks of a beautiful river, they are received by the Great Spirit, who is the judge of mankind. Wicked people are transferred to the Evil Spirit who lives under the earth in a wretched dungeon swarming with serpents. The good people enjoy every pleasure, the bad people endure great misery. The judgment takes place at the river of death where the souls have to cross the river on a narrow pole. Burdened with all their bad deeds in a bundle on the back the wicked people fall in the river and are swept away to the Evil Spirit's dominion. The good ones pass over and arrive in the blessed land "where husbands live with their wives and children, where society exists as it did before death" (Grant 1890: 354 f.).

We notice that the judgment, has been equalized with the ordeal of passing the river of death. The dualism between God and devil is, of course, Christian. However, these polar concepts may have been built on an earlier idea of two mythological beings, the divine twins, who had, in part, culture hero features. The younger twin was drowned by the underwater monsters and became the ruler of the land of the dead (cf. Fisher 1946: 240 f. For a general perspective, see Hultkrantz 1979d: 32 ff., in particular 39 ff.).

In a letter of January 31, 1822, the Indian agent (at Mackinac), George Boyd, adduces the retribution doctrine but says that good and bad people nevertheless go the same place, ruled by the Great Spirit. The wicked people have to suffer there from the sins they have committed on earth. Most interestingly, the world will be destroyed in a great conflagration, followed by a day of judgment (Kinietz 1947: 164, quoting Boyd, "Letter to Lewis Cass," Michigan Superintendency Letterbook, 1, 1822, National Archives). This is indeed eschatology in the theological sense of the term.

William Keating, a member of Long's expedition to Manitoba in 1823, seems in the main to agree with Boyd. The dead arrive at a stream which they have to cross on a large snake that serves as a bridge.[26] Those who have died from drowning fall into the river and remain there forever.[27] All the rest proceed to the land of the dead which is situated to the south, on the shores of the ocean. Here the good people spend a time of leisure, dancing, singing, and feeding upon mushrooms that are very abundant. The wicked persons, however, are haunted by the persons they have injured. Thus, "If a man has destroyed much property, the phantoms of the wrecks of this property obstruct his passage wherever he goes; if he has been cruel to his dogs or horses, they also torment him after death; the ghosts of those, whom during his life-time he wronged, are there permitted to avenge their injuries" (Keating 1825, 2: 154 f.).

In both Boyd's and Keating's reports the retribution finds place within the confines of one and the same realm of the dead.

Several documents on Ojibway eschatology date from the middle of the last century. Curiously enough these late sources deal with one, indivisible land of the dead, a place of happiness. William Warren, an Ojibway half-breed and theologist, tells us how the soul follows a wide, beaten path towards the west. It eats from the big strawberries along the path and reaches the rapid stream over which is lying the rolling and sinking bridge. After four days' travel it arrives in the land of spirits. There is game in abundance, dancing, and rejoicing. All departed relatives are congregated and greet the new arrival with gladness (Warren 1885: 73 f.; Warren, in Schoolcraft, ed. 1851–60, 2: 135). Schoolcraft, in whose great work on the Indians much of this information is included, also quotes a legend in which the beauty and the rich fauna of the happy land of the dead are mentioned (Williams, ed. 1956: 180 f.). He also imparts the information that Chebiabose, the brother of the culture hero, is the keeper of the country of souls (Schoolcraft, ed. 1851–60, 5: 149).

The most exhaustive description of this country has been given by the German explorer J. G. Kohl. An Ojibway drew a sketch

26. This snake may, of course, be interpreted, as some authors have done, as the mythical underworld monster so frequent in Algonkian (and North American) belief traditions. However, it may also be an interpretation of the fact that the bridge swings up and down, and this feature may—or may not—have relation to the Symplegades motif (cf. footnote 19 above).

27. Kinietz discredits this information which "was not reported by any other writer of his day for the Chippewa" and, he continues, cannot be substantiated in later beliefs (Kinietz 1947: 65). He is mistaken. In a book first printed in 1850 Susanna Moodie writes that a Mississauga who has drowned is not permitted to pass into the tribal realm of the dead but haunts the lake or river where he lost his life (Moodie 1870: 302; also Chamberlain 1888: 158).Cooper found in recent times an Ojibway woman at Lake of the Woods who gave the same information (Cooper 1936: 6).

for him of the way there with a pencil on a piece of paper and explained the details.[28] He pointed out how a dead person should avoid on his path the gigantic, sweet strawberries growing there, for otherwise he would be "lost."[29] After some three or four days the traveller meets the broad river over which a big tree trunk is stretched. It swings up and down, and many people fall into the river and turn into toads or fishes. The small children are in particular danger. (Another informant told Kohl that the trunk really is a big, winding snake.) On the other side of the river is the land of souls, ruled over by Menaboshu, the culture hero. It is a very happy place; people there are always glad and spent their time dancing and eating mushrooms (Kohl 1859a, 1: 288 ff., 300 n.).[30]

Of particular interest is the informant's statement that Christian people have a paradise of their own to which Indians have no entry. Kohl drew the conclusion that the Indians had modelled the idea expressed in the existence of double burial places at the mission villages along the beaches of Lake Superior: the Christians had one burial place, the pagan Indians another (Kohl 1859a, 1: 290 f.). This was a shrewd observation, and it may be a correct conclusion. Kohl furthermore relates a dream that an Ojibway at Fond du Lac had. In a fever-dream he went toward the Christian paradise but left the trail and returned when he could not discover any marks from moccasins. Certainly, he did not want to go to the Christian paradise if his own people were not there (Kohl 1859a, 2: 75 f.).

It then follows that the Ojibway denied any discrimination between good and bad people; all go to the same place, "and we Indians do not know if the Great Spirit makes such a difference between good and bad people, and how he would do it" (Kohl 1859a, 1: 294).

Again, Peter Jones testifies from the same time that wicked people have a fate different from that of good people. Brave warriors,

28. His informant was apparently a member of the Medicine Society for whom only initiated members could obtain, for themselves and others, a safe journey to the next world (cf. Landes 1968: 189–90).

29. The danger in eating the strawberries has been emphasized in several descriptions of the journey to the other world, all of them from the Great Lakes area (Gayton 1935: 274 f.). The rationale behind this enigmatic motif seems to be that persons who eat of the food of the dead partake of their world and are thus lost to the living (see MacCulloch 1922: 653; Hultkrantz 1957: 114 f.). In other words, the fears of living shamans in a trance have been transferred to narratives of dead persons on their path to the land beyond the grave.

30. Other sources also mention that Menaboshu lives, with his brother, in the realm of the dead (cf. Jenness 1935: 38, 107 f.).

good hunters, and virtuous people go to the happy spirit-land. The cowards, the lazy hunters, misers, liars, thieves, fornicators, and uncharitable people, on the other hand, are forced to wander about in a dark place where they are attacked by wolves, mountain lions, and bears (Jones 1861: 102 ff.).

Apparently, two different eschatological traditions coexisted, one with a retribution doctrine, another without the latter but with the idea of a separate afterlife for Christians, that is, mostly whites.

A. P. Reid gives us interesting details on the doctrine of retribution. According to him the dead wander for four days until they reach the river of death. In the happy realm of the virtuous people there is no war. There are plenty of moose, and once you have killed one and taken out the choicest pieces of meat, it stands up again, sound and whole. The bad people have another realm, extremely cold and devoid of game; as a result, they go hungry there. Some of them try to cross the river to the realms of the blessed but are thrown back again. Those who have committed, what we consider, crimes against members of another tribe are not punished in the hereafter (Reid 1873: 110 ff.).[31]

Toward the end of the last century William Hoffman supplied more information on Ojibway ideas of the future life in his treatise on the Medicine Society (*midewiwin*). In the realm of death, "the land of the sleeping sun," where Shadow Spirit, or Ghost Spirit, rules, the men initiated into this society assemble in a spiritual counterpart to the *mide* lodge of the living, the Ghost Lodge. The Ghost Spirit presides in this lodge (Hoffman 1891: 163, 171, 241, 278 ff.).[32] In other words, people continue their role behavior in the other world.

The two conceptions of life after death, a realm for all, and two different realms for the good and the bad, occur in the ethnographic descriptions from the present century. The majority of these descriptions emphasize the universal realm of the dead (Hugolin 1907: 334; William Jones in Landes 1968: 190 f., 198 f.; Jones 1916: 382; Lowie 1922a: 457; Jones 1919, 2: 7 ff.; Jenness 1934: 281; Cooper 1936: 6; Coleman 1937: 56 f.; Flannery 1940: 22 f.; Hallowell 1940; Landes 1968:

---

31. The reference to the revivified moose is modelled on current belief patterns in animal ceremonialism (Hultkrantz 1979d: 141 ff.).

32. Jenness 1935: 42, however, describes the Shadow Spirit as a psychopomp (cf. Landes 1968: 189 ff.; Dewdney 1975: 103 ff., 128 f.). Cf. the comments by John Wesley Powell, head of the Bureau of Ethnology: "In Mr. Hoffman's paper it is seen that two and a half centuries of association with the white man has ... inculcated in the minds of the Ojibwa a clearer conception of a Great Spirit and a future life than is normal to the savage mind" (Powell 1891: xxxix).

190, 194, 196 ff.). The universality is not unconditional, however. Clearer than earlier accounts, these modern reports tell us that to gain a future life people must live correctly (Jones 1916: 388). This does not mean that there is a place for the wicked, but that those who do not conform to tribal ethical standards have to stay behind (Flannery 1940: 23; Cooper 1936: 6). Perhaps they turn into wandering ghosts, as is the case in many other North American eschatologies.[33] One investigator has observed that there is no association between the dead and the Supreme Being; "evidently the dead did not go to the Supreme Being" (Coleman 1937: 56, cf. 34 ff.). In some descriptions we meet the motif, mentioned above, that the world of the departed is upside down: it is activity during the night, but silence and passivity during the day (Jones 1919, 1: 11; Densmore 1929: 75; Jenness 1935: 108).

Some authors mention a differentiation of the afterworld along the heaven (or paradise)/hell axis. "The Northern Saulteux concept of the Hereafter is," says Alanson Skinner, "that there are two roads leading into the sky. One road is traversed by the souls of the good who travel there as fast as a bird can fly, immediately on leaving the body. Evil doers travel the other road on foot, very slowly and at last come to an evil place from which they cannot escape." Skinner adds that "there is a strong possibility that missionary influence has altered the original beliefs" (Skinner 1911: 160). Another approach to the retribution idea is illuminated by Cooper. The Rainy Lake Ojibway claim that the wicked reach the village of the dead just as the good do, but there is a special place for them, "a small lodge on the side, outside the village proper. They are not wanted among the village people" (Cooper 1936: 21).

Jenness quotes the legend of Ogauns' vision, a fantastic panorama of the splendor of heavens, where the Great Spirit reigns, and the dismal depths of the lower world where the wicked dead, in particular the rich, are tormented and repent their sins (Jenness 1935: 56 ff.). This is an Indian counterpart to Dante's *Divine Comedy*, and as such of some interest; but the Christian penetration is obvious, and there are few traces of indigenous Ojibway beliefs.

The most extensive descriptions of the land of the dead in modern times come from Diamond Jenness (the Parry Island Ojibway) and Irving Hallowell (the Berens River Saulteaux). They refer to

---

33. This is a difficult question, however. Jenness assures us that at death the Ojibway Indian's soul goes to the land of souls in the west, whilst his shadow "roams about on earth but generally remains near the grave" (Jenness 1935: 18, see also, however, 108. Cf. Hultkrantz 1953: 77 f., 476).

experiences had by persons who have visited the other world, vision-aries and unconscious sick people. Jenness also refers to the Orpheus tradition. The latter contains several motifs belonging to the journey beyond: a dog devouring those who have tormented dogs, the bridge moving up and down (the passage is safe if the traveller offers to-bacco), a barrier of fire that burns up sorcerers, a man who extracts the traveller's brain with a knife and stores it, the wigwam of Grand-mother Earth (whose grandchildren are the culture hero and the ruler of the dead (Jenness 1935: 109). Jenness observes that the jumble of beliefs among Parry Islanders are more or less in accordance with this narrative. The obvious exceptions to the rule are the Christian Indians who believe in a hereafter where people come together irrespective of race and speech (Jenness 1935: 110).

Among the Berens River Saulteaux, Hallowell found people who had been to the land of the dead during a serious disease or approached it in a dream. It is described by these travellers as a beautiful country, very bright, and with many flowers (Hallowell 1940: 32). As far as one can see, there are wigwams (Hallowell 1940: 30), and people shouting and laughing (Hallowell 1940: 31). It is a happy land in the south where no one has trouble in making a living, although in other respects life there duplicates life on earth (Hallowell 1940: 34).[34] The Supreme Being is in no way associated with this realm; its lord is another person, "the master of the dead" (Hallowell 1940: 35, 37, 39).[35]

This is, then, the old, undifferentiated land of the dead, a happy realm for everybody. Certainly, Hallowell also notes instances, in the case of one old man, of the belief in a double destination—good people go to the Great Spirit, bad to the Evil Spirit; but he rightly ascribes this belief to a partial assimilation of Christian ideas. As he states, beliefs regarding life after death "did not embody sanctions of any great importance with respect to man's daily conduct during life" (Hallowell 1940: 35 f.). Nevertheless, there are two parallel versions of the afterlife. If the version of the universal destination predominates at Berens River, it may be due to the fact that these Ojibway live fairly isolated in the northwest, in a land that they had colonized during beaver-trapping days.

Also, the Ojibway vacillate between a terrestrial and a celes-tial interpretation of afterlife (and, moreover, between these and a

34. The Northern Ojibway seem to locate the realm of the dead to the south, whereas the Southern Ojibway seek it mostly in the east or west.

35. Hallowell emphasizes that we are dealing with the same concept as that of the master or boss of animals (Hallowell 1940: 39).

reincarnation on earth). We are informed that the land of the departed spirits is not necessarily toward the west but "somewhere—as though in *space*" (Densmore 1929: 75). They travel there along the Milky Way (Jenness 1935: 109). They become stars there (Jenness 1935: 111). Or, the stars are the campfires of the dead (Hagar 1922: 69) or their peeping holes (Macfie 1944: 14). The northern lights represent the dancing dead in the world beyond (Hallowell 1940: 32) or a span of dogs sent by the powers to meet and escort the newly deceased (Macfie 1944: 15). Skinner suspects the sky-home of the dead reveals missionary influence (Skinner 1911: 160). However, this need not be the case, as will be demonstrated.

Conclusion

An effort will now be made to summarize the most important findings of this investigation, and some conclusions will be drawn. The main issue is, of course, the Christian influence on Northern Algonkian eschatology, but the original Algonkian ideas of the other world will also be discussed and tentatively reconstructed.

In his extremely generalizing statements on the religions of the Algonkian tribes, Father Wilhelm Schmidt, the well-known Austrian ethnologist, makes a distinction between an older religious layer where the hereafter is in heaven, associated with the Supreme Being, and only a home for the virtuous—this is the *Urkultur*—and a later religious layer where the dead live in the underworld toward the west under a chief of the dead—this is the matrilinear-animistic culture (Schmidt 1935, 6: 78). Our presentation has demonstrated that Schmidt's reconstruction is misleading and incorrect. Conard's exposition of Algonkian beliefs is far closer to the truth, even if it has some evolutionistic drawbacks.

Our perusal has shown that when first encountered by missionaries the Northern Algonkians knew no retribution after death. They were astounded when they heard about this idea. Their immediate answer was to construct a realm for the Christians (whites), different from their own. During the eighteenth century the idea of retribution gained ground, however,[36] and from then on, there are

---

36. Because of the shortness of space very little has been said about what constitutes the "bad," the "evil." In the main the values may not be too different from Christian values, or civil values in a modern society (cf. Hallowell 1940: 35 n. 3); but the ethics usually concern only one's own tribe and have no application outside the ethnic boundaries.

two parallel traditions, one distinguishing between two realms of the dead (one for the good, one for the wicked), and another perpetuating the pre-Christian concept of one universal realm. The latter seems to have been the one predominating during the last hundred years, probably because the tradition of dual destinations was absorbed by local Christian traditions. The believer were formally Christians, their beliefs vacillated between a Christian and a native interpretation.

Similarly, the concept of the Supreme Being was originally no part of Northern Algonkian eschatology. There was on the whole no master of the dead, except among the Ojibway and some Cree who had been caught into the myth-cycle around the culture hero and his slain brother. Christian impulses partly remodelled this master concept, so that the Supreme Being replaced the dead twin divinity, and partly installed the Supreme Being as chief of the dead, in particular, the virtuous dead.

This reconstruction of the emerging role of the Supreme Being in eschatology should not conceal the fact that the Supreme Being has been an important figure in the Northern Algonkian pantheon since—probably—pre-Christian times.

The structure of the Northern Algonkian conception of the realm of the dead seems fairly clear in our source material. This realm has a vague profile, as could be expected since it is difficult to verbalize beliefs that are so little anchored in surrounding reality and may become so conflicting. Eschatological beliefs contain ideas that are mutually exclusive: life in the hereafter—life as a reincarnated person on earth, life in heaven—life in the grave or as a ghost on earth, life in the south—life in the east or west, and so on. Two principles decide the structure of the realm of the dead:

1. The principle of analogy: the afterworld is a duplicate of the world of the living, but generally more satisfactory, happier than this world (cf. Hultkrantz 1957: 38 ff.). This principle means that the economic pursuits and the social differentiation of tribal existence on earth are perpetuated on the other side of the grave: chiefs remain chiefs, hunters continue hunting, etc. People who are excluded from the Indian village—thieves, murderers, and some others—may be excluded from the spirit village. They remain as ghosts on earth, or are destroyed.

2. The principle of transcendence: the dead are invisible, have day when we have night, or have different food, all these features being expressions of the radically different, supernatural quality of the other life. Another manifestation of the same principle is the transference, in mythology (for understanding of mythology, cf.

Hultkrantz 1979c: in particular 87 ff., 92), of the land of the dead to the sky. The march of souls over the Milky Way or their dancing in the northern lights gives a cosmic dimension to eschatological thought.

These two principles may conflict with one another—no record of a journey to the otherworld refers, as far as I know, to the Milky Way or the northern lights, but pious conviction does. Christian influence probably paved the way for a reconciliation between the two ways of conceiving of the destiny of souls, but this cannot be proved.

The tale of the journey to the otherworld is, as has been stressed above, an epic narrative and includes as such several migratory motifs which, however, can be related both to local mythology and individual Indians' personal experiences during deathlike states. In this connection it is of interest that in several of these tales the dangers on the journey function as mechanisms for weeding out unworthy people. Among the Parry Island Ojibway, for instance, they strike persons who have died before their time, or have not had a proper burial, or are sorcerers, or have tormented dogs (Jenness 1935: 108 ff. Cf. Landes 1968: 199).

This was the only form of retribution there was in pre-Christian times, unless we also include here the ostracism of socially unworthy individuals (thieves, murderers, etc.) who are banned in this life and continue to be banned in the next life: they become wandering ghosts. However, this is not a regular feature. In fact, among the Ojibway, retribution thinking was absent from human society, since there were no organized penal sanctions (Hallowell 1967: 361 f., 365).[37] Impulses from Christianity changed this pattern: the virtuous became separated from the wicked.

This change also implied that the small children who in former days had been so endangered during the journey to the otherworld were rescued by an act of mercy of the Supreme Being.

37. A later source from the Western Ojibway maintains that sinners fall into the river: certainly as Ruth Landes remarks, a Christian intrusion (Landes 1968: 197).

12

Tribal and Christian Elements in the Religious Syncretism among the Shoshoni Indians of Wyoming

RELIGIOUS SYNCRETISM, IN THE WIDER SENSE OF THIS TERM,[1] is an expression for cultural contact, and in most cases it presupposes an advanced acculturation, as it is the focus of culture, its value system which is influenced. Religious syncretism must therefore be analysed in its connections with the changes of the whole cultural system. These changes cannot be confined to the present time. Theoreticians of acculturation have, however, all too often categorically contrasted the acculturation process with a conjectured earlier, static, and "original" state. Even if one defines, as the present author has previously done, acculturation as "the process of change in complete culture-contact" (Hultkrantz 1960a: 17), it is obvious that throughout the ages acculturation has formed a continually recurring process amongst all peoples with the exception of the most isolated tribes in marginal areas.

---

1. Some authors identify syncretism and fusion, that is, complete religious amalgamation (cf. Dozier 1962: 164). In this article the word syncretism will be used to indicate the process of religious fusion, irrespective of the presence of fusion in its advanced sense.

The Shoshoni Indians of Wyoming, amongst whom I have had the privilege of conducting field work, have, since they were first noticed by white men, undergone a continuous process of acculturation, not least concerning religion.[2] Since being primitive seed-collectors and hunters in the Great Basin in a remote past they have, during the last centuries, been influenced by the Plateau and Plains cultures, European-American civilization and Pan-Indian revitalization movements, respectively. All these cultural changes are reflected in the religious history of the Shoshoni, such as this can be determined with the aid of archeological discoveries and combinations, ethnological distribution studies and historical documents.

Historical Survey

If we turn to the historical documents (to which in this connection we can even add ethnographical reports from later days as well as certain statements made by my Shoshoni informants) we can find evidence that during the first decades of the nineteenth century the Plains Indian Sun Dance was inserted into the Shoshoni ceremonial organization which, up to that time, probably had been rather poor. Some modern Shoshoni Indians say that the Sun Dance antedates the birth of Christ, a supposition which could possibly be inspired by the claim of the closely situated Arapaho Indians that they own the oldest Sun Dance. It may, however, also give expression to the conviction that as a divinely established ceremony, the Sun Dance must have been instituted in a very ancient, "mythical" age.

Other knowledgeable Shoshoni are, however, aware that the Shoshoni form of Sun Dance was introduced by the legendary chieftain and medicine-man, Yellow Hand (*Ohamagweia*).[3] According to tradition he received it in a vision, a feat which could be true. It is very likely that an old Basin Shoshoni annual ceremony was remodelled

2. In his outline of types of religious adjustment in North America Dozier (1962) suggests six different alternatives, from "rejection" to "fusion" and "stabilized pluralism." In the present author's opinion, it is difficult to pinpoint the Shoshoni situation in such terms since the progression of the acculturation process in this instance is not the same for each individual or each religious phenomenon. The perspective must here be more dynamic and less classificatory.

3. *Ohamagweia*, properly "he dipped his hands in yellow." He was probably identical with the Hiding Bear (d. 1842) mentioned by Russell (Russell 1955: 7, 115, 145). Cf. also Hultkrantz 1958: 150.

into the Sun Dance by the mediation of Yellow Hand, who had probably found the prototype among his former tribesmen, the Comanche
Indians, or among the Kiowa Indians.[4]

During the 1830s the same chief endeavored to introduce the
form of "Christianity" which he had observed in the Northwest practiced by the Flatheaad and Nez Percé Indians. Bonneville who, at this
time, visited both the Shoshoni and their neighbors in the north and
west, has the following to say concerning Yellow Hand's initiative:
"The senior chief of the Shoshonies was a thinking man, and a man of
observation. He had been among the Nez Perces, listened to their
new code of morality and religion received from the white men, and
attended their devotional exercises. He had observed the effect of all
this, in elevating the tribe in the estimation of the white men; and
determined, by the same means, to gain for his own tribe a superiority over their ignorant rivals, the Eutaws [=the Ute Indians in Colorado and Utah]. He accordingly assembled his people, and promul-
gated among them the mongrel doctrines and form of worship of the
Nez Perces; recommending the same to their adoption. The
Shoshonies were struck with the novelty, at least, of the measure,
and entered into it with spirit. They began to observe Sundays and
holidays, and to have their devotional dances, and chants, and other
ceremonials, about which the ignorant Eutaws knew nothing"
(Irving 1954: 341).

However, the opinion of Bonneville and the historians who
have quoted him that it was a more or less barbaric sort of Christianity
which was thus introduced among the Shoshoni, is incorrect (Spier
1935: 20, 21, 34. Cf., e.g., Trenholm and Carley 1964: 84 f.). As put
forward by Spier, it is certainly true that around 1820 a group of
Catholic Iroquois trappers had arrived in Flathead country (southwest
Montana) and slightly influenced the local religion with several Christian traits (Spier 1935: 30 ff., 64 f.).[5] These Christian elements, in the
first place the keeping of the Sabbath and kneeling when praying,
were, however, implanted into an already existing Plateau Indian
religious movement, the so-called Prophet Dance, and transformed
by the latter. According to Spier, the native traits have dominated. It
was this superficially Christianized Plateau religion which Yellow

---

4. Certain traditions assert that Bazil, adopted son of Lewis and Clark's
guide, Sacajawea, should have introduced the Comanche Sun Dance in the Fort
Bridger country. Sometimes even Sacajawea herself is mentioned as the bearer.

5. It may be that the Christian elements were introduced at an earlier date
(cf. Walker 1968: 31 ff.).

Hand tried to propagate, and no traditional form of Christianity.

We do not know what effect this religious revolution had upon the Shoshoni, but apparently it only touched their religion on the outside so that their inherited religious pattern remained intact.

During the summer of 1840 Yellow Hand's Shoshoni—"the Green River Snakes"—were visited by the well-known Catholic missionary, Pierre-Jean de Smet. His energetic drive captivated the Shoshoni, not least their chief, who took the opportunity of stipulating new and harder laws against theft (Chittenden and Richardson, eds. 1905, 1: 216 ff.). One can say that de Smet's mission work marks the beginning of a, certainly, rather weak and superifical Christianization. This process was probably simplified by the fact that already in the 1820s the Shoshoni Indians had taken up permanent relations with and finally mixed together with trappers (mountain men) who married Shoshoni girls. The most famous of these fur-hunters, James Bridger, took a Shoshoni Indian (Mary Washakie) as his third wife. His trading post, Fort Bridger, in southwest Wyoming, became a center for a group of Indians and half-breeds, the so-called *haivo-dïka* ("pigeon-eaters"), who have been described in a rather derogatory manner in our sources (cf. Hultkrantz 1958: 153 f.). This group has however cultivated a type of wild Christianity containing many pagan elements (dream oracles, medicine bags, wonder cures, etc.). But even the main group of the Eastern Shoshoni soon mingled with trapper descendants, a fact which can possibly be detected in Yellow Hand's interest in Christian teachings.

The arrival in 1847 of Brigham Young and his followers started a full decade of lively contacts with Mormonism. In the main these contacts were rather strained, as the Mormons drove out the Shoshoni from their winter hunting grounds at Bear River and Salt Lake as well as decimated the wild animal life along the Green River in the heart of Shoshoni country (Trenholm and Carley 1964: 148 f.). Some Indians were, however, won over to the Mormon faith, among others the well-known chief of the Lemhi Shoshoni, Snag. But the more closely organized Eastern Shoshoni under Yellow Hand's successor, Washakie, put up strong resistance. In 1855 when missionaries dispatched from Salt Lake City showed a copy of the Book of Mormon to one of Washakie's braves, he declared: "This book is of no use. If the Mormon captain [= Young] has nothing better to send than this, we had better send it, his letter and these men, back to him, and tell him that they are no good to us, that we want powder, lead and caps, sugar, coffee, flour, paints, knives and blankets, for those we can use. Send these men away to their own land" (Brown 1900:

350 ff.). After reading through a few pages even Washakie stated that the book was no good for his people, but was for the white man (Brown 1900: 350 ff.). This attitude toward book religion is upheld even nowadays by many Shoshoni in spite of increasing literacy. Even younger Shoshoni have thus informed me of their conviction that the white people have been given the gospel through the Bible, whereas it has been revealed to the Indians in visions and the Sun Dance. They mean therefore that the Bible is unnecessary for them.

However, to return to the Mormons: their mission had very little success, and it was certainly not made easier by the fact that Fort Bridger was occupied by the "saints," an event which caused the diffidence of the trapper group to turn into hostility. The American army expedition against the Mormons in 1857–58 did not raise the prestige of the last-named in the eyes of the Shoshoni. The Indians had no reason to acknowledge a completely foreign doctrine which was not even honored by those in power, but which instead displeased them.

Even so it appeared for a while as if Mormonism should have a new chance. In the year 1868 Washakie's Shoshoni were allotted, at their own request, a reservation consisting of their old favorite hunting grounds alongside the Wind River. Unfortunately, they did not have this reservation to themselves for very long; for already in 1878 their old archenemies, the Northern Arapaho, were placed in the eastern part of the reservation. Shortly afterward the Indian agent could report a noticeable intensification of interest in the Mormon faith. In his report for the year 1879 he writes: "During the early part of the summer, quite a number of Shoshones left the reservation for Salt Lake. Not understanding the reason for their mysterious departure, as most of them slipped away in the night time, I inquired of Washakie the cause; his explanation was they were Mormons; they have gone to Salt Lake to get washed, and they can see their departed friends and relatives, next summer. I judge from this the Mormons have instructed them to be baptized in the Mormon Church, and in the future life they will meet their friends gone before" (Report of the Commissioner of Indian Affairs 1879: 168, 1880: 177).[6] Hebard's interpretation of this note is that those Shoshoni who were dissatisfied with the arrival of the Arapaho on their reservation found an excuse to leave this by joining the Mormon church (Hebard 1930: 214). However, this sounds rather unlikely: emigration to some of the

6. Steward mentions that a few Mormon converts drawn from Washakie's band live today under the care of the Mormon church at Washakie, Utah (Steward 1938: 177 f.).

Shoshoni reservations in Idaho would appear to have been more natural. Nor is it feasible that the Shoshoni suddenly to such a degree had been won over to Mormonism, that for religious reasons they would have left the tribe to join the new faith.

The true reason for the short "emigration" can be found in the statement, quoted above, that the following summer the Shoshoni should see their dead relations—certainly not the Mormon doctrine. This information should be seen in connection with Colonel Brackett's parallel report that almost every summer the Shoshoni were agitated by some prophet who predicted the end of the world, whereupon they all gathered near the Bear River to partake in "a series of dances, incantations and rites" in great excitement (Brackett 1880: 332). As clearly understood by Shimkin, these sentences refer to the first Ghost Dance (Tävibo's dance), an offshoot of the above-mentioned Prophet Dance, which had, at this time, a foothold in the Bridger Basin (Shimkin 1942: 456). Shimkin's supposition that this cult was connected in some way with Mormonism is certainly too precipitate; their willingness to become Mormons was most probably just a cover for those Shoshoni who wished to participate in the Ghost Dance.

Mormonism therefore did not make any inroads. Nowadays there is a Mormon mission at Fort Washakie which was founded in 1934, and it has its followers. But the results of the mission cannot be said to have gone down very deep. The knowledgeable medicine-man, Tudy Roberts, who belonged to the conservative Sage Creek group (see below), appeared as a "washed" Mormon during my first visits to the Wind River reservation.

The Shoshoni who moved to the Wind River reservation in the 1870s were thus, in the main, believers in their old tribal religion, even though many foreign traits, particularly from Catholicism, were brought in by the squaw-men and half-breeds who immigrated from the Fort Bridger country. In September 1876 the agent Irwin wrote that no attempt had been made to spread Christianity amongst the Shoshoni, "and they are almost entirely ignorant of the Christian religion" (Report of the Commissioner of Indian Affairs 1876: 153). A new situation arose however when an Episcopal mission was started at Wind River in 1883–84, under the leadership of a Welshman, John Roberts, a man of unusual stature (see Olden 1923, Nash 1932).[7] Nevertheless, in spite of his intensive efforts and backing from the agency and government, Roberts and his assistants had very little

7. Roberts' services to the mission on the Wind River reservation procured him later on a degree of doctor honoris causa.

success in the beginning. It was not only tribal conservatism and Indian distrust which stood in the way, but also other reasons can be perceived:

1. Contact between the whites and Indians was made difficult due to the fact that the Indians were not adept at English and the whites had no knowledge of the Shoshonean language. The Reverend Roberts certainly learned Shoshonean and even translated, amongst other things, a prayer book (with a rather heavy transcription of Shoshonean phonemes), but his assistants did not follow his example. The Shoshoni who had mixed with French trappers had a little knowledge of French phrases, but their knowledge of English was much more scanty. In 1882 the agent reported that out of all the Indians on the reservation—842 Shoshoni and 940 Northern Arapaho—only 10 could speak English (Report of the Commissioner of Indian Affairs 1882: 404). When it came to the chief, the reservation's previous licensed trader, J. K. Moore, Jr., informs us that "Washakie spoke very little English but understood more than he spoke and really understood more than he pretended. He also spoke French" (Hebard 1930: 240).

During the twentieth century the situation has naturally changed with the coming of regular school attendance. Nowadays the majority of the Shoshoni are English-speaking and bilingual (it would appear that the youngsters speak only English). There is only a small minority of the older generation who lack knowledge of English.

2. In spite of the settlements on the reservation, the old nomadic way of life carried on. Even after a certain amount of farming and cattle-breeding, particularly the last-mentioned, had been stabilized during the 1880s, there still remained seasonal variations between living in winter quarters down on the Wind River plain (or sometimes in the old Fort Bridger country or on the plains around Salt Lake City) and hunting and collecting expeditions up in the mountains and in Jackson Hole during spring, summer, and autumn. It is completely natural that this instability, which possibly also affected the Shoshoni personality type,[8] considerably hampered the efforts of the missionaries.

---

8. Efforts to determine the personality type among the Shoshoni have been made by Shimkin, although from other points of departure (Shimkin 1939, 1942, 1947a). As we shall find, the Reverend John Roberts called attention to the fickleness and inconstancy of the Shoshoni in comparison with the Arapaho whom he also knew well. However, since the Arapaho have been active participants in the same kind of seasonal working pattern as the Shoshoni (cf. below) it is doubtful whether this personality disposition can be connected with the migrations.

3. The first contact between tribal religion and missionary Christianity appeared strengthening to the first-named. Christian rituals and Christian symbols could, to a certain extent, be integrated with the inherited Shoshoni religion and make it more attractive. During the years around 1890 the old Shoshoni religion seemed to experience a type of renaissance, in that a Christianized form of the Sun Dance became established. It gained great popularity and soon swept through the neighboring tribes, among others the Ute and Bannock (see Lowie 1919; Shimkin 1953; Voget 1953). This tendency toward a "Sun Dance religion" has persisted up to modern times (see below).

4. The first missionary activity took place during a time when the tribe was experiencing a great crisis: the buffaloes disappeared, the newly introduced farming was on the decline, diseases prevailed and harvested many deaths (Shimkin 1942: 454). It was a time when, to cite Shimkin, "the Shoshone were open to all sorts of innovations" (Shimkin 1942: 459). Impulses from newly formed religious movements of a different, Pan-Indian type started to make inroads. Most noticeable amongst these revivalistic movements was the Ghost Dance in its second stage, Wovoka's dance. A mark of the times was that the bearers of this new dance, a few Shoshoni from Idaho, arrived by train at Lander, south of the Wind River reservation. Direct communication with Wovoka was established through some Wyoming Shoshoni who visited him in Nevada (Shimkin 1942: 457).[9] The Ghost Dance among the Shoshoni could, in a natural way, be connected with an existing dance pattern, the round dance, and it did not lead to the same excesses as, for example, among the Sioux. White Colt, William Washington, and Tudy Roberts were notable as prominent Shoshoni Ghost Dance leaders.

At the turn of the century the peyote cult spread among the Shoshoni, one of the main reasons for this being that the old Chief's son, Charlie Washakie, had been won over to peyotism. Ultimately peyotism, its conceptual system, and nightly rituals stemmed from the tribes around the Rio Grande. The Shoshoni assumed it in the first place from their old kinsfolk in Oklahoma, the Comanche, and from their neighbors, the Arapaho, who had begun to use peyote already around 1890. The peyote cult experienced some initial resistance, as with its closed doctrine it competed with the tribal religion. Only after a couple of decades did it gain a firm foothold among

9. Many years later, in 1910, Wovoka visited the Wind River reservation where a Ghost Dance was held in his honor.

a fraction of the Shoshoni, among whom were members of the Washakie family.

The Ghost Dance and peyote cult were forms of expressing a new Indian feeling of solidarity, a conscious Pan-Indianism which was stimulated by the conditions on the reservations—in the first place, the readjustment of the way of living and the change of old life values—as well as by the common Indian heritage and the bond of opposition against the whites. On a more restricted national or tribal level the revitalization of the Sun Dance brought about a new form of self-consciousness. Christianity was understood as an instrument for the white superiority and was associated with farming, cut hair, European clothes, and a way of life in accordance with the white man's.

As an example of the opposition to the Christian mission it has been pointed out that the main figurehead of the Shoshoni, the tribal chief, Washakie, who died in 1900 at a great age, had not agreed to become a member of the church until a few years before his death (1897) when he was baptized by the representative of the Episcopalian church, the Reverend John Roberts.[10] However, earlier Washakie had not at all opposed Christianity, but had maintained an amiable neutrality; for him the Christian faith represented a section of the new civilization in which he also wanted the Shoshoni to own a part. Washakie, as well as his family, had a rather indifferent attitude to religious questions, and right up until the last few years of his life he remained rather uninterested in the subject of life after death.[11] According to one of his white friends, the chief commented on Rev. Roberts' sermon on this topic in the following way: "Well, this world suits me pretty well. I like it here. ... I want to stay here with my friends, and I do not want to go to another world. [Still,] I may die tonight, I have to go sometime" (Hebard 1930: 236 f.). Washakie's indifference to religion may possibly be connected with his double

10. Our sources give different reasons for Washakie's baptism. According to Bishop Ziegler, the main reason was Roberts' courageous demeanor after the killing of a son of Washakie's. Out of fury the chief had menaced to kill any white man he came across, whereupon Roberts had appeared in front of him and offered his own life in exchange. In admiration of this courage Washakie decided to be converted to Christianity (see Ziegler 1944: 10). Bishop Talbot, however, says that Washakie was baptized by Roberts at a time when he was lying critically ill (Talbot 1906: 38 f.).

11. During a severe illness he had however travelled to the land of the dead in delirium (see Olden 1923: 61 f.).

ideological inheritance, his father being a Flathead Indian.[12] As is well known, value conflicts pave the way for relativism in religious matters.

After Washakie's baptism the following to the Christian church increased, and many became, like Washakie, regular church-goers. The Episcopal church accepted a donation from Washakie of 160 acres of land, meant to be used for the building of a church and a school (Hebard 1930: 246 f.). However, mission work advanced slowly. The first enthusiasm among the young missionaries had soon died out. Already in a letter in 1885 the missionary and teacher at Wind River, A. C. Jones, complained about the possibilities of teaching the gospel on the reservation: "Before taking up such a work as this, one is inclined to believe that very soon the effect of religious teaching will be seen, but after giving it a trial of some months and finding that little change has been wrought, there is a feeling created which if expressed would be somewhat like the following: Well, I see there is no use in trying to teach the Indians anything, for they don't seem to have any desire to be guided by our religious teaching, although they listen very attentively to the parables and miracles of our Lord and to the story of the cross told to them through an interpreter" (Trenholm and Carley 1964: 307 f.). In spite of the fact that the mission faced a difficult and almost hopeless task, the purposeful and energetic Roberts pressed on with his work.

Even difficulties of another character cropped up. The work of the missionaries was not wholeheartedly backed up by the whites. In a communication to the commissioner of Indian affairs, the chairman of the Shoshone Negotiating Commission, J. D. Woodruff, stated that the Shoshoni "spiritually ... should be left entirely as they are, for their intellects are not strongly enough developed to grapple with the different creeds and forms of the Christian religion. They no doubt would, as many more intelligent people have, become entangled and lost in doubt and waste their brain forces in matters of conjecture as to the future, which should be applied to better ways and methods of meeting the trials of this life."[13] On the other hand, there were representatives of the whites who more or less recognized

12. From a conversation he had with one of Wyoming's pioneers, J. D. Woodruff, it emerges that Washakie nevertheless cared for the next life when his own death drew near. Woodruff testifies that the chief was anxious he would come to the heaven of the whites and not to the old Shoshoni land of spirits where his own people were (see Hebard 1930: 275 f.).

13. Communication from J. D. Woodruff to the Office of Indian Affairs, October 15, 1891.

as the chief blessings of the mission its reforming effects on the ordinary everyday occupations. A commission, which had been appointed to examine the question of Shoshoni land cessions, was impressed by Reverend Roberts' ability to persuade the Indians to farm the land which had been donated to the church by Washakie. Among other things the report says: "Mr. Roberts should be encouraged and assisted in his good work, as, in our opinion, a more self sacrificing and earnest Christian worker never entered a field of labor; it being a fact, that cannot be successfully contradicted, that he has done more toward advancing these Indians in education, farming and mechanical pursuits than all other agencies combined."[14]

As time went by Roberts' persistent teachings, personal cure of souls, and conscious instruction of the younger generations seemed to bear fruit. The Shoshoni became nominal Christians, many of them believing in the Christian faith in their own way, and one or another even turned catechist. At the same time, however, the old religion, more or less modified, prevailed in the minds of the great majority. Christianity did not replace heathenism, it filled in those phases of existence which had been influenced by the western way of life or had been formed by the contact situation. In this respect the situation is unchanged even today. And it has, as far as I can judge, remained this way since Christianity made its first appearance among the Shoshoni.

This statement is important because it explains how the Shoshoni religion could remain comparatively unchanged after the first contact with the white man one hundred and fifty years ago. Up until modern times one has clearly differentiated between the inherited religion and Christianity, and not until comparatively recently—during this century—has Christ, for example, been coupled together with elements from the tribal religion. (It is another matter that he occurs, as a symbolic figure, in the Christianized Sun Dance of the 1890s.) During the entire nineteenth century the religious acculturation seems to have been an additive rather than a changing process. This can appear consternating—has not a well-known cultural anthropologist, Kroeber, been able to conclude that cultural changes on the material plane are accumulative, on the spiritual plane transformative (Kroeber 1952: 155, 165)? I consider that I have now provided the reason for the Shoshoni deviation from this pattern: the new religion was simply added as it corresponded to a new dimen-

14. Report, February 22, 1893, Bureau of Indian Affairs, Special Cases No. 147.

sion of existence. As I have stated in previous articles the vision-quest, Sun Dance, and mythology in the old religion corresponded to three cultural situations, the hunting life, the buffalo hunt, and the story telling of the winter evenings (Hultkrantz 1956a). The distinctive feature in these religious activities was, among other things, that they were exclusive of each other, each one constituting a total ideological complex which was actualized when the situation so demanded. In the same way the Christian religious complex became topical in certain given circumstances—at church attendance on Sundays, at weddings and funerals, and in company with white people, in particular in school.

During our own century these religious complexes have increasingly become more harmonized with each other, and even amalgamated. My own field investigations during the span of ten years, 1948–58, have clearly convinced me of this. One can in this connection talk about a "graded acculturation," as Christianity has not, to the same degree, become united with the different religious configurations. The Sun Dance, the axis of the Shoshoni religion since the end of the nineteenth century, has, as we have already noted, gained an ideological reinterpretation in a Christian direction. To a great extent the old vision complex has been pushed aside—who needs the special help of guardian spirits in the new, enclosed existence with public privileges, income from the cessions of old tribal hunting grounds and royalities from oil wells and timber-cutting? Only the medicine-men are in need of such visions. Otherwise this direct approach to the supernatural has been taken over by the peyote cult—which, for the rest, has a part-Christian (Catholic) background. The security which the vision of a guardian spirit provided in bygone days is today pursued, to a certain degree and with a different perspective, in eschatology. This development certainly depends upon incitement from the Christian faith. That hereby the conceptions of life after death, earlier rather unimportant, have been transformed and even enriched by the Christian doctrines is not surprising. The mythological tales, finally, with their roots in the hunting and collecting ways of life in the Basin culture, still form a closed configuration and are in the process of being transformed into a profane treasure trove of fictional tales. This process is a natural consequence of their isolation from the realities of the modern way of life (Hultkrantz 1960b: 568). The western motifs which have, in later days, been incorporated (e.g., dragon tales) do not increase the religious value of the tales.

Present-day Religious Acculturation

The new religious situation is characterized, first and foremost, by a pronounced confessional disunity. There are, as we have seen, several competing religious denominations within the reservation, the most important of which are the Episcopal church, and the Catholic church and the Latter Day Saints.[15] Also such an Indian religious product as the peyote cult causes dissension; many are for it, many against it. The peyote believers are now organized in an inter-Indian church of their own, The Native American church, with permanent religious rituals which are usually performed during the night between Saturdays and Sundays. Around 75 percent of the Shoshoni on the Wind River reservation are practicing peyotists.

But even apart from the split caused by these imported ideologies there occurs a religious factionalism, namely within the frame of the old Shoshoni religion. This factionalism is based partly on the old tribal partition. Washakie's Shoshoni usually consisted of four to six bands, sometimes more, as groups on the periphery such as Pocatello's Shoshoni (in Idaho) occasionally joined the tribe. Still today one can discern certain differences in the religious conceptions of the main Shoshoni group on the reservation, the earlier Plains Shoshoni, and the descendants of the so-called Sheepeaters (Mountain Snakes) up in the mountain regions (Hultkrantz 1966–67a). In our days when the old band solidarity has given way to the affinity ties within the local groups (which are often constituted by the descendants of a previous band) there reigns a local religious particularism in many places, and this particularism corresponds to a certain level of religious acculturation. One finds, thus, a stronger conservatism among peripheral groups such as the Sage Creek or Bull Lake Shoshoni than among the centrally situated Fort Washakie Shoshoni.

Naturally this religious pluralism has led to strong religious opposition between different factions. The chances of the Christian mission have diminished, the grip of the old religion has scarcely slackened, in any case not among the middle-aged and older people, whereas the younger generations show an increasing indifference toward religion as such. Many young men partake in the Sun Dance for social reasons, just as many of our young men attend confirmation

15. The Catholic church has for a long time had a stronghold among the Arapaho (St. Stephen's Mission), among some Shoshoni half-breed families (of partly French descent), and among Mexicans residing close by, in particular in the little town of Riverton.

classes for conventional reasons. G.I.s who have experienced existence in foreign countries, and the few youngsters who have attended colleges, willingly leave both the old religion with its ethnocentrism and the Christian faith whose world-view and animistic conceptions appear inadequate to them in the atomic age of this century. Indifference, weakness in character, and alcoholism are often the results of their deficient ideological foundation.

In this connection I shall, however, mainly concentrate upon the, in any case for the moment, receding Christian mission, and the persistence of the old faith, partly shadowed by Christian symbols. On the other hand, the peyote religion will not be handled here.

It would be emphatically wrong to suppose that the recession of the Christian faith as an active religious attitude depends on a qualitative deterioration in the missionary efforts. Dr. John Roberts, the first Episcopalian missionary, whom I met shortly before his death in 1949 (he died at the high age of 96), had mastered the Shoshoni language rather well, in contrast to his successors—in this instance one can speak about a negative development. Also perhaps the self-denial and first enthusiasm of the pioneering days are lacking in the modern representatives of the mission. Let us not forget, however, that already the first missionaries were heartily discouraged with their results. In the light of the particularly small inroads the mission has made during the past eighty years, it is easy to understand the present-day resignation in mission circles. In addition to this the interest for the Indian mission has cooled off within the diocese of Wyoming during the last few decades, a fact which has naturally influenced the possibilities of the mission.

Some characteristic features from the Shoshoni Christianity of the 1950s can serve to illustrate the difficulties which the mission experiences in trying to fulfill its aims. Church attendance was minimal, except at funerals; in this respect the Shoshoni were more negligent than their easterly neighbors on the reservation, the Arapaho Indians. (Dr. Roberts likened the Shoshoni to wild birds: he meant that one could not make agreements with them, nor could one pin them down to attend church services.) Their knowledge of the Bible and the Christian dogmas was incomplete, and the holy texts were incorrectly interpreted. Not least were they perplexed when it came to the figure of Christ and the Trinity, whereas the devil fitted more easily into place—he is called *ižap⁰*, "coyote" or "prairie wolf," which intimates that he has taken the place of the doubtful culture hero and trickster by this name. Eschatology was partly Christian, partly old Shoshoni. The clergyman was recognized as a medicine-man, *puha-*

gan, because he prayed for the sick. The rituals of the high church which were practiced during divine service had, undoubtedly, a certain effect on the Indians who were interested in rituals, but the import of the church rituals was not always fully clear to them.

This very general picture of the conditions must be seen in connection with, on the one hand, the strong Christian influences upon the Shoshoni religion—a point to which I shall soon return—and, on the other hand, the negative effects which the Christian teaching has had upon the Shoshoni religion. According to the Shoshoni the spirits of nature have thus fled from both electricity and the Christian gospel; an Indian told me how the powers had moved far up to the mountains in fear of the Christian cross. It is possible that the abandonment of the vision-quest, once eagerly promoted by the medicine-man, William Surrell, at the end of World War I, was ultimately inspired by Christian teachings. It is quite certain that the Christian mission loosened up the old tribal religion for many individuals, and members of the Washakie family have used the Christian eschatology as an argument against the old pagan conceptions of life after death.

It is thus possible to state that the Christian mission has had strong, unintentional side influences, while its positive, edifying results failed to fulfill expectations. I shall try here to supply a few of the reasons which, to my knowledge, have actively obstructed the Christian mission among the Shoshoni:

1. The existence of several competing Christian denominations counteracts the demands on exclusivism by the Christian religion and creates insecurity. Many Indians waver between different denominations; Tudy Roberts, for instance, wavered between the Episcopal church and Mormonism. According to tradition in Washakie's family, the chief is said to have been baptized three times: firstly as a Catholic (by de Smet?), then as a Mormon, and lastly as an Episcopalian (by Rev. Roberts). The medicine-man, John Trehero, who had been baptized as a child by Rev. Roberts, criticized the multibaptism. "So many are baptized in different churches," he maintained, "and yet Jesus said that one should only be baptized once."

2. Christianity in its Episcopalian or Catholic form is not an experienced religion in the same way as the Shoshoni religion. Therefore it does not fit in well in the existing religious pattern, nor is its doctrine understandable or convincing in comparison with the Shoshoni religion whose truth has been tested in visions. In this respect the peyote cult with its hallucinations has also an advantage

over the Christian religion. Inasmuch, however, as the frequency of visions has decreased the church has gained ground among many who had previously been indifferent or even hostile to Christian beliefs.

3. The Christian dogmatic is difficult to digest, and even professing Christians—or more explicitly those who consider themselves to be Christian—are unfamiliar with much of the Christian message. Sin, the last judgment, and hell are concepts which meet strong opposition, and since neither the terms nor the conceptions which they cover have occurred among the Shoshoni the Christian church has here a difficult task. Attempts have not been lacking on the part of the Indians to have the Christian doctrines adjusted. The medicine-man, Morgan Moon, who was a catechist of the Episcopalian church, discussed the Bible with Dr. Roberts and strongly emphasized that faults occurred in several places. One can assume that Moon was guided by his own visionary experiences.

4. The Shoshoni find it difficult to accept Christianity's claim to be the one and only religion. Their natural world is dominated by the tribe in the reservation milieu, and their religious world has the tribe's interest as its focal point. John Trehero, the medicine-man has, in his conversations with me, repeatedly referred to a tradition in which he fully believed and which he had heard as a child from several Shoshoni. According to this tradition Christ, after the crucifixion, had wandered up to the mountains to fast. Here he prayed to his Almighty Father that He should send his Holy Ghost down to the mountains to be at hand for those who could not read or write. And the Spirit appeared to the Indians in dreams at the rock drawings (where in the old days visions were sought by brave and lonely Shoshoni), and he gave them the Sun Dance. "The white man has been given the Creator's words written down, we know them through the spirits," said Trehero. "This is what *puha* [= the spirit] told the first Indian who got the medicine." To Trehero this version of Jesus' words of the Comforter, the Holy Ghost (John 14, 16), represents a convincing reason for the separation between the religion of the white man and the religion of the red Indian. "When I went to school," he said, "I took part in the Holy Communion" (Dr. Roberts confirmed this); "now I go to the Sun Dance." Trehero's personal enemies among the Shoshoni say that even in later times he has attended holy communion in the Episcopalian church but merely to gain more strength for his medicine séances.

Most of the Shoshoni believers in the old religion do not take exception to the Christian church but accept it as a religious institution suitable in certain situations, but at the same time they maintain that their own inherited religion suits them best. They can, moreover, point out that nowadays the main Christian principals—God the Father, Christ, the Holy Spirit, and the Apostles—are included in their old religion, and that up to a certain point even the Christian symbols have been integrated. We can establish that hereby only their mythological world has been enriched. They themselves maintain, however, that they have interpreted the Christian message in a better way than the representatives of the Christian church.

Tribal religion is today characterized by persistence, concentration—and to a certain extent—innovation. "Persistence" is a concept which, in this connection, has been introduced by Dusenberry (Dusenberry 1962). It indicates that a traditional religion holds its ground in an acculturative situation. It can appear surprising that a tribal religion can remain active when the way of life in the tribe has undergone such a radical change: gone is the old political, social, and economic structure, gone are the chieftains and the band organization, buffalo hunts, and tribal wars. Still, something very fundamental persists from the old days, namely the variation of the seasonal occupations, the yearly working rhythm, and hereby to a certain extent, the nomadic existence. Gross has shown that the close neighbors of the Shoshoni, the Arapaho, still rotate between different dwelling places and different occupations all according to the seasons (Gross 1949). In the same way this is the case with the Shoshoni: they alternate between their summer existence on the reservation, when the tribe comes together on the plain to celebrate the Sun Dance and the tribal solidarity is strengthened, their autumnal hunting and fishing activities up in the Wind River Mountains, and potato-picking in Idaho, their inactivity during the winter season in simple cottages scattered over the reservation, and the renewed hunting and fishing in the spring. That there exists a certain permanent engagement in farming and cattle breeding does not, in principle, interfere with this seasonal rotation which, as we have seen earlier, is modelled on the alternating seasonal pattern in the old Plains Indian days. Religion corresponds in an essential degree with the seasonal changes and in this way satisfies traditional needs.

Another contributive reason for the persistence of the old religion is the reservation system. As long as the majority of the Indians live on the reservation, where they are relatively isolated and referred to themselves and their own small collectivities, the old religious ideas and customs will persist. At the same time they keep a frontal position against the whites. The conservative Shoshoni, in particular, are aware that the European-American civilization and way of life disbands the foundations of the traditional society, and in their aims to preserve their old culture they cling to the old religion which incarnates the tribe and its values.

It would be too hasty to believe that this adhesion to the old religion comprehends all aspects of the traditional religious life. As in the spheres of social and material culture a disintegration has taken place which has resulted in the preservation only of vital culture elements, so has also the old religious system been exposed to a process of decomposition through which those religious aspects which had been attached to past, no longer pursued activities have fallen away. The vision complex has been affected especially badly; to seek visions among the rock-drawings up in the mountains is no longer a part of the religious pattern, the medicine-men excepted. The religious and social life has been concentrated to the Sun Dance which in this way has come to symbolize the continuity in the tribal life, its religious institutional foundation. The Sun Dance has absorbed the vision complex—exhausted dancers may receive visions—shamanism, and the ritual dances which previously existed separately. This process has been facilitated by the Christian reinterpretation of the Sun Dance, a point which will be demonstrated presently. According to the Shoshoni, Lynn St. Clair, the reinterpretation has deepened the import of the dance and secured its value.

The sacredness of the Sun Dance in modern times is shown best perhaps in the following incident. The Sun Dance is a "thirst-standing dance" (*taguwuned*), a ceremony which among other things comprises three days' abstinence from food and drink. During the Sun Dance of 1955, led by the medicine-man, John Trehero, a young man could not stand it any longer and rushed thoughtlessly to the nearest water. In shame he had to retreat from the scene. Trehero pointed out to me that the young man was, for all time, excluded from partaking in the dance. He could be likened to "that fellow who betrayed Jesus."

During the 1940s the Sun Dance was intensified, at the same time as it expanded outwardly—in 1941, with the cooperation of John Trehero, it was introduced among the Crow Indians in Montana (Voget 1948). The inner intensification was probably connected with the fact that the Sun Dance had recently been legitimatized after having for a long time been regarded as suspect by the whites and even been forbidden during a number of years. The Indian Reorganization Act of June 1934 meant, among other things, a change of thought in regard to Indian religions, and in spite of an initial opposition from the agency, the Shoshoni soon managed to re-establish their Sun Dance in the old form. In the summer of 1942 Wyoming's governor sent telegraphic felicitations for "a successful ceremonial."[16] Initiative for the resumption of this Medicine Dance had come from the ranks of the old believers, in particular the medicine-men. After the war they were joined by the war veterans who, in the Asiatic battlefields, had experienced the equality of all human beings and all religions, and who here found a way of self-assertion against the white supremacy. Enthusiasm expressed itself in innovations: the spirits appeared in dreams for the medicine-men and other religiously gifted people and gave instructions about new dance insignia, new color combinations for the center pole of the Sun Dance lodge, new Sun Dance songs, etc.

During the 1950s a decline in this intensification took place, and the dance became increasingly more commercialized and turned into a tourist attraction. But it continues to assert itself as the concentrated manifestation of the old Shoshoni religion.

The last-mentioned statement is not restricted by the circumstance that the aims and symbols of the dance have, so to speak, been "translated" to the Christian tongue. This has taken place in connection with a superficial Christianization of different aspects of the Shoshoni religion. The Christianization has in the main affected religious beliefs, whilst the rites have not changed but symbolically and the mythological tales principally remained intact. Likewise, the religious pattern stands unaltered; we have already discerned the reasons for this.

The religious conceptions have thus been adapted to Christian ideas but without the basic religious structure having thereby been changed. The concept of God, which is pre-Christian (Hultkrantz 1962b: 548 ff.), has been activated; one prays to "the Father above" even outside of the Sun Dance. On the other hand he is never experienced in dreams or visions. An old Shoshoni woman told me how she prayed every evening and every sun-rise to *Tam Apö* (Our Father), Jesus, and the sun. In the Sun Dance at least the medicine-man, Trehero, prays to Jesus, who is then called (*Tam)apanndú:a*, "(Our) Father's Son," or *Tam báBi*, "Our Older Brother." Visions of Jesus occur, but he is never *puha*, guardian spirit. Trehero saw Jesus in a dream. "He was just like he is in pictures, he was standing on a white cloud, floating away from me." The medicine-man, Tudy

16. Telegram, June 24, 1942, from Governor N. H. Smith to Herman St. Clair, chairman of the Shoshoni Sun Dance Committee (Wind River Agency Files, n.d.).

Roberts saw Jesus standing in the east with the sun surrounding his head, and underneath him there was a pleasant spot with high, green grass, and green sagebrush. But, he said, Jesus did not see him. Even the Holy Ghost has been integrated with Shoshoni religion, at least according to Trehero. He namely upholds that the power which emanates from the vision-spirits is sent by *puhanbaBi*, a sort of prototype of all supernatural potency. This being is "the third." "First comes the Father, then the Son and then the power," Trehero explained. As previously mentioned the Coyote, *ižap⁰*, is nowadays identified with the devil. According to the doctrine of the Ghost Dance, two brothers will come to earth in the fulfillment of time, one being the Coyote and the other our older brother. The Coyote will persuade people that he is our older brother. But do not listen to him, and notice that he has his tail twisted around his middle, so that it can be used as a belt.

Even the conceptions about life after death have been adjusted to Christian beliefs. In the old days people who were considered to be evil and anti-social were transformed into ghosts, *tzo:ap*, whilst the good people, and the majority were good, went to the land of the dead. Nowadays this representation has been modified by some Shoshoni: *tzo:ap* is an evil person's spirit which lives under the earth or "comes to the fire"; with the latter purgatory or hell are presumably meant. The peyote-eaters consider that the road to the land of the dead divides itself into one path which leads to heaven and one which leads to hell. Naturally the peyote people go to the more pleasant place.

The perhaps most interesting results of the Christian influences on the Shoshoni religion are offered in the Sun Dance. Its schedule of rituals is still the same as before, and its aims are, as previously, that people are cured and that animals and vegetation thrive. (One can possibly say, however, that the curing has taken the first place in the modern ceremony.) More consideration need not be given to the circumstance that one or another of the dancers wears a crucifix, or that Trehero calls upon Jesus in his prayer at the center pole. More important is the fact that the exterior attributes and symbols of the Sun Dance have been reinterpreted according to Christian ideas. This has apparently taken place in close connection with the Shoshoni around Pocatello, Idaho. One of the last-mentioned informed me that the Sun Dance illustrates how Jesus hung on the cross for three days and was then taken down. He likened the radiating roof poles at the top of the airy lodge to the Apostles, and the foliage which filled out the walls of the lodge he compared with the innumerable individuals who comprise the human race. The Shoshoni at Fort Washakie hold a similar opinion. The Sun Dance lodge is the grave of Christ, through which one passes to go out to a new life;[17] or it is Golgatha. (Besides these interpretations we glimpse the old religious idea that the lodge stands as a symbol for the whole world.) The roof poles are "the Brothers of Jesus," that is the twelve Apostles. It is also said that the western pole represents "the good influence," whilst the north and south poles symbolize the robbers at Golgatha. Since time immemorial one has placed a stuffed eagle on one of the roof poles; because this pole is clefted it is called the path of life or the Judas pole (Judas spoke with a forked tongue).

The main cultic symbol in the Sun Dance lodge is the center pole, comprised of the Y-formed trunk of a cotton tree. It has of old been regarded as a symbol of the Supreme Being, and this idea still persists. But also other associations are connected with it nowadays. It is thus said that the pole is "Our Brother," Jesus (Y is the sign for brother), or that it is the cross of Christ—this is a remarkable parallel case to the old World tradition that the cross of Christ is the pillar of the world. One of my informants considered however, that the center pole could not symbolize the cross, since the supernatural instructions concerning the founding of the Sun Dance had been given at the time of the birth of Christ, and not at the time of his death. Finally it has been suggested that the center pole represents the road through existence which divides itself into one path for the good, and one, the left, for the evil.

In this connection it should also be mentioned that the buffalo head attached to the center pole represents Christ (to my knowledge, however, this interpretation is not so common), and the doll which is often found under the buffalo head is sometimes regarded as a symbol of the Creation, and sometimes as another image of Christ—perhaps the crucified. According to Lynn St. Clair, the eagle was the supernatural instructor of the Sun Dance and in this attribute is likened to the New Testament. In bygone days the Sun Dance persisted for four days (nowadays three days), and this depended upon the fact that Christ fasted for forty days, and one day in the Bible is equal to ten common days.

An active adherent to the Christian reinterpretation of the Sun Dance was the Shoshoni, Lynn St. Clair (1903–52), whose gravestone is embellished with a picture of the Crucified One and

17. This interpretation ought however be compared with the old American Indian idea that the ordeals the dancers have to pass through represent a process in which they die and are revived to a new life as initiates.

with the motto "In thee I trust." Lynn told me how, as a boy during religious instruction at school, he had discovered similarities between the teachings of Christ and Christian symbols on the one hand, and the theology which was developed around the Sun Dance on the other hand. As a catechist with Rev. Lawrence D. Stueland, he became definitely convinced that there was a connection between the two, and during the years 1945–47, according to his own words, he presented his thoughts concerning this matter to the people. As far as we know the "Christian" version of the Sun Dance had not taken place before, at the earliest, the 1890s, but Lynn maintained that it had had its beginning much earlier—perhaps he meant that the dance had from the incipience been performed in conjunction with Christian ideas. According to the origin tales of the Sun Dance which Lynn communicated to me, the initial founder of the dance should have been the buffalo spirit whilst, the instructions for the appearance of the lodge were given in a later vision by the eagle spirit. Lynn thought that the buffalo vision had taken place before the birth of Christ and that it could be equalled to the Old Testament, while the eagle vision which he assigned to the time of the birth of Christ could be likened to the New Testament.

It is difficult to say how genuine the Christian reinterpretation is of the Sun Dance, and to what degree it has a propagandistic, superficial character. Some Shoshoni seem to take it seriously, others probably regard it in the main as a means of influencing the white man in a positive direction. In this connection one should remember that the revival of the dance after the time of prohibiton did not occur without interference from the agents, and also, that some of the white men on the reservation could not recall any Christian points in the Sun Dance until after its reintroduction.

Under Christian guise or not the Sun Dance is apprehended even by the younger Shoshoni as a religious holiday of greater importance than the Christian divine service. A man in his thirties, who had been a prisoner of the Japanese during the second world war, and had consequently encountered the world outside the boundaries of the reservation, became in a very bad humor after a Sun Dance in the 1950s because he had seen me film the dance. His remarks to me can serve as a conclusion to this short exposé: "You have come here to find out about things, to learn how to get in touch with the Old One above. But stop pestering us! You don't walk the right way. You try to find the Old One, and that shows that your religion is not the right one. I have been far away, and I know that only the Indian religion is the right one.—Look at this piece of wood. One side works and is good when one puts fire to it, the other side is charred and is no good for anything. This is how it is with the white man's Bible: you can use it, but we Indians do not benefit from it. We know better how one can come close to the Old One. If you really want to know the true faith, then you should take part in the Sun Dance and not question and trouble us here. For it is this you wish to know when you take pictures of the Sun Dance—yes, I know your intentions just as well as I know the wapiti, the white-tailed deer, and the birds. If you knew the right faith then you would not come here. We would not want to visit your country! Only Indians know God, that is my conviction."

13

The Traditional Symbolism of the Sun Dance Lodge among the Wind River Shoshoni

Introductory Remarks

OF ALL THE NORTH AMERICAN INDIAN RELIGIOUS CEREMONIES no one is as spectacular and as well-known as the Sun Dance of the Plains Indians.[1] The information collected on the subject since the turn of the century is quite extensive (cf. Hultkrantz 1966–67b: 29 ff.). However, while there is a mass of materials on the outer features of the dance, on behavioral and ritual aspects, there is very little information on its religious aspects, in particular the meaning of the ritual. As F. Eggan has stated, "despite all the studies of the Sun Dance we still do not have an adequate account giving us the meaning and significance of the rituals for the participants and for the tribe. One such account would enable us to revalue the whole literature of the Sun Dance" (Eggan 1954: 757. Cf. Hultkrantz 1965a: 88; cf. the critical remarks, Jorgensen: 177). Neither is there any thorough study of the religious symbolism of any Sun Dance, although for instance G. Dorsey's

---

1. The English name, Sun Dance, is a misnomer. The gazing at the sun in the Sioux Sun Dance inspired this designation. The sun plays a role in some Sun Dances; as the Crow say, it is the "mask" of the Supreme Being. The basic import of the Sun Dance will be given below. Cf. also footnote 23.

235

monograph on the Arapaho Sun Dance observes meticulously all pertinent details (Dorsey 1903; cf., however, Miller 1977).

The comparative studies of the Sun Dance dismiss the religious meaning of the dance as unessential. The following pronouncement by such an authority as Robert Lowie is representative: the Sun Dance "does not revolve about the worship of a particular deity, the popular English name for it being a misnomer, but is a composite of largely unintegrated elements prominent in the area at large. The remarkable thing about it is the wide distribution of many objective features, while the interpretations and ostensible motives for holding it vary widely. [. . . Yet] the alleged aims of the ceremony vary widely. We must infer that the ceremonial behavior in the festival was older and that the assumed objectives were subsequent additions. It is also clear that the Dance was only in part a religious ceremony and in large measure served for the aesthetic pleasure and entertainment of the spectators" (Lowie 1954: 178, 180). In a characteristic way Lowie here loses sight of the central perspective which joins all partakers of the dance, the religious meaning which is the motive for its performance. This meaning may be different in different tribes, but it is there. When formulated by the dancers or believers it is as "objective" as any other ceremonial trait. Lowie's assumption that behavior antedates objectives is just one of those behavioristic clichés.

Lowie belonged to the team of anthropologists who seventy years ago noted down the Sun Dance ceremonials of the Plains tribes. His general views mirror the spirit in which these investigations were undertaken. It is obvious that the interest in the symbolism of the dance[2] was minimal among these anthropologists. A new effort to appreciate this symbolism at its intrinsic value is pressing. Such an effort is possible because the material that was salvaged is—in spite of all shortcomings in our documents—partly satisfactory for analysis. Moreover, many Sun Dances are still performed, and may thus be observed in the field.[3]

The following account is an attempt to view the religious symbolism of the Wind River Shoshoni Sun Dance lodge in a "meaningful" perspective. Attention is paid not only to the ideology of the dance as such but also and foremost to the concrete elements of the

---

2. The word "dance" should not mislead: it expresses the dominant ritual action during the ceremony. Most Indian ceremonies are labelled "dances."

3. However, the new Indian secrecy as regards traditional religion prevents field observation in many places.

Sun Dance structure which together throw further light on this ideology. A particular place in the analysis will be devoted to a new scholarly interpretation according to which the Shoshoni Sun Dance serves as a revitalization cult.

The investigation is mainly based on my own field research among the Wind River Shoshoni in Wyoming 1948–58. There is, however, additional material in printed works, such as ethnographical accounts by Lowie and Shimkin and a folkloristic book by Olden (Lowie 1919; Shimkin 1953; Olden 1923). Besides there are archival documents and other unprinted sources in public or private ownership to which I have had access. The value of these sources is very different. Some are tall tales, like Allen's impossible story of the ceremony of the Sheepeater Indians, a mountain branch of the Wyoming Shoshoni (cf. Allen 1913: 9 f., 70 f.; Hultkrantz 1970c: 253 ff.). Others are most informative, as is (the Shoshoni) H. St. Clair's manuscript on the dance (1902), published as an appendix to Shimkin's book (cf. Shimkin 1953: 474 f.),[4] or his kinsman L. St. Clair's manuscript from 1936 which he amended and corrected for me in 1948, four years before his death. St. Clair's information goes back to Judge Ute, a Shoshoni traditionalist who died in 1927 (cf. Wind River Agency Files n.d.: death records).[5]

Our classic sources on the Plains Sun Dance have been presented in a "flat" perspective, that is, in the ethnographic present, regardless if the ceremony was celebrated at the time of recording or a hundred years earlier (cf. Hultkrantz 1967a: 102). The Wind River Shoshoni symbolism as described here refers primarily to the traditional pattern of symbols at the time of my field visits, and secondarily to the Christian symbolism at the same time. Some twenty years ago the Christian symbolic interpretation seemed superficially to supersede the traditional one. It is, however, less certain that this is the situation today, considering the renaissance of traditional Indian values.

The Plains Indian Sun Dance

The Sun Dance is, besides the ubiquitous vision-quest, the most typical exponent of Plains Indian religion (cf. Wissler 1950: 222). It is

4. St. Clair was Lowie's chief informant on the Wind River Shoshoni (cf. Lowie 1909b; 169).

5. F. Burnett, in a letter to Professor Hebard in 1929, gives the year 1928 (cf. Hebard 1933: 235).

closely tied up with the ancient way of life peculiar to these Indians: bison hunting on horseback, living in movable tents (teepees), a tribal organization, and graded war-societies. Whatever its antecedents— there are indications that it sprang forth in old archaic society—the Sun Dance as we know it from historical records was formed inside the dynamic Plains culture that emerged in the early eighteenth century. It became so firmly settled that it survived the downfall of the independent Plains socio-political organization and the abolition of the Plains Indian economy at the end of the last century.

Analysis of the distribution of Sun Dance traits convinced Leslie Spier that the dance had originated among, or diffused from, the Arapaho, Cheyenne, and Teton Dakota (cf. Spier 1921: 477, 491, 494 f., 498). Perhaps it would be more cautious to say that the Plains form of the ceremony was modelled in these societies (for it seems to belong to a widespread cultic complex). The Dakota dance was closely knit up with the military complex of the Plains Indians, whereas the Arapaho and Cheyenne Sun Dances strongly elaborated the religious import: the dance as a cultic drama, a re-creation of the primeval action through which the earth was once created (cf. Hultkrantz 1973b: 9 ff., and sources quoted there). Now, this religious idea is manifested in ritual and symbolic details in most Sun Dances all over the Plains area but is not always clearly recognized as such. The war complex ideology, for instance, often seems to have taken over, several recurrent features having a direct association with warfare. After the eclipse of the Plains military pattern a hundred years ago, the Sun Dance scene sometimes turned into an arena for the cure of diseases—a hypertrophy of a trait that had originally been subsumed under the re-creation aspect.

I am anxious to point out that this reconstruction is not in line with the opinion of many of my American colleagues (cf. Lowie above). It is, however, perfectly in harmony with the main tendencies in W. Schmidt's and W. Müller's interpretations (cf. Schmidt 1929: 811 ff.; Müller 1956: 303 ff. Cf. Underhill 1965: 151), and it backs up Eliade's view of the meaning of ritual drama (cf., e.g., Eliade 1971: 51 ff.).

As a New Year ceremony the Sun Dance was originally held in June when a fresh new verdure covered the ground. A typical Sun Dance like the one arranged by the Southern Arapaho contains the following elements (Dorsey 1903; cf. Hultkrantz 1973b: 11 ff.).

The man who has made the vow or been blessed by a dream (vision) to set up a Sun Dance, and the military society to which he belongs, prepare the tribe for the ceremony and select the time and place. When time is up the different bands come together, and their teepees form a big circle with the opening to the east, the sacred direction.

During four days of preparation the candidates of the ceremony are assembled in the so-called White Rabbit lodge, a teepee which has been erected to the west of the middle point of the big camp circle. Here a new fire is kindled, the sacred fetishes (a sacred wheel, a buffalo skull) are brought in, and the candidates rehearse the songs and rituals pertaining to the ceremony.

Renowned warriors from military societies, equipped with horses, lances, and guns charge on a particularly selected cottonwood tree, shoot at it, and make coup on it (i.e., touch it with their hand or a staff in order to count a point of honor). After prayers to the tree some other soldiers cut it down. It is dragged to the Sun Dance circle, but before reaching camp it is attacked by members of other societies in a sham battle. The latter ends with the victory of the pole-dragging soldiers. The tree is then ceremonially raised in the center of the dance ground. Other poles are attached to the tree as roof poles, peripheral uprights and cross-pieces, and the walls are covered with willow brush. The result is an airy, circular structure with a big opening toward east. It stands ready on the fourth day, and at the same time the rabbit teepee is taken down.

In the evening of the same day, the dancers enter the Sun Dance lodge in their ceremonial outfits. For three days and three nights they fast, dance (periodically) in front of the center pole, and pray to the powers. In the early mornings they perform the "sunrise dance." The body paint of the dancers is changed each day by the "grandfathers," or personal advisors of the dancers. The first day after the "dancing in" an altar is built on the west side of the center pole. It is formed by prairie sods representing the first ground in the creation myth and by the buffalo skull and sacred wheel mentioned before and a ceremonial pipe, among other items. The next day is "medicine day" when the dancers might receive visions from the powers above. This day there is also a display of supernatural power, and curing of the sick. On the final day each dancer may have a sip out of a bucket containing water from "the great lake in the sky." In the evening there is a great feast. The ceremony ends the next morning.

Some tribes, like the Teton Dakota and the Blackfoot, practiced self-torture in their dancing in the past. The aim was to call on the powers and ask for their pity. Recently, these tribes have resumed their mortifications.

The Wind River Shoshoni Dance: History and Phenomenology

The Sun Dance that is performed among the Wind River Shoshoni differs in some respects from the Arapaho Sun Dance, just as both differ from other Plains Sun Dances in ritual details and symbolism. The Shoshoni Dance is clearly marginal to other Sun Dances, in this respect reflecting the peripheral location of the Shoshoni on the Plains (cf. Shimkin 1953: 408). It has moreover changed with time, depending primarily upon three factors: the re-creating force that may be attributed to visions, influences from other Sun Dances, and, in later times, pressure from the European civilization resulting in an increasing adoption of white (Christian) values.

Everything seems to indicate that the Wind River Shoshoni Sun Dance is of comparatively recent origin.[6] It had, however, a predecessor of considerable age, a round dance called the "Father Dance" (*apönökar*), possibly also the "Thanksgiving Dance" (cf. Olden 1923: 37 f.; Lowie 1915b: 817; Shimkin 1953: 433 f.; Thompson n.d.). In this dance, which continued until recently, the people came together and shuffled around a cedar tree, while they thanked the Supreme Being (*Tam Apö*, "Our Father") for his gifts and asked him for bounty in the year to come. Similar prayer dances have existed among the Shoshoni and Paiute of the Basin area (cf. Hultkrantz in press).

Although the Father Dance and the Sun Dance have occurred independently of each other, some elements of the former could have found their way into the Sun Dance. According to my informants a round dance formerly took place inside or outside the Sun Dance lodge after the end of the regular Sun Dance ceremonies; some people found this being less proper, however. Informant L. St. Clair, an excellent historian, considered the preliminary dancing before a shelter (cf. below) a left-over of an original "Sun Dance." This seems, however, less probable.

The beginnings of the Shoshoni Sun Dance are veiled in mystery. Indeed, the dance escaped the attention of the explorers of the last century. Colonel Brackett's paper on the Shoshoni from 1879 does not mention it, which, however, may be due to his limited know **:**

---

6. I leave aside here the whole problem of the relationship, if there ever was one, between the archeological remains of the Medicine Wheel on Bald Mountain in the Big Horn range, other medicine wheels of the area and the ancient Sun Dance. Early on there was the idea among the whites that some sort of connection existed between medicine wheels and Shoshoni religion (cf. Comstock in Jones 1875: 265). However, knowledgeable Shoshoni Indians refer the wheels to the Crow.

edge.[7] H. St. Clair's manuscript from 1902 is the first authentic description (see Shimkin 1953: 474 f.). As to the age of the dance Robert and Yolanda Murphy seem to infer that it appeared only with the early reservation period (cf. Murphy and Murphy 1960: 308). Grace Raymond Hebard held the opinion that the dance was brought to the Shoshoni by the famous Sacajawea, the pilot of Lewis and Clark, when she returned from the Comanche in 1843, for some of her descendants claimed she was the introducer of the dance (cf. Hebard 1933: 157, 201, 259 f., 275).[8] Shimkin, again, basing his conclusions on the evidence of old informants and archival data, establishes the years 1800–20 as the probable date of the introduction of the Sun Dance (cf. Shimkin 1953: 413).[9] My own field information and research in old documents confirms his results. Moreover, I think a forgotten notice by J. Beckwourth on "the medicine lodge" in the Shoshoni camp at Weber River in 1825 refers to the Sun Dance (cf. Bonner, ed. 1931: 61 f.; cf. Hultkrantz 1970d: 297 f., 302).[10]

The man who brought the Sun Dance to the Shoshoni was apparently Ohamagweia, or Yellow Hand, a Shoshoni chief who was by birth a Comanche, and who in one or another way was related to Sacajawea.[11] It was probably an old Kiowa or Comanche form of the dance that was introduced.[12] Certainly, there is also another Shoshoni tradition according to which the Shoshoni Dance antedates all other Sun Dances.[13] This version is, however, more a testimony of pious belief than a record of historical facts. Yellow Hand is said by many people to have received the dance in a vision, and several versions of this vision have circulated on the reservation.

We do not know for sure the outlines of the original Shoshoni

7. He writes, for instance, "Material pleasures alone are those which a Shoshoni understands" (cf. Brackett 1880: 331).

8. The date for Sacajewea's arrival is not certain, and her role in the Sun Dance history is doubtful (cf. Shimkin 1953: 410 f.; Hultkrantz 1975: 154).

9. There is in the agency files a copy of a letter (June 15, 1937) from Mr. F. Stone, superintendent, in which he gives the date "about the year 1819" for the first Sun Dance. He does not say how he arrived at this date.

10. According to Beckwourth, the ceremony took place in the winter season. However, this is in agreement with what some informants have to tell, cf. below.

11. This relationship was, in my view, different from the one postulated by Shimkin (cf. Hultkrantz 1970d: 294 f., 296 n. 17). On Ohamagweia as introducer of the dance, cf. Shimkin 1953: 409 ff.; Hultkrantz 1970d: 294, 301 f.

12. I follow here Shimkin's interpretation (Shimkin 1953: 414 ff.).

13. St. Clair n.d.: "The first Indians to dance the Sun Dance were the Shoshone Indians. The Sun Dance was founded by a Shoshone Indian." Other Shoshoni Indians corroborated this "information," and one of them asserted that the Shoshoni had exported the dance to the Arapaho, Sioux, and other Indians.

Dance, although Shimkin has tried to reconstruct it (cf. Shimkin 1953: 417 ff.). So much is certain that in the main it followed the general Plains pattern as illustrated here with the Arapaho dance. It also showed some peculiarities of its own. Thus elderly informants could still in the 1940s tell us that the Sun Dance was also formerly celebrated in wintertime (cf. Hultkrantz 1970d: 302).[14]

The general motives for the dance to be arranged were wishes for a long life and good luck in general, and particularly success in war and cure for diseases (cf. Shimkin 1953: 431). It is difficult to judge if these goals were collectivistic, aiming at the tribe as a whole, or individualistic. In any case, they were expressed in the ceremony leader's prayer before the center pole immediately prior to the beginning of the dancing. The center pole was adorned with a buffalo skull, facing west, an eagle in a nest of willows, and a small "Sun Dance doll" made from wood or buckskin. On the other hand, there was no altar and no buffalo skull at the foot of the pole. During the four nights prior to the proper ceremony, the leader and a few other participants practiced Sun Dance songs at a particular windbreak erected for the purpose. The lodge ceremony then started in the evening and lasted three nights and days.[15] The dancers jogged steadily up and down looking upon the center post and its sacred images. Occasionally they also danced up to the center pole. On the second full day relatives helped to construct a small booth around the place where the dancer lay down to rest, just behind his dancing position. The skin of the booth was, according to Shimkin, painted with "records of visions of war experiences" (Shimkin 1953: 425); I have no such information. An interesting detail is that when the dancers received a sip from the sacred water (the event that marked the termination of the dance) they vomited (cf. Olden 1923: 36; Jayne, ed. 1952: 9). Such vomiting occurred also in the Arapaho and Cheyenne dances. One is furthermore reminded of the sacred vomiting in the New Year rituals of the southeastern Indians.

The great change in the Sun Dance occurred around 1890 when the Shoshoni had adapted themselves to reservation life, buffalo hunting and warfare was gone, and the old religion was on the

14. My chief informant here, Nadzaip (a medicine-woman), had a brother, Morgan Moon, whose innovations as a Sun Dance leader—due to his visionary experiences—created strong counter-reactions among the Shoshoni (cf. Shimkin 1953: 435 f.).

15. The number three is sacred west of the Rocky Mountains, the number four east of them; the Wind River Shoshoni having geographically an intermediate position keep both numbers sacred.

verge of becoming suppressed by the white rulers and the Christian missions. Ritual traits referring to war disappeared to a large extent, and the emphasis on blessings for success in war was replaced by prayers for good health and cure from disease. The new political organization with a tribal council (1893) instead of chieftainship and informal meetings was reflected in the creation of a Sun Dance committee. The date of the dance was postponed from June to late July, the time when the harvest had been taken care of. Some old traits like the putting up of a Sun Dance doll and the vomiting went out of use, at least temporarily, whilst others, such as the dancing up to the center pole, became more common. Influences from other Sun Dances—particularly from the one of their eastern neighbors, the Northern Arapaho, who in the 1870s had settled on the reservation— resulted in some new ritual elements. The most conspicuous change, however, was the reinterpretation of the Sun Dance symbolism into Christian concepts (cf. Hultkrantz 1969: 22, 33, 36 ff.).

The reformulation of the Sun Dance in the 1880s and 1890s, and the new emphasis on health and curing, saved the Shoshoni dance in a time when the old hunting life was gone, most Sun Dance ceremonies were forbidden by white authorities, and several of them—in particular among the tribes practicing torture in their dance—became extinct. Indeed, it was during this difficult time that the Wind River Shoshoni version of the Sun Dance spread to the Northern Ute (1890), the Fort Hall Shoshoni and Bannock (1901), and the Shoshoni of Nevada (1933) (cf. Jorgensen 1972: 19 ff., 25 f.; Hoebel 1935: 578 f.).

After the Indian Reorganization Act (1934) there was a new resurge of Sun Dance celebration on the Wind River reservation (cf. Hultkrantz 1969: 34). More people than ever before took part in the Sun Dance. Since the Sun Dance was now mainly a means of achieving spiritual power—which in the old days could only be procured on solitary vision-quest expeditions—and a ritual for the removal of disease, and therefore its presumably old interpretation of a New Year's rite had become vague and even obsolete, it was possible to arrange several Sun Dances each summer.[16] For instance, one dance is usually arranged by conservative believers, another by peyotists. The latter deviate from other sun dancers in not expecting visions of super-

---

16. This notwithstanding I was informed, during my visit to the Stoney (Assiniboin) of Alberta in the autumn of 1977, that these Indians had held six Sun Dances that summer.

natural power during the dance, and in wearing a pouch with a peyote button around the neck.

One of the renewers of the Sun Dance in recent times has been the famous medicine-man John Trehero, now in his nineties (and no longer active). Being a descendant of Yellow Hand, he reintroduced the Sun Dance doll for the ceremonies in which he or his close kinsmen took part. He also transferred the Shoshoni Dance to the Crow Indians (1941) (see Voget 1948: 634 ff.).[17]

The 1950s brought tendencies of commercialization into the Sun Dance celebration. However, the sacred character was not lost and has since been strengthened under the pressure of resurging Indian nationalism.

Looking back we may say that in modern times the Shoshoni Sun Dance has absorbed almost all expressions of earlier religious rituals, in particular the vision complex and the "shamanism."[18] With a certain justification we may consider the Sun Dance as the aboriginal religion of today. As such it is the core of Shoshoni traditionalism, and the ideological center of ethnic cohesion.

Shoshoni Sun Dance Ideology and the Revitalization Theory

The foregoing reconstruction of the Wind River Shoshoni Sun Dance presupposes continuity in patterns and ideas up to our own time. This interpretation has recently been challenged by J. Jorgensen in a provocative book, *The Sun Dance Religion*. He suggests that the modern vigorous Sun Dance among the Ute and Shoshoni (which both belong to the Numic-speaking peripheral Plains and Basin groups) constitutes a so-called redemptive movement, and thus has little connection with the old Sun Dance. He puts this new "Sun Dance religion," as he calls it, on a par with nativistic, contra-acculturative movements (although he refuses to use a term like acculturation).

Jorgensen points out that the main motivations for the dance are an oppressed population's need for health and happiness in a white-dominated world, and for tribal coherence against white

17. There is testimony that, in spite of Shimkin's denial, dolls had been used in the time between the two World Wars by Sun Dance leaders Andrew Bazil and Morgan Moon.

18. In Shimkin's words, the Sun Dance is "going far in socializing shamanism" (cf. Shimkin 1939: 9).

power, furthermore the single individual's need for personal status and esteem within his community (cf. Jorgensen 1972: 234 ff., 244, 246 ff.). It is the ritual participant's conscious intention to gain supernatural power in the dance. He does it in order to forward his own health, or that of others, or to help those who are mourning by injecting into them resources from the power-filled ceremony. If possible, he also tries to become a medicine-man through visions during the dance (cf. Jorgensen 1972: 247). In Jorgensen's view the Shoshoni Sun Dance is not just a ceremony, it is the nucleus of a religious movement, a Sun Dance religion. He adopts the view that in the 1880s, "at a time when the Wind Rivers had lost access to the strategic resources on which they once subsisted, when their movements were restricted, and when their death rate greatly outstripped their birth rate, a few Wind River shamans began to retool the Sun Dance ritual" (Jorgensen 1972: 18). There was a change in focus from hunting and warfare to curing of illness and maintenance of communal unity, and "a few Shoshone shamans sought a solution to the illness, death, and petty factionalism that became pervasive in the 1870s and 1880s" (Jorgensen 1972: 19). Thus the Sun Dance was reworked and crystallized into a redemptive movement (cf. Jorgensen 1972: 77).

Jorgensen observes that the restructuring of the Sun Dance took place when the people had lost faith in another revitalization movement, the Ghost Dance. Using D. Aberle's terminology, he states that when the transformative movement the Ghost Dance failed, people turned to a redemptive movement, the new Sun Dance. According to Aberle, a transformative movement seeks total change of social or natural order, whilst a redemptive movement seeks total change of the individual (cf. Aberle 1966: 318 ff.). It stands to reason that in North America a movement of the latter kind should be more successful during reservation time. The Sun Dance "religion" has persisted for almost a century and will, in Jorgensen's view, continue to persist.

Is Jorgensen's picture correct? His description of the changes about 1890 are certainly to the point: this was the time when Christian symbolism began to be accepted, when references to war and hunting were dampened down, and problems of tribal cohesion and, in particular, concerns of health took precedence in prayers and rituals. The gradual reduction of other ritual complexes, such as the vision-quest, have given a strengthened importance to the dance, and perhaps the visions received in the dance. Thus the Sun Dance has become the focus of Shoshoni religious life, an observation that I was able to make during my field research (cf. Hultkrantz 1969: 27, 33).

However, I do not agree with Jorgensen when he defines this modified Sun Dance as a redemptive movement in the sense referred to. In the minds of the participants this "western form" of the Sun Dance is not separated from other Sun Dances. Nor is it alien to other Plains tribes, and it attracts visitors from these peoples. The Shoshoni are conscious of its supposed origin in a very ancient time, and the procedures follow basically the old Sun Dance pattern. The Sun Dance is not considered a separate "religion" but part of the old religion. At the most we may say that the old religion has been condensed into a "Sun Dance religion" (I used this expression in Hultkrantz 1969: 22).

If my reasoning here is correct, as I think it is, the present leaders of the Sun Dance would still today cling to a traditional, possibly cosmological interpretation of the ceremony. In the following I shall try to demonstrate that this is the case to a large extent, through three consecutive operations:

1. an investigation of Shoshoni opinion on the meaning of the Sun Dance;

2. an analysis of traditional symbolism of the cultic lodge; and

3. a short examination of the nature and function of Christian symbolism attached to the Sun Dance lodge.

The Meaning of the Sun Dance

As has emerged from the foregoing, the manifest meaning of the Sun Dance has change considerably over the generations. Still, due to the conservatism of religious thought it should be possible to reveal some very old tenets still held by practitioners. The investigator has to be aware of the fact that the Shoshoni generally confuse the meaning of the dance with the motives behind the arrangement of individual dances or the joining in the dance by individual believers.

The presumably original existential interpretation turns up occasionally. Said informant L.S.C.,[19] "we dance the Sun Dance so

19. In the following the informants will be rendered by their initial letters. Two main informants who have already been mentioned are John Trehero (J. T.) and L. St. Clair (L. S. C.). Of these Clair (1903–1952) was my foremost informant on the symbolism of the Sun Dance. He had, as I have indicated, written an account of the Sun Dance which, however, deviated in part from what he told me. He explained that this was due to his reticence to present the true facts in the manuscript. Lynn had received his information from the knowledgeable old-timer Judge Ute, or Yutatsi (1843–1927).

that we may live during the winter, survive it and manage to live until next summer, when we have a new Sun Dance." The same informant also said that people pray "for strength, happiness, many animals to kill, berries and roots and good health and happiness for the people." Or as J. T. put it, he hoped for good spiritual gifts in the days to come. Closely connected with prayers for the future is the thanksgiving for past blessings. For instance, when at the sunrise rite the dancers face the east they thank the Supreme Being for the sun and its light and for the life that he bestows on the earth (L. S. C.). J. T. felt good when his grandson returned unhurt from Korea. God was good, and he wanted to thank him by sponsoring a Sun Dance for the people; "I could not thank God in any other way."

It is a common observation today, also conceded by an idealist like L. S. C., that all Shoshoni have different views of what the Sun Dance stands for.[20] L. S. C. could even see that "people enjoy meeting, it always makes you glad to see your friend and relative." He was quite aware that many interpretations are possible. Foremost among them all he stressed the curative aspect (cf. St. Clair n.d.). According to him, the buffalo spirit of the inauguration vision[21] said the following to the hero who was granted the message to set up the first Sun Dance: "Our Father on high sent me to you to tell you that a certain power will be imparted to you. It will enable you to cure those who are sick. You may cure any sickness by faith and prayer. I shall give you that power. ... When you have gone through [the Dance] the power will help you to extract those agents that make people sick." Other informants (T. R., P. C., and others) agreed that this was the chief message of the Sun Dance. One of medicine-man J. T.'s guardian spirits once urged its client to go into the Sun Dance and pray with the other dancers for the sick.

Some other interpretations are also given, probably spoils from the one more comprehensive program and import of the dance. There is still a vague remembrance that the Sun Dance gives divinatory visions of war. L. S. C. told me that in the old days a person who fainted from exhaustion in the dance was covered with a buffalo robe. When he came to he vomited white horsehair, for instance—a sure

20. In her unpublished notes Miss Marion Roberts states that all dancers have different reasons for going into the dance: some think they will recover from illness, others ask for a good harvest, and still others go in for renown (Roberts n.d.).

21. L S. C., quoting Ute (see above), embraced the tradition that the Sun Dance was first entrusted to the Shoshoni by a buffalo spirit. This tradition is at variance with another tradition according to which Yellow Hand dreamt about a human spirit he had seen as a white man in a picture.

sign that the people would win a battle and catch a white horse from the enemy, or make a coup on that horse. Several features of the old ceremony indicated that it was once coupled with military purposes, such as the formal "killing" of the tree selected to become the center post, the singing of a war song in front of the center post during the dance by a woman or an old man, and the fire-bringers' songs about their stealing horses from the enemy. These rites are, of course, now obsolete. However, wars are still topical. T. W. put up a Sun Dance in 1948 because some young Shoshoni had been drafted for military service, and he feared there would be a new war. He wanted the boys to be safe and out of danger, so he prayed for them.

Another motive for arranging or joining a Sun Dance is to attain supernatural power. Nobody prays for such power, as one does in the vision-quest; if it comes, this is coincidental (L. S. C.). When in 1955 T. R. found that he recently had had bad luck and made bad medicine he decided to put up next year's Sun Dance; this way he thought he could bring about a change for the better. Many medicine-men use their powers in the Sun Dance, either in curing people, or prophesying or calling forth a soothing rain. Some are granted such power in the visions they receive during the dance.

My chief informant on the Sun Dance and its ideology, L. S. C., made a remarkable connection between the dance and Shoshoni eschatology. "If," he said, "I believe in the Sun Dance and go in and believe that I shall be free from my sickness, then I shall recover. If I am a good Indian and pray to the Father to help me, I have a straight road to walk after death. However, if I do not believe in the Sun Dance, and I live a no good life, I shall walk the other road and do not come to the Father." It is easy to see Christian reminiscences in this pronouncement. However, the double path of afterlife has a definite association to the old symbolism of the center post, as we shall soon see.

It is, as we observed, necessary to make a distinction between the ideological frame, or meaning, of the Sun Dance and the causes (motives) of joining it or putting it up. Too often the issues are confused by the Shoshoni, as in the cases of T. R. and T. W., related above. In a few instances they are kept distinct, in most cases only individual motives are given. For instance, the sponsor of the Sun Dance in 1955, J. T., was urged in a vision to arrange it, no reason being provided. "I dreamt this year," said J. T., "that the eagle wanted me to put up the Sun Dance, for three nights and three days, for all my people. . . . The spirit pointed out to me the place of the Sun Dance lodge." Such a commandment has, certainly, some interior meaning, but it is hidden from human beings. The spirits have their reasons which man cannot grasp.

All the variety of interpretations which have been reproduced here indicate that the meaning of the Sun Dance, vaguely perceived in some statements, is mostly obscured behind individual motives (which may be considered to represent parts of this meaning). It is furthermore obvious that, although the Shoshoni may be aware of a cosmic symbolism in their Sun Dance, the idea of a cyclic renewal as a re-creation of the world is not present in their thoughts. We have to keep this in mind when the account now turns to the symbolism of the Sun Dance lodge and its particulars.

Cultic Symbolism

In the following presentation only such cultic objects as I found associated with the Sun Dance lodge will be referred to. Thus the heap of stones and the digging-stick, mentioned by Shimkin, will not be discussed (for pictures of the Shoshoni Sun Dance, cf. Shimkin 1953: pl. 30–37; Hultkrantz 1973b: pl. xvii–xxv).

1. The dance lodge. The dance lodge is called *taguwunexa*, "thirst-standing-lodge," or *taguwunögani*, "thirst-standing-house"; *taguwunö*, or thirst-standing, being the name of the Sun Dance. The name thus refers to the physical exertion, not to the sacred import of the lodge.

This does not mean to say that the lodge is not sacred. "The Sun Dance lodge is a symbol of the world," said L. S. C. "It is round because it is the world.[22] The rafters are supposed to extend over the earth. It is the first place where the humans could pray." Here is the original idea of the lodge as a microcosmos, a sacred replica of the earth or the world, clearly expressed.

Those who take part in the preparation dance—which is sometimes performed at the place where the dancing lodge will be erected—"dance to make the ground sacred place." "After the last preliminary night's singing the ground of the Sun Dance lodge is sacred ground" (L. S. C.). This means that in principle only the dancers are allowed in the section of the lodge where dancing takes place; not even a reputed medicine-man is supposed to be there unless he is

---

22. The Indians represent the earth as a round disc (cf. Müller 1970: 203 ff., Sioux Indians).

The Sun Dance lodge.

one of the dancers. Outsiders coming in to receive blessings from dancing medicine-men are often requested to take off their moccasins and, if men, their hats. Women in the process of menstruation and men who are drunk have to keep away from the lodge. L. S. C. was most upset when after a Sun Dance in 1948 mounted youths played around inside the lodge.

The normal procedure is that the lodge rots away, or that its timbers are sold to interested buyers, whites, and half-breeds. This is a new custom, said N., but "it spoils the medicine": diseases return to those who have been cured during the dance. However, even today the central pole is left to decay.

2. The center pole. The middle post, or "forked pole" (*wurušagar*), is the most sacred part of the lodge. Ideally it should be a cottonwood tree which is quite juicy when green; however, nowadays also a pine tree may be chosen, for cottonwood grows sixteen miles up the river, whereas pine is available up in the foothills. A cottonwood center pole "is always cool, however much the sun shines on it; this is not the case with common cottonwood trees" (L. S. C.). Stories circulate that during the dance the center pole opens, and water comes out. It is spiritual water that blesses the dancers but only can be seen by some. Dancers may drink it through their whistles.

These wonderful qualities of the center post, as well as the ceremonial felling of the tree, the sham battle around it, and the circumstantial ritual at its raising, testify to its symbolic importance. N. told me that the center pole "from way back, when the Sun Dance was given to my people," was a vehicle for prayers. "The Father above told us that we must not destroy this pole, it should be left standing to decay naturally, for all the prayers and the ailments of the sick who attended the Dance still remain on this pole." However, my informants were careful to point out that the prayers were not directed to the center pole as such, just as they were not meant for the sun.[23] The pole thus serves as an intermediary between man and God. Sacred power emanates from the pole. L. S. C. admonished me to observe how the medicine-man J. B., when attending to the sick in the dance, first stroked his medicine-feathers against the center post before he made them touch his patients.

It is obvious that the center pole, besides being a communication channel for prayers, represents divine power. "Many sun dancers pray before the center pole, for it stands for Christ. Before this was done they prayed there nevertheless, for it stood for Our Father above," said G. W., a man in his thirties in 1948. Chief Dick Washakie told Grace Hebard in 1926 that the cottonwood tree of the Sun Dance hall represented God.[24] L. S. C.'s opinion was that this forked pole "is a sign for the Milky Way. The Milky Way is believed to be a great path over which travel the people who have passed to the beyond"

23. Cf. L. S. C.: "The dancers pray to God to bless them through the centre pole. But I have never heard anybody pray to the centre pole or the sun; they always pray to Our Father."

24. Chief Dick Washakie was the son of old Chief Washakie, the last tribal chief (Hebard 1930: 294).

(St. Clair n.d.).²⁵ Thus the center pole has the function of being a replica of God and of the "backbone of the sky," as the Shoshoni call the Milky Way (*tugungu:himp*). The cosmic associations are obvious. The center, God, the Milky Way, the communication channel—this is the world pole, the *axis mundi,* and the road to God and the powers above.

In this light the very last ritual gesture becomes understandable. When the dance is over the dancers throw their aprons at the foot of the center pole, and some of the spectators tie on some pieces of clothing, and also tobacco or feathers, to the pole. In the old days, N. told me, the center pole was sometimes covered with the clothing of the participants and their relatives. They should obviously be interpreted as prayers to the Supreme Being, a kind of communicative offerings. N. informed me further that the supplicant first made a prayer to God, and then placed a dress or a blanket as an offering. The custom seems to be the same today. J. T. said that anybody who is sick—not necessarily a dancer—could "throw away [*witēin*] his disease" by laying down his clothes by the pole. The disease would, he meant, dwindle away with the clothes. On the plain outside of Fort Washakie, one can still observe those lonely forked poles with clothing attached to them, the last remnants of a Sun Dance celebrated months or perhaps years before.

3. The buffalo head. A head of buffalo, *kwïc,* is fixed on the center pole just where the forked branches come together, or slightly below. It faces west and is the center of attention during dancing. In the old days it was painted with white clay, and sweetsage was put into its nostrils (L. S. C.). The latter custom is still extant. Another old custom, counting coup on the buffalo head by an old man before it was put in place (L. S. C.), has become obsolete.

The symbolism of the buffalo head was explained in the following way by L. S. C.: The buffalo represents the buffalo spirit of the founding vision, "the first message"; the sweetsage in its nostrils is "the symbol of the vapor" of this spirit, for "that had the smell of sweet sage." Also, the buffalo on the pole stands for food and nourishment. J. T. made the following statement: "The buffalo was created here on earth for food. He is the biggest eatable animal that

25. L. S. C. explained to me that from the fork there is a bad path to the left, and a good one to the right, and in the Sun Dance you should ask God to be admitted to walk the right path. This echoes Christian teaching. However, the idea of a road of the dead which is split in two, one for those who embraced the tribe's values and conformed to them in their lives, and one for those who lived unworthy lives and are excluded from the community in afterlife, is known from many parts of North America.

Buffalo head in the Sun Dance lodge.

has a split hoof. And all animals that have a foot like the buffalo are eatable. For that reason he represents the eatable animals on the pole." Several dancers who have been staring at the buffalo head while dancing during the potent second day, the day of visions, have experienced how the buffalo head moves, its eyes roll violently, and steam stands around its nostrils. Such signs predict a vision, perhaps of the buffalo spirit itself.

The stuffed buffalo head has replaced the buffalo skull of

earlier days, but the symbolism is apparently the same. It represents the most important economic resource of the heyday of Plains culture, when enormous bison herds strolled over the grounds. Its association with a ceremony that means the rejuvenation of all nature's resources is therefore natural. If the spirit that revealed the ceremony to the people had the form of a buffalo, this points to the importance the buffalo had in comparison to other animals. Indeed, there are hints that the buffalo spirit was a kind of a master of the game in Plains Indian ideology. "He is the chief of all animals," said the well-informed L.S.C. (cf. Hultkrantz 1961a: 208 f., 216).

4. The willows. A bunch of willows (*sihö^{wi}*) or grass is attached to the fork of the center pole. I heard that in former days the buffalo skull should have been fastened over this bunch, but I have only seen Sun Dances where the buffalo head was placed under the willows (cf. D. Washakie in Hebard 1930: 294). It seems more reasonable to imagine that the eagle (cf. below) had the willows as its nest, as was the case among other Plains Indians.

The willows are tied in such a way that the ends point south and north (St. Clair n.d.). I do not know if this arrangement has any symbolic implication.

According to L. S. C., the willows are symbols of the growing food.[26] They have been produced by Mother Earth. They stand for "the branches carrying nourishment for the living." L. S. C. drew a parallel between berry bushes and willows on one side, human beings on the other: the former are more reliable than the humans, they have a duty to fulfill, and that is to feed the humans.

It strikes us that this description is not quite accurate: willows and grass may be food for buffaloes but not for men. The original idea was possibly that the willows symbolized the new verdure that would provide the animals—horses, buffaloes, antelopes, and so on—with food. Unless, of course, the eagle nest idea was basic.

5. The eagle. One of the rafters that serve as a "roof" carries at its top end an eagle, or eagle feathers. This rafter, which runs in an east-west direction from its anchorage in the center pole, is usually called "the backbone," and is deeply forked. In the old days people caught an eagle (*pia kwina*) for each, or every second, Sun Dance. Like other Prairie and Plains tribes the Shoshoni constructed small hidea-

---

26. The willows that are shaken by the female choir seated close to the drummers left of the lodge entrance have the same symbolism. "It is the women's task to pick berries and roots," said L. S. C., "and the shaking of the willows is a prayer of much vegetational food."

ways made from stones on mountain ridges, and caught the eagles alive there (C. S.).[27] Nowadays the bird is usually replaced by its tailfeathers, or a stuffed bird is fetched. I have seen both alternatives used. When the dance has ended the eagle, or eagle feathers, are brought back to a pine in the mountains.

Like the buffalo the eagle is a most sacred being. L. S. C. told me that he represents "the second message" in the Sun Dance legend, at the same time as he symbolizes peace and purity. "The second message" was handed down to L. S. C. by Judge Ute and begins in the following way: "Many years after the introduction of the Sun Dance [through the buffalo vision], when the first sun dancers had long been dead, a young Shoshoni had a nightly vision. It was an eagle that came flying from the place of sunset towards east, into the tipi of the sleeping young man.[28] The spirit said that he should make new the endurance dance." The eagle ordered some new ritual performances, prescribed that an eagle bird was appended to the "backbone" pole, and that black rings should be painted on the nether part of the center pole for the number of days the dance should run. (Since the painting should be done by a brave warrior who at the same time recounted his war deeds this custom has become abandoned.) Finally, the eagle instructed the people to put up as many roof poles as he had tailfeathers—twelve in number—and to make whistles to be used in the dance from the bones of his shoulder wings and to use his wings as a fan in healing sick persons.

The same informant, L. S. C., remarked that the Supreme Being had selected the eagle for his second message because "he is superior to all birds, and in his flight he will soar; his body is free from impurity." (On the other hand, L. S. C. underlined that the eagle is not, like the U.S. eagle emblem, a symbol of freedom.) Before the eagle is fastened to the rafter, a man chosen for the task offers a prayer in which he asks the Supreme Being to bless the people "as you have this eagle to whom you have given power to fly in the sky, where there is fresh clean air, where there is no sickness" (St. Clair n.d.).

The eagle is the bird of peace. His feathers are used "for peaceful meeting." If two Indian groups come together, they hold up eagle feathers as a token of peace, said L. S. C. This is, of course, an echo of calumet and peace pipe ceremonies on the central and northern Plains. At the same time the custom conforms to conceptions of

27. The procedure is described in Wilson 1928: 108 ff., Hidatsa Indians.
28. The buffalo in the first vision arrived, on the other hand, from the rising sun, for "like the sun he gives life and food for man" (L. S. C.).

the eagle held all over North America. On the other hand, the Sun Dance eagle's association with the thunderbird is not as clear-cut with the Shoshoni, as for instance, it is among the Oglala Sioux.

It seems that the symbolism of the eagle as expressed here is a reformulation of its role—known all over the northern hemisphere—as the heavenly bird (the messenger of God, or God himself) at the top of the world tree.[29] Such a reformulation could easily take place within the frame of the vision pattern so characteristic for the Plains Indians and for the Shoshoni. L. S. C., who was a chairman of the Sun Dance committee, had witnessed many cases where dancers had experienced visions of a spiritual eagle, groped after it with their arms and then fallen backward or sideways, losing their consciousness. J. T. was visited in his sleep by an eagle who urged him to put up a Sun Dance. "The eagle gave me the Sun Dance." It is most probable that the so-called second message (insofar as it really contained any innovations) had a similar origin.

6. The flags. The forks of the center pole are topped by two square flags. Tradition prescribes that they should be one white, the other blue. However, also other colors are possible, provided they express the opposition between light and dark. L. S. C. saw them as symbols of day and night, sky and earth (cf. St. Clair n.d.). In other words, the two branches of the tree are supposed to express the cosmic duality.

I noticed that at one Sun Dance the northern fork had a yellow and the southern a whitish flag, which does not conform to this interpretation; also, the center pole had been painted yellow up to shoulder height. The reason for this was a vision that the medicine-man T. R., one of the Sun Dance leaders, had had. T. R. told me he was visited by one of those spirits that had instructed the people about the first Sun Dance. The spirit, that looked like a human being, approached him from the north and said, "When you put up the Sun Dance, use yellow paint. Tell the tribe that whenever they are going to have a Sun Dance to paint it yellow."[30]

29. According to Dick Washakie, eagle feathers could be fastened to the high forked branches of the center pole (Hebard 1930: 294). Other observers have like myself seen the eagle lashed to the tip of a long rafter (Hart and Carlson 1948: 8). Reports that the eagle was tied to the lower end of a rafter just over the entrance seem less trustworthy (Stafford 1938; this paper is apparently a copy of an anonymous ms. in Wind River Agency Files n.d.).

30. It should be added that the medicine-man Morgan Moon, active during the time between the World Wars, and mentioned in the foregoing, demanded all dancers to have yellow paint the first dancing day (information by L. S. C.).

This example shows how easily symbols may change character in the Plains area. L. S. C. was aware of this: "In the eagle vision [=the second message] people were told to make the flags green and blue, since the eagle and Our Father have their abodes in the sky. Later on, since we introduced two Sun Dances [each season], the colors have been revealed in the sponsor's vision."

7. The manikin. The Sun Dance doll (*puēlk*) is no regular feature of the modern Sun Dance. B. S. C. remembered that before about 1918 a doll was carved for each new Sun Dance by a certain man selected for the job. It was made from wood, had feathers sticking up from the back of the head, and its cheeks were decorated with the lightning sign. According to B. S. C., this wooden doll was the spirit that imparted the first instructive vision to the founder of the Sun Dance.[31] T. R. called the doll "the spirit of the Sun Dance" (cf. Shimkin 1953: 418, 441 n. 48), and L. S. C. said vaguely that "it represents creation."

What T. R. and L. S. C. said holds good for the present doll spirit as well, although its import is slightly different. As B. S. C. stressed, the doll used by Andrew Bazil in the 1920s was his personal medicine, and the same goes for the present doll which is in the possession of J. T. The latter puts it up when he himself, or a relative of his, dances and needs protection. It is then fixed on the west side of the center pole, about two meters from the ground. It portrays a little Indian, thirty cm. in height, made from buckskin and thus white and yellow in color. There is a little green feather at the back of the head. The facial features are sown with a black thread, and the eyes are small black crosses. J. T. received this spirit in a vision. It is a "desert spirit" that helps when a person is strained, and J. T. called it "the great medicine-man that gives power in the Sun Dance." At the same time he regarded it as a link in the chain of Sun Dance dolls: he had, he said, received it from the old-timers. It connected him with his ancestor, Yellow Hand, who owned the first Sun Dance doll.

All the data presented here clearly show that the Sun Dance lodge and its parts have a cosmological symbolism. It could be easily demonstrated that also the paraphernalia of the dancers and the ritual actions before and during the dance may express a similar symbolism.

31. B. S. C. probably refers to the spirit of the picture revealed to Yellow Hand (cf. footnote 21).

However, our special object of analysis has been the cultic lodge, and its symbolic language is unequivocal.

Compared with the preceding account of the meaning of the Sun Dance, the analysis of cult symbolism brings out more readily the ulterior import of the dance. Some statements on the meaning of the Dance seem to get along with the symbolic interpretation of the dancing lodge, others are mixed up with the particular motives for arranging a dance.

In addition, there is the confusion caused by the application of Christian symbolism.

Christian Reinterpretation

The main lines of Christian reinterpretation of the Sun Dance were presented in an earlier paper (cf. Hultkrantz 1969: 36 ff.). Here I shall restrict the account to the Christian symbolism in the Sun Dance lodge but at the same time present some more details.

One strong difference from the foregoing description will immediately catch the attention: whereas there was a fair consensus about traditional symbolism, there is not the same agreement among informants as to the Christian interpretation. Indeed, one and the same individual may even suggest different Christian symbols to denote one and the same cultic phenomenon. Thus L. S. C. identified the center pole as the cross, Christ, and the path through life. The same persons who ascribe a traditional tribal symbolism to the dancing lodge will, as an addition to this, and as an afterthought, present a Christian interpretation. This attitude fits in with my observations of the Shoshoni tendency to conceive alternating religious configurations (Cf. Hultkrantz 1969: 26 f., and literature referred to there). At the same time it bears testimony that the Christian symbolism is imposed upon the Sun Dance and does not constitute its ideological premises.

The Christian reinterpretation represents a process that certainly took its beginning about 1890 but, since that date, has gone on incessantly. As an example could be mentioned the case of L. S. C. When studying to become a catechist in the Episcopal church this faithful guardian of Shoshoni traditions found out that Christ and his Apostles were represented in the upright main poles of the Sun Dance lodge. After 1945 he and his companions made these findings public in the Shoshoni Sun Dance camp.

Here are some examples of Christian reinterpretation.

1. The dance lodge is, according to Y. S., the grave of Christ. "When you get out of it you go to a renewed life, like Christ." An imaginative Idaho Shoshoni (J. R., belonging to the *hukandïka* group (cf. Hultkrantz 1975: 139 f.)) told me that the dance symbolizes how Jesus hung on the cross for three days and then was taken down. He also said that the rafters of the lodge stand for the apostles, and the brush intertwined in the "wall" for the innumerable members of the people.

2. The center pole is in most cases Christ or, as he is designed in this connection, "Our Brother." L. S. C. explained that by its fork the center pole forms the sign for brother in the sign language: two fingers drawn out of the mouth into the air (cf. Clark 1885: 82). Another interpretation is that the center pole represents the cross of Christ, for the bunch of willows forms the arms of the cross (L. S. C.).[32] Finally, it is our path through life, a conception which may have Christian patterning, as noted in the foregoing.

In contradistinction to traditional symbolism also other poles may have a symbolic value in Christian reinterpretation. The twelve main corner poles are designated the Apostles of Christ. Also the twelve rafters are so called ("Jesus' brothers"). One informant, J. T., agreed with the first interpretation, but at the same time he suggested that the poles standing directly north and south of the center pole represent the robbers of Golgotha. L. S. C. who was not very sympathetic to J. T. denied the truth of this interpretation.

3. The buffalo head was identified as Christ by T. W. and G. W., father and son. I did not find that other Shoshoni applied a Christian interpretation in this case. See however the paragraph on the eagle, below.

4. The willows may be seen as part of the cross (see above). One of Shimkin's informants held that the willows symbolize the holy water that Christ made in the mountains (cf. Shimkin 1953: 441).

5. The eagle, the "second messenger" according to L. S. C., might be a representative of the New Testament (just as the buffalo, in a vague sense, might be the Old Testament) in L. S. C.'s opinion. It was his thought that the eagle vision was sent at the birth of Christ. The rafter that the eagle is resting on is, said the same informant, the Judas pole, for it is the only rafter that is forked. L. S. C. is referring here to the sign language where "talking with a forked tongue"

32. The missionaries translated "cross" into Shoshoni "branched tree" (cf. Roberts 1925: 13).

stands for lying (cf. Clark 1885: 234). Judas was, of course, a liar, hence the association.

6. There is to my knowledge no Christian symbolism attached to the flags.

7. The doll is a symbol of Jesus. L. S. C. admitted this interpretation, although he rightly suspected that the doll then (1948) in use was made by J. T.'s wife.

Conclusions

It is now possible to arrive at some valid conclusions concerning the original idea and later religious change of the Shoshoni Sun Dance. The analysis of the symbolism of the lodge itself provides us with means to make this evaluation, and it also helps us to judge Jorgensen's theory that the modern dance is a revitalization movement.

First of all, it is obvious that the Shoshoni Sun Dance lodge, like many other Sun Dance lodges, evinces a symbolism that stresses its character of being a renewal ceremony with cosmological implications.[33] The symbolism of the cultic lodge brings out that, whatever the motives for the arrangement of the Sun Dance, its basic ideology must once have been largely identical with that of the modelling western Algonkian tribes (Cheyenne, Arapaho). This is an important statement. It furthermore generates the hypothesis that the original idea behind all the older Sun Dance performances among the Plains tribes had the same contents.

We may here pause and make some other inferences. It seems reasonable to presuppose that the old Shoshoni way of life and its values were expressed in the original thanksgiving ceremony, the "Father Dance." When, however, this hunting-and-gathering existence was superimposed by the more nomadic and colorful Plains culture—with its roots in highly developed cultures farther east—the Father Dance was replaced by the Sun Dance in importance and slowly dwindled away. The Sun Dance embodied the ideas and values of the bison hunting, warlike Plains tribes (cf. Hultkrantz 1949:

---

33. Wissler's statement, that Plains Indian art "is strongly geometric, but as a whole, not symbolic" (Wissler 1950: 222), is apparently erroneous (cf. Wissler 1941: 132 ff., in particular 137).

153). It also contained the cosmogonic and cosmological symbolism of the eastern cultures. The deep impact of the Sun Dance in Shoshoni culture is obvious to anyone studying their traditional religion. There is even a tale of rats dancing a Sun Dance in a buffalo skull, and J. T. told me he had seen one morning bears perform the Sun Dance at a creek (cf. Hultkrantz 1970a: 72 f.)!

Our second conclusion is that the Christian reinterpretation of the symbolism of the Sun Dance lodge is accidental rather than integrative. From the outset it represented a kind of reconciliation between Christian and Shoshoni religions. The Christian symbolism was an additive element in the Sun Dance designed to make the latter more acceptable to Christian missionaries. We must remember that from the 1880s onward missionaries and superintendents made efforts to prohibit the Plains Sun Dances, and some clergymen on the Wind River reservation succeeded in closing the ceremony for a number of years. The religious liberalism initiated by the government after 1934, and the proclamation of the free exertion of American Indian religions in 1978, have, of course, made such reasons for a Christian reinterpretation increasingly superfluous. In later years the Christian symbolism has served as an alibi for the participation in the dance by Indians with a predominating Christian faith. There is reason to believe that with the new religious situation the Christian reinterpretation will gradually weaken.

The third conclusion we can draw is that Jorgensen's view of the Shoshoni Sun Dance as a redemptive movement is misleading. It is true that health and curing of disease are prominent issues in today's Sun Dancing. However, this is not a testimony of a restructuring of the dance, its transformation into a new religion. It only means that one of the moments of the Sun Dance mystery, the renewal of life and health, has received a central position in a daily existence no longer marked by anxieties for the survival of the tribe and the world, but by worries of the individual's fate in a multi-dimensional human situation.

Finally, a comparison with the modern Crow Sun Dance is rewarding. The Crow, situated in southwestern Montana, earlier had a Sun Dance which, however, on account of its close association with military life disappeared with the cessation of warfare in the 1870s (cf. Lowie 1915c: 5). In 1941 the Shoshoni J. T. introduced the Shoshoni form of the Sun Dance among the Crow (cf. Voget 1948: 634 ff.). The Crow Dance thus shares the peculiar traits of the Shoshoni Dance, such as the concentration on health and curing, and the back-and-forth dancing.[34] Recently, the symbolism of the Crow Sun Dance lodge has been studied by Miller (cf. Miller 1977). He was not able to find any clear cut Crow statements on the renewal-of-the-world motif,[35] but the cosmic symbolism seems clear.

Miller states that to the Crow the center pole and the circle of forked poles surrounding it are "symbols of the cosmos as a whole." The shape of the lodge provides "a visual image of the cosmos of the Crow." The center pole is the center of the sacred space of the lodge, and the place where power is concentrated. One of its forks represents heaven, the other earth, and their merging at the fork signifies the unity of these cosmic principles. At the base of the pole cigarettes are collected which have been smoked in prayer by dancers. "With these objects the center pole becomes a representation both of the powers to whom the Dance is directed and of the silent and verbal offerings which invite them to sanctify the Lodge by their presence."

The buffalo head, the eagle, and the buckskin doll are appended to or near the center pole as they are in the Shoshoni Dance. They have here the same symbolic implications. The eagle is said to be very closely associated with the Supreme Being.

The cosmic symbolism of the Crow Sun Dance, an offshoot of the modern Shoshoni Sun Dance, is thus most evident. Perhaps it partly derives from the old Crow Dance, although the hiatus of sixty-seven years between the two dance forms seems to preclude this possibility. The parallels with Shoshoni symbolism are so intimate that the latter has probably been the chief source of inspiration. It seems, however, that in both Sun Dances the basic ideological struc-

---

34. For some reasons unknown to me Jorgensen identifies the "new" Sun Dance as a particular expression of the aspirations of the Numic-speaking peoples. The Crow are not mentioned. In this way he can easier keep the new dance apart from the "true" Plains ceremony.

35. In a letter to me (Miller May 10, 1978), Miller states that he was surprised by its absence. "I probed for it with a number of Crow friends, but in vain. It is all the more unusual in that the Crow do feel that the performance of the Sun Dance has a revitalizing effect on the community. I spoke with a number of dancers who said that one of the main reasons for their participation was the promotion of the general welfare of the Crow for the coming year. I also encountered a general, but rather vague, understanding that there is some danger, not clearly or specifically defined, in allowing a summer to go by without performing a Sun Dance. This in spite of the decidedly non-cyclical nature of the Sun Dance ritual itself. ... The emphasis seems to be on the present moment and the potential for future events, rather than upon a primordial past which must be re-created and renewed annually. Hence, the perception of the revitalization of the community without the attendant notion, which we could expect, of re-creation and renewal of the cosmic order."

ture to which the cosmic symbolism refers has fallen away as a conscious thought: the idea of the re-creation of the world. Among the Shoshoni we have no origin myth to substantiate this idea (cf. Hultkrantz 1960b: 565; Hultkrantz 1972a: 348 f.). The origin legend, instanced in the foregoing, sheds no light on the cosmological interpretation. What remains of the latter is the symbolism, and its language is clear.

14

The Changing Meaning of the Ghost Dance as Evidenced by the Wind River Shoshoni

Introduction

In THIS CHAPTER it is my intention to demonstrate how the Ghost Dance of the North American Indians, considered in its greater historical context, has changed its meaning over time. The Wind River Shoshoni of Wyoming will furnish materials for this perspective. The conclusions reached ought to have importance for our understanding of the background of the Ghost Dance movement which swept over great parts of the United States in 1889–90.

In order to set our theme within its larger framework, we shall discuss here firstly the main features of the Ghost Dance and the modern discussion around it.[1] Although the term "Ghost Dance" is not very concise,[2] it will be used here concerning two related movements, both of which stem from Northern Paiute Indians (formerly called Paviotso) in westernmost Nevada, and spread over large areas

1. For a convenient literary survey, see La Barre 1971.
2. The term has also been used more freely about cults associated with the dead and about revivalistic religious movements. The former case is illustrated by, for example, Dempsey's report on the Blackfoot "ghost dance " (Dempsey 1968). The term was used as a designation of all new religious movements in La Barre 1970.

of the American West. It will be shown that the Ghost Dance has its roots both in the Plateau and in the Basin areas. Next, the Wind River Shoshoni dance will be described and analyzed. It will be demonstrated that it continues a specific cultic pattern with a corresponding religious ideology. Finally, it will be suggested that this pattern occurred all over the Basin area before the appearance of the historical Ghost Dance, giving birth to the latter jointly with the Plateau Prophet Dance.

While data on the Basin and Plateau groups have been culled from the ethnographic literature, the Wind River data presented here are mainly based on my own and Dmitri Shimkin's field research among these Indians, as well as on historical and archival records.

The Ghost Dance and the Discussion around Its Antecedents

There are reasons to consider the 1890 Ghost Dance as a continuation of the 1870 Ghost Dance. The ideas and actions of the older Ghost Dance were reinforced and had a major breakthrough in the younger.

The 1870 Ghost Dance originated with Wodziwob ("grey hair"), also called Fish Lake Joe (because he apparently had spent his early life among the Fish Lake Paiute), 1844–1918 (?). When entering the scene of history, he was a resident of Walker Lake Reservation.[3] Some time about 1870 he went into a trance and received the divine message that the dead would be resurrected, the game restored, and the old-time tribal life returned to the earth. It seems that the prophet thence had repeatedly similar trance experiences, with the same general message (cf. Mooney 1896: 702 f.; Du Bois 1939: 5). The new doctrine was accompanied by a cultic dance which had to be performed at night. The dancers formed a circle, and they were supposed to have no fire in the center (Mooney 1896: 703; Du Bois 1939: 6 f.).

This Ghost Dance was of a short duration—just some few years—and did not have a very wide diffusion. It reached all Paiute, had some distribution in California, from the Yokuts-Chumash and

3. James Mooney, the famous ethnologist of the Second Ghost Dance, asserts that Wovoka's father, Tävibo, was the initiator of the first Ghost Dance. However, as proved by Cora Du Bois, the founder was Wodziwob (who was mentioned by Mooney as one of the prophets). See Mooney 1896: 701; Du Bois 1939: 3 ff.; Hittman 1973: 250 f., 260 ff.

northward, and had some converts in Oregon (Spier 1927; Gayton 1930; Du Bois 1939). In the east it made some impression on the Shoshoni and Bannock (Mooney 1896: 701; Jorgensen in press).

When speaking of the Ghost Dance we usually refer to the movement that was started in 1889 by a Paiute living in Mason Valley, Nevada, Wovoka ("the cutter") or Kwohitsauq ("big rumbling belly"), 1858–1932. He was also known as Jack Wilson, a name given to him by his white employers, a farming family bearing this name. He was the son of Tävibo, a man who apparently took part in the Ghost Dance of 1870 (Mooney 1896: 701 ff.; cf. above, footnote 3). Wovoka may have been influenced by his father. It is in any case striking that his message did not basically deviate from the gospel of the first Ghost Dance.

Wovoka had charismatic gifts. He could suck out diseases from his sick tribesmen, and he possessed the power of causing rain and snow (Mooney 1896: 772 f.; Bailey 1957: 207). Sometimes he relapsed into deep trances, and in consequence of one such trance, or more probably a whole series of trance experiences, he was called by the Supreme Being to prophesy a reunion between the living and the dead. The exact wording of the message seems to have varied. While in 1892, after the Sioux Ghost Dance disaster, Wovoka told James Mooney that people would gather in the other world, provided they lived righteous lives and danced the round dance given to him by the Lord (Mooney 1896: 771 f.), he had a more active message of the coming of the blessed realm to this world in a letter addressed to Arapaho and Cheyenne visitors (August 1891). The basic tenets were the following: the dead are arisen and are on their way to this earth, conducted by a spirit in a cloud-like appearance. The game is returning. There will be peace with the whites. There was also talk of the whites disappearing from Indian grounds (Mooney 1896: 779 ff., cf. 818). It is quite probable that Wovoka's message was more revolutionary than eschatological from the beginning, but that he tempered it down after the military campaign against the Sioux (cf. Overholt 1974: 41 ff., 49). Of course, the Sioux reinterpreted his original message in a violent way, anticipating, and thus indirectly contributing to, military action (Overholt 1974: 44, 54 ff.).

The dancing pattern in Wovoka's religion was probably identical with Wodziwob's, as, for instance, Gayton's material seems to demonstrate (Gayton 1930). Since the dancing structure is of importance to our main theme it will be briefly described here (cf. Mooney 1896: 802, 920 f.). The dancers, men and women, formed a circle, with their fingers interlocked. They progressed clockwise by taking small steps to the left, in a kind of shuffling movement. The dancers were surrounded by round structures of willow branches. The dancing which went on for four consecutive nights and a morning was accompanied by singing. The songs meditated the arrival of Old Man (God) and the dead. Mooney emphasizes that dancers never fell in a trance in the Paiute Ghost Dance (Mooney 1896: 772, 803; cf. Bailey 1957: 195). The trance states occurred in the Ghost Dance of the Plains Indians.[4]

Wovoka's Ghost Dance spread over great areas of western North America. Plains, Basin, and Desert tribes of the Southwest were all caught in its grip.[5] The reasons for its success may be sought in several factors, such as the precarious situation of the Plains tribes after the Indian wars and their confinement to reservations, spiritual depression as a result of cultural deprivation in many tribes, new means of intertribal communication (railroads), and so on. In the long run, of course, the Ghost Dance in its original form was doomed. The dead were supposed to come back in the spring of 1891 (Mooney 1896: 778). Even if the Sioux war had not interfered, the movement would have declined almost certainly after that date.

The discussion among scholars has concerned three themes: the distribution, antecedents, and revivalism of the Ghost Dance. The nature of its revivalism has, as could be expected, attracted most scholarly attention.[6] In this connection, however, the debate about the antecedents of the Ghost Dance will be of primary interest.

The discussion opened with Alice Fletcher's short paper on the Indian messiah, in which she tried to show that the major features of the Ghost Dance were integrating parts of the indigenous religions (Fletcher 1891).[7] To these features she adduced details of the ritual dancing, the faith in visions, and the eschatological beliefs. Subsequent research by Alfred Kroeber, Leslie Spier, Ann Gayton, and Cora Du Bois centered on the diffusion of the 1870 Ghost Dance in

4. Overholt is mistaken when he says that the trance was a common feature of the Ghost Dance (Overholt 1974: 56).

5. Cf. the distribution map in Mühlmann 1964. See also the study on the Ghost Dance in this work (Lindig and Dauer 1964).

6. I am thinking here primarily of phenomenological, sociological, and psychological works like those written by Clemhout, Guariglia, La Barre, Lanternari, Ljungdahl, Mühlmann, Smith, Thrupp, Voget, and Wallace. An original line of reasoning is represented by Hans-Peter Müller who considers that the Ghost Dance development was primarily determined by the situations on the Indian reservations (Müller 1975: 198).

7. This article should be distinguished from N. P. Phister's like-named article the same year (Phister 1891).

California (Kroeber 1904; Spier 1927; Gayton 1930; Du Bois 1939). In this connection Du Bois made it explicit that a study of the Ghost Dance process necessarily implies the use of the concept of diffusion (DuBois 1939: 135). Actually, some modern writers tend to create an opposition between process and diffusion in the handling of the Ghost Dance material.[8]

Spier's foremost contribution to the subject was a monograph in which he tried to establish an identity in doctrine between the first Paiute Ghost Dance and the so-called Prophet Dance of the Plateau (Spier 1935). The latter was an aboriginal Indian ritual complex since at least the 1800s, elaborated around prophets who during trance experiences had visited the other world and received information that the world would be destroyed and renewed, and the dead would return. By dancing a dance imitating the dances of the dead, the believers thought they could hasten these events (Spier 1935: 5, and passim). Spier could make it probable that the Prophet Dance had its roots in an ideological complex centering on beliefs around the dead: visits by the living, in particular shamans in a trance, to the dead, or shamans retrieving the lost souls of sick persons in the other realm, or—in the Orpheus tale—journeys of a hero of long ago to this realm (Spier 1935: 13 ff., 16). As Du Bois has remarked, the idea of a restoration of a soul from the dead may be embroidered upon to cover the return of many dead (Du Bois 1939: 3, 137). The epidemics that swept the Plateau and Northwest after the appearance of the white man could have been the trigger releasing such a wider concept, as Walker has tried to show, following suggestions made by Aberle (Walker 1969; Aberle 1959).[9]

Another anthropologist, William Strong, follows along the same lines. He has indicated that a late art style on the lower Columbia, characterized by rib cage motifs and other death motifs, points to a protohistoric ghost cult in the same area as the Prophet Dance (Strong 1945; cf. also Hultkrantz 1978: 124). Epidemics may indeed lie behind these religious expressions, as also Strong suggests.

However, many Prophet Dance manifestations contain a message of earth destruction which clearly refers to earthquakes (see,

8. Cf. the criticism of Du Bois in Müller 1975: 34. Hittman distinguishes between two types of explanation, replacing each other (Hittman 1973: 248). David Aberle has correctly demonstrated the logical error in this type of reasoning: Aberle 1959: 82.

9. However, Walker wrongly dismisses the importance of the Plateau death complex (Walker 1969: 250). Without it the Prophet Dance had scarcely taken form. Concerning possible Christian influences, see the end of the present chapter.

e.g., Ray 1936: 72). Since the Plateau is a region often affected by such natural disturbances the death cult could—as Spier, Herskovits, and Suttles mean—have purely indigenous motivation (Spier, Suttles, and Herskovits 1959). Be that as it may, the Prophet Dance occurred early in the Plateau area, penetrated the coast Salish area in the years about 1840 (Suttles 1957), and thus was a precursor of the Ghost Dance which it resembled in most aspects.

Was it, then, the inspirative force behind the Ghost Dance? Most scholars have taken this for granted after Spier's revelations, but Michael Hittman is of a different opinion. Hittman thinks that Wodziwob was a "crisis-broker" who cured the Walker River reservation Paiute from their deprivation due to loss of lands, frustration, epidemics, and starvation. Stressing the importance of the food quest and the shamanistic-curing complex in Northern Paiute culture, and adducing the disruption of the subsistence economy around 1870 and the grave epidemics 1867–68, Hittman suggests that the Ghost Dance of 1870 had two functions, that of an increase rite and that of a curing rite. "The 1870 Ghost Dance functioned as a curing rite, and since it was grafted upon the Round Dance, a traditional ceremony whose function was the increase of food supplies, the 1870 Ghost Dance also functioned as an increase rite" (Hittman 1973: 248, 264). It was thus the recently deceased, those who had lost their lives in the epidemics, who should return to earth: a collective extension of Wodziwob's accomplishments as a shaman who could fetch the souls of the seriously ill persons from the realm of death (Hittman 1973: 260 ff).[10]

I think Hittman has found some very good reasons for the immediate "outbreak" of the 1870 Ghost Dance, and that he has rightly combined it with extant ceremonial life. At the same time he has, in my view, overemphasized the shamanic role and in a faulty way dismissed the Prophet Dance heritage (Hittman 1973: 270 f.). It is true that there is no evidence of a Ghost Dance, or Prophet Dance, among the Northern Paiute of western Nevada before 1870 (Du Bois 1939: 3, quoting Willard Park). However, the following circumstances seem to indicate that about this time the Prophet Dance had repercussions among these Paiute:

---

10. Hittman's reconstruction of the Ghost Dance as possibly a transformed annual mourning ceremony brought by Wodziwob from his original people, the Paiute of Fish Lake Valley, is not at all convincing. For Hittman, this would explain how a death-shunning people like the Walter Lake Paiute could embrace the doctrine of the return of the dead (Hittman 1973: 264 ff.). However, Spier has referred to a similar fear of the dead among the Prophet-Dancing Plateau groups (Spier 1935: 13 f.).

1. The similarities in doctrine between the Ghost Dance and the Prophet Dance are astounding. Spier sees in the Southern Okanagon Prophet Dance a duplicate of the Paiute Ghost Dance: he mentions as common elements "the impending end and renewal of the world, the returning dead, the portent or the prophet's visit to the dead precipitating the dance anew, proselytizing, dances and songs learned from the dead, renewed contacts with the dead in trances during the dance, and so on" (Spier 1935: 9). The similarities are too obvious to allow a simplistic explanation à la Bastian.

2. According to the Prophet Dance doctrine on the Plateau, the culture hero and trickster, Coyote, will return with the dead before the high god proper (Spier 1935: 11, 18; Nash 1937: 415, 425). The idea of the returning culture hero, disseminated among Salishan and Algonkian peoples, is probably influenced by Christianity (Hultkrantz 1977: 429). When, however, the idea recurs among the Wind River Shoshoni in the Ghost Dance doctrine (cf. below) this very fact makes a direct connection between these Shoshoni and the Salish of the Plateau quite possible: in both cases Coyote leads the dead. We may presume that the northern Paiute had been affected in a similar way. Moreover, their relations with the Bannock and Shoshoni of Idaho and Wyoming were very vivid at this time.[11]

3. Spier suggested that the Northern Paiute had received the Prophet Dance via their kinsmen, the Oregon Paiute (Spier 1935: 22 f.; cf. Du Bois 1939: 136). This seems now quite probable. Du Bois reports that Wodziwob was assisted by another Paiute prophet, Weneyuga, who spread the Ghost Dance to the Washo, the Pyramid Lake Paiute, and those Northern Paiute who had been placed on the Klamath Indian Reservation after the treaty of 1864 (Du Bois 1939: 4 ff., 130). The interesting thing about Weneyuga is that he apparently contributed with the doctrine of the returning dead to the Ghost Dance (Du Bois 1939: 5). We know that the Modoc of the Klamath reservation had the Prophet Dance before 1870 (Spier 1935: 10 f.). In view of the connections between the Indians on this reservation and the Walker Lake Paiute, a direct Prophet Dance influence on the latter, possibly through Weneyuga, is not out of the question.

If the Northern Paiute imported their Ghost Dance doctrine, they certainly grafted it, as Hittman says, on their traditional round

---

11. Personal relationships, kinship relations, and folk narratives speak for these contacts. The wanderings and communication ties of individual Wind River Shoshoni were extensive, as Shimkin has shown and I have myself experienced among the Shoshoni.

dance. Spier was the first one to observe this double descent of the Ghost Dance, although he was uncertain whether the round dance was not originally, perhaps, Modoc (Spier 1935: 24).

In order to determine the nature of this dance, and establish its potentials to change over time, we now turn to a study of the Wind River Shoshoni Ghost Dance.

The Wind River Shoshoni Ghost Dance and Its Antecedents

The Wind River Shoshoni are named after their reservation in the Wind River Valley of western Wyoming. Before the treaty at Fort Bridger in 1868, the Wyoming Shoshoni (or Eastern Shoshoni) were divided in three fractions, the Plains Shoshoni who roamed the country between Salt Lake, the Sweetwater and the Bighorn Basin in the north, and who represented the Plains culture; the Sheepeaters who inhabited the mountainous areas where they dedicated themselves to the hunt of the bighorn sheep; and the small ethnic groups in southwestern Wyoming who were hunters and collectors (Hultkrantz 1958, 1966–67a, 1975). The Plains Shoshoni were more or less united under Chief Washakie, a great personality who sometimes also controlled the other Shoshoni groups. He remained the domineering Indian power in the reservation existence that started about 1870 (the wars with the Sioux and Cheyenne forced the Shoshoni to abandon their reservation on several occasions).

As noted above, these Shoshoni remained in touch with their kin, other Shoshoni, Bannock, and Paiute on the other side of the Rocky Mountains and in the western part of the Great Basin area. In May 1870, the Ghost Dance message reached the Shoshoni in the Bear River Valley, Utah, and the Bridger Basin, Wyoming, and the pertaining ceremonial dance was held (Jorgensen in press). What happened thereafter is difficult to tell. It seems, however, that new "prophets" emerged who repeated the same message. Thus in a Smithsonian report for the year 1879, Colonel Albert Brackett writes about the Wind River Shoshoni: "Almost every summer they get thoroughly frightened by some prophet predicting the speedy end of the world" (Brackett 1880: 332). It is more doubtful whether this testimony may be interpreted as proof that the Shoshoni "in times of calamity" had such prophets who announced the return of the dead, as Shimkin thinks (Shimkin 1939).

There is more information on the 1890 Ghost Dance. James

Mooney, who visited the reservation in the summer of 1892 (Mooney 1896: 654), has the following to tell us. Early in 1889 a Bannock from Fort Hall who had just returned from the Paiute country brought the news of the dead people coming back to the Wind River Shoshoni and the Northern Arapaho (who also had been referred to the Wind River reservation). A delegation of five Shoshoni headed by Täbinshi, and one Arapaho went by railroad to Nevada where they saw the messiah (Jack Wilson) and took part in a Ghost Dance performance that lasted a whole night. The messiah told them that they would meet all their dead when the leaves turned yellow in 1891. He also urged them to dance frequently, "because the dance moves the dead." So this they did on their return to the Wind River country.

When in the autumn of 1890 a dense smoke from forest fires in the mountain drifted down in the reservation, this was taken as the first sign of the great world change, and the Shoshoni danced more intensely than ever (Mooney 1896: 807 f.).[12] According to the Shoshoni, it was expected that a deep sleep would come on the believers. This sleep would continue four days and nights. On the morning of the fifth day all people would open their eyes in a new world, where Indians and whites would live together forever (Mooney 1896: 786). However, this new world never came. The smoke that had settled over the Wind River Valley evaporated. The dancing was kept up for another year, but when the changes that were expected in the autumn of 1891 did not materialize the Shoshoni—sceptical realists according to Mooney—gave up the dance (Mooney 1896: 808).

They did, and they did not. The ties with the Paiute were not disrupted; indeed, Wovoka visited the reservation in 1917 (according to my informant J. T.). Occasionally Shoshoni Indians visited their congeners in Nevada. One such visitor was Egon Edmo Bonatsie (1872–1939). He went on horseback to the *tukanait* Shoshoni in western Nevada to take part in sprinting races, and afterward attended a Ghost Dance, led by a woman. This dance terminated in what he considered a fraud: a supposed dead woman appeared in buckskin clothes and moccasins and shook hands with the dancers. However, a

12. A second deputation of Plains Indians to Wovoka arrived in March 1890 at Wind River, see Mooney 1896: 894. There were, however, no Wind River Shoshoni among them. Shimkin (1942: 456) mentions that three Idaho Shoshoni and one Bannock spread the Ghost Dance to the Wind River Shoshoni in 1890. This piece of information is at variance with Mooney's and, in my view, of minor value. Mooney appeared on the scene shortly after the events of 1890, Shimkin's informant (Dick Washakie) relied on his memory almost fifty years afterward.

young man peeped into the leader's tent after the ceremony and saw how her daughter took off the dead woman's clothes (information by E. B.).[13] Such experiences, if true, did not cement the Shoshoni faith in the Ghost Dance. One knowledgeable informant assured me that most Shoshoni were negative to Wovoka's message (J. T.).

Some, however, continued to believe in it. White Colt (*tošа bugkutua*, 1853–1936) was a reputed medicine-man who often went in a trance to the land of the dead. Once when he was there a message arrived that the dead were not yet supposed to see God's face. They all have to abide till Our Brother (Jesus) comes; that's why the realm of the dead is called the place of waiting. The dead told each other that one day Our Brother will arrive. "You will find two brothers: the first one is *ižapö* (the Coyote), and he will make himself look like the real brother, Jesus. But do not listen to him who is the first one: you can tell that he is not the true brother, because he will have his tail wrapped around his waist, using it as a belt. If you listen to him, he will take you as one of his children." "That's what the people tell one another in the land of the dead when they have Ghost Dances there" (L. S.).

White Colt sponsored Ghost Dances at Fort Washakie. He had learnt them from the dead, although—said my informant—they had existed among the Shoshoni before his time. A later leader of the Ghost Dances was William Washington (*pambiduwi:ji*, "long-haired young man"). He had the dances "in the brush at Little Wind River" and was succeeded by John Dick. Another Ghost Dance leader was Toorey Roberts (*tu:di*, "to stretch," 1882–1957) at Sage Creek. During my stay among the Shoshoni, he arranged the Ghost Dances at Sage Creek for those who lived there, a most conservative lot. He put up the Ghost Dance once or twice a year. Sometimes he did it in the winter, at a selected place in the brush where there is no wind. Toorey told me that he could see the dead in his dreams. Although they were not his guardian spirits, they counseled him what to do. In the Ghost Dance he said he was together with the dead and sang with them.[14]

The Ghost Dance ritual was held for four consecutive nights at the time of the full moon and was sponsored by Toorey and his family. It lasted from early evening to midnight. The attendants formed a circle which, however, was never complete. Both men and

13. There were ghost impersonations in some Northern Paiute Ghost Dances, cf. Kelly 1932: 179 f.; Park 1941: 190 f.

14. Some participants in the Ghost Dance were given sweetsage in order that they would learn ghost songs in their dreams (information by L. S.).

women participated in the dance (it was one of the few dances where this occurred), and they alternated in the circle, or the men danced on the left side and the women on the right side of the leader. In the middle of the circle a fire was kept burning to illuminate the dancing ground; it lacked symbolic implications. Facing the east the leader prayed for God's blessing. The dance then started, all dancers moving clockwise, hand in hand, the men pushing, the women following. I never heard that any dancers fell in a trance, receiving messages from the dead. No instruments were used, but the dancers were singing Ghost Dance songs. The final song had the text, *muga pEish^ö hukumanto yezegina*, "the soul—already—in the dust—flying."[15] This phrase was repeated until, after some ten or twelve times, each dancer reached the point from where he had started.

Until recently the belief in the Ghost Dance has, among some individuals, been steadfast. Nadzaip Rogers (1871–1952), a medicine-woman, was a believer until the very end. She confided to D. T. that when she slept her soul went up to heaven. She claimed she knew the trail up there. In her dream she saw the dead in heaven. Another old Shoshoni woman, P. C., was convinced that some day all the dead would return in some form. "I have heard," she told me, "that almost every day some of the spirits of the dead are around us. They appear like whirlwinds."

We notice two important features in the Shoshoni Ghost Dance. The first one is the strong element of Christian influence, beside the eschatological perspective as such: the dead are waiting for God, they are assembled in heaven, Coyote appears as a devil and tries to recruit people as his disciples. I was told expressly by the Ghost Dance adherents that Coyote is, in fact, the devil. The other point to be made is that the coming of the dead is projected into a vague future. This is in line with Wovoka's teaching in 1892 and has become a dogma accepted by other tribes as well (cf. Kehoe 1968: 300). White Colt who joined the Ghost Dance of the dead in their realm was urged by them to perform it also on earth, for, he was told, for each step you take Our Brother comes closer. "That is the reason you have Ghost Dances still today" (L. S.). The promise is there, but no date is fixed.[16]

Alice Kehoe has observed that the Ghost Dance continued long after the massacre at Wounded Knee (1890), partly in Oklahoma,

15. On the concept of *mugua,* see Hultkrantz 1951.
16. One informant (G. W.) told me that, according to the revelation by a guardian spirit, the world will come to an end when a tail of light (*tabehoBonet*) from Mars touches Earth.

partly among the Dakota (Kehoe 1968: 298, 302). She says that the Dakota of Saskatchewan may be the last group practicing the Ghost Dance religion (Kehoe 1968: 296). However, the dancing was abandoned there about 1950 (Kehoe 1968: 301). I know for sure that the Wind River Shoshoni held traditional Ghost Dances still at the end of the 1950s.

However, our picture of the Shoshoni Ghost Dance becomes confused when we take into consideration that a Sun Dance is usually finished by a Ghost Dance.[17] Thus when the Sun Dance had ended on the morning of August 31, 1948, it was announced that a Ghost Dance would be arranged that evening at the Sun Dance place, and a Wolf or War Dance in the community hall. The Ghost Dance was then held outside of the eastern entrance to the Sun Dance lodge. It had the same character of a round dance with shuffling steps as the Ghost Dance at Sage Creek but was definitely a merry occasion, a piece of entertainment.[18]

The explanation is simple: this round dance was in effect no Ghost Dance but used the same dancing pattern as the Ghost Dance. As we know, the latter term is the white man's invention. A secular round dance and a Ghost Dance are called by the same name, *narayar, naraya'ndo,* meaning "dancing sideways, shuffling." When the round dance had a religious meaning this was not expressed by its name, with one important exception.

It will be remembered that according to my informants, the Ghost Dance had existed among the Shoshoni prior to the acceptance of the Paiute message. It was firmly anchored in myth. J. T. said it existed "way back when Coyote was ruling the world." In a myth which is compounded with the well-known story of "the hoodwinked dancers," Coyote institutes the round dance as a protective means against diseases. One informant showed me some rock-drawings at the Sage Creek foothills and explained one of them as a bat that instructs you how to dance the Ghost Dance, another—a doglike head—as Coyote who "belongs to the Ghost Dance and tells you how to cure." My informant L. S. said, however, that the dance had been adopted, in its present form, from Nevada Indians. In Nevada, he went on, there are cliff-drawings on a mountain wall showing spirits dancing the Ghost Dance.

17. At the time of my visit another dance mostly supplanted it, the popular "forty-nine dance" that had come in during the 1920s.

18. Nadzaip Rogers, who was a stout defender of the sacred Ghost Dance, considered that it was against the wish of the Supreme Being to dance on sacred ground in a round dance "with bells on."

Mooney states, "However novel may have been the doctrine, the Shoshoni claim that the Ghost Dance itself as performed by them was a revival of an old dance which they had had fully fifty years before" (Mooney 1896: 809, cf. 791). The same opinion was expressed by my informant J. T. He asserted that an old Shoshoni dance had been given a new meaning by the followers of Wovoka, as a dance for the return of the dead, and lately had turned into a dance for pleasure only.

The old round dance was *apönökar* (also *narayahEkap*), the "Father Dance." It was a seasonal dance in which prayers were directed to *Tam Apö*, "Our Father," the Supreme Being. It is described in the following way by Rev. Sherman Coolidge in the 1890s: "The thanksgiving dance takes place about the end of September or the beginning of October each year. The whole tribe is brought together in some appointed locality. A hemlock or cedar tree is planted. The tribe, men, women and children, in close order, form a circle about this tree and move very slowly around, with some keeping time in a low, monotonous chant, in which they thank the Great Spirit for his bounty and invoke a continuance. They ask him to look upon the mountains, the rivers and trees, and entreat him to send rain upon them and into the rivers. They also invoke him to bid the earth cease to swallow their fathers, mothers and children."[19]

This description is quoted almost verbatim by Sarah Olden who otherwise received her information mainly from the knowledgeable Episcopal missionary, John Roberts.[20] She adds, however, some Shoshoni words in the chant, meaning "send rain on the mountains." These words, she asserts, were repeated a thousand times (Olden 1923: 37 f.). The source of this information was probably John Roberts.

Anthropologist Robert Lowie has additional material on this dance. It was, according to a short myth fragment rendered by Lowie, instituted by Coyote for mankind just after the world was created. Lowie's informant asserted that the dance could be given by any person at any time of the year, and was usually arranged when somebody in the family had a cold or some more serious disease. By shaking their blankets, the sick partakers of the dance were supposed to

19. Coolidge's writing are included in John C. Thompson's manuscript, "In Old Wyoming," University of Wyoming Archives, and in an anonymous author's article, "Wyoming Indians," in *Collections of the Wyoming Historicial Society*, 1 (Cheyenne 1897), p. 103.

20. Roberts could, of course, have referred Olden to his colleague Coolidge's writings which should have been known to him.

remove the disease. Men and women alternated in the dance circle, and sometimes several circles were formed in a concentric pattern. Near the circumference of the smallest circle was a pine tree that afterward was left there to be used for subsequent ceremonies. A big fire was lit in the center of the circle if the dance was held at night. The dance lasted five consecutive nights and one day, and was finished by everybody taking a bath (Lowie 1915b: 817).

Our first impression is that Lowie has here confounded the Father Dance and the later Ghost Dance. The curing aspects were part of the latter; it may seem less appropriate that they also occurred in the former. Lowie calls the dance "naroya" which is, as we know, a neutral name for any round dance. However, one of his informants likened it to the "nuakin" or food dance of the Lemhi Shoshoni, as well as to the Father Dance of these Shoshoni. Lowie's description of the former gives a conventional round dance with the aim "to ensure a plentiful supply of food, especially of salmon and berries." It was celebrated toward the end of winter or in the beginning of spring (Lowie 1909b: 217 f.). Concerning the Father Dance among the Lemhi, Lowie only says that it was danced like the food dance but had "different songs, which were usually without words, but partly in the nature of a prayer." It was performed mostly by old men (Lowie 1909b: 219). No tree is mentioned for either dance. As Lowie portrays the Wind River "naroya" it is only vaguely identical with the Lemhi dances. The common denominator is the round dance.

Still, Dmitri Shimkin's account of the Father Dance comes close to Lowie's description of the "naroya." Shimkin stresses the importance of the medicine-man as initiator of the ceremony and says that the purposes of the dance varied according to the supernatural gifts of the medicine-man: one had power over food, another over smallpox, and so on. The dance itself is described in the following manner: "A cedar is placed upright in an open plot of ground, and a brush enclosure is built around it. The shaman stands by the center pole, and the dancers form a circle in which men and women alternate. They clasp hands and shuffle sideways. At the end of each dance, they shake their blankets to shake away illness." Shimkin also mentions that the medicine-man addresses Our Father in prayer during the dance (Shimkin 1953: 433 n. 41).

I think we have to accept Lowie's and Shimkin's information as it stands but make the following elucidations. The Father Dance was a cultic expression of man's appreciation of the gifts that the Supreme Being had given him and was celebrated in the autumn. It was, in other words, an annual thanksgiving ceremony, perhaps connected with prayers for a good coming year. Like some other tribal anniversary ceremonies it encompassed prayers for food, health, and curing of the sick. These aims, however, also could be served at separate ceremonies along the same pattern. I am less certain that these rites, as Shimkin thinks, could be called Father Dance but cannot prove my point. They were all certainly round dances.

The cedar tree, which probably symbolized the world-tree—a concept well developed in the Sun Dance symbolism (cf. Hultkrantz 1979f.)—was part of the Ghost Dances that Mooney witnessed on the Wind River reservation (Mooney 1896: 809).[21] It later dropped out of this ceremony.

As an annual thanksgiving ceremony the Father Dance was by and by succeeded by the Sun Dance, the foremost Plains Indian ritual that may have reached the Plains Shoshoni in the 1820s (Shimkin 1953: 409 ff., 417; Hultkrantz 1970d).[22] Shimkin finds that the concern about food and general welfare was not as conspicuous in the Sun Dance as in the Father Dance, and he states that the latter had much more emotional appeal to many of his informants (Shimkin 1953: 434). This appeal was evidently transferred to its offspring, the Ghost Dance.

An Old Ceremony with a New Meaning

The anniversary rite among the Wind River Shoshoni had its close counterpart in the Great Basin area, and particularly among the Shoshoni and Northern Paiute (Park 1941: 193; Harris 1940: 53 f.). Willard Park called the Basin religious dances indiscriminately round dances, but he emhasized that among the Northern Paiute the praying was as much a part of the occasion as was the dancing. The dancers circulated around a pole in the middle, and their dance-leader asked for rain, wild seeds, pine nuts, fish, game, and good health for all (Park 1941: 186). There was no connection with ghosts, animal spirits, and shamanistic powers (Park 1941: 187). Park makes it

---

21. Mooney remarks that the cedar tree also appeared in the center of the Kiowa Ghost Dance circle. He ascribes its position to its never-dying green, its aromatic fragrance, durability, and the dark red color of its heart, as if it was dyed in blood.

22. I do not know how long the Father Dance continued; I did not find any traces of it during my first field visit in 1948, nor at my later visits. Mooney's information that it had ended about 1840 is perhaps of doubtful value. Much depends, of course, on what we mean by Father Dance.

clear that "the Round Dance ... is the backbone of the [dancing] complex and the other parts are supported by it" (Park 1941: 184). It seems perhaps less to the point when Park refers this ceremony to a southwestern pattern of rain and fertility beliefs (Park 1941: 194, cf., however, 199 f.). It is in fact the "desert culture pattern" as defined by Jennings (1964: 152 f.) that finds expression in the Paiute ceremonialism.

It is true that in an appreciation of the Basin round dance Julian Steward has characterized it as recreational, with secondary religious motives (Steward 1939: 265). It would be more fitting to say that it was basically religious and secondarily recreational. In a separate investigation I have pointed out that the round dance varied in symbolic content according to changing ecology (seed dance, pine nut dance, etc.) but was always directed to the Supreme Being. Due to shifting economic pursuits the seed dance, pine nut dance, fish dance, etc. were celebrated at different seasons. First-fruit rites were, in the northernmost Basin, connected with these thanksgiving ceremonies. Possibly there was also a conscious idea of world renewal, whereas it is less certain that curing was always a part of the ceremony (Hultkrantz in press, 1976b: 144 f.).

This Father Dance, or God Dance or Wolf Dance (Ute, Paiute), was the ritual and, to a certain extent, the ideological model of the Ghost Dance. If we accept the hypothesis that the cedar was the world-tree, and the original dance a renewal ceremony (as it clearly was among some Western Shoshoni, cf. Steward 1941: 267), then we may say that with the Ghost Dance the annual cosmic rejuvenation turned into the final cosmic rejuvenation. The eschatology and concept of the dead of the Plateau Prophet Dance mixed with the annual Basin thanksgiving ceremony and changed its meaning. The return of the dead became the top priority, and the Orpehus myth—which the Northern Paiute might have taken over from the Plateau peoples—formed a kind of foundation myth (or legend) (Spier 1935: 15 f.; Gayton 1930: 77 ff., 82; Hultkrantz 1957: 40, 124, 145 f., 147, 261 ff., 306 f., 311) . The dance on earth was supposed to imitate the dance of the dead (Spier 1935: 13).

Some words should be said here about the background of the Prophet Dance. It was certainly based on native ideas, but the force that molded it may have been extraneous. In contradistinction to Spier I presume that a stimulus diffusion took place through which Christian ideas supplied the frame and ferment of the Prophet Dance. It is highly likely that Iroquois Christian Indians gone west, or Hudson Bay and Northwest Company tradesmen, were influential in this process.

Likewise, the Ghost Dance eschatology most certainly was also inspired by Christian teaching, in this case from missionaries and Christian farmers. It is less certain, however, to what extent Christianity added any new elements to the ones already existing in the Prophet Dance. We could at least expect that Christian notions backed up and strengthened the eschatological message.

The fusion between Plateau and Basin religious ideas started among the Northern Paiute of western Nevada, where the Prophet Dance was grafted on the old round dance.[23] Due to the diminished importance of the cosmic pole in the new setting the latter often fell away in the Ghost Dance ritual, as was the case among the Northern Paiute and the Shoshoni.[24] The existence of the round dance in the Basin area facilitated the quick spread of the Ghost Dance there and among the Wind River Shoshoni who had a Basin origin. Perhaps the experience of the Ghost Dance on the Father Dance pattern contributed toward the quiet, purely religious interpretation it received among these peoples.

The hypothesis put forward by Hittman, that the 1870 Ghost Dance originally functioned as a postmortal curing rite after the epidemics at the Walker River Reservation, seems wide of the mark (Hittman 1973: 248, 257, 258, 260 ff., particularly 262). As noted by Spier, before the Ghost Dance revivals there was no preoccupation with the dead in the Great Basin similar to the constant concern with them in the Northwest Coast and Plateau areas (Spier 1935: 16). Hittman has, however, rightly stressed the importance of the food rites in the Basin, and he has correctly understood the importance of Park's round dance observations (Hittman 1973: 257 f., 263 f.). Like most other anthropologists he has undervalued Christian influences. We may conclude that it is the combination of Christian beliefs, collective deprivation (emphasized by Hittman), Prophet Dance doctrine, and Basin annual ceremony pattern that brought forth and provided a meaning for the Ghost Dance.

Meaning is a loaded word, and meaning in Ghost Dance

23. Cf. also Lowie 1939: 315, 323; and Du Bois 1939: 7 for an appreciation of the close connection between the Ghost Dance and Paiute ceremonialism. It should be observed, however, that round dances around a pole also occurred in the Plateau Prophet Dance, cf. Spier 1935: 12, 20, 24.

24. On this subject, cf. also Mooney 1896: 80. The Modoc Ghost Dance pole was a shamanic symbol, see Nash 1937: 418, 420. The cosmic symbolism of the Basin pole was sometimes associated with the Milky Way, the communications channel to the other world. It is perhaps revealing that Wovoka was said to be able to go to heaven by way of the Milky Way, see Dangberg 1957: 287 n. 13.

context a relative concept (Overholt 1978, 1974: 57). Still, if we look at it from a point of view which leaves room for continuity and a reasonable public consensus, the building up of the Ghost Dance pattern as presented in this account seems to validate a most conspicuous religious meaning.

15

Conditions for the Spread of the Peyote Cult in North America

A<small>S IS WELL KNOWN</small>, large parts of native North America with the Prairies and Plains in the middle of the continent as the center of diffusion have constituted, since the end of the last century, the scene of a nativistic Indian movement, the so-called peyote cult.[1] Through the mediation of Indian tribes like the Kiowa, Kiowa Apache, and Comanche (who also to a large extent were responsible for its ritual form) the peyote cult has spread from the areas of the Rio Grande northward over the whole Prairie and Plains area up to the Saskatchewan River. In the west it has gained ground among Great Basin groups and among the Navajo and Taos Indians on the high plateaus of Arizona and New Mexico. In the east some groups of the former Woodland Indians at the Great Lakes have been won for peyotism. The number of peyotists in an ethnic group may fluctuate, but often the main part of the Indians belong to the peyote cult.

---

1. The term "nativism" is here used in a very wide sense, corresponding to Voget's "reformative nativism" that presupposes a synthesis of traditional and alien cultural components (Voget 1956: 250). "Traditional" includes in this case not only tribal but also general Indian traits.

The peyote cult—or, as it should have been called, the peyote religion[2]—is named after its central cultic action, the consumption (by eating, drinking, or smoking) of the spineless cactus peyote (*Lophophora williamsii*). This cactus that may be found growing wild along theRio Grande and in the country south of this river contains several alkaloids, among them the morphinelike, hallucinogeneous mescaline. Peyote produces colorful visions, hallucinations of movement and audition, strengthens the capacity for observation, and brings forth sentiments of solidarity and personal surrender. In pre-Columbian days peyote was used in connection with certain public ceremonies among the Indians of Mexico, for instance, at the annual thanksgiving ceremonies. In its modern form the peyote ritual constitutes a religious complex of its own, considered to promote health, happiness, and welfare among its adepts. Many peyotist groups have (since 1918) joined the peyote ecclesiastical organization, The Native American Church. Today, the peyote cult is almost the only one besides shakerism of the revivalistic Indian movements of the nineteenth century still prevailing. Its diffusion is steadily going on, and in many reservations where it has had a hold for some time it is gaining more and more converts.[3]

The peyote cult has been described and analyzed in several instructive works, foremost among them the monographs by La Barre and Slotkin (see, e.g., La Barre 1938, 1960; Slotkin 1956. Cf. Gusinde 1939).[4] Most problems of a major scope have been dealt with in these publications. However, one special problem seems to me to deserve a greater attention: whether the spread of peyote and the peyote cult was facilitated by particular historical, social, or other conditions in Indian North America, or even whether the cult had a precursor. In the following I shall briefly illuminate this problem and to this end formulate two leading questions: what were the conditons for the diffusion of the peyote cult? what particular factors accounted for the spread of the cult to just those areas that were mentioned above, and for its obstruction in other areas? It is obvious that in many respects the task undertaken here is too complicated to be dealt with

2. It is unfortunately due to Kroeber's influence that so many religions, in particular of a sectarian character, have been misnamed "cults" in North American anthropology.

3. Conversely, in many other reservations the peyote cult is receding. The history of peyote has always been a backward and forward movement.

4. The leading authority is La Barre. The best discussions of the peyote cult in a tribal setting may be found in Aberle 1966; Aberle and Stewart 1957; and Stewart 1944.

adequately in a short chapter. Only the main lines of my investigation can therefore be presented here. A more detailed account will follow in a separate paper already completed and waiting for publication.

Students of peyotism have suggested a variety of preformative factors, but the dissension between their opinions is considerable. It is safe to say that most interpreters are agreed upon one thing, viz., that the growth and spread of the peyote cult should be seen as a concomitant of the radical change that Indian society in the Plains and Prairie area has undergone during the past hundred years. In this perspective the peyote cult offers an example of religious acculturation, that is, religious change following a "complete culture-contact" (or complete interaction between two different cultures) (see Hultkrantz 1969: 15).[5] There is, however, no unanimous opinion among researchers as to what factors had the decisive influence in this process. Most students are inclined to single out one or two factors. We shall here survey the main views on this matter, and then continue with factors that have been referred to as proofs of a religio-historical continuity.

If, first, we concentrate on proposed factors of acculturation it goes without saying that external changes in the environment have facilitated this process, and thereby peyotism. Thus Aberle and Stewart have primarily explained peyote diffusion with reference to geographic availability—which is an important ecological point of view—and possible communications (cf. Aberle 1957). As we know, railroads and dust roads for wagons quickly spread over the central distribution area—the Plains and Prairies—in the 1860s and thereafter, thus transforming the intercommunicative possibilities here. This is exactly the time when the peyote cult began to spread. The diffusion took place between reservations, since Indians were now confined to such areas.

Many authors have adduced circumstances that should underline the role of peyotism in the ideological adaptation of Indian groups. Some points that have been proposed are absurd, for instance, the claim that the peyote cult strengthens the old tribal religion in an acculturative situation. Such a stand disregards the fact that peyotism is an intrusive, new religion that shakes the tribal sol-

5. Aberle however asserts that acculturation was a nonessential factor for the growth of peyotism among the Navajo (Aberle 1966: 243). Cf. further below.

idarity and some old religious values. If, however, the reference is not to the traditional tribal religion but to traditional *Indian* religion seen as a token of Indian identity—what has been called Pan-Indianism—the standpoint is more realistic. As a matter of fact, peyote has been an instrument for the creation of this feeling of Indian commonness (cf. Shonle 1925: 57); séances often include members of many tribes, and the sensation of intimacy and transference that was earlier said to accompany the eating of peyote contributes to intertribal understanding among peyotists.

A student and peyotist like Slotkin has seen peyote as a weapon in the Indian fight against white domination (cf. Slotkin 1956: 17 ff.). Not in any militant sense, however; peyotism, he says, "provided a supernatural means of accommodation to the existing domination-subordination relation" (cf. Slotkin 1956: 20). Peyote provided the ideological foundation for the opposition to white supremacy.

Some observers think that in this encounter peyote legitimated Indian efforts by appearing as a counterpart to Christianity. It is commonly said among peyotists that just as the whites learned the right way from Christ, Indians learned it from peyote. In other words, two equal religions confront each other, the one as good as the other. The peyote religion has the advantages that it is native Indian and well adapted to the prevalent situation. In comparison with orthodox Christianity it is much easier to learn—some few concepts like God, Jesus, thunderbird, and (mother) peyote, some ethical prescriptions, a very elementary ritual—and it is inspirational. It meets traditional Indian requirements in a way orthodox Christianity never does.

And still, there is the opinion among scholars that the peyote cult attained its position of a Pan-Indian, ideological institution in virtue of its Christian affinities. There is no doubt that a central part of the ideology is, as could just be seen, decidedly Christian. We know also that Ute and Winnebago peyote groups have made petitions to Christian organizations to be approved as members of the Christian church. Some students who, although not Indian, regard themselves as peyotists, in particular Slotkin, define the peyote cult as an Indian version of Christianity (cf. Slotkin 1956: 46). This is a surprising statement. For all we know there were only a few Christian traits among the Kiowa and Comanche when the peyote cult spread from this nucleus area around 1890 (cf. Mooney 1892: 65). In later days it assumed a veneer of Christian ideology, as La Barre has underscored (cf. La Barre 1971: 22). Altogether it is a question of an additive process, not a fundamental change of the ideological pattern. As such, however, it most certainly has stimulated the diffusion of the peyote religion.

If thus the importance of the social factors of acculturation has been emphasized by many writers in their assessment of peyote distribution, others have put the adaptation of the individual to a new cultural situation in the foreground. They have proceeded from the fact that man in acculturation suffers from a cultural shock; and Geertz is perhaps quite right when he pinpoints suffering as a gateway to religion (cf. Geertz 1966: 19).[6] The arrival of European civilization deprived the Indians not only of the externals of traditional culture but also of existential meaning and religious values. The loss was expressed in spiritual terms among the Plains Indians: they were, says Ruth Underhill, "apparently deserted by their spirit helpers" (Underhill 1952: 143). The scientists who have analyzed the situation think they have found deeper causes behind such manifest religious formulations: anxiety for life and health, or for social and personal security, or for economic safety. The dissolution of these anxieties should then be offered by peyote.

There is, for instance, the thesis proposed by Richard Schultes, a botanist who has written several articles on the peyote cult, that peyote spread as a remedy, a medicine to ensure health and survival (cf. Schultes 1938). Now, Schultes does not mean that it was because of narcotic qualities that peyote met such a quick response; from a medical point of view peyote is not narcotic since the use of it does not create any dependence whatsoever (a fact not always recognized by American courts). Schultes is concerned with the Indian idea that peyote is medicine. There is much evidence at our disposal that persons have joined the peyote cult for curative reasons. However, Schultes has neglected to place the curative aspect into its spiritual frame: medicine is for the Indians a comprehensive concept referring to origins in visions and supernatural qualities (cf. La Barre 1960: 52, 54).

Another proposition is that the peyote cult is a refuge for people who suffer mentally from cultural loss. An investigation made at the Navajo reservation in the Southwest has indicated that

6. His dictum that the problem of suffering is "not to avoid suffering but how to suffer" is too narrow however. The theory of cultural shock comes close to "the cultural disintegration theory," so called by Stewart who does not find it adequate to explain peyote diffusion, however. This theory that has been applied in practice by, e.g., Kroeber says that "peoples experiencing cultural disintegration and degradation will readily accept new religions, especially those which promise the miraculous restoration of former conditions of life" (Stewart 1944: 90). Cf. also, e.g., Ljungdahl 1969: 168.

peyotists show more disturbances in their dreams than other individuals (cf. Dittmann and Moore 1957). The same lack of stability has been demonstrated among Menomini on a reservation in Wisconsin: Rorschach tests provide evidence that peyotists as a transitional group in society have difficulties in coping with cultural change and therefore, according to the investigators, exhibit great anxiety (cf. Spindler 1955). There is, in the view of the present author, reason to believe that the real cause of this anxiety is the loss of the old, tribal religious value system which could not be restored in the peyote cult. Confessions of sins, i.e., transgressions of the ethical code of the peyote religion, may, however, to a certain point reduce this anxiety. On the social side, peyote membership may be a ladder to distinction both for the old elite, at least on the Plains, and for newcomers striving for status. Of course, the religious problem is not solved in this way.

Not surprisingly, some authors have developed the theory that peyote has been resorted to in a situation of economic depression. This theory could naturally be linked with the general theory of deprivation on account of cultural loss in acculturation. However, one author, Aberle, denounces the latter at the same time as he embraces the former as cause of Navajo peyotism. Aberle has observed that the peyote cult was established at the same time as there was a forced stock reduction (of sheep and goats) in the Navajo country, in the 1930s; he also points out that the Navajo at that time were the least acculturated tribe in the United States (cf. Aberle 1966: 3, 243, 308 f.). However, since the action was ordered by white authorities it is difficult to avoid the conclusion that acculturative pressure was responsible for the weakened economic situation that emerged. It is important to note that it was not the economy as such, but the loss of cultural stability and religious balance that drove the stock owners into peyotism. For, as Aberle remarks himself, the elimination of so much of the stock upset the world order (cf. Aberle 1966: 200).

After having observed factors that could account for social and individual adaptation to peyote we shall, finally mention two general ideological patterns into which, according to several authors, the peyote cult could easily be framed. We are here thus dealing with arguments for a religio-historical continuity.

La Barre, Howard, and others have noted that a "mescal bean cult" preceded the peyote cult in the central and southern parts of the Prairie and Plains area (cf. La Barre 1938: 105 ff.; Howard 1957: 75 ff.).[7]

---

7. In later publications the two authors have disagreed in some matters of diffusion, partly due to misunderstandings (cf. La Barre 1960: 48; Howard 1960).

The mescal bean or "red bean" is (the fruit of) an evergreen, *Sophora secundiflora*. It was consumed in the same way as peyote and brought on vomiting—to some peoples, like the Iowa, considered ceremonial cleansing—and hallucinations. The mescal eaters formed secret societies, and their ritual paraphernalia were those of the later peyotists. It seems indeed very likely that the peyote cult was formed on the pattern of the ancient mescal bean cult. This would also explain why the mescal and the peyote have so often been confused in the debate (cf. Howard 1957: 86).

The importance of the vision complex in furthering the course of the peyote cult was pointed out by Ruth Shonle as early as 1925. In particular she aligned its diffusion on the Prairies and Plains with the vision-quest here, since in this area the seeking of visions preceded all kinds of significant undertakings (cf. Shonle 1925: 53, 58 f.). Some students have followed suit, but many who have developed other ideas on the spread of peyote disagree. There are especially two objections that have been raised by critics: that peyote has spread outside the true vision complex area, and that visions have little meaning in the peyote cult. The validity of the first objection has been illustrated with examples taken from the Southwest area, traditionally an area where, at least among the agricultural Pueblo Indians, subjective experiences have played a subordinated role (cf. Benedict 1923b: 40). If in this area we find the peyote cult represented in the pueblo of Taos, this may be defended by referring to its peripheral position and the influx of Plains cultural elements. However, the recent spread of peyotism to the Navajo Indians offers a more delicate problem. The Navajo have a negative attitude to visions (cf. Haile 1940), and Aberle plays down the role of visions in the Navajo peyote cult (cf. Aberle 1966: 6). We know, however, that peyotism had great difficulties to gain ground on the Navajo reservation, and that it was introduced very late. A similar reasoning is applied by La Barre in defense of Miss Shonle's standpoint (cf. La Barre 1960: 51).

The second objection is tied up with the first one, for it is just in an area like the Navajos' that the reduced significance of visions in the peyote cult can be demonstrated (cf. Stewart 1944: 86). Nevertheless, it is hard to see how a direct experience with the supernatural in visions can have as little meaning as the propounders of this thesis think it has.

We have seen that an array of motivations has been mobilized in order to account for the accommodation of the peyote cult on North American Indian reservations. Some of them appear less convincing, others well taken. We certainly come closer to the truth if we proceed from the assumption that several of these propositions combined indicate the conditions for the spread of the peyote cult. A similar stand has been taken earlier by authors like La Barre, Ruth Shonle, Arth, and Slotkin. They do not, however, La Barre excepted, take stock of other possibilities than those they find useful. A survey of opinions like the one here presented seems to the present author more likely to bring creative results. Otherwise, Slotkin's list of causes is both elaborate and suggestive (although perhaps too much attention is paid to ethical and sociological issues) (cf. Slotkin 1956: 18 f., 35 ff.).

An attempt will now be made to assess the conditions for the diffusion. It is based on some of the earlier proposals and adds some further points of view.

In this connection it is important to make a distinction between the functions of peyote in a certain society and the original circumstances at the time when peyote was accepted by this group (or by certain individuals in this group). In other words, I do not find certain psychological considerations very helpful which take their departure from peyotist reactions in a modern Indian community. The functions of the peyote cult change with locality and time in one and the same tribal group.[8]

Furthermore, consistent with this point is another, that any proposition regarding the general conditional factors of peyote distribution should ignore special local developments, unless these illustrate the former. Since the distribution is so intimately tied up with the Prairie and Plains area—or, to be more exact, the Plains Indian reservations—there should be a heavy reliance on factual materials from this region. However, other regions are interesting not least because they demonstrate factors operative in impeding diffusion.

Finally, there is reason to lay more stress on religion and faith in evaluating the conditioning factors. Among the Omaha, says Malcolm Arth, "the (peyote) religion is first and foremost an expression of the spiritual and aesthetic needs of many of the people" (Arth 1956: 25). It is certainly so among all groups that have adopted peyotism, although, when reading many of the papers that have been quoted in the foregoing, one often receives the impression that religion is forgotten. Or, the manifest religion is reduced to latent personality trouble. In my discussion of cultural shock and anxiety, above, I suggested that disturbance of religious values lies behind

---

8. The interesting problem of differential diffusion has been observed by several anthropologists, for instance, George and Louise Spindler and Wesley Hurt, Jr.

these states. My anthropological colleagues have, to my understanding, been too eager to avoid the obvious conclusion.

After these considerations I offer the following scheme as my contribution to the understanding of the factors that paved the way for the peyote cult.

1. The change in the North American Indian situation at the end of the nineteenth century supplied new facilities for religious innovations and for the introduction of a foreign religious movement, the peyote cult. Slotkin has mentioned some of the salient features in the new situation: cessation of intertribal warfare (and, we may add, of wars with the whites), settlements within reservations, often bordering on each other (and several tribes joined in one reservation, *vide* the Indian Territory, or Oklahoma), easy travel on highways and railroads, use of English as a common language, and use of mail service by those who can read and write (cf. Slotkin 1956: 19).

In the cultural and religious fields, these environmental changes had various repercussions that may be covered with the word acculturation. Religious acculturation implied a demand for continued religious faith in molds that were both anchored in the past heritage and adapted to new ideas. We note specifically:

A. There was a cultural change, sometimes bordering on cultural loss. The old religious rites, for instance war rituals, buffalo-hunting rituals, were not adapted to the new situation on the reservations. The major Plains Indian ceremony, the Sun Dance, was forbidden or repressed by the white authorities. At the same time the men now found leisure time to indulge in ceremonialism. It seems that the peyote rite filled in the vacuum left by the Sun Dance.

B. There ensued a relativism of values, and this fostered a crisis that had to be overcome. The old religion was insufficient. So was white man's Christianity to those who did not want to be incorporated in the western civilization. Peyote, with a structure like the church and concepts competing with Christian ideas, offered a solution. At the same time incorporation of Christian concepts facilitated the acceptance of peyotism on reservations where Christian missions were influential.

2. The ideological structures of the vanishing Indian cultures constituted preformative patterns into which the peyote religion could be framed, or else, by which the peyote religion was blocked.

A. Positive adaptations. In these cases, mostly represented in the Prairie and Plains area, there was a rapport in structure and function between the old religious pattern and the peyote cult. Several examples could be adduced, but we single out the following:

a. The mescal bean cult which, as we have seen, had many features in common with the peyote cult, preceded the latter in the middle and southern parts of the Plains area. Indeed, there is archeological testimony that the red bean cult existed in southwestern Texas during the first millenium A.D. (cf. Campbell 1958).

b. Ritual structure and ritual symbolism have on the whole been fairly identical in the whole area under consideration here, with the exception of the Great Basin (cf. Lowie 1915a: 231 ff.). They are also reflected in the peyote cult. As pointed out by La Barre, Slotkin, and others, specific ritual traits in the peyote cult can be derived from Mexican Indian ceremonials, Apache and Kiowa rituals, mescal bean rituals, and Christian rituals (prayer forms, Bible reading, etc.).

c. The preformative influence of the vision complex, or the vison-quest pattern, should indeed be considered the most important single factor for the spread of peyotism, exactly as suggested by Ruth Shonle. In ascribing this importance to visions I want to stress that they should not be regarded as having an intrinsic value in themselves, but as constituting forms for a direct experience of the supernatural world—for it is this immediate contact and its blessings that mean so much. As one of my Shoshoni informants on peyote told me, the importance lies in the power, not in the vision. Seen in this perspective the Navajo peyote experiences also move along the pattern set by the visionary experiences.

The significance of the vision pattern for the acceptance of peyote may be best observed in the Plains area, the stronghold of the vision complex (cf. above). When the Indians moved to reservations the vision-quest declined, and that for mainly two reasons. Firstly, the old, sacred places were no longer accessible, now being situated in white man's land.[9] Secondly, the reservation life meant an ideological change, and the acquisition in visions of guardian spirits for war, hunting of game and other formerly topical pursuits was experienced as superfluous. There was now a need for spiritual communion and a faith in Indian religious values on a more general scale. However, having been defeated in combat and exposed to competing ideologies the Plains Indians had difficulties in realizing their will to believe. The vision had been succeeded by the religious doubt.

In this deplorable situation the peyote cult was actualized. It was well adapted to the new situation on the reservations, and the old vision pattern could be transferred to it. However, within the

9. There are exceptions. The Cheyenne, for instance, still seek visions at their sacred mountain, Bear Butte, in the Black Hills, far from the reservation.

general structure there appeared some novelties. The visions were no longer individualistic, as in the old nomadic and hunting culture, but were received in a collective frame, and this added, of course, to the visionary's sense of safety and spiritual reality. Furthermore, if formerly the vision-quest had been associated with vicissitudes, and not always was successful, it was now a comparatively easy task, and visions were attainable for everybody who tried. Indeed, the peyote vision could be very strong, a true hallucination, and as such superior in quality and more compelling than earlier visionary dreams (cf. Hultkrantz in La Barre 1960: 57 n. 4). Finally, the vision no longer revealed spirits and conferred special powers, except in some cases; it mediated a direct experience of a spiritual sphere of existence, and it showed in symbolical form a spiritual way of living. Sometimes the vision could tell the future, or it imparted a general consciousness and feeling of divine power.

B. Obstructive factors. In this context we shall review some patterns that were responsible for the restriction of peyote diffusion to certain areas, mainly the Prairie and Plains and the Great Basin, while the Southwest with some exceptions (Apache and Navajo, Taos) did not take part in the expansion.

a. Conservatism and traditionalism have everywhere constituted a hindrance to the diffusion of the peyote cult, but particularly so in the Pueblo area (or subarea of the Southwest) where a well-ingrained ceremonialism and an agrarian type of religion well adjusted to the needs of Pueblo culture and society had been left intact for many centuries. White expansion has only slowly infringed upon the Pueblo Indian traditions.

The individualism of the Plains Indians that admitted so many religious innovations was entirely absent here. But even on the Plains the peyote cult has represented something new and foreign when first known, and it has therefore been opposed by individuals as well as tribal councils. As time passed it gained in reputation, particularly so when it had been integrated with old cultic elements or obtained a Christian veneer.

b. Hierarchical structure has sometimes been a strong impediment. The medicine-men on the Prairies and Plains and in the Great Basin have occasionally tried to oppress peyotism since it threatened to take over their healing and divinatory functions but with little success; after all, their position was already attenuated through the presence of other visionaries. In the Pueblo area, however, the richly differentiated priestly and healing associations put up an effective barrier against new institutional religious systems that upset the ruling order.

c. There have been other "psychotropic" (La Barre) means beside peyote, and where these prevailed they prevented the spread of peyote. Thus the diffusion of peyote westward was checked by the presence of the Jimsonweed or *toloache* (cf. Driver 1961: 102).

3. Peyote had, of course, an attraction of its own, not in its taste or in the aesthetic layout of its ceremonials—the former is horrid, the latter rather simple—but in its effects.

A. The peyote experience provides religious assurance, an assurance that is strengthened by the positive reactions of all those who partake in the rite. The experiences of colored visions, voices, and strong positive sentiments to other peyotists present convince the participant of the ceremony of the supernatural quality of the herb.

B. As a consequence of its supernatural character all kinds of blessings are expected from peyote: good health, personal security, family happiness, endurable economic support, etc. These conditions are all thus considered in a religious perspective.

C. The peyote cult is characterized by great flexibility, not least in its conceptual system, and can therefore, in the long run, be integrated with different cultures. The Pueblo religions are however obvious exceptions to this rule.

D. The peyote cult furthers Pan-Indianism, the Indian community in interests over tribal boundaries. Over great areas we find the peyote cult to be the creed of Indians of many nations, and members of different tribes may sit together at the same cultic meetings.

These are, as far as the present writer can see, the main conditions and the main obstacles, respectively, in the diffusion of the peyote cult. With all respect to those who think differently, I consider that to a large extent this diffusion took place because there was a religious situation that facilitated it. The foregoing short analysis, although incomplete, should have borne out this conclusion.

BIBLIOGRAPHY

Aberle, David F. 1959. "The Prophet Dance and Reactions to White Contact," *Southwestern Journal of Anthropology* 15(1), pp. 74–83.

———. 1966. *The Peyote Religion among the Navaho.* New York: Viking Fund Publications in Anthropology, 42.

Aberle, David F., and Omer C. Stewart. 1957. *Navaho and Ute Peyotism: A Chronological and Distributional Study.* Boulder, Colo.: University of Colorado Studies, Series in Anthropology, 6.

Alexander, Hartley Burr. 1916. *North American Mythology.* Boston: Marshall Jones, The Mythology of All Races, 10.

Allen, William Alonzo. 1913. *The Sheep Eaters.* New York: Shakespeare Press.

Almqvist, Kurt. 1966. "Les Trois Cercles de l'Existence," *Etudes Traditionelles* 87 (393), pp. 25–33.

Anderson, Frank G. 1955. "The Pueblo Kachina Cult: A Historical Reconstruction," *Southwestern Journal of Anthropology* 11 (4), pp. 404–419.

Andrae, Tor. 1926. *Mystikens Psykologi.* Uppsala: Sveriges Kristliga Studentrörelses.

Angulo, Jaime de, and William Ralganal Benson. 1932. "The Creation Myth of the Pomo Indians," *Anthropos* 27, pp. 261–74, 779–96.

Anisimov, A. F. 1963. "The Shaman's Tent of the Evenks and the Origin of the Shamanistic Rite," *Studies in Siberian Shamanism,* ed. Henry N. Michael. Toronto: Arctic Institute of North America, pp. 84–123.

[Anonymous]. n.d. "The Indian Sundance." Fort Washakie, Wyo.: Wind River Agency Files, manuscript.

Arbman, Ernst. 1939. *Mythic and Religious Thought.* Lund, Sweden: Dragma, Martino P. Nilsson.

———. 1963. *Ecstasy or Religious Trance* 1: *Vision and Ecstasy.* Norstedts, Sweden: Svenska Bokförlaget.

Arth, Malcolm J. 1956. "A Functional View of Peyotism in Omaha Culture," *Plains Anthropologist* 7, pp. 25–29.

Baal, J. van. 1979. "The Scandal of Religion," *Science of Religion: Studies in Methodology,* ed. Lauri Honko. The Hague: Mouton.

Bahnson, Kristian. 1882. "Gravskikke hos Amerikanske Folk," *Aarbog for Nordisk Oldkyndighed og Histoire.* Kjøbenhavn, Denmark: n.p., pp. 128–215.

Bailey, Paul. 1957. *Wovoka, The Indian Messiah.* Los Angeles, Calif.: Westernlore.

Barnett, H. G. 1957. *Indian Shakers.* Carbondale, Ill.: Southern Illinois University.

Bascom, William R. 1965. "The Forms of Folklore: Prose Narratives," *Journal of American Folklore* 78, pp. 3–20.

Bates, Marston. 1953. "Human Ecology," *Anthropology Today,* ed. Alfred Louis Kroeber. Chicago: University of Chicago, pp. 700–713.

Bauer, Clyde Max. 1948. *Yellowstone—Its Underworld.* Albuquerque, N. Mex.: University of New Mexico.

Beals, Ralph Leon. 1933. *The Acaxee.* Berkeley, Calif.: University of California, Ibero-Americana, 6.

———. 1943. *The Aboriginal Culture of the Cáhita Indians.* Berkeley, Calif.: University of California, Ibero-Americana, 19.

Bechmann, S. 1958. *Der Schamanismus bei den Indianern des Subarktischen Amerika.* Wien: n.p.

Beckwith, Martha Warren. 1938. *Mandan-Hidatsa Myths and Ceremonies.* New York: G. E. [Stechert], Memoirs of the American Folklore Society, 32.

Benedict, Ruth Fulton. 1922. "The Vision in Plains Culture," *American Anthropologist* 24(1), pp. 1–23.

———. 1923a. "A Matter for the Field Worker in Folk-Lore," *Journal of American Folklore* 36, p. 104.

———. 1923b. *The Concept of the Guardian Spirit in North America.* Menasha, Wis.: George Banta, American Anthropological Association Memoir, 29.

———. 1938. "Religion," *General Anthropology,* ed. Franz Boas. Boston and New York: D. C. Heath, pp. 627–65.

Benz, Ernst. 1971. *Neue Religionen.* Stuttgart: Klett.

Biggar, H. P., ed. 1925, 1932. *The Works of Samuel de Champlain,* 6 vols. Toronto: Champlain Society, 2 and 4.

Birket-Smith, Kaj. 1930. *Contributions to Chipewyan Ethnology.* Copenhagen: Gyldendal, Report of the Fifth Thule Expedition, 6 (3).

———. 1967. *Studies in Circumpacific Culture Relations 1: Potlatch and Feasts of Merit.* Copenhagen: Munksgaard.

Birket-Smith, Kaj, and Frederica de Laguna. 1938. *The Eyak Indians of the Copper River Delta, Alaska.* Copenhagen: Levin & Munksgaard, E. Munksgaard, Det Kgl. Danske Videnskabernes Selskab.

Black, A. K. 1934. "Shaking the Wigwam," *The Beaver* 265 (3), pp. 13, 39.

Blair, Emma Helen, ed. 1911. *The Indian Tribes of the Upper Mississippi Valley and Region of the Great Lakes,* 2 vols. Cleveland, Ohio: Arthur H. Clark, 1.

Blumensohn, Jules. 1933. "The Fast among North American Indians," *American Anthropologist* 35 (3), pp. 451–69.

Boas, Franz. 1888. *The Central Eskimo.* Washington, D.C.: Bureau of American Ethnology, 6th Annual Report, pp. 399–669.

———. 1915. "Mythology and Folk-tales of the North American Indians," Franz Boas et al. *Anthropology in North America.* New York: G. E. Stechert, pp. 306–349.

———. 1916. *Tsimshian Mythology.* Washington, D.C.: Bureau of American Ethnology, 31st Annual Report, pp. 29–1037.

———. 1917. "The Origin of Death," *Journal of American Folklore* 30, pp. 486–91.

———. 1932. "Current Beliefs of the Kwakiutl Indians," *Journal of American Folklore* 45, pp. 177–260.

———. 1966. *Kwakiutl Ethnography,* ed. Helen Codere. Chicago and London: University of Chicago.

Bogoras, Waldemar. 1907. *The Chukchee.* New York: G. E. Stechert, American Museum of Natural History Memoirs, 11; The Jessup North Pacific Expedition, 7.

Bonner, T. D., ed. 1931. *The Life and Adventures of James P. Beckwourth.* New York: Knopf.

Bouteiller, Marcelle. 1950. *Chamanisme et Guérison Magique.* Paris: Presses Universitaires de France.

Bowers, Alfred W. 1950. *Mandan Social and Ceremonial Organization.* Chicago: University of Chicago.

———. 1965. *Hidatsa Social and Ceremonial Organization.* Washington, D. C.: Bureau of American Ethnology, Bulletin 194.

Brackett, A. G. 1880. *The Shoshonis, or Snake Indians, Their Religion, Superstitions, and Manners.* Washington, D.C.: Annual Report of the Smithsonian Institution for the Year 1879, Government Printing Office, pp. 328–33.

Brinton, Daniel G. 1868. *The Myths of the New World.* New York: Leypoldt & Holt.

———. 1882. *American Hero-Myths.* Philadelphia: H. C. Watts.

Brosses, Charles de. 1760. *Du Culte des Dieux Fétiches.* Paris: n.p.

Brown, James Stephens. 1900. *Life of a Pioneer.* Salt Lake City, Utah: G. Q. Cannon and Sons.

Brown, Joseph Epes. 1953. *The Sacred Pipe: Black Elk's Account of the Seven Rites of the Oglala Sioux.* Norman, Okla.: University of Oklahoma.

———. 1964. *The Spiritual Legacy of the American Indian.* Lebanon, Pa.: Pendle Hill, Pamphlet 135.

———. 1970. "Conceptions of the Animals among the Oglala Sioux: A Study of Religious Values." Ph.D. diss., University of Stockholm.

———. 1972. *The North American Indians: A Selection of Photographs by Edward S. Curtis.* Millerton, N.Y.: Aperture.

———. 1976. "The Roots of Renewal," *Seeing with a Native Eye,* ed. Walter Holden Capps. New York: Harper and Row, pp. 25–34.

Bunzel, Ruth L. 1932a. *Introduction to Zuni Ceremonialism.* Washington, D.C.: Bureau of American Ethnology, 47th Annual Report, pp. 467–544.

———. 1932b. *Zuñi Katcinas: An Analytical Study.* Washington, D.C.:

Bureau of American Ethnology, 47th Annual Report, pp. 837–1086.

———. 1932c. *Zuñi Origin Myths.* Washington, D.C.: Bureau of American Ethnology, 47th Annual Report, pp. 545–609.

———. 1932d. *Zuñi Ritual Poetry.* Wshington, D.C.: Bureau of American Ethnology, 47th Annual Report, pp. 611–835.

Burgesse, J. Allen. 1944. "The Spirit Wigwam as Described by Tommie Moar, Pointe Bleue," *Primitive Man* 17 (3–4), pp. 50–53.

Burlingame, Merrill G. 1942. *The Montana Frontier.* Helena, Mont.: State Publishing Company.

Burstein, S. R. 1950. "Tabu," *Encyclopaedia Brittanica* 21.

Bushnell, David I., Jr. 1920. *Native Cemeteries and Forms of Burial East of the Mississippi.* Washington, D.C.: Bureau of American Ethnology, Bulletin 71.

———. 1927. *Burials of the Algonquian, Siouan and Caddoan Tribes West of the Mississippi.* Washington, D.C.: Bureau of American Ethnology, Bulletin 83.

Campbell, T. N. 1958. "Origin of the Mescal Bean Cult," *American Anthropologist* 60(1), pp. 156–60.

Carter, John G. 1938. *The Northern Arapaho Flat Pipe and the Ceremony of Covering the Pipe.* Washington, D.C.: Bureau of American Ethnology, Bulletin 119, pp. 69–202.

Casagrande, Joseph B. 1952. "Ojibwa Bear Ceremonialism: The Persistence of a Ritual Attitude," *Acculturation in the Americas,* ed. Sol Tax. Chicago: University of Chicago, Proceedings of the 29th International Congress of Americanists, pp. 113–17.

Catlin, George. 1841. *Letters and Notes on the Manners, Customs, and Condition of the North American Indians,* 2 vols. London: George Catlin, 2.

Chamberlain, Alexander F. 1888. "Notes on the History, Customs, and Beliefs of the Mississauga Indians," *Journal of American Folklore* 1, pp. 150–60.

———. 1901. "Kootenay 'Medicine-Men,'" *Journal of American Folklore* 14, pp. 95–99.

Chapman, John W. 1921. "Tinneh Animism," *American Anthropologist* 23 (3), pp. 298–310.

Chase, Richard. 1949. *Quest for Myth.* Baton Rouge, La.: Louisiana State University.

Chittenden, Hiram Martin. 1918. *The Yellowstone National Park.* Cincinnati, Ohio: Stewart & Kidd.

Chittenden, Hiram Martin, and Alfred Talbot Richardson, eds. 1905. *Life, Letters and Travels of Father Pierre-Jean De Smet, S. J.,* 4 vols., New York: F. P. Harper.

Christiansen, Reidar Thoralf. 1946. *The Dead and the Living.* Oslo: [Aschehoug], Studia Norvegica, 2.

Clark, William Philo. 1885. *The Indian Sign Language.* Philadelphia: L. R. Hamersly.

Clements, Forrest E. 1932. "Primitive Concepts of Disease," *University of California Publications in American Archaeology and Ethnology* 32 (2), pp. 185–252.

Clerk of California, The. 1748–49. *An Account of a Voyage for the Discovery of a North-west Passage*, 2 vols. London: Mr. Jolliffe.

Cline, Walter Buchanen, et al. 1938. *The Sinkaietk or Southern Okanagon of Washington.* Menasha, Wis.: George Banta, General Studies in Anthropology, 6.

Coe, Ralph T. 1976. *Sacred Circles: Two Thousand Years of North American Indian Art.* London: Arts Council of Great Britain.

Coleman, (Sister) Bernard. 1937. "The Religion of the Ojibwa of Northern Minnesota," *Primitive Man* 10 (3–4), pp. 33–57.

Collier, Donald. 1944. "Conjuring among the Kiowa," *Primitive Man* 17 (3–4), pp. 45–49.

Collins, June McCormick. 1950. "The Indian Shaker Church: A Study of Continuity and Change in Religion," *Southwestern Journal of Anthropology* 6 (4), pp. 399–411.

Conard, E. Laetitia Moon. 1900. "Les Idées des Indiens Algonquins Relatives a la Vie d'Outre-Tombe," *Revue de l'Histoire des Religions* 42, pp. 9–49, 220–74.

Converse, Harriet Maxwell. 1908. *Myths and Legends of the New York State Iroquois,* ed. Arthur C. Parker. Albany, N.Y.: New York State Museum, Bulletin 125.

Cooper, John M. 1933. "The Northern Algonquian Supreme Being," *Primitive Man* 6 (3–4), pp. 41–111.

———. 1936. *Notes on the Ethnology of the Otchipwe of Lake of the Woods and of Rainy Lake.* Washington, D.C.: Catholic University of America, Anthropological Series, 3.

———. 1944. "The Shaking Tent Rite among Plains and Forest Algonquians," *Primitive Man* 17 (3–4), pp. 60–84.

———. 1946. "The Culture of the Northeastern Indian Hunters: A Reconstructive Interpretation," *Man in Northeastern North America,* ed. Frederick Johnson. Andover, Mass.: Papers of the Robert S. Peabody Foundation for Archaeology, 3, pp. 272–305.

———. 1956. *The Gros Ventres of Montana* 2: *Religion and Ritual.* Washington, D.C.: The Catholic University of America, Anthropological Series, 16.

Corlett, William Thomas. 1935. *The Medicine-Man of the American Indian and His Cultural Background.* Springfield, Ill.: Charles C. Thomas.

Count, Earle W. 1952. "The Earth-Diver and the Rival Twins," *Indian Tribes of Aboriginal America,* ed. Sol Tax. Chicago: University of Chicago, pp. 55–62.

Craig, Steve, and Chester King. 1978. "The Religious and Historical Significance of the Point Conception-Shisholop Area to Native Americans." Santa Barbara (Calif.) Indian Center, manuscript.

Cramton, Louis C. 1932. *Early History of Yellowstone National Park and Its Relation* to *National Park Policies*. Washington, D.C.: U.S. Department of the Interior, National Park Service.

Crooke, William. 1908. "Ancestor-Worship and Cult of the Dead," *Encyclopaedia of Religion and Ethics*, 12 vols., ed. James Hastings. New York and Edinburgh: Scribner's and T. & T. Clark, 1, pp. 425–32.

Crumrine, N. Ross. 1977. *The Mayo Indians of Sonora: A People Who Refuse to Die*. Tucson, Ariz.: University of Arizona.

Czaplicka, Marie Antoinette. 1914. *Aboriginal Siberia*. Oxford: Clarendon Press.

Dangberg, Grace M., ed. 1957. *Letters to Jack Wilson, The Paiute Prophet, Written between 1908 and 1911*. Washington, D.C.: Bureau of American Ethnology, Bulletin 164, pp. 279–96.

David, Robert Beebe. 1937. *Finn Burnett, Frontiersman*. Glendale, Calif.: Arthur H. Clark.

Deloria, Ella. 1944. *Speaking of Indians*. New York: Friendship Press.

Deloria, Vine, Jr. 1973. *God Is Red*. New York: Grosset & Dunlap.

Dempsey, Hugh Aylmer. 1968. *Blackfoot Ghost Dance*. Calgary: Glenbow-Alberta Institute Occasional Paper, 3.

Denig, Edwin Thompson. 1930. *Indian Tribes of the Upper Missouri*, ed. J. N. B. Hewitt. Washington, D.C.: Bureau of American Ethnology, 46th Annual Report, pp. 375–628.

———. 1953. *Of the Crow Nation*, ed. John C. Ewers. Washington, D.C.: Bureau of American Ethnology, Bulletin 151, pp. 1–74.

Densmore, Frances. 1918. *Teton Sioux Music*. Washington, D.C.: Bureau of American Ethnology, Bulletin 61.

———. 1929. *Chippewa Customs*. Washington, D.C.: Bureau of American Ethnology, Bulletin 86.

———. 1932. "An Explanation of a Trick Performed by Indian Jugglers," *American Anthropologist* 34 (2), pp. 310–314.

———. 1948. "Notes on the Indians' Belief in the Friendliness of Nature," *Southwestern Journal of Anthropology* 4 (1), pp. 94–97.

———. 1953. *The Belief of the Indian in a Connection between Song and the Supernatural*. Washington, D.C.: Bureau of American Ethnology, Bulletin 151, Anthropological Papers, 37, pp. 217–23.

Dewdney, Selwyn. 1975. *The Sacred Scrolls of the Southern Ojibway*. Toronto: University of Toronto.

Dittmann, Allen T., and Harvey C. Moore. 1957. "Disturbance in Dreams as Related to Peyotism among the Navaho," *American Anthropologist* 59 (4), pp. 642–49.

Dittmer, Kunz. 1954. *Allgemeine Völkerkunde*. Braunschweig, Germany: F. Vieweg.

Dixon, Roland B. 1908. "Some Aspects of the American Shaman," *Journal of American Folklore* 21, pp. 1–12.

Dockstader, Frederick J. 1954. *The Kachina and the White Man*. Bloomfield Hills, Mich.: Cranbrook Institute of Science, Bulletin 25.

Dorsey, George A. 1903. *The Arapaho Sun Dance.* Chicago: Field Columbian Museum, Anthropological Series, 4.

———. 1904. *Traditions of the Skidi Pawnee.* Boston: Memoirs of the American Folklore Society, 8.

———. 1905a. *The Cheyenne* 1: *Ceremonial Organization.* Chicago: Field Columbian Museum, Anthropological Series, 9 (1).

———. 1905b. *The Cheyenne* 2: *The Sun Dance.* Chicago: Field Columbian Museum, Anthropological Series, 9 (2).

———. 1906a. "Legend of the Teton Sioux Medicine Pipe," *Journal of American Folklore* 19, pp. 326–29.

———. 1906b. *The Pawnee: Mythology.* Washington, D.C.: The Carnegie Institution.

———. 1907. "The Skidi Rite of Human Sacrifice," *Proceedings of the 15th International Congress of Americanists* 2, pp. 65–70.

Dorsey, James Owen. 1889. "Teton Folk-Lore," *American Anthropologist,* o.s., 2 (2), pp. 143–58.

———. 1894. *A Study of Siouan Cults.* Washington, D.C.: Bureau of American Ethnology, 11th Annual Report, pp. 351–544.

Dozier, Edward P. 1961. "The Rio Grande Pueblos," *Perspectives in American Indian Culture Change,* ed. Edward H. Spicer. Chicago: University of Chicago, pp. 94–186.

———. 1962. "Differing Reactions to Religious Contacts among North American Indian Societies," *Akten des 34. Internationalen Amerikanistenkongresses.* Wien: Ferdinand Berger, Horn, pp. 161–71.

———. 1971. "The American Southwest," *North American Indians in Historical Perspective,* ed. Eleanor Burke Leacock and Nancy Oestreich Lurie. New York: Random House, pp. 228–56.

Driver, Harold E. 1961. *Indians of North America.* Chicago: University of Chicago.

Driver, Harold E., and William C. Massey. 1957. *Comparative Studies of North American Indians.* Philadelphia: Transactions of the American Philosophical Society, 47 (2).

Drucker, Philip. 1940. *Kwakiutl Dancing Societies.* Berkeley, Calif.: University of California, Anthropological Records, 2 (6).

———. 1941. *Culture Element Distributions* 17: *Yuman-Piman.* Berkeley, Calif.: University of California, Anthropological Records, 6 (3).

DuBois, Cora. 1935. *Wintu Ethnography.* Berkeley, Calif.: University of California Publications in American Archaeology and Ethnology, 36 (1).

———. 1939. *The 1870 Ghost Dance.* Berkeley, Calif.: University of California, Anthropological Records, 3 (1), pp. 1–151.

Dumarest, Noël. 1919. *Notes on Cochiti, New Mexico,* ed. and trans. Elsie Clews Parsons. Lancaster, Pa.: Memoirs of the American Anthropological Association, 6 (3).

Dundes, Alan. 1964. *The Morphology of North American Indian Folktales.* Helsinki: FF Communications, 195.

———. 1967. "North American Indian Folklore Studies," *Journal de la Societe des Americanistes* 56, pp. 53–79.

Durkheim, Émile. 1954. *The Elementary Forms of the Religious Life.* London: George.

Dusenberry, Verne. 1962. *The Montana Cree: A Study in Religious Persistence.* Stockholm: Acta Universitatis Stockholmiensis, Stockholm Studies in Comparative Religion, 3.

Dyke, A. P. 1970. "Montagnais-Naskapi or Montagnais and Nascaupi? An Examination of Some Tribal Differences," *Ethnohistory* 17 (1–2), pp. 43–48.

Eastman, Charles Alexander. 1911. *The Soul of the Indian.* Boston and New York: Houghton-Mifflin.

Eggan, Fred. 1954. "Social Anthropology and the Method of Controlled Comparison," *American Anthropologist* 56 (5), pp. 743–63.

———. 1966. *The American Indian.* Chicago: University of Chicago.

Eliade, Mircea. 1949. *Le Myth de l'Eternel Retour.* Paris: Gallimard.

———. 1950. "Shamanism," *Forgotten Religions,* ed. Vergilius Ferm. New York: Philosophical Library, pp. 299–308.

———. 1951. *Le Chamanisme et les Techniques Archaïques de l'Extase.* Paris: Librairie Payot.

———. 1971. *The Myth of the Eternal Return.* Princeton, N.J.: Princeton University.

Elkin, Henry. 1940. "The Northern Arapaho of Wyoming," *Acculturation in Seven American Indian Tribes,* ed. Ralph Linton. New York: D. Appleton-Century, pp. 207–255.

Evans, Ivor Hugh Norman. 1937. *The Negritos of Malaya.* Cambridge: The University Press.

Evans-Pritchard, E. E. 1956. *Nuer Religion.* Oxford: Oxford University.

———. 1965. *Theories of Primitive Religion.* Oxford: Clarendon.

Ewers, John C. 1955a. "The Bear Cult among the Assiniboin and Their Neighbors of the Northern Plains," *Southwestern Journal of Anthropology* 11 (1), pp. 1–12.

———. 1955b. *The Horse in Blackfoot Indian Culture.* Washington, D.C.: Bureau of American Ethnology, Bulletin 159.

Fahey, John. 1974. *The Flathead Indians.* Norman, Okla.: University of Oklahoma.

Fay, George E. 1950. "A Calendar of Indian Ceremonies," *El Palacio* 57 (6), pp. 166–72.

Feest, Johanna E., and Christian F. Feest. 1978. "Ottawa," *Handbook of North American Indians* 15: *Northeast,* ed. Bruce G. Trigger. Washington, D.C.: Smithsonian Institution, pp. 772–86.

Fenton, William N. 1936. *An Outline of Seneca Ceremonies at Coldspring Longhouse.* New Haven, Conn.: Yale University Publications in Anthropology, 9.

———. 1953. *The Iroquois Eagle Dance: An Offshoot of the Calumet Dance.* Washington, D.C.: Bureau of American Ethnology, Bulletin 156.

———. 1978. "Northern Iroquoian Culture Patterns," *Handbook of North American Indians* 15: *Northeast,* ed. Bruce G. Trigger. Washington, D.C.: Smithsonian Institution, pp. 296–321.

Feraca, Stephen E. 1961. "The Yuwipi Cult of the Oglala and Sicangu Teton Sioux," *Plains Anthropologist* 6 (13), pp. 155–63.

———. 1963. *Wakinyan: Contemporary Teton Dakota Religion.* Browning, Mont.: Studies in Plains Anthropology and History.

Fewkes, Jesse Walter. 1897. *Tusayan Katcinas.* Washington, D.C.: Bureau of American Ethnology, 15th Annual Report, pp. 245–313.

———. 1901. "An Interpretation of Katcina Worship," *Journal of American Folklore* 14 (53), pp. 81–94.

———. 1920. *Sun Worship of the Hopi Indians.* Washington, D.C.: Smithsonian Institution Annual Report for 1918, Government Printing Office, pp. 493–526.

———. 1923. "Ancestor Worship of the Hopi Indians," *Smithsonian Institution Annual Report for . . . 1921.* Washington, D.C.: Government Printing Office, pp. 485–506.

Findeisen, Hans. 1956. *Das Tier als Gott, Dämon und Ahne.* Stuttgart: Kosmos.

———. 1960. "Das Schamanenentum als Spiritistische Religion," *Ethnos* 25 (3–4), pp. 192–213.

Fisher, John F. 1975. "An Analysis of the Central Eskimo Sedna Myth," *Temenos* 11, pp. 27–42.

Fisher, Margaret W. 1946. "The Mythology of the Northern and Northeastern Algonkians in Reference to Algonkian Mythology as a Whole," *Man in Northeastern North America,* ed. Frederick Johnson. Andover, Mass.: Papers of the Robert S. Peabody Foundation for Archaeology, 3, pp. 226–62.

Flannery, Regina. 1939a. *An Analysis of Coastal Algonquian Culture.* Washington, D.C.: Catholic University of America, Anthropological Series, 7.

———. 1939b. "The Shaking-Tent Rite among the Montagnais of James Bay," *Primitive Man* 12 (1), pp. 11–16.

———. 1940. "The Cultural Position of the Spanish River Indians," *Primitive Man* 13 (1), pp. 1–25.

———. 1944. "The Gros Ventre Shaking Tent," *Primitive Man* 17 (3–4), pp. 54–59.

———. 1946. "The Culture of the Northeastern Indian Hunters: A Descriptive Survey," *Man in Northeastern North America,* ed. Frederick Johnson. Andover, Mass.: Papers of the Robert S. Peabody Foundation for Archaeology, 3, pp. 263–71.

Fletcher, Alice C. 1883. "The White Buffalo Festival of the Uncpapas," *Reports of the Peabody Museum of American Archaeology and Ethnology* 16–17, pp. 260–75.

———. 1884. *The Shadow or Ghost Lodge: A Ceremony of the Ogallala Sioux.*

Cambridge, Mass.: Annual Report of the Trustees of the Peabody Museum, 3 (3–4).

———. 1891. "The Indian Messiah," *Journal of American Folklore* 4, pp. 57–60.

Fletcher, Alice C., and Francis La Flesche. 1911. *The Omaha Tribe*. Washington, D.C.: Bureau of American Ethnology, 27th Annual Report, pp. 16–672.

Forde, C. Daryll. 1949. *Habitat, Economy and Society: A Geographical Introduction to Ethnology*, 7th ed. London: Methuen.

Franklin, John. 1823. *Narrative of a Journey to the Shores of the Polar Sea*. London: John Murray.

Fraser, Thomas M., Jr. 1963. "Malay Spiritualistic Ritual in Southern Thailand," *International Journal of Parapsychology* 5 (4), pp. 387–410.

Frazer, James George. 1933. *The Fear of the Dead in Primitive Religion* 1. London: Macmillan.

———. 1955. *The Golden Bough*, 12 vols., London: Macmillan, 5 (2).

Freud, Sigmund. 1950. *Totem and Taboo*. London: Routledge & Kegan Paul.

Fridegård, Jan. 1963. *Den Gåtfulla Vägen*. Göteborg, Sweden: Zinderman.

Friederici, Georg. 1906. *Skalpieren und Ähnliche Kriegsgebräuche in Amerika*, Braunschweig, Germany: Druck von F. Vieweg und Sohn.

———. 1929. "Zu den Vorkolumbischen Verbindungen der Südsee-Völker mit Amerika," *Anthropos* 24, pp. 441–87.

Funk & Wagnalls Standard Dictionary of Folklore, Mythology, and Legend. 1949. New York, 1.

Garfield, Viola Edmundson, and Linn A. Forrest. 1948. *The Wolf and the Raven*. Seattle, Wash.: University of Washington.

Garrestson, Martin S. 1938. *The American Bison*. New York: New York Zoological Society.

Gauvreau, E. 1907. "Les Dakotas, Religion, Moeurs, Coutumes," *Proceedings of the 15th International Congress of Americanists*, 2 vols. Québec: Dussault & Proulx, 1, pp. 311–13.

Gayton, A. H. 1930. "The Ghost Dance of 1870 in South-Central California," *University of California Publications in American Archaeology and Ethnology* 28 (3), pp. 57–82.

———. 1935. "The Orpheus Myth in North America," *Journal of American Folklore* 48, pp. 263–93.

———. 1946. "Culture-Environment Integration: External References in Yokuts Life," *Southwestern Journal of Anthropology* 2 (3), pp. 252–68.

Geertz, Clifford. 1966. "Religion as a Cultural System," *Anthropological Approaches to the Study of Religion*, ed. Michael Banton. London: Tavistock, A.S.A Monographs, 3, pp. 1–46.

Gennep, Arnold van. 1909. *Les Rites de Passage*. Paris: É. Nourry.

Gifford, E. W., and Stanislaw Klimek. 1936. *Cultural Element Distributions* 2: *Yana*. Berkeley, Calif.: University of California Publications in American Archaeology and Ethnology, 37 (2), pp. 71–100.

Gilmore, Melvin R. 1929. *Prairie Smoke*. New York: Columbia University.

Ginsberg, Morris. 1934. *Sociology.* Oxford: Oxford University.

Goddard, Ives. 1978. "Eastern Algonquian Languages," *Handbook of North American Indians* 15: *Northeast,* ed. Bruce G. Trigger. Washington, D.C.: Smithsonian Institution, pp. 70–77.

Goddard, Pliny Earle. 1916. *The Beaver Indians.* New York: Anthropological Papers of the American Museum of Natural History, 10 (4).

Goldenweiser, Alexander. 1946. *Anthropology: An Introduction to Primitive Culture.* New York: F. S. Crofts.

Goldfrank, Esther S. 1927. *The Social and Ceremonial Organization of Cochiti.* Menasha, Wis.: Memoirs of the American Anthropological Association, 33.

Goode, William J. 1951. *Religion among the Primitives.* Glencoe, Ill.: Free Press.

Graburn, Nelson H., and B. Stephen Strong. 1973. *Circumpolar Peoples: An Anthropological Perspective.* Pacific Palisades, Calif.: Goodyear Publishing.

Grant, Peter. 1890. "The Sauteux Indians about 1804," *Les Bourgeois de la Compagnie Nord-Ouest,* ed. L. R. Masson. Québec: A. Cote, 2, pp. 303–366.

Grimm, Jakob. 1966. *Teutonic Mythology,* 4 vols. New York: Dover.

Grinnell, George Bird. 1923. *The Cheyenne Indians,* 2 vols. New Haven, Conn.: Yale University Press, 2.

Gross, Feliks. 1949. "Nomadism of the Arapaho Indians of Wyoming," *Ethnos* 14 (2–3), pp. 65–88.

Gunther, Erna. 1926. "An Analysis of the First Salmon Ceremony," *American Anthropologist* 28 (4), pp. 605–617.

———. 1928. "A Further Analysis of the First Salmon Ceremony," *University of Washington Publications in Anthropology* 2 (5), pp. 129–73.

———. 1949. "The Shaker Religion of the Northwest," *Indians of the Urban Northwest,* ed. Marian W. Smith. New York: Columbia University Contributions to Anthropology, 36, pp. 37–76.

———. 1950. "The Westward Movement of Some Plains Traits," *American Anthropologist* 52 (2), pp. 174–80.

Gusinde, Martin. 1939. "Der Peyote-Kult, Entstehung und Verbreitung," *Festschrift zum 50 Jahrigen Bestandsjubilaum des Missionshauses St. Gabriel Wien-Mödling,* Wien-Mödling: St. Gabriel-Studien, 8, pp. 401–499.

Haas, Mary R. 1958. "A New Linguistic Relationship in North America: Algonkian and the Gulf Languages," *Southwestern Journal of Anthropology* 14 (3), pp. 231–64.

Haeberlin, Herman Karl. 1916. "The Idea of Fertilization in the Culture of the Pueblo Indians," *Memoirs of the American Anthropological Association* 3 (1), pp. 1–55.

Haekel, Josef. 1938. "Zum Problem des Individualtotemismus in Nordamerika," *Internationales Archiv für Ethnographie* 35, pp. 14–22.

———. 1955. "Zur Problematik des Heiligen Pfahles bei den Indianern Brasil-

iens," *Acts of the 31st International Congress of Americanists,* 2 vols. São
    Paulo: Editora Anhembi, 1, pp. 229–43.

———. 1958. "Religion," *Lehrbuch der Völkerkunde,* ed. Leonhard Adam and
    Hermann Trimborn. Stuttgart: Ferdinand Enke, pp. 40–72.

———. 1959. "Der 'Herr der Tiere' im Glauben der Indianer Mesoamerikas,"
    Mitteilungen aus dem Museum für Völkerkunde in Hamburg 25, pp. 60–69.

Hagar, Stansbury. 1908. "Ancestor-Worship and Cult of the Dead (American),"
    Encyclopaedia of Religion and Ethics, 12 vols., ed. James Hastings. New
    York and Edinburgh: Scribner's and T. & T. Clark, 1, pp. 433–37.

———. 1922. "Sun, Moon and Stars (American)," *Encyclopaedia of Religion
    and Ethics,* 12 vols., ed. James Hastings. New York and Edinburgh:
    Scribner's and T. & T. Clark, 12, pp. 65–71.

Haile, Berard. 1938. "Navajo Chantways and Ceremonials," *American Anthro-
    pologist* 40 (4), pp. 639–52.

———. 1940. "A Note on the Navaho Visionary," *American Anthropologist* 42
    (2), p. 359.

———. 1942. "Navajo Upward-reaching Way and Emergence Place," *Ameri-
    can Anthropologist* 44 (3), pp. 407–420.

Hale, Horatio. 1883. *The Iroquois Book of Rites.* Philadelphia: D. G. Brinton.

Hallowell, A. Irving. 1926. "Bear Ceremonialism in the Northern Hemis-
    phere," *American Anthropologist* 28 (1), pp. 1–175.

———. 1940. "The Spirits of the Dead in Saulteaux Life and Thought," *Journal
    of the Royal Anthropological Institute* 70 (1), pp. 29–51.

———. 1942. *The Role of Conjuring in Saulteaux Society.* Philadelphia: University
    of Pennsylvania, Publications of the Philadelphia Anthropological
    Society, 2.

———. 1946. "Concordance of Ojibwa Narratives in the Published Works
    of Henry R. Schoolcraft," *Journal of American Folklore* 59,
    pp. 136–53.

———. 1947. "Myth, Culture and Personality," *American Anthropologist* 49 (4),
    pp. 544–56.

———. 1967. *Culture and Experience.* New York: Schocken.

Harrington, M. R. 1921. *Religion and Ceremonies of the Lenape.* New York:
    Museum of the American Indian, Heye Foundation, Indian Notes
    and Monographs.

Harris, J. S. 1940. "The White Knife Shoshoni of Nevada," *Acculturation in
    Seven American Indian Tribes,* ed. Ralph Linton. New York: D. Apple-
    ton Century, pp. 39–116.

Harris, Marvin. 1978. *Cannibals and Kings: The Origins of Cultures.* Glasgow:
    Fontana/Collins.

Harrison, Jane Ellen. 1912. *Themis.* Cambridge: University Press.

Hart, Sheila, and Vada F. Carlson. 1948. *We Saw the Sun Dance.* Concord, Calif.:
    Concord Graphic Arts.

Hartland, Edwin Sidney. 1914. *Mythology and Folktales: Their Relation and Inter-
    pretation,* 2nd ed. London: D. Nutt, Popular Studies in Mythology,
    Romance, & Folklore, 7.

Hartmann, Horst. 1973. *Die Plains—und Prärieindianer Nordamerikas.* Berlin: Museum für Völkerkunde.

———. 1978. *Kachina-Figuren der Hopi-Indianer.* Berlin: Museum für Völkerkunde.

Harva, Uno. 1938. *Die Religiösen Vorstellungen der Altaischen Völker.* Helsinki: FF Communications, 125.

Hatt, Gudmund. 1951. "The Corn Mother in America and in Indonesia," *Anthropos* 46, pp. 853–914.

Hauge, Hans-Egil. 1945. "Tabu som Religionsvitenskaplig Begrep," *Folkkultur,* pp. 119–39.

Hawley, Florence. 1950. "Big Kivas, Little Kivas, and Moiety Houses in Historical Reconstruction," *Southwestern Journal of Anthropology* 6 (3), pp. 286–302.

Haynes, Jack Ellis. 1947. *Haynes' Guide: Handbook of Yellowstone National Park,* 49th ed. Yellowstone Park, Wyo.: Haynes.

Hebard, Grace Raymond. 1930. *Washakie.* Cleveland: Arthur H. Clark.

———. 1933. *Sacajawea.* Glendale, Calif.: Arthur H. Clark.

Heizer, Robert Fleming, and Gordon W. Hewes. 1940. "Animal Ceremonialism in Central California in the Light of Archaeology," *American Anthropologist* 42 (4), pp. 587–603.

Henry, Alexander. 1809. *Travels and Adventures in Canada and the Indian Territories, between the Years 1760 and 1776.* New York: I. Riley.

Henshaw, Henry W. 1905. "Popular Fallacies Respecting the Indians," *American Anthropologist* 7 (1), pp. 104–113.

———. 1910. "Popular Fallacies," *Handbook of American Indians North of Mexico,* ed. Frederick W. Hodge, 2 vols. Washington, D.C.: Bureau of American Ethnology, Bulletin 30 (2), pp. 282–86.

Herskovits, Melville J. 1949. *Man and His Works: The Science of Cultural Anthropology.* New York: Knopf.

Hilger, (Sister) M. Inez. 1951. *Chippewa Child Life and Its Cultural Background.* Washington, D.C.: Bureau of American Ethnology, Bulletin 146.

———. 1952. *Arapaho Child Life and Its Cultural Background.* Washington, D.C.: Bureau of American Ethnology, Bulletin 148.

Hill, W. W. 1944. "The Navajo Indians and the Ghost Dance of 1890," *American Anthropologist* 46 (4), pp. 523–27.

Hind, Henry Youle. 1860. *Narrative of the Canadian Red River Exploring Expedition,* 2 vols. London: Longman, Green, Longman and Roberts.

Hittman, Michael. 1973. "The 1870 Ghost Dance at the Walker River Reservation: A Reconstruction," *Ethnohistory* 20 (3), pp. 247–78.

Hoebel, E. Adamson. 1935. "The Sun Dance of the Hekandika Shoshone," *American Anthropologist* 37 (4), pp. 570–81.

Hoffman, Walter James. 1891. *The Midē'winwin or "Grand Medicine Society" of the Ojibwa.* Washington, D.C.: Bureau of American Ethnology, 7th Annual Report, pp. 143–300..

———. 1896. *The Menomini Indians.* Washington, D.C.: Bureau of American Ethnology, 14th Annual Report, Pt. 1, pp. 3–328.

Holm, Gustav. 1914. "Ethnological Sketch of the Angmagssalik Eskimo," *Meddelelser fra Grønland* 39 (1), pp. 1–147.

Holmberg, Henrik Johan. 1855. *Ethnographische Skizzen über die Völker des Russischen Amerika.* Helsingfors, Finland: Acta Societatis Scientiarum Fennicae.

Holmberg, Uno [Harva]. 1917. *Gudstrons Uppkomst.* Uppsala, Sweden: Lindblad.

———. 1925. "Vänster Hand och Motsols," *Rig* 1–2, pp. 23–36.

Honko, Lauri. 1964. "Memorates and the Study of Folk Beliefs," *Journal of the Folklore Institute* 1 (1–2), pp. 5–19.

———. 1968. "Genre Analysis in Folkloristics and Comparative Religion," *Temenos* 3, pp. 48–64.

———. 1975. "Zur Klassifikation der Riten," *Temenos* 11, pp. 61–77.

Hornaday, William T. 1889. *The Extirmination of the American Bison.* Washington, D.C.: Annual Report of the Smithsonian Institution, 1887, 2.

Howard, James H. 1957. "The Mescal Bean Cult of the Central and Southern Plains: An Ancestor of the Peyote Cult?" *American Anthropologist* 59 (1), pp. 75–87.

———. 1960. "Mescalism and Peyotism Once Again," *Plains Anthropologist* 5 (10), pp. 84–85.

———. 1965a. *The Plains-Ojibwa or Bungi.* Vermillion, S.D.: South Dakota Museum Anthropological Papers, 1.

———. 1965b. *The Ponca Tribe.* Washington, D.C.: Bureau of American Ethnology, Bulletin 195.

———. 1968. *The Southeastern Ceremonial Complex and Its Interpretation,* Columbia, Mo.: Memoirs of the Missouri Archaeological Society, 6.

Hudson, Charles. 1976. *The Southeastern Indians.* Knoxville, Tenn.: University of Tennessee.

Hudson, J. W. 1902. "An Indian Myth of the San Joaquin Basin," *Journal of American Folklore* 15, pp. 104–106.

Hugolin, R. P. 1907. *L'Idée Spiritualiste et l'Idée Morale chez les Chippewas.* Québec: International Congress of Americanists, 15th Congress, pp. 329–35.

Hultkrantz, Åke. 1947. "Naturfolk och Kulturfolk," *Världens Länder och Folk efter Andra Världskriget,* ed. Sven Dahl. Stockholm: Natur och Kultur, 1, pp. 518–605.

———. 1949. "Kulturbildningen hos Wyomings Shoshoni-indianer," *Ymer* 2, pp. 134–57.

———. 1951. "The Concept of the Soul Held by the Wind River Shoshone," *Ethnos* 16 (1–2), pp. 18–44.

———. 1953. *Conceptions of the Soul among North American Indians.* Stockholm: The Ethnographical Museum of Sweden, Monograph Series, 1.

———. 1954a. "Indianerna i Yellowstone Park," *Ymer* 2, pp. 112–45. Translated as "The Indians in Yellowstone Park," *Annals of Wyoming* 29 (2), p. 125–49.

———. 1954b. "The Indians and the Wonders of Yellowstone. A Study of the Interrelations of Religion, Nature and Culture," *Ethnos* 19 (1–4), pp. 34–68.

———. 1955. "The Origin of Death Myth as Found among the Wind River Shoshoni Indians," *Ethnos* 20 (2–3), pp. 127–36.

———. 1956a. "Configurations of Religious Belief among the Wind River Shoshoni," *Ethnos* 21 (3–4), pp. 194–215.

———. 1956b. "Religious Tradition, Comparative Religion and Folklore," *Ethnos* 21 (1–2), pp. 11–29.

———. 1956c. "Shoshonerna i Klippiga Bergs-området," *Ymer* 3, pp. 161–89.

———. 1957. *The North American Indian Orpheus Tradition.* Stockholm: The Ethnographical Museum of Sweden, Monograph Series, 2.

———. 1958. "Tribal Divisions within the Eastern Shoshoni of Wyoming," *Proceedings of the 32nd Congress of Americanists (1956).* Copenhagen, pp. 148–54.

———. 1959. "Indianer, 1: Religionsgeschichtlich," *Die Religion in Geschichte und Gegenwart,* 3rd ed., 3, pp. 699–702.

———. 1960a. *General Ethnological Concepts.* Copenhagen: Rosenkilde and Bagger, International Dictionary of Regional European Ethnology and Folklore, 1.

———. 1960b. "Religious Aspects of the Wind River Shoshoni Folk Literature," *Culture in History: Essays in Honor of Paul Radin,* ed. Stanley Diamond. New York: Columbia University, pp. 552–69.

———. 1961a. "The Masters of the Animals among the Wind River Shoshoni," *Ethnos* 26 (4), pp. 198–218.

———. 1961b. "The Owners of the Animals in the Religion of the North American Indians," *The Supernatural Owners of Nature,* ed. Åke Hultkrantz. Stockholm: Acta Universitatis Stockholmiensis, Stockholm Studies in Comparative Religion, 1, pp. 53–64.

———. 1961c. "The Shoshones in the Rocky Mountain Area," *Annals of Wyoming* 33 (1), pp. 19–41.

———. 1962a. "Die Religion der Amerikanischen Arktis," *Die Religionen Nordeurasiens und der Amerikanischen Arktis: Die Religionen der Menschheit,* ed. Christel Matthias Schröder. Stuttgart: Kohlhammer, pp. 357–415.

———. 1962b. "Religion und Mythologie der Prärie-Schoschen," *Akten des 34. Internationalen Amerikanistenkongresses (1960),* Wien, pp. 546–54.

———. 1963. *Les Religions des Indiens Primitifs de l'Amérique, Essai d'une Synthèse Typologique et Historique.* Stockholm: Acta Universitatis Stockholmiensis, Stockholm Studies in Comparative Religion, 4.

———. 1965a. "The Study of North American Indian Religion," *Temenos* 1, pp. 87–121.

———. 1965b. "Type of Religion in the Arctic Hunting Cultures: A Religio-Ecological Approach," *Hunting and Fishing, Nordic Symposium on Life in a Traditional Hunting and Fishing Milieu in Prehistoric Times and up to the Present Day,* ed. Harald Hvarfner, Luleå: Norbottens Museum, pp. 265–318.

———. 1966a. "An Ecological Approach to Religion," *Ethnos* 31, pp. 131–50.

———. 1966b. "The Ethnographers and Other Field-Workers. Some Aspects of Religio-Ethnographical Field-Work," *Ethnos* 31 (supplement), pp. 65–82.

———. 1966–67a. "The Ethnological Position of the Sheepeater Indians in Wyoming," *Folk* 8–9, pp. 155–63.

———. 1966–67b. "North American Indian Religion in the History of Research: A General Survey," 4 parts, *History of Religions* 6 (2), pp. 91–107; 6 (3), pp. 183–207; 7 (1), pp. 13–34; 7 (2), pp. 112–48.

———. 1967a. "Historical Approaches in American Ethnology: A Research Survey," *Ethnologia Europaea* 1 (2), pp. 96–116.

———. 1967b. "Spirit Lodge, a North American Shamanistic Séance," *Studies in Shamanism*, ed. Carl-Martin Edsman. Stockholm: Scripta Instituti Donneriani Aboensis, 1, pp. 32–68.

———. 1968a. "'Miscellaneous Beliefs': Some Points of View Concerning the Informal Religious Sayings," *Temenos* 3, pp. 67–82.

———. 1968b. "Shoshoni Indians on the Plains: An Appraisal of the Documentary Evidence," *Zeitschrift für Ethnologie* 93 (1–2), pp. 4–72.

———. 1969. "Pagan and Christian Elements in the Religious Syncretism among the Shoshoni Indians of Wyoming," *Syncretism*, ed. Sven S. Hartman. Stockholm: Scripta Instituti Donneriani Aboensis, 3, pp. 15–40.

———. 1970a. "Attitudes to Animals in Shoshoni Indian Religion," *Studies in Comparative Religion* 4 (2), pp. 70–79.

———. 1970b. "The Phenomenology of Religion: Aims and Methods," *Temenos* 6, pp. 68–88.

———. 1970c. "The Source Literature on the 'Tukudïka' Indians in Wyoming: Facts and Fancies," *Languages and Cultures of Western North America*, ed. Earl Swanson, Jr. Pocatello, Idaho: Idaho State University, pp. 246–64.

———. 1970d. "Yellow Hand, Chief and Medicine-man among the Eastern Shoshoni," *Proceedings of the 38th International Congress of Americanists* 2. Munich. pp. 293–304.

———. 1971. "The Structure of Theistic Beliefs among North American Plains Indians," *Temenos* 7, pp. 66–74.

———. 1972a. "An Ideological Dichotomy: Myths and Folk Beliefs among the Shoshoni Indians of Wyoming," *History of Religions* 11 (4), pp. 339–53.

———. 1972b. "Review of Werner Müller, *Glauben und Denken der Sioux*, and Peter J. Powell, *Sweet Medicine*," *Temenos* 8, pp. 163–69.

———. 1973a. "The Hare Indians: Notes on Their Traditional Culture and Religion, Past and Present," *Ethnos* 38 (1–4), pp. 113–52.

———. 1973b. *Prairie and Plains Indians*. Leiden: E. J. Brill, Iconography of Religions, 10 (2).

———. 1973c. *Metodväger inon den Jämförande Religionforskningen*. Stockholm: Esselte Studium.

———. 1975. "Haivodïka, an Acculturated Shoshoni Group in Wyoming," *Zeitschrift für Ethnologie* 100, pp. 135–56.

———. 1976a. "The Contribution of the Study of North American Indian Religions to the History of Religions," *Seeing with a Native Eye*, ed. Walter Holden Capps. New York: Harper and Row, pp. 86–106.

——. 1976b. "Religion and Ecology among the Great Basin Indians," *The Realm of the Extra-Human, Ideas and Actions*, ed. Agehananda Bharati. The Hague and Paris: Mouton, pp. 137–50.

——. 1977. "Amerikanische Religionen," *Theologische Realenzyklopädie* 2 (3–4). Berlin: Walter de Gruyter, pp. 402–450.

——. 1977a. "History of Religions in Anthropological Waters: Some Reflections against the Background of American Data," *Temenos* 13, pp. 81–97.

——. 1978. "The Cult of the Dead among North American Indians," *Tenemos* 14, pp. 97–126.

——. 1979a. "Ecology of Religion: Its Scope and Methodology," *Studies in Methodology*, ed. Lauri Honko. The Hague: Mouton, pp. 221–36.

——. 1979b. "The Fear of Geysers among Indians of the Yellowstone Park Area," *Lifeways of Intermontane and Plains Montana Indians*, ed. Leslie B. Davis. Bozeman, Mont.: Museum of the Rockies Occasional Papers, 1, pp. 33–42.

——. 1979c. "Myths in Native North American Religions," *Native Religious Traditions*, ed. Earle H. Waugh and K. Dad Prithipaul. Waterloo, Ontario: Wilfred Laurier University for the Canadian Corporation for Studies in Religion, Studies in Religion, 8, pp. 77–97.

——. 1979d. *The Religions of the American Indians*. Berkeley, Calif.: University of California.

——. 1979e. "Ritual in Native North American Religions," *Native Religious Traditions*, ed. Earle H. Waugh and K. Dad Prithipaul. Waterloo, Ontario: Wilfred Laurier University for the Canadian Corporation for Studies in Religion, Studies in Religion, 8, pp. 135–47.

——. 1979f. "The Traditional Symbolism of the Sun Dance Lodge among the Wind River Shoshoni," *Religious Symbols and Their Functions*, ed. Haralds Biezais. Stockholm: Scripta Instituti Donneriani Aboensis, 10, pp. 70–95.

——. 1980a. "The Concept of the Supernatural in Primal Religion." Paper delivered at Northwestern University, Evanston, Ill.

——. 1980b. "The Problem of Christian Influence on Northern Algonkian Eschatology," *Studies in Religion* 9 (2), pp. 161–83.

——. 1981. "Indianen som Naturskyddare," *De Tog Vårt Land*, ed. Lennart Lindberg and Lars Wennersten. Stockholm: Bok Förlaget Plus, pp. 85–100.

——. in press. "Mythology and Religious Concepts." To be published in *Handbook of North American Indians* 11: *Basin*.

——. n.d. "Wind River Shoshone Field Notes," manuscript. Lidingö, Sweden.

Hultkrantz, Åke, ed. 1955. *Primitiv Religion och Magi*. Stockholm: Svenska Bokförlaget, Bonniers.

Hurt, Wesley R., Jr. 1960. "A Yuwipi Ceremony at Pine Ridge," *Plains Anthropologist* 5 (10), pp. 48–52.

————. 1961. "Correction on Yuwipi Color Symbolism," *Plains Anthropologist* 6 (11), p. 43.

Hurt, Wesley R., Jr., and James H. Howard. 1952. "A Dakota Conjuring Ceremony," *Southwestern Journal of Anthropology* 8 (3), pp. 286–96.

Hyde, George E. 1959. *Indians of the High Plains.* Norman, Okla.: University of Oklahoma.

Hyman, Stanley Edgar. 1955. "The Ritual View of Myth and the Mythic," *Journal of American Folklore* 88, pp. 462–72.

Irving, Washington. 1954. *The Adventures of Captain Bonneville.* Portland, Oreg.: Binfords and Mort.

Jacobs, Wilbur R. 1980. "Indians as Ecologists and Other Environmental Themes in American Frontier History," *American Indian Environments: Ecological Issues in Native American History,* ed. Christopher Vecsey and Robert W. Venables. Syracuse, N.Y.: Syracuse University Press, pp. 46–64.

Jayne, C. D., ed. 1952. *Fremont County and Its Communities.* Laramie, Wyo.: n.p.

Jenness, Diamond. 1934. *The Indians of Canada.* Ottawa: National Museum of Canada, Bulletin 65.

————. 1935. *The Ojibwa Indians of Parry Island, Their Social and Religious Life.* Ottawa: National Museum of Canada, Bulletin 78.

Jennings, Jesse D. 1964. "The Desert West," *Prehistoric Man in the New World,* ed. Jesse D. Jennings and Edward Norbeck. Chicago: University of Chicago, pp. 149–74.

Jensen, Adolf E. 1963. *Myth and Cult among Primitive Peoples.* Chicago and London: University of Chicago.

Jetté, J. 1911. "On the Superstitions of the Ten'a Indians (Middle Part of the Yukon Valley, Alaska)," *Anthropos* 6, pp. 95–108, 241–59, 602–615, 699–723.

Jones, James Athearn. 1830. *Traditions of the North American Indians,* 3 vols. London: Henry Colburn and Richard Bentley.

Jones, Peter. 1861. *History of the Ojebway Indians.* London: A. W. Bennett.

Jones, W. A. 1875. "Report upon the Reconnaissance of Northwestern Wyoming including Yellowstone National Park Made in the Summer of 1873." Washington, D.C.: 43rd Congress, 1st Session.

Jones, William. 1911. "Notes on the Fox Indians," *Journal of American Folklore* 24 (92), pp. 209–237.

————. 1916. "Ojibwa Tales from the North Shore of Lake Superior," *Journal of American Folklore* 29, pp. 368–91.

————. 1919. *Ojibwa Texts,* 2 vols. Leyden: E. J. Brill, Publications of the American Ethnological Society, 7 (1–2).

————. 1939. *Ethnography of the Fox Indians.* Washington, D.C.: Bureau of American Ethnology, Bulletin 125.

Jorgensen, Joseph G. 1972. *The Sun Dance Religion.* Chicago and London: University of Chicago.

———. in press. "Ghost Dance, Bear Dance, Sun Dance," to be published in *Handbook of North American Indians* 11: *Basin*.

Juel, Eric. 1945. "Notes on Seal-Hunting Ceremonialism in the Arctics," *Ethnos* 10 (2–3), pp. 143–64.

Kane, Paul. 1925. *Wanderings of an Artist among the Indians of North America*. Toronto: The Radisson Society of Canada.

Karsten, Rafael. 1935. *The Origins of Religion*. London: K. Paul, Trench, Trubner.

Kaut, Charles R. 1959. "Notes on Western Apache Religious and Social Organization," *American Anthropologist* 61 (1), pp. 99–102.

Keating, William H. 1825. *Narrative of an Expedition to the Source of St. Peter's River*, 2 vols. London: G. B. Whittager.

Kehoe, Alice B. 1968. "The Ghost Dance Religion in Saskatchewan, Canada," *Plains Anthropologist* 13 (42), pp. 296–304.

Kehoe, Thomas, and Alice B. Kehoe. 1977. "Stones, Solstices and Sun Dance Structures," *Plains Anthropologist* 22 (76), pp. 85–95.

Kelley, J. Charles. 1966. "Mesoamerica and the Southwestern United States," *Handbook of Middle American Indians*, 16 vols., ed. Gordon F. Ekholm and Gordon R. Willey. Austin, Tex.: University of Texas, 4, pp. 95–110.

Kelly, Isabel T. 1932. *Ethnography of the Surprise Valley Paiute*. Berkeley, Calif.: University of California Publications in American Archaeology and Ethnology, 31 (3), pp. 67–210.

Kenton, Edna, ed. 1954. *The Jesuit Relations and Allied Documents*. New York: Vanguard.

Kidwell, Clara Sue. 1973. "Science and Ethnoscience," *The Indian Historian* 6 (4), pp. 43–54.

Kinietz, W. Vernon. 1940. *The Indians of the Western Great Lakes 1615–1760*. Ann Arbor, Mich.: University of Michigan.

———. 1947. *Chippewa Village: The Story of Katikitegon*. Bloomfield Hills, Mich.: Cranbrook Institute of Science, Bulletin 25.

Kirk, G. S. 1970. *Myth: Its Meaning and Function in Ancient and Other Cultures*. Berkeley, Calif.: University of California.

Kluckhohn, Clyde. 1942. "Myths and Rituals: A General Theory," *The Harvard Theological Review* 35 (1), pp. 45–79.

Koch-Grünberg, Theodore. 1920. *Indianermärchen aus Südamerika*. Jena, Germany: Diederich.

Kock, Gösta. 1956. "Der Heilbringer. Ein Beitrag zur Aufklärung seiner Religionsgeschichtlichen Voraussetzungen," *Ethnos* 21 (1), pp. 118–29.

Kohl, Johann Georg. 1859a. *Kitschi-Gami oder Erzählungen vom Obern See*, 2 vols. Bremen: C. Schünemann.

———. 1859b. *Reisen im Nordwesten der Vereinigten Staaten*, 2nd. ed., St. Louis, Mo.: Conrad Witter.

Krause, Aurel. 1885. *Die Tlinkit-Indianer*. Jena, Germany: H. Costenoble. English trans. *The Tlingit Indians*. Seattle, Wash.: 1956.

Krickeberg, W. 1935. "Beiträge zur Frage der Alten Kulturgeschichtlichen Beziehungen Zwischen Nord- und Südamerika," *Zeitschrift für Ethnologie* 66 (4–6), pp. 287–373.

Kroeber, Alfred Louis. 1902. *The Arapaho.* New York: American Museum of Natural History, Bulletin 18 (1).

———. 1904. "A Ghost Dance in California," *Journal of American Folklore* 17, pp. 32–35.

———. 1908. *Ethnology of the Gros Ventre.* New York: Anthropological Papers of the American Museum of Natural History, 1 (4).

———. 1916. "Thoughts on Zuñi Religion," *Anthropological Essays Presented to William Henry Holmes.* Washington, D.C.: privately printed, pp. 269–77.

———. 1925. *Handbook of the Indians of California.* Washington, D.C.: Bureau of American Ethnology, Bulletin 78. Reprinted by California Book Co., Ltd., Berkeley, Calif., 1953.

———. 1939. *Cultural and Natural Areas of Native North America.* Berkeley, Calif.: University of California.

———. 1948. *Seven Mohave Myths.* Berkeley, Calif.: University of California, Anthropological Records, 11 (1).

———. 1952. *The Nature of Culture.* Chicago: University of Chicago.

———. 1957. *Ethnographic Interpretations.* Berkeley, Calif.: Publications in American Archaeology and Ethnology, 47 (2).

Kroeber, Alfred Louis, and E. W. Gifford. 1949. *World Renewal: A Cult System of Native Northwest California.* Berkeley, Calif.: University of California, Anthropological Records, 13 (1).

Kunike, H. 1926. "Zur Astralmythologie der Nordamerikanischen Indianer," *Internationales Archiv für Ethnographie* 27, pp. 1–29, 55–78, 107–134.

Kurath, Gertrude Prokosch. 1961. *Effects of Environment on Cherokee-Iroquois Ceremonialism, Music, and Dance.* Washington, D.C.: Bureau of American Ethnology, Bulletin 180 (18), pp. 173–95.

La Barre, Weston. 1938. *The Peyote Cult.* New Haven, Conn.: Yale University Publications in Anthropology, 19.

———. 1947. "Primitive Psychotherapy in Native American Cultures: Peyotism and Confession," *Journal of Abnormal and Social Psychology* 42 (3), pp. 294–309.

———. 1960. "Twenty Years of Peyote Studies," *Current Anthropology* 1 (1), pp. 45–60.

———. 1970. *The Ghost Dance: Origins of Religion.* Garden City, N.Y.: Doubleday.

———. 1971. "Materials for a History of Studies of Crisis Cults: A Bibliographic Essay," *Current Anthropology* 12 (1), pp. 3–44.

La Farge, Oliver. 1956. *A Pictorial History of the American Indian.* New York: Crown.

Lafitau, Joseph François. 1724. *Moeurs des Sauvages Ameriquains, Comparées aux Moeurs des Premiers Temps,* 2 vols. Paris: Saugrain l'Aîné, 1.

Lambert, R.S. 1956. "The Shaking Tent," *Tomorrow* 4 (3), pp. 113–28.

Landes, Ruth. 1968. *Ojibwa Religion and the Midéwiwin.* Madison, Wis.: University of Wisconsin.

Lantis, Margaret. 1938. "The Alaskan Whale Cult and Its Affinities," *American Anthropologist* 40 (3), pp. 438–64.

———. 1947. *Alaskan Eskimo Ceremonialism*. New York: Monographs of the American Ethnological Society, 11.

Leeuw, G. van der. 1933. *Phänomenologie der Religion*. Tübingen, Germany: J. C. B. Mohr.

Leh, L. L. 1934. *The Shaman in Aboriginal American Society*. Boulder, Colo.: University of Colorado Studies, 20.

Lehmann, Friedrich Rudolf. 1930. *Die Polynesischen Tabusitten. Eine Ethnosoziologische und Religionswissenschaftliche Untersuchung*. Leipzig: R. Voigtländer, Veröffentlichungen des Sächsischen Staatlichen Forschungsinstituts für Völkerkunde, 1 (10).

Lévi-Strauss, Claude. 1958. "La Geste d'Asdiwal," *L'Annuaire 1958–59*. Paris: École Pratique des Hautes Études, pp. 3–43.

———. 1967. "The Story of Asdiwal," *The Structural Study of Myth and Totemism*, ed. Edmund Leach. London: Tavistock Publications, pp. 1–47.

———. 1969. *Claude Levi-Strauss och strukturalismen*. Stockholm: Cavefors.

Lévy-Bruhl, Lucien. 1927. *L'Âme Primitive*. Paris: F. Alcan.

Lindig, Wolfgang H. Von, and Alfons M. Dauer. 1964. "Prophetismus und Geistertanzbewegung bei Nordamerikanischen Eingeborenen," *Chiliasmus und Nativismus*, ed. Wilhelm Emil Mühlmann, 2nd ed. Berlin: Dietrich Reimer, pp. 41–74.

Linford, Velma. 1947. *Wyoming, Frontier State*. Denver, Colo.: Old West.

Linton, Ralph. 1936. *The Study of Man*. New York: D. Appleton-Century.

———. 1943. "Nativistic Movements," *American Anthropologist* 45 (2), pp. 230–40.

Ljungdahl, Axel. 1969. *Profetrörelser, Deras Orsaker, Innebörd och Förutsättningar*. Stockholm: Stockholm Studies in Comparative Religion, 10.

Loeb, E. M. 1933. "The Eastern Kuksu Cult," *University of California Publications in American Archaeology and Ethnology* 33 (2), pp. 139–232.

Long, James Larpenteur. 1961. *The Assiniboines*, ed. Michael Stephen Kennedy. Norman, Okla.: University of Oklahoma.

Long Lance, (Chief) Buffalo Child. 1928. *Long Lance*. New York: Cosmopolitan Book Corporation.

Lowie, Robert H. 1909a. *The Assiniboine*. New York: Anthropological Papers of the American Museum of Natural History, 4 (1).

———. 1909b. *The Northern Shoshone*. New York: Anthropological Papers of the American Museum of Natural History, 2 (2), pp. 163–306.

———. 1915a. "Ceremonialism in North America," Franz Boas et al., *Anthropology in North America*. New York: G. E. Stechert, pp. 229–58.

———. 1915b. *Dances and Societies of the Plains Shoshone*. New York: Anthropological Papers of the American Museum of Natural History, 11 (10), pp. 803–835.

———. 1915c. *The Sun Dance of the Crow Indians*. New York: Anthropogical Papers of the American Museum of Natural History, 16 (1), pp. 1–50.

———. 1919. *The Sun Dance of the Shoshoni, Ute, and Hidatsa*. New York: Anthropological Papers of the American Museum of Natural History, 16 (5), pp. 391–431.

———. 1922a. "Ojibwa," *Encyclopaedia of Religion and Ethics*, 12 vols., ed. James

Hastings. New York and Edinburgh: Scribner's and T. & T. Clark, 9, pp. 454–58.

———. 1922b. *The Religion of the Crow Indians.* New York: Anthropological Papers of the American Museum of Natural History, 25 (2), pp. 309–444.

———. 1925. *Primitive Religion.* London: G. Routledge.

———. 1934a. *An Introduction to Cultural Anthropology.* New York: Farrar & Rinehart.

———. 1934b. "Religious Ideas and Practices of the Eurasiatic and North American Areas," *Essays Presented to C. G. Seligman,* ed. E. E. Evans-Pritchard et al. London: Kegan Paul, Trench, Trubner, pp. 183–88.

———. 1935. *The Crow Indians.* New York: Holt, Rinehart and Winston.

———. 1939. "Ethnographic Notes on the Washo," *University of California Publications in American Archaeology and Ethnology* 36 (5), pp. 301–352.

———. 1940. *An Introduction to Cultural Anthropology,* 2nd ed. New York: Farrar & Rinehart.

———. 1953a. "Alleged Kiowa-Crow Affinities," *Southwestern Journal of Anthropology* 9 (4), pp. 357–68.

———. 1953b. "The Relations between the Kiowa and the Crow Indians," *Societé Suisse des Americanistesâ Bulletin* 7, pp. 1–5.

———. 1954. *Indians of the Plains.* New York: McGraw-Hill.

Lumholtz, Carl. 1900. *Symbolism of the Huichol Indians.* New York: Memoirs of the American Museum of Natural History, 3 (1).

Lynd, James William. 1889. *The Religion of the Dakotas.* St. Paul, Minn.: Collections of the Minnesota Historical Society, 2.

McClintock, Walter. 1910. *The Old North Trail.* London: Macmillan.

———. 1923. *Old Indian Trails.* Boston and New York: Houghton Mifflin.

MacCulloch, John Arnott. 1922. "Descent to Hades (Ethnic)," *Encyclopaedia of Religion and Ethics,* 12 vols., ed. James Hastings. New York and Edinburgh: Scribner's and T. & T. Clark, 4, pp. 648–54.

McElwain, Thomas. 1980. "Methods in Mask Morphology: Iroquoian False Faces in the Ethnographical Museum, Stockholm," *Temenos* 16, pp. 68–83.

McFeat, Tom, ed. 1967. *Indians of the North Pacific Coast.* Seattle, Wash.: University of Washington.

Macfie, Harry. 1944. *Lägereldar Längesen.* Stockholm: Bonnier.

McGee, W. J. 1900. *The Seri Indians.* Washington, D.C.: Bureau of American Ethnology, 17th Annual Report, 1, pp. 128–344.

Macgregor, Gordon. 1946. *Warriors without Weapons.* Chicago: University of Chicago.

McIlwraith, Thomas Forsyth. 1948. *The Bella Coola Indians,* 2 vols. Toronto: University of Toronto, 1.

McKenney, Thomas. 1846. *Memoirs, Official and Personal, with Sketches of Travels among the Northern and Southern Indians,* 2 vols., New York: Paine and Burgess.

McLean, John. 1892. *The Indians of Canada: Their Manners and Customs*, 3rd ed. London: Charles H. Kelly.

MacLeod, William Christie. 1936. "Conservation among Primitive Hunting Peoples," *Scientific Monthly* 43, pp. 562–66.

———. 1938. "Self-Sacrifice in Mortuary and Non-Mortuary Ritual in North America," *Anthropos* 33, pp. 349–400.

Mandelbaum, David Goodman. 1940. *The Plains Cree*. New York: Anthropological Papers of the American Museum of Natural History, 37 (2).

Marett, Robert Ranulph. 1909. *The Threshold of Religion*. London: Methuen.

———. 1922. "Tabu," *Encyclopaedia of Religion and Ethics*, 12 vols., ed. James Hastings. New York and Edinburgh: Scribner's and T. & T. Clark, 12, pp. 181–85.

Maringer, Johannes. 1956. *Vorgeschichtliche Religion*. Einsiedeln: Benziger.

Martin, Calvin. 1974. "The European Impact on the Culture of a Northeastern Algonquian Tribe: An Ecological Interpretation," *William and Mary Quarterly* 31 (1), pp. 3–26.

———. 1978. *Keepers of the Game: Indian-Animal Relationships and the Fur Trade*. Berkeley, Calif.: University of California.

———. 1980. "Subarctic Indians and Wildlife," *American Indian Environments: Ecological Issues in Native American History*, ed. Christopher Vecsey and Robert W. Venables. Syracuse, N.Y.: Syracuse University Press, pp. 38–45.

Matthews, Washington. 1877. *Ethnography and Philology of the Hidatsa Indians*. Washington, D.C.: United States Geological and Geographical Survey, Miscellaneous Publications, 7.

———. 1897. *Navajo Legends*. Boston: Memoirs of the American Folklore Society, 5.

———. 1899. "The Study of Ethics among the Lower Races," *Journal of American Folklore*, 12, pp. 1–9.

———. 1902. *The Night Chant*. New York: Memoirs of the American Museum of Natural History, 6.

Mauss, Marcel. 1947. *Manuel d'Ethnographie*. Paris: Payot.

Mead, Margaret. 1934. "Tabu," *Encyclopaedia of the Social Sciences*, 15 vols., ed. Edwin R. A. Seligman. New York: Macmillan, 14, pp. 502–505.

Mead, Margaret, and Ruth L. Bunzel, eds. 1960. *The Golden Age of American Anthropology*. New York: G. Braziller.

Meggers, Betty J. 1954. "Environmental Limitation on the Development of Culture," *American Anthropologist* 56 (5), pp. 801–824.

Mensch, Cornelis. 1937. *Taboe, Een Primitieve Vreesreactie*. Amsterdam: H. J. Paris.

Métraux, Alfred. 1943. "The Social Organization and Religion of the Mojo and Manasi," *Primitive Man* 16 (1–2), pp. 1–30.

Michelson, Truman. 1925. *Notes on Fox Mortuary Customs and Beliefs*. Washington, D.C.: Bureau of American Ethnology, 40th Annual Report, pp. 351–496.

Miller, F. 1977. "The Crow Sun Dance Lodge: Form, Process, and Geometry in the Creation of Sacred Space." Philadelphia: Temple University. Published in *Temenos* 16 (1980), pp. 92–102.

———. May 10, 1978. Letter to Åke Hultkrantz. Lidingö: Private Archive, Åke Hultkrantz.

Miranda, Daniel E. 1977. "The Grounding of an Interdisciplinary Study of Death in the Phenomenology of Religion," *Religion: Journal of Religion and Religions* 7 (1), pp. 86–90.

Mokler, Alfred James. 1927. *Transition of the West*. Chicago: Lakeside Press.

Moodie, Susannah. 1870. *Roughing It in the Bush*. Toronto: Maclear.

Mooney, James. 1892. "A Kiowa Mescal Rattle," *American Anthropologist*, o.s., 5 (1), pp. 64–65.

———. 1896. *The Ghost-Dance Religion and the Sioux Outbreak of 1890*. Washington, D.C.: Bureau of American Ethnology, 14th Annual Report, 2, pp. 641–1136.

———. 1907. "Arapaho," *Handbook of American Indians North of Mexico*, 2 vols., ed. Frederick Webb Hodge. Washington, D.C.: Bureau of American Ethnology, Bulletin 30 (1), pp. 72–73.

———. 1910. "Scalping," in *Handbook of American Indians, North of Mexico*, 2 vols., ed. Frederick Webb Hodge. Washington, D.C.: Bureau of American Ethnology, Bulletin 30 (2), pp. 482–83.

Moore, John H. 1974. "Cheyenne Political History, 1820–1894," *Ethnohistory* 21 (4), pp. 329–59.

Morgan, Lewis H. 1901. *League of the Ho-de-no Sau-nee or Iroquois*, 2 vols., 2nd ed. New York: Dodd, Mead.

Mühlmann, Wilhelm Emil, ed. 1964. *Chiliasmus und Nativismus*, 2nd ed. Berlin: Dietrich Reimer.

Müller, Hans-Peter. 1975. *Tradition und Abweichendes Verhalten: der Nordamerikanische Geistertanz als Entwicklungsproblem*. Wiesbaden: B. Heymann.

Müller, Johann Georg. 1855. *Geschichte der Amerikanischen Urreligionen*. Basel: Schweighausersche.

Müller, Werner. 1954. *Die Blaue Hütte*. Wiesbaden: Franz Steiner.

———. 1956. *Die Religionen der Waldlandindianer Nordamerikas*. Berlin: Dietrich Reimer.

———. 1961. "Die Religionen der Indianervölker Nordamerikas," *Die Religionen der Menschheit: Die Religionen des Alten Amerika*, ed. Christel Matthias Schröder. Stuttgart: Kohlhammer, pp. 171–267.

———. 1970. *Glauben und Denken der Sioux*. Berlin: Reimer.

———. 1972. *Geliebte Erde: Naturfrömmigkeit und Naturhass im Indianischen und Europäischen Nordamerika*. Bonn: Bouvier Verlag Herbert Grundmann.

———. 1976. *Indianische Welterfahrung*. Stuttgart: Ernst Klett.

Mulloy, William. 1952. "The Northern Plains," *Archeology of Eastern United States*, ed. James B. Griffin. Chicago: University of Chicago, pp. 124–38.

Murphy, Robert Francis, and Yolanda Murphy. 1960. *Shoshone-Bannock Subsistence and Society*. Berkeley, Calif.: University of California, Anthropological Records, 16.

Nabakov, Peter. 1967. *Two Leggings.* New York: Thomas Y. Crowell.

Nash, A. B. 1932. "The Hidden Hero of Wyoming—John Roberts," *The Churchman* 146 (8), n.p.

Nash, Philleo. 1937. "The Place of Religious Revivalism in the Formation of the Intercultural Community on Klamath Reservation," *Social Anthropology of North American Tribes,* ed. Fred Eggan. Chicago: University of Chicago, pp. 375–442.

Nelson, Richard K. 1973. *Hunters of the Northern Forest.* Chicago: University of Chicago.

Niblack, Albert Parker. 1890. *The Coast Indians of Southern Alaska and Northern British Columbia.* Washington, D.C.: Report of the United States National Museum, 1888, pp. 225–386.

Norris, Philetus W. 1881. *Annual Report of the Superintendent of the Yellowstone National Park ... for the Year 1880.* Washington, D.C.: Government Printing Office.

———. 1882. *Annual Report of the Superintendent of the Yellowstone National Park ... for the Year 1881.* Washington, D.C.: Government Printing Office.

Odum, Howard W. 1947. *Understanding Society: The Principles of Dynamic Sociology.* New York: Macmillan.

Ohlmarks, Åke. 1939. *Studien zum Problem des Schamanismus.* Lund: C. W. K. Gleerup.

Olden, Sarah Emelia. 1923. *Shoshone Folk Lore: As Discovered from the Rev. John Roberts, A Hidden Hero, On the Wind River Indian Reservation in Wyoming.* Milwaukee, Wis.: Morehouse Publishing Company.

Olson, Ronald L. 1936. *The Quinault Indians.* Seattle, Wash.: University of Washington Publications in Anthropology, 6 (1).

O'Neil, Paul. 1977. *The Frontiersmen.* Alexandria, Va.: Time-Life.

Opler, Marvin K. 1941. "A Colorado Ute Indian Bear Dance," *Southwestern Lore* 7 (September), pp. 21–30.

Opler, Morris Edward. 1945. "The Lipan Apache Death Complex and Its Extensions," *Southwestern Journal of Anthropology* 1 (1), pp. 122–41.

Opler, Morris Edward, and William E. Bittle. 1961. "The Death Practices and Eschatalogy of the Kiowa Apache," *Southwestern Journal of Anthropology* 17 (4), pp. 383–92.

Osgood, Cornelius B. 1932. *The Ethnography of the Great Bear Lake Indians.* National Museum of Canada, Annual Report for 1931, Bulletin 70, pp. 31–97.

———. 1959. *Ingalik Mental Culture.* New Haven, Conn.: Yale University Publications in Anthropology, 56.

Overholt, Thomas W. 1974. "The Ghost Dance of 1890 and the Nature of the Prophetic Process," *Ethnohistory* 21 (1), pp. 37–63.

———. 1978. "Short Bull, Black Elk, Sword, and the 'Meaning' of the Ghost Dance," *Religion* 8 (2), pp. 171–95.

Pallis, Svend A. 1944. "Religionsvidenskab," *Videnskaben i Dag*, ed. F. Brandt and K. Linderstrøm. Copenhagen: n.p.

Park, Willard Z. 1934. "Paviotso Shamanism," *American Anthropologist* 36 (1), pp. 98–113.

———. 1938. *Shamanism in Western North America*. Chicago and Evanston: Northwestern University.

———. 1941. "Culture Succession in the Great Basin," *Language, Culture, and Personality*, ed. Leslie Spier et al. Menasha, Wis.: Sapir Memorial Publication Fund, pp. 180–203.

Parker, Arthur C. 1928. "Indian Medicine and Medicine Men," *Annual Archaeological Report* Toronto, pp. 9–17.

Parkman, Francis. 1950. *The Oregon Trail*. New York: New American Library.

Parsons, Elsie Clews. 1921–22. "A Narrative of the Ten'a of Anvik, Alaska," *Anthropos* 16–17, pp. 51–71.

———. 1922. "Winter and Summer Dances Series in Zuni," *University of California Publications in American Archaeology and Ethnology*, 17, pp. 171–216.

———. 1926. *Tewa Tales*. New York: G. E. Stechert, Memoirs of the American Folklore Society, 19.

———. 1928. "Notes on the Pima 1926," *American Anthropologist* 30 (3), pp. 445–64.

———. 1929a. *Kiowa Tales*. New York: G. E. Stechert, Memoirs of the American Folklore Society, 22.

———. 1929b. *The Social Organization of the Tewa of New Mexico*. Menasha, Wis.: Memoirs of the American Anthropological Association, 36.

———. 1930. *Spanish Elements in the Kachina Cult of the Pueblos*. New York: Proceedings of the 23rd International Congress of Americanists, pp. 582–603.

———. 1933. *Hopi and Zuñi Ceremonialism*. Menasha, Wis.: Memoirs of the American Anthropological Association, 39.

———. 1936. *Taos Pueblo*. Menasha, Wis.: George Banta, General Series in Anthropology, 2.

———. 1939. *Pueblo Indian Religion*, 2 vols. Chicago: University of Chicago.

Paulson, Ivar. 1958. *Die Primitiven Seelenvorstellungen der Nordeurasischen Volker*. Stockholm: Statens Etnografiska Museum, Monograph Series, 5.

———. 1959. "Zur Aufbewahrung der Tierknochen im Nordlichen Nördamerika," *Amerikanistische Miszellen, Mitteilungen aus dem Museum für Völkerkunde in Hamburg* 25, pp. 182–88.

———. 1962. "Wildgeistvorstellungen in Nordeurasien," *Paideuma* 8 (2), pp. 70–8.

———. 1965. "Die Rituelle Erhebung des Bärenschädels bei Arktischen und Subarketischen Völkern," *Temenos* 1, pp. 150–69.

Petitot, Émile. 1886. *Traditions Indiennes du Canada Nord-Ouest*. Paris: Maisonneuve Frères et C. Leclerc.

Pettazzoni, Raffaele. 1931. *La Confession des Péchés*. Paris: E. Laroux.

———. 1954. *Essays on the History of Religions*. Leiden: E. J. Brill, Studies in the History of Religions, 1.

———. 1956. *The All-Knowing God*. London: Methuen.

Pettersson, Olof. 1966. "Monotheism or Polytheism? A Study of the Ideas about Supreme Beings in African Religion," *Temenos* 2, pp. 48–67.

Phister, Nat. P. 1891. "The Indian Messiah," *American Anthropologist*, o.s., 4 (2), pp. 105–108.

Pond, Gideon H. 1889. "Dakota Superstitions," *Minnesota Historical Collections* 2 (3), pp. 215–55.

Pond, Samuel William. 1908. "The Dakotas or Sioux in Minnesota as They Were in 1834," *Collections of the Minnesota Historical Society*, 12, pp. 319–501.

Powell, John Wesley. 1891. *Report to the Director*. Washington, D.C.: Bureau of American Ethnology, 7th Annual Report, pp. xv–xli.

Powell, Peter J. 1969. *Sweet Medicine: The Continuing Role of the Sacred Arrows, the Sun Dance, and the Sacred Buffalo Hat in Northern Cheyenne History*, 2 vols. Norman, Okla.: University of Oklahoma.

Powers, Stephen. 1877. *Tribes of California. Contributions to North American Ethnology*. Washington, D.C.: Government Printing Office.

Prescott, Philander. 1852. "Contributions to the History, Customs, and Opinions of the Dacota Tribe," *Historical and Statistical Information Respecting the History, Condition and Prospects of the Indian Tribes of the United States*, 6 vols., ed. Henry Rowe Schoolcraft. Philadelphia: J. B. Lippincott, 2, pp. 168–99.

———. 1853. "The Dacotahs or Sioux of the Upper Mississippi," *Historical and Statistical Information Respecting the History, Condition and Prospects of the Indian Tribes of the United States*, 6 vols., ed. Henry Rowe Schoolcraft. Philadelphia: J. B. Lippincott, 3, pp. 225–46.

Preuss, K. Th. 1929. "Indianer, Religionsgeschichtlich," *Die Religion in Geschichte und Gegenwart*, 2nd ed., 3, pp. 209–212.

Radcliffe-Brown, Alfred Reginald. 1952. *Structure and Function in Primitive Society*. London: Cohen & West.

Radin, Paul. 1915. "Religion of the North American Indians," Franz Boas et al., *Anthropology in North America*. New York: G. E. Stechert, pp. 259–305.

———. 1920. "The Autobiography of a Winnebago Indian," *University of California Publications in American Archaeology and Ethnology*, 16 (7), pp. 381–473.

———. 1923. *The Winnebago Tribe*. Washington, D.C.: Bureau of American Ethnology, 37th Annual Report, pp. 35–550.

———. 1926. "Literary Aspects of Winnebago Mythology," *Journal of American Folklore* 39, pp. 18–52.

———. 1937. *Primitive Religion: Its Nature and Origin*. New York: Viking.

———. 1945. *The Road of Life and Death*. New York: Pantheon.

———. 1948. *Winnebago Hero Cycles: A Study in Aboriginal Literature*. Bloomington, Ind.: Indiana University, Memoirs of the International Journal of American Linguistics, 1.

──────. 1951. *Die Religiöse Erfahrung der Naturvölker.* Zürich: Rhein, Albae Vigiliae, 2.

──────. 1956. *The Trickster: A Study in American Indian Mythology.* New York: Philosophical Library.

Radisson, Peter Esprit. 1885. *Voyages of Peter Esprit Radisson.* Boston: The Prince Society.

Rasmussen, Knud. 1929. *Intellectual Culture of the Iglulik Eskimos.* Copenhagen: Report of the Fifth Thule Expedition, 7 (1).

Rawcliffe, Donavan Hilton. 1959. *Illusions and Delusions of the Supernatural and the Occult.* New York: Dover.

Ray, Verne F. 1936. "The Kolaskin Cult: A Prophet Movement of 1870 in Northeastern Washington," *American Anthropologist* 38 (1), pp. 67–75.

──────. 1941. "Historic Backgrounds of the Conjuring Complex in the Plateau and the Plains," *Language, Culture, and Personality: Essays in Memory of Edward Sapir,* ed. Leslie Spier et al. Menasha, Wis.: George Banta, pp. 204–216.

Reagan, Albert B. 1930. *Notes on the Indians of the Fort Apache Region.* New York: Anthropological Papers of the American Museum of Natural History, 31 (5).

Reichard, Gladys A. 1947. *An Analysis of Coeur d'Alene Myths.* Philadelphia: Memoirs of the American Folklore Society, 41.

──────. 1949. "The Navaho and Christianity," *American Anthropologist* 51 (1), pp. 66–71.

Reid, A. P. 1873. "Religious Beliefs of the Ojibois or Sauteux Indians," *Journal of the Anthropological Institute* 3, pp. 106–113.

Report of the Commissioner of Indian Affairs. Washington, D.C.: 1876, 1879, 1880, 1881, 1882.

Rich, E. E. 1960. "Trade Habits and Economic Motivation among the Indians of North America," *Canadian Journal of Economics and Political Science* 26 (1), pp. 35–53.

Ridington, Robin, and Tonia Ridington. 1970. "The Inner Eye of Shamanism and Totemism," *History of Religions* 10 (1), pp. 49–61.

Riggs, Stephen Return. 1883. "Mythology of the Dakotas," *American Antiquarian and Oriental Journal* 5 (2), pp. 147–49.

──────. 1893. *Dakota Grammar, Texts, and Ethnography.* Washington, D. C.: Government Printing Office, Contributions to North American Ethnology, 9.

Riley, Carroll L. 1974. Mesoamerican Indians in the Early Southwest," *Ethnohistory* 21 (1), pp. 25–36.

Roberts, John. 1925. *Indians of the Rockies and the Pacific Coast: Shoshone and Arapaho, Wind River Reservation.* Hartford, Conn.: Indian Tribes and Missions, 4; The Church in Story and Pageant, 8.

Roberts, Marion. n.d. "The Shoshone Sun-Dance." Lidingö: Private Archive, Åke Hultkrantz, manuscript.

Roe, Frank Gilbert. 1951. *The North American Buffalo: A Critical Study of the Species in Its Wild State.* Toronto: University of Toronto.

Róheim, Geza. 1952. "Culture Hero and Trickster in North American Mythology," *Indian Tribes of Aboriginal America,* ed. Sol Tax. Chicago: University of Chicago, pp. 190–94.

Rooth, Anna Birgitta. 1957. "The Creation Myths of the North American Indians," *Anthropos* 52, pp. 497–508.

Rousseau, Jacques. 1955. "Rites Païens de la Forêt Québécoise: La Tente Tremblante et la Suerie," *Cahiers des Dix* 18–19, pp. 130–232.

Rousseau, Madeleine, and Jacques Rousseau. 1948. "La Cérémonie de la Tente Agitée chez les Mistassini," *Actes du XXVIIIᵉ Congrès International des Américanistes.* Paris: Musée de l'Homme, pp. 307–315.

———. 1952. "Le Dualisme Religieux des Peuplades de la Forêt Boréale," *Acculturation in the Americas,* ed. Sol Tax. Chicago: University of Chicago, Proceedings of the 29th International Congress of Americanists, 2 vols., 2, pp. 118–26.

Ruby, Robert H. 1955. *The Oglala Sioux.* New York: Vantage.

Russell, Osborne. 1955. *Journal of a Trapper,* ed. Aubrey L. Haines. Portland, Ore.: Oregon Historical Society.

St. Clair, L. n.d. "The So-called Shoshone Sundance, Which the Shoshones Call: Da-g-oo Wi-n-o-de." Fort Washakie: Wind River Agency Files, manuscript.

Sapir, Edward. 1922. "Vancouver Island Indians," *Encyclopaedia of Religion and Ethics,* 12 vols., ed. James Hastings. New York and Edinburgh: Scribner's and T. & T. Clark, 12, pp. 591–95.

Sauer, Carl. 1936. *American Agricultural Origins: A Consideration of Nature and Culture. Essays in Anthropology,* ed. by Robert H. Lowie. Berkeley, Calif.: University of California Press.

Schebesta, Paul. 1927. *Bei den Urwaldzwergen von Malaya.* Leipzig: F. A. Brockhaus.

Schmidt, Wilhelm. 1929, 1935. *Der Ursprung der Gottesidee,* 8 vols. Münster: Aschendorff, 2, 6.

———. 1930. *Handbuch der Vergleichenden Religionsgeschichte.* Münster: Aschendorff.

Schoolcraft, Henry Rowe, ed. 1851–60. *Historical and Statistical Information Respecting the History, Condition and Prospects of the Indian Tribes of the United States,* 6 vols. Philadelphia: J. B. Lippincott.

Schultes, Richard E. 1938. "The Appeal of Peyote *(Lophophora williamsii)* as a Medicine," *Amerian Anthropologist* 40 (4), pp. 698–715.

Schuster, Meinhard. 1960. "Die Schamanen und Ihr Ritual," *Völkerkunde,* ed. B. Freudenfeld. München: C. H. Beck, pp. 27–40.

Sears, William H. 1954. "The Sociopolitical Organizaton of Pre-Columbian Cultures on the Gulf Coastal Plain," *American Anthropologist* 56 (3), pp. 339–46.

Seligman, Brenda Z. 1951. *Notes and Queries on Anthropology,* 6th ed. London: Routledge and Kegan Paul.

Sheridan, Philip Henry. 1882. *Report of an Exploration of Parts of Wyoming, Idaho and Montana in August and September, 1882.* Washington, D.C.: Government Printing Office.

Shimkin, Demitri Boris. 1939. "Some Interactions of Culture, Needs, and Personalities among the Wind River Shoshone." Ph. D. diss., University of California, Berkeley.

———. 1942. "Dynamics of Recent Wind River Shoshone History," *American Anthropologist* 44 (3), pp. 451–62.

———. 1947a. *Childhood and Development among the Wind River Shoshone.* Berkeley, Calif.: University of California, Anthropological Records, 5 (5).

———. 1947b. *Wind River Shoshone Ethnogeography.* Berkeley, Calif.: University of California, Anthropological Records, 5 (4).

———. 1947c. "Wind River Shoshone Literary Forms: An Introduction," *Journal of the Washington Academy of Sciences* 37 (10), pp. 329–52.

———. 1953. *The Wind River Shoshone Sun Dance.* Washington, D.C.: Bureau of American Ethnology, Bulletin 151, Anthropological Papers, 41, pp. 397–484.

Shonle, Ruth. 1925. "Peyote, the Giver of Visions," *American Anthropologist* 27 (1), pp. 53–75.

Sieroszewski, Wenceslas. 1902. "Du Chamanisme d'après les Croyances des Yakoutes," *Revue de l'Histoire des Religions,* 46, pp. 204–233, 299–338.

Skinner, Alanson. 1909. "The Lenapé Indians of Staten Island," *The Indians of Greater New York and the Lower Hudson,* ed. Clark Wissler. New York: Anthropological Papers of the American Museum of Natural History, 3, pp. 3–62.

———. 1911. "Notes on the Eastern Cree and Northern Saulteaux," *Anthropological Papers of the American Museum of Natural History* 9 (1), pp. 119–77.

———. 1913. *The Menomini Indians* 1: *Social Life and Ceremonial Bundles of the Menomini Indians.* New York: Anthropological Papers of the American Museum of Natural History, 13 (1), pp. 1–165.

———. 1920. *Medicine Ceremony of the Menomini, Iowa, and Wahpeton Dakota.* New York: Museum of the American Indian, Heye Foundation, Indian Notes and Monographs, 4.

Slotkin, J. S. 1956. *The Peyote Religion.* Glencoe, Ill.: Free Press.

Slotkin, Richard. 1973. *Regeneration through Violence: The Mythology of the American Frontier, 1600–1860.* Middletown, Conn.: Wesleyan University.

Smith, Huron Herbert. 1933. *Ethnobotany of the Forest Potawatomi Indians.* Milwaukee, Wis.: Bulletin of the Public Museum of the City of Milwaukee, 7 (1).

Smith, Jonathan Z. 1980. "The Bare Facts of Ritual," *History of Religions* 20 (1–2), pp. 112–27.

Smith, Marian W. 1954. "Shamanism in the Shaker Religion of Northwest America," *Man* 54 (181), pp. 119–22.

Snow, (Chief) John. 1977. *These Mountains Are Our Sacred Places.* Toronto: Samuel-Stevens.

Speck, Frank G. 1931. *A Study of the Delaware Indian Big House Ceremony.* Harrisburg, Pa.: Publications of the Pennsylvania Historical Commission, 2.

———. 1935. *Naskapi: The Savage Hunters of the Labrador Peninsula.* Norman, Okla.: University of Oklahoma.

———. 1949. *Midwinter Rites of the Cayuga Long House.* Philadelphia: University of Pennsylvania.

Spence, Lewis. 1914. *Myths and Legends of the North American Indians.* Boston: Nickerson.

Spencer, Herbert. 1876. *Principles of Sociology.* London: Williams & Norgate, 1.

Spencer, Robert F. 1952. "Native Myth and Modern Religion among the Klamath Indians," *Journal of American Folklore* 65 (257), pp. 217–26.

Spencer, Robert F. and Jesse D. Jennings. 1965. *The Native Americans.* New York and London: Harper & Row.

Spier, Leslie. 1921. *The Sun Dance of the Plains Indians: Its Development and Diffusion.* New York: Anthropological Papers of the American Museum of Natural History, 16 (7), pp. 451–527.

———. 1927. "The Ghost Dance of 1870 among the Klamath of Oregon," *University of Washington Publications in Anthropology* 2 (2), pp. 39–56.

———. 1930. *Klamath Ethnography.* Berkeley, Calif.: University of California Publications in American Archaeology and Ethnology, 30.

———. 1933. *Yuman Tribes of the Gila River.* Chicago: University of Chicago.

———. 1935. *The Prophet Dance of the Northwest and Its Derivatives: The Source of the Ghost Dance.* Menasha, Wis.: George Banta, General Series in Anthropology, 1.

———. 1936. *Cultural Relations of the Gila River and Lower Colorado Tribes.* New Haven, Conn.: Yale University Publications in Anthropology, 3.

Spier, Leslie, Wayne Suttles, and Melville J. Herskovits. 1959. "Comment on Aberle's Thesis of Deprivation," *Southwestern Journal of Anthropology* 15 (1), pp. 84–88.

Spinden, Herbert J. 1908. *The Nez Percé Indians.* Menasha, Wis.: George Banta, Memoirs of the American Anthropological Association, 2 (3).

Spindler, George. 1955. *Sociocultural and Psychological Processes in Menomini Acculturation.* Berkeley, Calif.: University of California Publications in Culture and Society, 5.

Spiro, Melford E. 1970. *Buddhism and Society: A Great Tradition and Its Burmese Vicissitudes.* New York: Harper & Row.

Sproat, Gilbert Malcolm. 1868. *Scenes and Studies of Savage Life.* London: Smith, Elder.

Stafford, C. B. 1938. "Shoshone Indian Sun Dance," *Wyoming Wild Life* 3 (7), n.p.

Standing Bear, Luther. 1933. *Land of Spotted Eagle.* Boston: Houghton Mifflin.

Stern, Theodore. 1956. "Some Sources of Variability in Klamath Mythology," *Journal of American Folklore* 69, pp. 1–12.

Stevenson, Matilda Coxe. 1898. "Zuni Ancestral Gods and Masks," *American Anthropologist*, o.s., 11 (1), pp. 33–40.

———. 1904. *The Zuñi Indians*. Washington, D.C.: Bureau of American Ethnology, 23rd Annual Report, pp. 1–608.

Steward, Julian H. 1936. "The Economic and Social Basis of Primitive Bands," *Essays in Anthropology Presented to A. L. Kroeber*, ed. by Robert H. Lowie. Berkeley, Calif.: University of California, pp. 331–50.

———. 1938. *Basin-Plateau Aborginal Sociopolitical Groups*. Washington, D.C.: Bureau of American Ethnology, Bulletin 120.

———. 1939. "Some Observations on Shoshonean Distributions," *American Anthropologists* 41 (2), pp. 261–65.

———. 1941. *Culture Element Distributions* 13: *Nevada Shoshone*. Berkeley, Calif.: University of California, Anthropological Records, 4 (2), pp. 209–359.

———. 1955. *Theory of Culture Change*. Urbana, Ill.: University of Illinois.

Steward, Julian H. et al. 1946, 1949. *Handbook of South American Indians*, 7 vols. Washington, D.C.: Bureau of American Ethnology, Bulletin 143, 2, 5.

Stewart, Kenneth M. 1946. "Spirit Possession in Native America," *Southwestern Journal of Anthropology* 2 (3), pp. 323–39.

———. 1956. "Spirit Possession," *Tomorrow* 4 (3), pp. 41–49.

Stewart, Omer C. 1941. *Culture Element Distributions* 14: *Northern Paiute*. Berkeley, Calif.: University of California, Anthropological Records, 4 (3), pp. 361–466.

———. 1944. *Washo-Northern Paiute Peyotism: A Study in Acculturation*. Berkeley, Calif.: University of California Publications in American Archaeology and Ethnology, 40 (3).

Stiglmayr, E. 1962. "Schamanismus, eine Spiritistiche Religion?," *Ethnos* 27, pp. 40–48.

Stirling, Matthew Williams. 1955. *Indians of the Americas*. Washington, D.C.: National Geographic Society.

Strong, William D. 1945. "The Occurrence and Wider Implications of a 'Ghost Cult' on the Columbia River Suggested by Carvings in Wood, Bone and Stone," *American Anthropologist* 47 (2), pp. 244–61.

Suttles, Wayne. 1957. "The Plateau Prophet Dance among the Coast Salish," *Southwestern Journal of Anthropology* 13 (4), pp. 352–96.

Swanson, Guy E. 1960. *The Birth of the Gods: The Origin of Primitive Beliefs*. Ann Arbor, Mich.: University of Michigan.

Swanton, John R. 1904. "The Development of the Clan System and of Secret Societies among the Northwestern Indians," *American Anthropologist* 6 (4), pp. 477–85.

———. 1905. *The Haida of Queen Charlotte Islands*. New York: Memoirs of the American Museum of Natural History, 8 (1).

———. 1908. *Social Condition, Beliefs, and Linguistic Relationship of the Tlingit Indians*. Washington, D.C.: Bureau of American Ethnology, 26th Annual Report, pp. 391–485.

———. 1909. *Contributions to the Ethnology of the Haida*. New York: Memoirs of the American Museum of Natural History, 8.

———. 1911. *Indian Tribes of the Lower Mississippi Valley and Adjacent Coast of the Gulf of Mexico.* Washington, D.C.: Bureau of American Ethnology, Bulletin 43.

———. 1928. *Aboriginal Culture of the Southeast.* Washington, D.C.: Bureau of American Ethnology, 42nd Annual Report, pp. 473–672.

———. 1946. *The Indians of the Southeastern United States.* Washington, D.C.: Bureau of American Ethnology, Bulletin 137.

Talbot, Ethelbert. 1906. *My People of the Plains.* New York and London: Harper & Brothers.

Tanner, Väinö. 1944. *Outlines of the Geography, Life and Customs of Newfoundland-Labrador.* Helsingfors, Finland: Tilgmann, Acta Geographica, 8.

Tatje, Terrence, and Francis L. K. Hsu. 1969. "Variations in Ancestor Worship Beliefs and Their Relation to Kinship," *Southwestern Journal of Anthropology* 25 (2), pp. 153–72.

Teicher, Morton I. 1960. *Windigo Psychosis.* Seattle, Wash.: Proceedings of the American Ethnological Society.

Teit, James. 1900. *The Thompson Indians of British Columbia.* New York: Memoirs of the American Museum of Natural History, 2 (4), pp. 163–392.

———. 1906. *The Lillooet Indians.* New York: Memoirs of the American Museum of Natural History, 4 (5), pp. 193–300.

———. 1909. *The Shuswap.* New York: Memoirs of the American Museum of Natural History, 4 (7), pp. 443–789.

Thomas, Northcote Whitridge. 1911. "Taboo," *Encyclopaedia Britannica*, 11th ed., 26, pp. 337–41.

Thompson, David. 1916. *David Thompson's Narrative of His Explorations in Western America, 1784–1812*, ed. J. B. Tyrell. Toronto: Champlain Society.

Thompson, J. n.d. "In Old Wyoming." Laramie, Wyo.: University of Wyoming Archives, manuscript.

Thompson, Stith. 1919. "European Tales among the North American Indians," *Colorado College Publications, Language Series* 2 (34), pp. 319–471.

———. 1953. "The Star Husband Tale," *Studia Septentrionalia* 4, pp. 93–163.

Thouless, Robert H. 1923. *An Introduction to the Psychology of Religion*, 2nd ed. Cambridge: Cambridge University.

Thwaites, Reuben Gold, ed. 1896–1901. *The Jesuit Relations and Allied Documents,* 73 vols. Cleveland, Ohio. Reprint, Totowa, N.J.: Rowman & Littlefield, 1959.

Titiev, Mischa. 1944. *Old Oraibi.* Cambridge, Mass.: Papers of the Peabody Museum of American Archaeology and Ethnology, 22 (1).

Trenholm, Virginia Cole, and Maurine Carley. 1964. *The Shoshonis: Sentinels of the Rockies.* Norman, Okla.: University of Oklahoma.

Turner, Lucien M. 1894. *Ethnology of the Ungava District, Hudson Bay Territory.* Washington, D.C.: Bureau of American Ethnology, 11th Annual Report, pp. 159–350.

Turner, Victor W. 1967. *The Forest of Symbols: Aspects of Ndembu Ritual.* Ithaca, N.Y.: Cornell University.

――――. 1969. *The Ritual Process: Structure and Anti-Structure.* London: Routledge & K. Paul.

Turney-High, Harry Holbert. 1941. *Ethnography of the Kutenai.* Menasha, Wis.: American Anthropological Association Memoirs, 56.

Tybjerg, Tove. 1977. "Nordvestkyst-Indianerne: Tlingit-Indianernes Dødefester," *Religion/77* (3), pp. 32–53.

Tyler, Hamilton A. 1964. *Pueblo Gods and Myths.* Norman, Okla.: University of Oklahoma.

Tylor, Edward Burnett. 1871. *Primitive Culture,* 2 vols. London: John Murray.

――――. 1873. *Primitive Culture,* 2 vols., 2nd ed. London: John Murray, 2.

――――. 1891. *Primitive Culture,* 2 vols., 3rd ed. London: John Murray.

Udall, Stewart L. 1972. "The Indians," *Look to the Mountain Top,* ed. Charles Jones. San Jose, Calif.: Gousha, pp. 1–6.

Umfreville, Edward. 1790. *The Present State of Hudson's Bay.* London: C. Stalker.

Underhill, Ruth Murray. 1938. *Singing for Power.* Berkeley, Calif.: University of California.

――――. 1946a. *Papago Indian Religion.* New York: Columbia University Contributions to Anthropology, 30.

――――. 1946b. *Workaday Life of the Pueblos.* Phoenix, Ariz.: U. S. Office of Indian Affairs, Indian Life and Customs, 4.

――――. 1948. *Ceremonial Patterns in the Greater Southwest.* New York: J. J. Augustin, Monographs of the American Ethnological Society, 13.

――――. 1952. "Peyote," *Proceedings of the 30th International Congress of Americanists.* London: The Royal Anthropological Institute, pp. 143–48.

――――. 1954. "Intercultural Relations in the Greater Southwest," *American Anthropologist* 56 (4), pp. 645–56.

――――. 1957. "Religion among American Indians," *The Annals of the American Academy of Political and Social Science* 311, pp. 127–36.

――――. 1965. *Red Man's Religion.* Chicago: University of Chicago.

Vastokas, Joan M. 1977. "The Shamanic Tree of Life," *Stones, Bones and Skin: Ritual and Shamanic Art,* ed. Anne Trueblood Brodzky et al. Toronto: Society for Art Publications, pp. 93–117.

Vecsey, Christopher. 1980. "American Indian Environmental Religions," *American Indian Environments: Ecological Issues in Native American History,* ed. Christopher Vecsey and Robert W. Venables. Syracuse, N.Y.: Syracuse University Press, pp. 1–37.

Vecsey, Christopher, and Robert W. Venables, eds. 1980. *American Indian Environments: Ecological Issues in Native American History.* Syracuse, N.Y.: Syracuse University Press.

Vestal, Stanley. 1957. *Sitting Bull, Champion of the Sioux,* 2nd ed. Norman, Okla.: University of Oklahoma.

Voegelin, Charles F. 1936. *The Shawnee Female Deity.* New Haven, Conn.: Yale University Publications in Anthropology, 10.

Voegelin, [Charles] F., and Erminie W. Voegelin. 1946. "Linguistic Considerations of Northeastern North America," *Man in Northeastern North America,* ed. Federick Johnson. Andover, Mass.: Papers of the Robert S. Peabody Foundation for Archeology, 3, pp. 178–94.

Voget, Fred W. 1948. "Individual Motivation in the Diffusion of the Wind River Shoshone Sundance to the Crow Indians," *American Anthropologist* 50 (4), pp. 634–46.

———. 1953. *Current Trends in the Wind River Shoshone Sun Dance.* Washington, D.C.: Bureau of American Ethnology, Bulletin 151, Anthropological Papers, 42, pp. 485–99.

———. 1956. "The American Indian in Transition: Reformation and Accommodation," *American Anthropologist* 58 (2), pp. 249–63.

Wach, Joakim. 1947. *Sociology of Religion.* London: Kegan Paul.

Wachmeister, Arrid. 1957. *Själavandringsforestallningar hos Nordamerikas Indianer.* Stockholm: Natur och Kultur.

Walker, Deward E., Jr. 1968. *Conflict and Schism in Nez Perce Acculturation.* Pullman, Wash.: Washington State University.

———. 1969. "New Light on the Prophet Dance Controversy," *Ethnohistory* 16 (3), pp. 245–55.

Walker, J. R. 1917. *The Sun Dance and Other Ceremonies of the Oglala Division of Teton Dakota.* New York: Anthropological Papers of the American Museum of Natural History, 16 (2), pp. 51–221.

Wallace, Ernest, and E. Adamson Hoebel. 1952. *The Comanches: Lords of the South Plains.* Norman, Okla.: University of Oklahoma.

Wallis, Wilson Dallam. 1947. *The Canadian Dakota.* New York: Anthropological Papers of the American Museum of Natural History, 41 (1).

Warren, William Whipple. 1885. "History of the Ojibways, Based upon Traditions and Oral Statements," *Collections of the Minnesota Historical Society* 5, pp. 21–394.

Washburn, Wilcomb E. 1961. "Ethnohistory: History 'in the Round,'" *Ethnohistory* 8 (1), pp. 31–48.

Wassén, S. Henry. 1961. "Cunaindianernas Medicinmän och Deras Värld," *Nytt och Nyttigt* 3, pp. 13–27.

Waterman, T. T. 1914. "The Explanatory Element in the Folk-Tales of the North-American Indians," *Journal of American Folklore* 27, pp. 1–54.

———. 1924. *The Shake Religion of Puget Sound.* Washington, D.C.: Annual Report, Smithsonian Institution, 1922, pp. 499–507.

Waters, Frank. 1963. *Book of the Hopi.* New York: Ballantine.

Waugh, Earle H., and K. Dad Prithipaul, eds. 1979. *Native Religious Traditions.* Waterloo, Ontario: Wilfred Laurier University for the Canadian Corporation for Studies in Religion, Studies in Religion, 8.

Webster, Hutton. 1942. *Taboo, A Sociological Study.* London: Oxford University.

Wedel, Waldo R. 1959. *An Introduction to Kansas Archeology.* Washington, D.C.:
    Bureau of American Ethnology, Bulletin 174.
Wheeler-Voegelin, Erminie, and Remedios W. Moore. 1957. "The Emergence
    Myth in Native North America," *Studies in Folklore,* ed. W. Edson
    Richmond. Bloomington, Ind.: Indiana University, pp. 66–91.
Widengren, Geo. 1945. *Religionens Värld.* Stockholm: Svenska Kyrkans
    Diakonityrelses.
———. 1968. "Mythos und Glaube im Lichte der Religionsphänomenologie,"
    Theologische Forschung 45, pp. 129–49.
Wike, Joyce. 1952. "The Role of the Dead in Northwest Coast Culture," *Indian
    Tribes of Aboriginal America,* ed. Sol Tax. Chicago: University of
    Chicago, pp. 97–103.
Willey, Gordon R. 1966. *An Introduction to American Archaeology* 1: *North and
    Middle America.* Englewood Cliffs, N.J.: Prentice-Hall.
Williams, Mentor L., ed. 1956. *Schoolcraft's Indian Legends.* East Lansing, Mich.:
    Michigan State University.
Wilson, Gilbert, 1928. *Hidatsa Eagle Trapping.* New York: Anthropological
    Papers of The American Museum of Natural History, 30 (4).
Wind River Agency Files. n.d. "Various Letters; Death Records." Fort
    Washakie, Wyo.; manuscript.
Wissler, Clark. 1912. "The Psychological Aspects of the Culture Environment
    Relation," *American Anthropologist* 14 (2), pp. 217–25.
———. 1926. *The Relation of Nature to Man in Aboriginal America.* New York:
    Oxford University.
———. 1941. *North American Indians of the Plains.* New York: American
    Museum of Natural History.
———. 1950. *The American Indian,* 3rd ed. New York: Douglas C. McMurtie.
Witthoft, John. 1949. *Green Corn Ceremonialism in the Eastern Woodlands.* Ann
    Arbor, Mich.: Occasional Contributions from the Museum of
    Anthropology of the University of Michigan, 13.
Wright, Muriel H. 1951. *A Guide to the Indian Tribes of Oklahoma.* Norman, Okla.:
    University of Oklahoma.
Wyman, Leland, W. W. Hill, and Iva Ósanai. 1942. *Navajo Eschatology.*
    Albuquerque, N. Mex.: University of New Mexico Bulletin, Anthro-
    pological Series, 4 (1).

Yarrow, H. C. 1880. *Introduction to the Study of Mortuary Customs among the North
    American Indians.* Washington, D.C.: Bureau of Ethnology.

Zerries, Otto. 1954. *Wild- und Buschgeister in Südamerika.* Wiesbaden: F. Steiner.
———. 1959. "Wildgeister und Jagdritual in Zentralamerika," *Mitteilungen aus
    dem Museum für Völkerkunde in Hamburg* 25, pp. 144–50.
———. 1961. "Die Religionen der Naturvölker Südamerikas und Westin-
    diens," *Die Religionen der Menschheit,* ed. Christel Matthias Schröder.
    Stuttgart: Kohlhammer, 7, pp. 269–384.
Ziegler, Winfred Hamlin. [1944]. *Wyoming Indians.* Laramie, Wyo.: The Dioce-
    san Office.

BELIEF AND WORHSIP IN NATIVE NORTH AMERICA

was composed in 10-point VIP Palatino and leaded two points,
with display type in Palatino Bold and Molé Foliate,
by Utica Typesetting Company, Inc.;
printed on 50-pound, acid-free Glatfelter Antique Cream,
Smythe-sewn and bound over boards in Joanna Arrestox B,
with jackets printed and laminated by Philips Offset Co, Inc.,
by Maple-Vail Book Manufacturing Group, Inc.;
and published by

SYRACUSE UNIVERSITY PRESS

SYRACUSE, NEW YORK 13210